# Good Housekeeping™

## BEST

# ONE-DISH MEALS

### Casseroles, Stir-Fries, Pizzas & More

# Good Housekeeping

## BEST

# ONE-DISH MEALS

## Casseroles, Stir-Fries, Pizzas & More

Time Inc.
HOME ENTERTAINMENT

Hearst Communications, Inc.

# Good Housekeeping ⟨BEST⟩ ONE-DISH MEALS

### GOOD HOUSEKEEPING

| | |
|---|---|
| *Editor in Chief:* | Ellen Levine |
| *Food Director:* | Susan Westmoreland |
| *Associate Food Director:* | Susan Deborah Goldsmith |
| *Food Associates:* | Lisa Brainerd, Lori Perlmutter, Mary Ann Svec, Lisa Troland |
| *Nutrition Director:* | Delia Hammock |
| *Food Appliances Director:* | Sharon Franke |
| *Art Director:* | Scott Yardley |
| *Photo Editor:* | Maya Kaimal |
| *Hearst Brand Development:* | Fran Reilly, Jenifer Kramer |

### TIME INC. HOME ENTERTAINMENT

| | |
|---|---|
| *Managing Director:* | David Gitow |
| *Director, Continuities and Single Sales:* | David Arfine |
| *Director, Continuities and Retention:* | Michael Barrett |
| *Director, New Products:* | Alicia Longobardo |
| *Group Product Managers:* | Robert Fox, Michael Holahan |
| *Product Managers:* | Chris Berzolla, Stacy Hirschberg, Roberta Harris, Jennifer McLyman, Daniel Melore |
| *Manager, Retail and New Markets:* | Tom Mifsud |
| *Associate Product Managers:* | Louisa Bartle, Alison Ehrmann, Dawn Perry, Daria Raehse, Carlos Jimenez |
| *Assistant Product Managers:* | Meredith Shelley, Betty Su, Lauren Zaslansky |
| *Editorial Operations Manager:* | John Calvano |
| *Fulfillment Director:* | Michelle Gudema |
| *Financial Director:* | Tricia Griffin |
| *Assistant Financial Manager:* | Amy Maselli |
| *Marketing Assistant:* | Sarah Holmes |

### CONSUMER MARKETING DIVISION

| | |
|---|---|
| *Production Director:* | John E. Tighe |
| *Book Production Manager:* | Jessica McGrath |
| *Book Production Coordinator:* | Joe Napolitano |
| *Special Thanks:* | Donna Miano-Ferrara, Anna Yelenskaya |

GOOD HOUSEKEEPING BEST ONE-DISH MEALS
Produced by Rebus, Inc.
New York, NY

First Edition
ISBN# 0-688-16373-4
Library of Congress Catalog Card Number: 98-60456
**Good Housekeeping** is a Registered Trademark of Hearst Communications, Inc.

Printed in the United States of America

# Contents

*Welcome to Good Housekeeping's* collection of great one-dish meals—over 400 recipes just right for worry-free weeknight suppers (and great for company, too). Like all our recipes, these were developed and triple-tested in the *Good Housekeeping* kitchens; they call for readily available ingredients and employ techniques that every home cook can manage. And, of course, the results are guaranteed to please. These recipes are just what you need if you want to serve hearty, satisfying meals but have too little time for meal planning, let alone for doing a juggling act in the kitchen. With one-dish meals, you don't have to set two or three timers so you know when to take one thing out of the oven before you burn whatever you're cooking on the stovetop. When the "main dish" is done, the whole meal is ready.

The recipes in *Best One-Dish Meals* were devised with an eye to today's love-affair with comfort food, starting with robust, warming soups and stews like Vegetable & Black-Eyed Pea Soup and Chicken Stew with Rosemary Dumplings. Our selection of stir-fries and skillet dinners offers Asian-inspired meals as well as one-pan wonders like Spring Risotto and Smoked Pork-Chop Dinner. With a nod to the growing popularity of main-dish salads, we offer hearty Steak Salad with Buttermilk Dressing, Sesame Noodle & Chicken Salad, and many more. Our pasta recipes include stovetop specials such as Tortellini Primavera and Noodles Paprikash as well as ten super variations on the ever-popular lasagna. Can a sandwich be a meal? Sure, if it's as substantial as our Hot Barbecued Chicken Sandwiches, Turkey Sloppy Joes, and Stuffed Mushroom-Beef Burgers. Take a break from take-out and serve up a homemade pizza loaded with tasty, good-for-you toppings like chicken, spinach, or feta cheese. Or bake a golden-crusted deep-dish dinner pie filled with vegetables and cheese or cream-sauced seafood. Last but not least, we've come up with an array of simple desserts, some of them quick enough to put together while the main dish is cooking. Choose from fresh-fruit creations, frozen delights or baked goods—from crisps to cookies.

One-dish meals are a fine old-fashioned idea whose time has come again—a classic concept that's perfectly suited to the way we eat today. Why not try one tonight?

# Hearty Soups & Stews

# Minestrone with Pesto

PREP: 20 MINUTES PLUS OVERNIGHT TO SOAK BEANS
COOK: 1 HOUR

In Genoa, this hearty soup is traditionally topped with a dollop of pesto.

8 ounces dry Great Northern beans (about
   1⅓ cups)
2 tablespoons olive oil
3 medium carrots, peeled and sliced
2 celery stalks, sliced
1 large onion, diced
2 ounces sliced pancetta or bacon, diced
1 pound all-purpose potatoes, peeled and cut into
   ½-inch cubes
2 medium zucchini (8 ounces each), quartered
   lengthwise then cut crosswise into ¼-inch
   pieces
½ medium head savoy cabbage (1 pound), sliced to
   equal 4 cups
1 large garlic clove, crushed with garlic press
2 cans (14½ ounces each) chicken broth or
   3½ cups homemade (page 24)
1 can (14½ ounces) diced tomatoes
½ teaspoon salt
2 tablespoons pesto, homemade (page 141) or
   store-bought

1 Rinse beans under cold running water and discard any stones or shriveled beans. In large bowl, place beans and *6 cups water*. Allow to stand at room temperature overnight. (Or, in 4-quart saucepan, heat beans and *6 cups water* to boiling over high heat; cook 2 minutes. Remove from heat; cover and let stand 1 hour.) Drain and rinse beans.

2 In 4-quart saucepan, heat beans and *enough water to cover* by 2 inches to boiling over high heat. Reduce heat to low; cover and simmer 40 minutes to 1 hour or until beans are tender, stirring occasionally. Drain beans.

3 Meanwhile, in 5-quart Dutch oven, heat olive oil over medium-high heat until hot. Add carrots, celery, onion, and pancetta; cook 10 minutes or until onion begins to brown, stirring occasionally.

4 Add potatoes, zucchini, cabbage, and garlic; cook, stirring constantly, until cabbage wilts.

5 Add chicken broth, tomatoes with their juice, and *1 cup water*; heat to boiling over high heat. Reduce heat to low; cover and simmer 30 minutes or until vegetables are tender.

6 In blender or food processor, with knife blade attached, blend ½ cup beans with 1 cup soup until pureed. Stir salt, bean puree, and remaining beans into soup; heat to boiling. Reduce heat to low; cover and simmer 10 minutes.

7 Top each serving of soup with 1 teaspoon pesto. *Makes 6 servings.*

Each serving: About 360 calories, 16 g protein, 52 g carbohydrate, 11 g total fat (3 g saturated), 6 mg cholesterol, 1100 mg sodium.

# Vegetable & Black-Eyed Pea Soup

PREP: 20 MINUTES ～ COOK: 10 MINUTES

2 tablespoons vegetable oil
6 ounces cooked ham, in one piece, diced
4 medium carrots, peeled and thinly sliced
3 medium celery stalks, chopped
2 medium onions, chopped
1 medium zucchini (about 8 ounces), quartered
   lengthwise, then cut crosswise into ¼-inch
   pieces
2 cans (16 ounces each) black-eyed peas, rinsed
   and drained
2 cans (14½ ounces each) no-salt-added stewed
   tomatoes
1 can (14½ ounces) chicken broth or 1¾ cups
   homemade (page 24)
¼ teaspoon coarsely ground black pepper

1 In 5-quart Dutch oven or saucepot, heat vegetable oil over medium-high heat until hot. Add ham, carrots, celery, and onions and cook, stirring frequently, until vegetables are almost tender, about 10 minutes. Add zucchini and cook about 5 minutes longer or until vegetables are tender.

2 Stir in black-eyed peas, stewed tomatoes, chicken broth, pepper, and *3 cups water*; heat to boiling over high heat. *Makes 6 servings.*

Each serving: About 305 calories, 17 g protein, 43 g carbohydrate, 9 g total fat (2 g saturated), 17 mg cholesterol, 1265 mg sodium.

*Minestrone with Pesto* ➤

# Lentil Soup with Tubettini

PREP: 15 MINUTES ∿ COOK: 30 MINUTES

2 tablespoons olive oil
2 medium carrots, peeled and diced
1 medium onion, chopped
2 garlic cloves, minced
1 can (16 ounces) whole tomatoes in puree
1 can (14½ ounces) vegetable broth
¾ cup dry lentils, rinsed
½ teaspoon salt
½ teaspoon coarsely ground black pepper
½ teaspoon dried thyme leaves
½ small head escarole, torn into 2-inch pieces (about 4 cups firmly packed)
¾ cup tubettini pasta (about 4 ounces)
Grated Parmesan cheese (optional)

**1** In 5-quart Dutch oven or saucepot, heat olive oil over medium-high heat until hot. Add carrots, onion, and garlic and cook until tender and golden. Add tomatoes with their puree, vegetable broth, lentils, salt, pepper, thyme, and *6 cups water*; heat to boiling, stirring with spoon to break up tomatoes. Reduce heat to low; cover and simmer 20 minutes or until lentils are almost tender.

**2** Stir in escarole and tubettini; heat to boiling over high heat. Reduce heat to medium; cook, uncovered, until tubettini are tender, about 10 minutes. Serve with Parmesan if you like. *Makes 6 servings.*

Each serving without Parmesan: About 260 calories, 12 g protein, 42 g carbohydrate, 6 g total fat (1 g saturated), 0 mg cholesterol, 345 mg sodium.

# Quick "Split Pea" Soup

PREP: 15 MINUTES ∿ COOK: 10 MINUTES

2 tablespoons vegetable oil
4 ounces Virginia ham, in one piece, cut into ½-inch cubes
1 medium onion, chopped
1 large potato (about 8 ounces), peeled and cut into 1-inch chunks
3 cups frozen peas

1 can (14½ ounces) chicken broth or 1¾ cups homemade (page 24)
½ cup half-and-half or light cream

**1** In 4-quart saucepan, heat 1 tablespoon vegetable oil over medium-high heat until hot. Add ham and cook until golden; transfer to plate. To drippings in saucepan, add remaining 1 tablespoon vegetable oil and onion; cook until golden.

**2** Add potato chunks, frozen peas, chicken broth, and *3¼ cups water* to saucepan; heat to boiling over high heat. Reduce heat to low; cover and simmer 10 minutes or until potato chunks are fork-tender. Remove saucepan from heat.

**3** Working in batches, puree mixture in blender, with center part of cover removed, at low speed.

**4** Return pureed soup to saucepan. Add ham and half-and-half. Heat through over medium heat, stirring often. *Makes 4 servings.*

Each serving: About 300 calories, 16 g protein, 28 g carbohydrate, 14 g total fat (4 g saturated), 31 mg cholesterol, 1350 mg sodium.

# Miso Soup

PREP: 20 MINUTES ∿ COOK: 35 MINUTES

1 tablespoon vegetable oil
2 large carrots, peeled and thinly sliced
2 garlic cloves, minced
1 small onion, diced
1 tablespoon grated, peeled fresh ginger
½ small head Napa (Chinese cabbage), about 8 ounces, cut crosswise into ½-inch-thick slices to make about 4 cups
1 tablespoon seasoned rice vinegar
¼ teaspoon coarsely ground black pepper
1 package (16 ounces) firm tofu, drained and cut into ½-inch cubes
¼ cup red miso, diluted with ¼ cup hot tap water
2 green onions, sliced for garnish

**1** In 5-quart Dutch oven, heat vegetable oil over medium heat until hot. Add carrots, garlic, onion, and ginger and cook, stirring occasionally, about 10 minutes or until onion is lightly browned.

**2** Add cabbage, rice vinegar, pepper, and *6 cups water*; heat to boiling over high heat. Reduce heat to low; cover and simmer 20 minutes or until vegetables are tender.

**3** Stir in tofu and miso; heat through, about 2 minutes. Sprinkle with green onions to serve. *Makes 6 servings.*

Each serving: About 185 calories, 14 g protein, 13 g carbohydrate, 10 g total fat (1 g saturated), 0 mg cholesterol, 510 mg sodium.

**2** In 4-quart saucepan, heat *8 cups water* to boiling over high heat. Add soup mix, noodles, carrot, red pepper, lemon peel, crushed red pepper, and tofu mixture; heat to boiling. Reduce heat to low; simmer soup 8 to 10 minutes or until noodles are cooked (if using linguine, cooking time will be slightly longer) and vegetables are tender. Stir in watercress until it wilts. Serve immediately because noodles will absorb liquid quickly. *Makes 4 servings.*

Each serving: About 135 calories, 5 g protein, 21 g carbohydrate, 4 g total fat (0 g saturated), 0 mg cholesterol, 405 mg sodium.

## Japanese Noodle Soup

PREP: 15 MINUTES ∾ COOK: 20 MINUTES

1 tablespoon vegetable oil
6 ounces firm tofu, cut into 1-inch pieces
3 medium green onions, thinly sliced
1 tablespoon grated, peeled fresh ginger
1 package (1.1 ounces) instant shiro miso soup mix
   (white soybean-paste soup)
8 ounces dried udon noodles or linguine
1 large carrot, peeled and cut crosswise into
   thirds, then cut lengthwise into matchsticks
1 medium red pepper, cut into thin strips
3 strips (3" by 1" each) lemon peel
¼ teaspoon crushed red pepper
1 small bunch watercress, tough stems trimmed

**1** In nonstick 10-inch skillet, heat vegetable oil over medium-high heat until hot. Add tofu, green onions, and ginger and cook 5 minutes or until golden.

### ▮▮▮ FOOD EDITOR'S TIP ▮▮▮

**Q.** I've had miso soup in Japanese restaurants and was wondering if there's any way to make it at home. What is miso and where can I get it?

**A.** Miso is a highly concentrated, fermented paste made from a combination of soybeans and a grain such as rice or barley. It comes in a variety of flavors, colors, and textures that fall into three basic categories: Red, which has a strong flavor; golden, which is mild; and white, which is mellow and slightly sweet. Miso can be purchased in health food stores and Oriental markets. You might also want to try an instant miso soup mix for a quick meal such as the recipe for Japanese Noodle Soup, above.

## Pasta e Piselli

PREP: 10 MINUTES ∾ COOK: 15 MINUTES

Dust with freshly grated Parmesan for an irresistible touch.

2 cups mixed pasta shapes (about 8 ounces) or
   elbow macaroni
Salt
2 tablespoons olive oil
3 garlic cloves, crushed with side of chef's knife
2 cans (14½ ounces each) chicken broth or
   3½ cups homemade (page 24)
1 can (14½ ounces) diced tomatoes
¼ cup packed fresh basil leaves, coarsely chopped
1 package (10 ounces) frozen peas, thawed
Grated Parmesan cheese

**1** In large saucepot, prepare pasta in *boiling salted water* as label directs; drain.

**2** Meanwhile, in 4-quart saucepan or saucepot, heat olive oil over medium heat until hot. Add garlic; cook until golden, about 5 minutes.

**3** Remove saucepan from heat. Then carefully add chicken broth, tomatoes with their juice, basil, and *½ cup water*. Return to heat; heat to boiling. Reduce heat to low; cover and simmer 5 minutes; discard garlic.

**4** Add peas and pasta; heat through. Serve soup with grated Parmesan. *Makes 5 servings.*

Each serving without Parmesan: About 290 calories, 11 g protein, 46 g carbohydrate, 7 g total fat (1 g saturated), 8 mg cholesterol, 705 mg sodium.

*Winter Vegetable Chili*

# Winter Vegetable Chili

PREP: 15 MINUTES ~ COOK: 1 HOUR

4 teaspoons olive oil

1 medium butternut squash (1¾ pounds), peeled and cut into ¾-inch cubes

2 medium carrots, peeled and diced

1 medium onion, diced

3 tablespoons chili powder

1 can (28 ounces) tomatoes in juice

1 can (4 ounces) chopped mild green chiles

1 cup vegetable broth

¼ teaspoon salt

2 cans (15 to 19 ounces each) black beans, rinsed and drained

¼ cup chopped fresh cilantro leaves

4 tablespoons nonfat sour cream (optional)

1 In 5-quart Dutch oven, heat 2 teaspoons olive oil over medium-high heat until hot. Add butternut squash and cook, stirring occasionally, until golden; transfer to bowl.

2 In same Dutch oven, heat remaining 2 teaspoons olive oil; add carrots and onion and cook until well browned. Stir in chili powder; cook 1 minute, stirring.

3 Add tomatoes with their juice, chiles with their liquid, vegetable broth, and salt; heat to boiling over high heat. Reduce heat to low; cover and simmer 30 minutes, stirring occasionally with spoon to break up tomatoes.

4 Stir in black beans and butternut squash; heat to boiling over high heat. Reduce heat to low; cover and simmer 15 minutes or until squash is tender and chili thickens. Stir in cilantro. Serve with sour cream if you like. *Makes 6 servings.*

Each serving without sour cream: About 225 calories, 14 g protein, 44 g carbohydrate, 5 g total fat (1 g saturated), 0 mg cholesterol, 930 mg sodium.

# Country Vegetable Stew with Couscous

PREP: 20 MINUTES ～ COOK: 50 MINUTES

2 tablespoons olive oil
1 pound medium mushrooms, halved
1 medium eggplant (about 1 pound), cut into
    1-inch chunks
2 small zucchini (about 6 ounces each), cut into
    ½-inch chunks
1 pound carrots, peeled and cut into ¼-inch-thick
    slices
1 medium onion, coarsely chopped
1 can (28 ounces) tomatoes in juice
1 teaspoon sugar
¾ teaspoon salt
½ teaspoon ground cumin
1 can (14½ ounces) vegetable broth
1 cup couscous (Moroccan pasta)
2 teaspoons chopped fresh parsley leaves
1 tablespoon all-purpose flour
1 can (15 to 19 ounces) garbanzo beans, rinsed
    and drained

1 In nonstick 5-quart Dutch oven or saucepot, heat
2 teaspoons olive oil over medium-high heat until hot.
Add mushrooms and cook until golden brown and all
liquid from mushrooms evaporates; transfer to bowl.

2 In same Dutch oven, heat 2 teaspoons olive oil
until hot. Add eggplant and zucchini and cook until
golden brown; transfer to bowl with mushrooms. In
same Dutch oven, heat remaining 2 teaspoons olive
oil; add carrots and onion and cook until golden
brown. Stir in tomatoes with their juice, sugar, salt,
and cumin; heat to boiling. Reduce heat to low; cover
and simmer 10 minutes, stirring occasionally with
spoon to break up tomatoes.

3 Add mushrooms, eggplant, zucchini, and any juices
in bowl to Dutch oven; heat to boiling. Reduce heat to
low; cover and simmer 10 minutes or until vegetables
are tender.

4 Meanwhile, in 2-quart saucepan, heat vegetable
broth to boiling over high heat. Add couscous; cover
and remove from heat; let stand 5 minutes. Stir in
chopped parsley.

5 In cup, mix flour with *2 tablespoons water*. Stir flour
mixture and garbanzo beans into vegetables; heat to
boiling over high heat. Boil 2 minutes until stew thickens slightly and beans are heated through. Serve stew
over couscous. *Makes 6 servings.*

Each serving: About 335 calories, 12 g protein, 59 g carbohydrate,
7 g total fat (1 g saturated), 0 mg cholesterol, 915 mg sodium.

# Vegetable & Pasta Chili

PREP: 20 MINUTES ～ COOK: 40 MINUTES

If you like your chili hot, garnish this with shredded
chile-studded Monterey Jack.

1 cup elbow macaroni (about 4 ounces)
2 tablespoons vegetable oil
2 medium carrots, peeled and thinly sliced
1 large onion, chopped
1 medium zucchini (about 8 ounces), cut into
    ½-inch pieces
1 medium yellow straightneck squash (about
    8 ounces), cut into ½-inch pieces
3 tablespoons chili powder
½ teaspoon salt
1 can (28 ounces) tomatoes in juice
1 can (16 ounces) whole-kernel corn, drained
1 can (4 ounces) chopped mild green chiles
⅓ cup tomato paste
½ teaspoon hot pepper sauce
2 cans (15½ to 19 ounces each) red kidney beans,
    rinsed and drained

1 In large saucepot, prepare pasta in *boiling water* as
label directs; do not use salt. Set macaroni aside.

2 Meanwhile, in 5-quart Dutch oven, heat vegetable
oil over medium-high heat until hot. Add carrots and
onion and cook, stirring occasionally, until vegetables
begin to brown. Add zucchini and yellow squash;
cook, stirring, until all vegetables are tender-crisp.

3 Stir in chili powder and salt; cook 1 minute. Add
tomatoes with their juice, corn, chopped green chiles
with their liquid, tomato paste, hot pepper sauce, and
*2½ cups water*; heat to boiling over high heat. Reduce
heat to low; simmer, uncovered, 20 minutes. Stir in
red kidney beans and macaroni; heat through. *Makes
6 servings.*

Each serving: About 340 calories, 15 g protein, 59 g carbohydrate,
7 g total fat (1 g saturated), 0 mg cholesterol, 980 mg sodium.

# Hearty Mushroom-Barley Soup

PREP: 20 MINUTES ～ COOK: 1¼ HOURS

Get a head start by partially cooking the barley a day ahead, as in step 1; cool and refrigerate.

¾ cup barley
2 tablespoons olive oil
3 medium celery stalks, sliced
1 large onion, chopped
1½ pounds mushrooms, thickly sliced
2 tablespoons tomato paste
2 cans (14½ ounces each) beef broth
5 medium carrots, peeled, halved lengthwise, then
    cut crosswise into ¼-inch-thick slices
¼ cup dry sherry
1 teaspoon salt

1 In 3-quart saucepan, heat barley and *4 cups water* to boiling over high heat. Reduce heat to low; cover and simmer 30 minutes. Drain barley; set aside.

2 Meanwhile, in 5-quart Dutch oven or saucepot, heat olive oil over medium-high heat until hot. Add celery and onion; cook 8 to 10 minutes or until golden, stirring occasionally. Increase heat to high; add mushrooms and cook 10 to 12 minutes or until liquid evaporates and mushrooms are lightly browned, stirring occasionally.

3 Reduce heat to medium-high; add tomato paste and cook, stirring, 2 minutes. Add beef broth, carrots, sherry, salt, barley, and *4 cups water*; heat to boiling. Reduce heat to low; cover and simmer 20 to 25 minutes or until carrots and barley are tender. *Makes 6 servings.*

Each serving: About 215 calories, 8 g protein, 32 g carbohydrate, 5 g total fat (0 g saturated), 0 mg cholesterol, 835 mg sodium.

# Curried Vegetable Stew

PREP: 10 MINUTES ～ COOK: 20 MINUTES

Serve the stew with an Indian bread, such as naan.

2 teaspoons olive oil
1 large sweet potato (about 12 ounces), peeled
    and cut into ½-inch chunks
1 medium onion, cut into ½-inch pieces
1 medium zucchini (about 8 ounces), cut into
    1-inch chunks
1 small green pepper, cut into ¾-inch pieces
1½ teaspoons curry powder

---

# A TOAST TO SOUPS & STEWS

All you need to turn a soup or a stew into a satisfying meal is a simple salad and a loaf of crusty bread to mop up the juices. If you have the time, try one of the following soup-friendly recipes.

## Herb & Garlic Bread

Preheat oven to 425°F. Cut *1 loaf Italian bread* (16 inches long) crosswise into 1-inch-thick slices, but do not cut all the way through. With the flat side of a knife, or a mortar and pestle, crush *1 garlic clove* to form a paste. In cup, mix garlic paste, *¼ cup olive oil, 1 tablespoon chopped fresh parsley leaves, ½ teaspoon salt, ½ teaspoon dried oregano,* and *¼ teaspoon coarsely ground black pepper.* With pastry brush, brush garlic mixture lightly on cut sides of bread slices, brushing any remaining garlic mixture on top of loaf. Wrap loaf loosely in foil, leaving top seam of foil slightly open. Bake loaf 20 minutes or until heated through. Makes 8 servings.

Each serving: About 215 calories, 5 g protein, 29 g carbohydrate, 9 g total fat (1 g saturated), 0 mg cholesterol, 475 mg sodium.

## Rosemary Toast Hearts

Preheat broiler. With 3¼-inch heart-shaped cookie cutter, cut a heart from each of *4 slices white bread.* Drizzle *1½ teaspoons olive oil* over hearts; sprinkle with *1 tablespoon grated Parmesan cheese, ¼ teaspoon crushed dried rosemary,* and *⅛ teaspoon black pepper.* Broil hearts on cookie sheet until golden, turning once. Makes 2 servings.

Each serving: About 135 calories, 4 g protein, 18 g carbohydrate, 5 g total fat (1 g saturated), 2 mg cholesterol, 235 mg sodium.

1 teaspoon ground cumin
1 can (15 to 19 ounces) garbanzo beans, rinsed
    and drained
1 can (14½ ounces) diced tomatoes
¾ cup vegetable broth
½ teaspoon salt

1 In nonstick 12-inch skillet, heat olive oil over medium-high heat until hot. Add sweet potato, onion, zucchini, and green pepper; cook 8 to 10 minutes or until vegetables are golden, stirring occasionally. Add curry and cumin; cook 1 minute, stirring.

2 Add garbanzo beans, tomatoes with their juice, vegetable broth, and salt; heat to boiling over high heat. Reduce heat to medium-low; cover skillet and simmer 10 minutes or until vegetables are fork-tender. *Makes 4 servings.*

Each serving: About 295 calories, 10 g protein, 55 g carbohydrate, 6 g total fat (1 g saturated), 0 mg cholesterol, 785 mg sodium.

# Butternut & Lentil Stew

PREP: 15 MINUTES ᕽ COOK: 30 MINUTES

In the fall, try this with fresh pumpkin in place of butternut squash.

1 can (14½ ounces) chicken broth or 1¾ cups
    homemade (page 24)
1 cup dry lentils, rinsed
1 bay leaf
1 tablespoon olive oil
1 medium onion, chopped
2 garlic cloves, crushed with garlic press
1 medium butternut squash (2½ pounds), peeled
    and cut into ¾-inch chunks
1 tablespoon chopped fresh sage, basil, or parsley
    leaves
¾ teaspoon salt
¼ teaspoon coarsely ground black pepper
2 plum tomatoes, coarsely chopped

1 In 2-quart saucepan, combine chicken broth and *enough water* to equal 3 cups. Stir in lentils and bay leaf; heat to boiling over high heat. Reduce heat to low; cover and simmer 25 minutes or until lentils are tender. Set aside.

2 Meanwhile, in nonstick 12-inch skillet, heat olive oil over medium heat until hot. Add onion and garlic and cook 5 minutes, stirring occasionally. Stir in butternut squash, sage, salt, and pepper. Cook, covered, 15 minutes or until squash is tender, stirring frequently.

3 Stir lentils with any cooking liquid into squash mixture. Discard bay leaf. Stir in tomatoes. Increase heat to medium-high and cook, uncovered, 1 minute longer. *Makes 4 servings.*

Each serving: About 255 calories, 12 g protein, 45 g carbohydrate, 5 g total fat (1 g saturated), 0 mg cholesterol, 750 mg sodium.

# Skillet Eggplant Stew

PREP: 15 MINUTES ᕽ COOK: 35 MINUTES

2 tablespoons plus 1 teaspoon olive oil
1 large onion, cut into ¾-inch pieces
2 medium eggplants (about 1 pound each), cut into
    2-inch pieces
⅓ cup pimiento-stuffed olives
2 tablespoons dark brown sugar
1 tablespoon balsamic vinegar
½ teaspoon salt
1 package (9 ounces) fresh mozzarella cheese balls,
    drained and each cut in half
1 large tomato (about 8 ounces), cut into ¾-inch
    pieces
¼ cup loosely packed fresh basil leaves, coarsely
    chopped

1 In nonstick 12-inch skillet (2 inches deep) or nonstick 5-quart saucepot, heat 1 teaspoon olive oil over medium heat until hot. Add onion and cook 10 minutes or until golden, stirring occasionally.

2 Increase heat to medium-high. Add remaining 2 tablespoons olive oil and eggplant to onion in skillet. Cook vegetables about 10 minutes longer or until eggplant is browned. Stir in olives, sugar, balsamic vinegar, salt, and *½ cup water*; heat to boiling. Reduce heat to low; cover and simmer 10 to 15 minutes longer or until eggplant is tender.

3 Remove skillet from heat; stir in mozzarella, tomato, and basil. *Makes 4 servings.*

Each serving: About 385 calories, 15 g protein, 31 g carbohydrate, 23 g fat (1 g saturated), 45 mg cholesterol, 625 mg sodium.

# PUMPKIN-POT STEW

When fresh pumpkins are in season, not only can they be called on to provide a delicious stew ingredient, but they can also be used as an interesting serving vessel. In this recipe, the pumpkin is cooked separately in the oven while the stew cooks on the stovetop. The stew is ladled into the cooked pumpkin and taken to the table. As the stew is served, chunks of cooked pumpkin are carved out and added to the bowls

PREP: 20 MINUTES  ∾  COOK: 1½ HOURS

1 medium pumpkin (12 pounds)
2 tablespoons vegetable oil
1 pound small white onions, peeled but left whole
4 large carrots (about 1 pound), peeled, halved lengthwise, and cut crosswise into thirds
2 pounds beef for stew
1 can (14½ ounces) beef broth
¼ cup ketchup
1 teaspoon salt
½ teaspoon coarsely ground black pepper
½ teaspoon dried thyme leaves
2 pounds all-purpose potatoes, peeled and cut into 1½-inch chunks
4 ounces small mushrooms, halved if large
1 package (12 ounces) frozen cut Italian green beans, thawed
2 tablespoons all-purpose flour

**1** Preheat oven to 450°F. Cut top from pumpkin; set aside. Scoop out seeds and membranes. Place pumpkin shell with top in place in pie plate; set in large roasting pan. Place pan on oven rack; pour in *boiling water* to come up just under rim of pie plate. Cover loosely with foil; bake 1½ hours or until tender.

**2** Meanwhile, in 8-quart Dutch oven, heat vegetable oil over medium-high heat until hot. Add onions and carrots and cook until golden; with slotted spoon, transfer to bowl. In oil remaining in Dutch oven, cook beef chunks, half at a time, until browned.

**3** Return all beef to Dutch oven; stir in beef broth, ketchup, salt, pepper, and thyme; heat to boiling, scraping to loosen brown bits. Reduce to low; cover and simmer 20 minutes.

**4** Add potatoes to stew along with carrots, onions, and mushrooms; heat to boiling. Reduce heat to low; cover and simmer 40 minutes longer or until meat and vegetables are tender. Stir in Italian green beans; heat through.

**5** Skim fat from liquid. In cup, blend flour with *2 tablespoons water*. Stir into liquid in Dutch oven; heat to boiling over high heat; boil 1 minute.

**6** Discard any liquid in pumpkin shell. Place pumpkin on platter; spoon stew into pumpkin. To serve, spoon out stew, scooping some pumpkin meat with each serving. Makes 8 servings.

Each serving: About 495 calories, 26 g protein, 39 g carbohydrate, 27 g total fat (10 g saturated), 82 mg cholesterol, 745 mg sodium.

# Moroccan Vegetable Stew

PREP: 15 MINUTES  ∾  COOK: 40 MINUTES

A hearty vegetarian stew sweetened with cinnamon and prunes.

1 tablespoon olive oil
2 medium carrots, peeled and cut into ¼-inch-thick slices
1 medium butternut squash (about 1¾ pounds), peeled and cut into 1-inch cubes
1 medium onion, chopped
1 can (15 to 19 ounces) garbanzo beans, rinsed and drained
1 can (14½ ounces) stewed tomatoes
½ cup pitted prunes, chopped
½ teaspoon ground cinnamon
½ teaspoon salt
⅛ to ¼ teaspoon crushed red pepper
1 cup couscous (Moroccan pasta)
2 tablespoons chopped fresh cilantro or parsley leaves

1  In nonstick 12-inch skillet, heat olive oil over medium-high heat. Add carrots, squash, and onion and cook until golden, about 10 minutes.

2  Stir in garbanzo beans, stewed tomatoes, prunes, cinnamon, salt, crushed red pepper, and *1½ cups water*; heat to boiling. Reduce heat to low; cover and simmer 30 minutes or until all vegetables are tender.

3  Meanwhile, prepare couscous as label directs.

4  Stir cilantro into stew. Spoon stew over couscous to serve. *Makes 4 servings.*

Each serving: About 475 calories, 15 g protein, 94 g carbohydrate, 5 g total fat (1 g saturated), 3 mg cholesterol, 780 mg sodium.

# Curried Lentil Soup

PREP: 30 MINUTES  ∾  COOK: 1 HOUR

Serve with toasted whole-wheat pitas.

2 tablespoons olive oil
4 medium carrots, peeled and diced
2 large celery stalks, diced
1 large onion, chopped
1 medium Granny Smith apple, peeled, cored, and diced
1 tablespoon grated, peeled fresh ginger
1 large garlic clove, crushed with garlic press
2 teaspoons curry powder
¾ teaspoon ground cumin
¾ teaspoon ground coriander
2 cans (14½ ounces each) vegetable or chicken broth (or 3½ cups homemade chicken broth, page 24)
1 package (16 ounces) dry lentils, rinsed
¼ cup chopped fresh cilantro leaves
½ teaspoon salt
Plain low-fat yogurt

1  In 5-quart Dutch oven or saucepot, heat olive oil over medium-high heat until hot. Add carrots, celery, onion, and apple; cook, stirring occasionally, 10 to 15 minutes or until lightly browned.

2  Add ginger, garlic, curry, cumin, and coriander; cook, stirring, 1 minute.

3  Add vegetable broth, lentils, and *5 cups water*; heat to boiling over high heat. Reduce heat to low; cover and simmer 45 to 55 minutes or until lentils are tender, stirring occasionally. Stir in cilantro and salt. Serve with yogurt. *Makes 5 servings.*

Each serving without yogurt: About 370 calories, 20 g protein, 60 g carbohydrate, 7 g total fat (1 g saturated), 0 mg cholesterol, 315 mg sodium.

# Caldo Verde

PREP: 15 MINUTES ～ COOK: 45 MINUTES

This thick green soup is a Portuguese classic made with potatoes and very thinly sliced kale.

2 tablespoons olive oil
1 large onion, diced
3 garlic cloves, minced
2½ pounds all-purpose potatoes (about 8 medium), peeled and cut into 2-inch chunks
2 cans (14½ ounces each) chicken broth or 3½ cups homemade (page 24)
½ teaspoon salt
¼ teaspoon coarsely ground black pepper
1 pound kale, coarse stems and veins removed, very thinly sliced

1 In 5-quart Dutch oven, heat olive oil over medium heat until hot. Add onion and garlic; cook until lightly browned, about 10 minutes.

*Mussel Soup*

2 Add potatoes, chicken broth, salt, pepper, and *3 cups water*; heat to boiling over high heat. Reduce heat to low; cover and simmer until potatoes are fork-tender, about 20 minutes.

3 With potato masher, mash potatoes in broth until potatoes are lumpy.

4 Stir in kale; simmer, uncovered, until tender, about 5 to 8 minutes. *Makes 5 servings.*

Each serving: About 250 calories, 8 g protein, 42 g carbohydrate, 7 g total fat (1 g saturated), 8 mg cholesterol, 925 mg sodium.

# Mussel Soup

PREP: 15 MINUTES ～ COOK: 20 MINUTES

1 tablespoon olive oil
1 large onion, sliced
2 garlic cloves, minced
1 can (28 ounces) plum tomatoes in puree
1 bottle (8 ounces) clam juice
½ cup dry white wine
¼ teaspoon salt
⅛ teaspoon crushed red pepper
2 pounds small mussels, scrubbed and debearded
2 tablespoons chopped fresh parsley
Green onions for garnish

1 In 5-quart Dutch oven, heat olive oil over medium heat until hot. Add onion and cook until tender and lightly browned, about 10 minutes. Add garlic; cook 2 minutes longer.

2 Stir in tomatoes with their puree, clam juice, white wine, salt, crushed red pepper, and *2 cups water*. Heat to boiling over high heat, stirring and breaking up tomatoes with spoon. Boil 3 minutes.

3 Add mussels; heat to boiling. Reduce heat to low; cover and simmer, stirring occasionally, until mussels open, about 4 minutes. Discard any mussels that do not open. Stir in parsley just before serving. Garnish with green onions. *Makes 4 servings.*

Each serving: About 160 calories, 11 g protein, 16 g carbohydrate, 6 g total fat (1 g saturated), 22 mg cholesterol, 790 mg sodium.

# Bouillabaisse

This classic Mediterranean seafood stew is easy to prepare and makes a terrific dinner for a crowd (the recipe serves 12). With crusty bread and a big green salad, it makes for a memorable meal.

1 dozen littleneck clams, scrubbed
1 dozen medium mussels, scrubbed and debearded
2 tablespoons olive oil
3 medium leeks (about 1 pound), rinsed to remove sand, then cut crosswise into 1-inch pieces
1 garlic clove, minced
2 cans (14½ to 16 ounces each) whole tomatoes
1 teaspoon salt
¾ teaspoon dried thyme leaves
½ teaspoon saffron threads
2 pounds boneless cod or scrod, cut into 1½-inch pieces
1 pound large shrimp, shelled and deveined
1 pound sea scallops, sliced horizontally in half
2 tablespoons chopped fresh parsley leaves

1 In 8-quart Dutch oven or saucepot, heat *1 cup water* to boiling over high heat; add clams and mussels and heat to boiling. Reduce heat to medium; cover and cook until shells just open, about 5 minutes, stirring occasionally. With slotted spoon, remove clams and mussels to large bowl. Rinse each clam and mussel in cooking broth in Dutch oven to remove any sand. Let broth stand until sand settles to bottom of Dutch oven. Pour clear broth into bowl with shellfish; discard gritty broth remaining in Dutch oven. Wipe Dutch oven dry.

2 In same Dutch oven, heat olive oil over medium heat until hot. Add leeks and garlic and cook until leeks are tender. Add tomatoes with their juice, salt, thyme, saffron, *2 cups water*, and reserved clam broth; heat to boiling.

3 Add cod, shrimp, and scallops; heat to boiling. Reduce heat to medium-low; cook, uncovered, 5 to 8 minutes or until cod flakes easily when tested with a fork, shrimp turn opaque throughout, and scallops are opaque. Add clams and mussels; heat through. Sprinkle with parsley. *Makes 12 servings.*

Each serving: About 205 calories, 30 g protein, 11 g carbohydrate, 4 g total fat (1 g saturated), 99 mg cholesterol, 500 mg sodium.

# Italian Seafood Stew

4 medium all-purpose potatoes (about 1 pound), peeled and quartered
1 medium zucchini (about 8 ounces), cut into bite-size chunks
2 teaspoons olive oil
1 small onion, minced
1 garlic clove, minced
½ cup chicken broth, canned or homemade (page 24)
8 cherrystone clams, scrubbed
8 large mussels, scrubbed and debearded
1 can (28 ounces) tomatoes in juice
½ cup dry white wine
1 teaspoon sugar
½ teaspoon salt
8 large shrimp, shelled and deveined
8 ounces red snapper fillets, cut into 2-inch chunks
1 tablespoon chopped fresh basil leaves

1 In 4-quart saucepan, cook potatoes with *enough water to cover* until almost tender, about 15 minutes. Add zucchini; cook until just tender, about 5 minutes. Drain.

2 Meanwhile, in 8-quart Dutch oven, heat olive oil over medium heat until hot. Add onion and cook until tender. Add garlic, chicken broth, clams and mussels; heat to boiling. Cover and cook about 5 minutes, removing clams and mussels to large bowl as shells just open.

3 To broth in Dutch oven, add tomatoes with their juice, wine, sugar, and salt; heat to boiling. Stir in clams, mussels, potatoes, zucchini, shrimp, and red snapper; heat to boiling. Reduce heat to medium; cook, uncovered, until shrimp turn opaque throughout and snapper flakes easily when tested with a fork, about 5 minutes. Sprinkle with chopped basil. *Makes 4 servings.*

Each serving: About 280 calories, 27 g protein, 28 g carbohydrate, 5 g total fat (1 g saturated), 69 mg cholesterol, 895 mg sodium.

## Shrimp & Sausage Gumbo

PREP: 10 MINUTES ～ COOK: 40 MINUTES

This Creole specialty is served with rice. Bake a pan of your favorite corn bread (from a mix or from scratch) to round out the meal.

1 cup regular long-grain rice
1 pound hot Italian-sausage links, casings pierced
    with a fork
2 tablespoons vegetable oil
¼ cup all-purpose flour
2 medium celery stalks, diced
1 medium green pepper, diced
1 medium onion, diced
1 can (14½ ounces) chicken broth or 1¾ cups
    homemade (page 24)
1 package (10 ounces) frozen whole okra
2 teaspoons hot pepper sauce
¼ teaspoon dried thyme leaves
¼ teaspoon dried oregano leaves
1 bay leaf
1 pound large shrimp, shelled and deveined
Oregano sprigs for garnish

1  In 2-quart saucepan, prepare rice as label directs; keep warm.

2  Meanwhile, heat 5-quart Dutch oven or saucepot over medium-high heat until hot. Add sausages and cook until very brown, about 10 minutes, turning often. Transfer sausages to plate to cool slightly. Slice each sausage into thirds.

3  Discard all but 1 tablespoon drippings from Dutch oven. Add vegetable oil and heat over medium heat until hot. Stir in flour until blended and cook, stirring frequently, until flour is dark brown but not burned. Add celery, green pepper, and onion and cook 8 to 10 minutes or until tender, stirring occasionally.

4  Return sausages to Dutch oven. Gradually stir in chicken broth, okra, hot pepper sauce, thyme, oregano, bay leaf, and *½ cup water*; heat to boiling. Reduce heat to low; cover and simmer 15 minutes.

Add shrimp and cook, uncovered, until shrimp turn opaque throughout, about 2 minutes. Discard bay leaf. Serve gumbo in bowls with a scoop of hot rice in center of each bowl. Garnish with oregano sprigs. *Makes 6 servings.*

Each serving: About 470 calories, 28 g protein, 37 g carbohydrate, 22 g total fat (7 g saturated), 138 mg cholesterol, 970 mg sodium.

## New England Cod Chowder

PREP: 20 MINUTES ～ COOK: 30 MINUTES

A creamy winter warmer made with potatoes, fennel, carrots, and chunks of codfish.

4 slices bacon
3 medium carrots, peeled, halved lengthwise, then
    cut crosswise into slices
1 fennel bulb (1 pound), diced, or 3 celery stalks,
    diced
1 medium onion, diced
3 medium all-purpose potatoes (1 pound), peeled
    and cut into ½-inch cubes
3 bottles (8 ounces each) clam juice
1 can (14½ ounces) chicken broth or 1¾ cups
    homemade (page 24)
1 bay leaf
1 pound boneless cod, cut into 1½-inch pieces
1 cup half-and-half or light cream

1  In 5-quart Dutch oven or saucepot, cook bacon over medium heat until browned. Remove bacon to paper towels to drain; crumble.

2  Discard all but 2 tablespoons bacon fat in Dutch oven. Add carrots, fennel, and onion and cook 6 to 8 minutes or until lightly browned, stirring occasionally. Add potatoes, clam juice, chicken broth, and bay leaf; heat to boiling. Reduce heat to low; cover and simmer 10 to 15 minutes until vegetables are tender.

3  Add cod; cover and cook 2 to 5 minutes or until cod flakes easily when tested with a fork. Carefully stir in half-and-half; heat through. Discard bay leaf. Serve soup with crumbled bacon. *Makes 5 servings.*

Each serving: About 335 calories, 24 g protein, 30 g carbohydrate, 14 g total fat (6 g saturated), 72 mg cholesterol, 780 mg sodium.

*Shrimp & Sausage Gumbo* ➤

# TAKING STOCK

Nothing beats the flavor of a soup made with fresh chicken broth. Though canned or even reconstituted broths are fine in a pinch, broth made from scratch lends a real depth of flavor. Use our classic long-simmering version or the superquick pressure-cooker one (and the reserved chicken) in our Sunday Chicken Soup (opposite page) or South-of-the-Border Chicken Soup (page 26). The broth also freezes well in sturdy containers for up to 3 months.

## Old-Fashioned Chicken Broth

PREP: 15 MINUTES PLUS OVERNIGHT TO CHILL
COOK: 4 HOURS 15 MINUTES

*1 whole chicken (about 3½ pounds)*
*2 carrots, peeled and cut into 2-inch pieces*
*1 celery stalk, cut into 2-inch pieces*
*1 medium onion, unpeeled and cut into quarters*
*5 parsley sprigs*
*1 garlic clove, unpeeled*
*½ teaspoon dried thyme leaves*
*½ bay leaf*

**1** In 8-quart Dutch oven or saucepot, place whole chicken with its neck (refrigerate or freeze giblets for use another day), carrots, celery, onion, parsley, garlic, thyme, and bay leaf. Add *3 quarts water*; heat to boiling over high heat. With slotted spoon, skim any foam from surface. Reduce heat to low; cover and simmer 1 hour, turning chicken once and skimming foam occasionally.

**2** Remove Dutch oven from heat and transfer chicken to cutting board. When chicken is cool enough to handle, remove meat from bones (refrigerate or freeze meat for use another day). Return chicken bones, skin, and scraps to Dutch oven; heat to boiling over high heat. Reduce heat to low; simmer, uncovered, 3 hours.

**3** Drain broth through colander into large bowl. Strain broth through sieve into another large bowl. Discard solids in sieve; cool broth slightly. Cover and refrigerate overnight.

**4** When cold, discard fat from surface of broth. Makes about 5 cups broth.

Each ½ cup: About 10 calories, 1 g protein, 1 g carbohydrate, 0 g total fat, 0 mg cholesterol, 30 mg sodium.

## Pressure-Cooker Chicken Broth

PREP: 15 MINUTES ∿ COOK: 20 MINUTES

**1** In 6-quart pressure cooker, place all ingredients called for in Old-Fashioned Chicken Broth, but use only *4 cups water*.

**2** Following manufacturer's directions, cover pressure cooker and bring up to high pressure (15 pounds). Cook 15 minutes. Remove cooker from heat and allow pressure to drop for 5 minutes, then follow manufacturer's directions for quick release of pressure.

**3** Drain broth through colander into large bowl. Strain broth through sieve into another large bowl. Transfer chicken to cutting board; discard solids in sieve. When chicken is cool enough to handle, remove meat from bones (refrigerate or freeze meat for use another day); discard skin and bones. Skim fat from broth (or refrigerate overnight to make skimming easier). Makes about 5½ cups broth.

Each ½ cup: About 10 calories, 1 g protein, 1 g carbohydrate, 0 g total fat, 0 mg cholesterol, 30 mg sodium.

Editor's note: We made our broths without salt so they're versatile enough to use in a variety of recipes. If you want to serve the broth on its own, stir in 2 teaspoons salt (or to taste) after cooking.

# Chicken Stew with Rosemary Dumplings

PREP: 20 MINUTES ⌒ COOK: 1 HOUR

It doesn't take hours to make this home-style recipe when you use quick-cooking chicken breasts.

2 tablespoons vegetable oil
6 large chicken-breast halves with bones (about
    3¼ pounds), skin removed
4 large carrots, peeled and cut into 1-inch pieces
2 large celery stalks, cut into ¼-inch-thick slices
1 medium onion, diced
2 teaspoons baking powder
1½ teaspoons chopped fresh rosemary or
    ½ teaspoon dried rosemary leaves, crushed
1 cup plus 2 tablespoons all-purpose flour
1¼ teaspoons salt
1½ cups milk
1 large egg
1 can (14½ ounces) chicken broth or 1¾ cups
    homemade (page 24)
¼ teaspoon coarsely ground black pepper
1 package (10 ounces) frozen peas, thawed

1  In 8-quart Dutch oven, heat 1 tablespoon vegetable oil over medium-high heat until hot. Add half the chicken and cook until lightly browned, 8 to 10 minutes. Transfer chicken to bowl. Repeat with remaining chicken.

2  To drippings in Dutch oven, add remaining 1 tablespoon vegetable oil. Add carrots, celery, and onion; cook until vegetables are browned and tender, about 10 minutes, stirring frequently.

3  Meanwhile, prepare dumplings: In small bowl, mix baking powder, rosemary, 1 cup flour, and ½ teaspoon salt. In cup, mix ½ cup milk with egg. Stir milk mixture into flour mixture just until blended.

4  Return chicken to Dutch oven; add chicken broth, pepper, remaining ¾ teaspoon salt, and *2 cups water*; heat to boiling. Drop dumpling mixture by rounded tablespoons on top of chicken and vegetables to make 12 dumplings. Cover; reduce heat to low and simmer 15 minutes.

5  Transfer dumplings, chicken, and vegetables to large bowl, reserving broth in Dutch oven.

6  In cup, mix remaining 2 tablespoons flour with remaining 1 cup milk until blended; stir into broth mixture. Heat to boiling over high heat; boil 1 minute to thicken slightly. Add peas and heat through. Return dumplings, chicken, and vegetables to Dutch oven. *Makes 6 servings.*

Each serving: About 400 calories, 40 g protein, 37 g carbohydrate, 10 g total fat (3 g saturated), 124 mg cholesterol, 940 mg sodium.

# Sunday Chicken Soup

PREP: 20 MINUTES ⌒ COOK: 2 HOURS

1 tablespoon olive oil
2 large carrots, peeled and cut into ¼-inch-thick
    slices
2 medium celery stalks, cut into ¼-inch-thick slices
1 medium onion, chopped
1 whole chicken (about 3½ pounds)
½ cup barley
1 teaspoon salt
¼ teaspoon coarsely ground black pepper
1 can (14½ to 16 ounces) stewed tomatoes
1 small head escarole (about 1 pound), coarsely
    chopped

1  In 8-quart Dutch oven or saucepot, heat olive oil over medium-high heat until hot. Add carrots, celery, and onion and cook, stirring frequently, until vegetables are golden.

2  Meanwhile, remove skin and as much fat as possible from chicken. Into Dutch oven with vegetables, place chicken, breast-side down. Add *10 cups water* and heat to boiling over high heat. Reduce heat to low; cover and simmer 45 minutes or until chicken is fork-tender. Remove chicken to bowl; refrigerate until chicken is cool enough to handle.

3  While chicken is cooling, add barley, salt, and pepper to vegetable mixture; heat to boiling over high heat. Reduce heat to low; cover and simmer 1¼ hours or until barley is tender.

4  Discard the bones and any skin and fat from the chicken; tear chicken meat into bite-size pieces.

5  When barley is tender, stir in chicken, stewed tomatoes, and escarole; heat to boiling over high heat. Reduce heat to low; cover and simmer 5 minutes to wilt escarole and blend flavors, stirring occasionally. Skim fat from soup, if any. *Makes 6 servings.*

Each serving: About 285 calories, 32 g protein, 25 g carbohydrate, 7 g total fat (1 g saturated), 89 mg cholesterol, 710 mg sodium.

# French Chicken Stew

PREP: 15 MINUTES ~ COOK: 40 MINUTES

3 teaspoons olive oil
4 medium skinless, boneless chicken-breast halves
    (about 1 pound), cut into 2-inch chunks
4 medium carrots, peeled and cut into 1½-inch
    pieces
2 medium potatoes (about ¾ pound), peeled and
    cut into 2-inch chunks
1 medium onion, coarsely chopped
¼ cup dry red wine
1 can (14½ to 16 ounces) stewed tomatoes
1¼ cups chicken broth, canned or homemade
    (page 24)
1 teaspoon fresh thyme or ¼ teaspoon dried
    thyme leaves
1 tablespoon all-purpose flour
1 package (10 ounces) frozen peas, thawed

1 In nonstick 12-inch skillet, heat 2 teaspoons olive oil over medium-high heat. Add chicken and cook until golden brown and juices run clear when pierced with tip of knife; transfer to bowl.

2 To drippings in skillet, add remaining 1 teaspoon olive oil and heat until hot. Add carrots, potatoes, and onion; cook until browned. Stir in red wine; cook 1 minute. Stir in stewed tomatoes, broth, and thyme; heat to boiling over high heat. Reduce heat to low; cover and simmer 25 minutes or until vegetables are tender.

3 In cup, mix flour with *2 tablespoons water*. Stir flour mixture, peas, and chicken into skillet; heat to boiling over high heat. Boil 1 minute or until mixture thickens slightly and is heated through.

4 Spoon stew onto 4 dinner plates. *Makes 4 servings.*

Each serving: About 350 calories, 34 g protein, 41 g carbohydrate, 6 g total fat (1 g saturated), 66 mg cholesterol, 785 mg sodium.

# South-of-the-Border Chicken Soup

PREP: 25 MINUTES ~ COOK: 1 HOUR

Except for the finishing touches (in step 6), this can be made a day ahead.

1 whole chicken (about 4 pounds), cut up
3 large celery stalks, cut into thirds
3 medium carrots, peeled and cut into thirds
2 medium onions, unpeeled and each cut into
    quarters
10 cilantro sprigs
2 bay leaves
1 teaspoon whole black peppercorns
8 medium all-purpose potatoes (about 2½ pounds)
1 can (15½ to 16 ounces) whole-kernel corn,
    drained
1½ teaspoons salt
¼ cup fresh lime juice
¼ cup chopped fresh cilantro leaves
Garnishes: 2 medium avocados, cut into ½-inch
    cubes, tortilla chips, lime wedges, cilantro sprigs

1 In 8-quart Dutch oven or saucepot, combine chicken, celery, carrots, onions, cilantro, bay leaves, black peppercorns, 3 whole peeled potatoes, and *10 cups water*; heat to boiling over high heat. Reduce heat to low; cover and simmer 35 to 45 minutes or until chicken and vegetables are tender.

2 Transfer chicken and potatoes to separate bowls.

3 Pour broth through sieve into large bowl. Skim fat from broth and return broth to Dutch oven; discard vegetables and spices. With potato masher, mash potatoes with 1 cup broth; stir mashed-potato mixture into broth in Dutch oven.

4 Peel and dice 5 remaining potatoes. Add potatoes to broth; heat to boiling over high heat. Reduce heat to low; cover and simmer 10 minutes or until potatoes are fork-tender.

5 Meanwhile, discard skin and bones from chicken; cut chicken into bite-size pieces. Stir chicken, corn, and salt into broth; heat through.

6 Just before serving, stir lime juice and chopped cilantro into soup. Serve soup with garnishes. *Makes 8 servings.*

Each serving without garnishes: About 325 calories, 29 g protein, 28 g carbohydrate, 11 g total fat (3 g saturated), 71 mg cholesterol, 590 mg sodium.

# Texas-Style Chili

PREP: 25 MINUTES ~ COOK: 1½ HOURS

A pot of this chili simmering on the range brings our children in from the cold mighty quickly. Small chunks of tender beef with onions and green peppers—but no beans—are simmered in a thick tomato sauce.

¼ cup vegetable oil
3½ pounds beef for stew, cut into ½-inch cubes
2 medium onions, chopped
3 medium green peppers, diced
4 garlic cloves, crushed with garlic press
2 cans (28 ounces each) tomatoes in juice
1 can (12 ounces) tomato paste
⅓ cup chili powder
¼ cup sugar
2 teaspoons salt
2 teaspoons dried oregano leaves
¾ teaspoon cracked black pepper

1 In 8-quart Dutch oven, heat vegetable oil over high heat until hot. Add meat, one-third at a time, and cook until browned. With slotted spoon, transfer meat cubes to bowl as they brown; set aside.

2 Reserve ½ cup onions; cover and set aside. To drippings in Dutch oven, add green peppers, garlic, and remaining onions; cook 10 minutes over medium-high heat, stirring occasionally.

3 Return meat to Dutch oven; add tomatoes with their juice, tomato paste, chili powder, sugar, salt, oregano leaves, cracked black pepper, and *2 cups water*; heat to boiling over high heat. Reduce heat to low; cover and simmer 1½ hours or until meat is fork-tender, stirring occasionally.

4 Spoon chili into large bowl. Pass reserved onions to sprinkle over each serving. ***Makes 12 servings.***

Each serving: About 470 calories, 26 g protein, 21 g carbohydrate, 32 g total fat (11 g saturated), 95 mg cholesterol, 950 mg sodium.

*South-of-the-Border Chicken Soup*

# Lean Beef Stroganoff

PREP: 20 MINUTES ∾ COOK: 30 MINUTES

1 package (12 ounces) extrawide curly noodles
Salt
1 boneless beef top sirloin steak, ¾ inch thick
   (1 pound)
Olive-oil nonstick cooking spray
3 teaspoons olive oil
1 pound medium mushrooms, thickly sliced
1 medium onion, chopped
1 teaspoon cornstarch
1 cup beef broth
½ cup chili sauce
2 tablespoons spicy brown mustard
12 ounces sugar snap peas or snow peas, strings
   removed
2 bags (6 ounces each) radishes, halved if large
6 tablespoons nonfat sour cream
2 tablespoons chopped fresh parsley leaves

1 In large saucepot, prepare noodles in *boiling salted water* as label directs; drain. Keep warm.

2 Meanwhile, with knife held in slanting position, almost parallel to cutting surface, slice steak crosswise into very thin slices.

3 Spray nonstick 12-inch skillet lightly with olive-oil nonstick cooking spray. In hot skillet, cook half the meat over medium-high heat, stirring quickly and constantly, about 2 minutes or until meat just loses its pink color; transfer to bowl. Repeat with remaining meat but do not use nonstick spray again.

4 In same skillet, heat 2 teaspoons olive oil over medium-high heat until hot. Add mushrooms and onion and cook until tender. In cup, mix cornstarch and beef broth; stir into mushroom mixture with chili sauce and mustard. Cook until mixture boils and thickens slightly. Return beef to skillet; heat through.

5 Meanwhile, in nonstick 10-inch skillet, heat remaining 1 teaspoon olive oil and *2 tablespoons water* over medium-high heat until hot. Add sugar snap peas and cook 5 to 7 minutes or until tender-crisp. Transfer to bowl. In same skillet, cook radishes and ¼ *cup water* over medium-high heat 5 to 7 minutes or until tender-crisp. Add sugar snap peas and ½ teaspoon salt to radishes; heat through.

6 Spoon noodles onto 6 dinner plates. Spoon beef mixture over noodles; top each serving with 1 tablespoon sour cream and sprinkle with parsley. Serve with sugar snap peas and radishes. *Makes 6 servings.*

Each serving: About 430 calories, 30 g protein, 58 g carbohydrate, 9 g total fat (2 g saturated), 90 mg cholesterol, 740 mg sodium.

# Orange Beef & Barley Stew

PREP: 25 MINUTES ∾ BAKE: 1¾ HOURS

2 tablespoons vegetable oil
1½ pounds beef for stew, cut into 1½-inch chunks
4 medium carrots, peeled and cut into 2-inch
   pieces
2 medium onions, each cut into 6 wedges
2 garlic cloves, crushed with garlic press
1 can (28 ounces) tomatoes with juice
1 can (14½ ounces) beef broth
1 cup dry red wine
3 strips (3" by 1" each) orange peel
1 bay leaf
½ teaspoon salt
¾ cup barley

1 Preheat oven to 350°F. In 5-quart Dutch oven, heat 1 tablespoon vegetable oil over medium-high heat until hot. Add beef chunks, half at a time, and cook until browned; transfer to bowl.

2 To drippings in Dutch oven, add remaining 1 tablespoon vegetable oil and heat until hot. Add carrots and onions and cook until browned. Add garlic; cook 1 minute, stirring. Return beef to Dutch oven; add tomatoes with their juice, beef broth, red wine, orange peel, bay leaf, and salt. Heat to boiling over high heat, stirring with spoon to break up tomatoes.

3 Cover and bake 45 minutes. Stir in barley; cover and bake 45 to 60 minutes longer or until beef and barley are tender. Discard bay leaf. *Makes 6 servings.*

Each serving: About 385 calories, 31 g protein, 32 g carbohydrate, 14 g total fat (4 g saturated), 55 mg cholesterol, 720 mg sodium.

*Orange Beef & Barley Stew*

# Burgundy Beef Stew

PREP: 30 MINUTES ~ BAKE: 1½ HOURS

The long baking time (no constant stirring and watching) frees you to do other things.

2 tablespoons vegetable oil
1 pound medium mushrooms, halved
1 package (½ ounce) dried mushrooms
2 pounds beef for stew, cut into 1½-inch chunks
¾ teaspoon salt
1 large onion, diced
2 garlic cloves, minced
2 tablespoons tomato paste
2 medium carrots, peeled, halved lengthwise, then cut crosswise into thirds
1 cup chicken broth, canned or homemade (page 24)
¾ cup dry red wine
¼ teaspoon dried thyme leaves
1 bay leaf

1 In 5-quart Dutch oven, heat 1 tablespoon vegetable oil over medium-high heat. Add fresh mushrooms and cook until tender and lightly browned and most of liquid evaporates, about 10 minutes; transfer to small bowl.

2 Meanwhile, in 2-cup glass measuring cup, add dried mushrooms to *1 cup boiling water*. Set aside.

3 Toss beef with salt. In same Dutch oven, heat remaining 1 tablespoon vegetable oil. Add beef chunks, half at a time, and cook until browned, 10 to 12 minutes per batch; transfer to bowl.

4 With slotted spoon, remove dried mushrooms from soaking liquid and coarsely chop; strain liquid. Set aside mushrooms and liquid.

5 Preheat oven to 350°F. In drippings in Dutch oven, cook onion with *2 tablespoons water* for 10 minutes or until tender and lightly browned, stirring occasionally. Add garlic and cook 2 minutes longer. Stir in tomato paste; cook 1 minute, stirring.

6 Return beef to Dutch oven; add dried mushrooms with their strained liquid, carrots, chicken broth, red wine, thyme, and bay leaf. Heat to boiling over high heat. Cover Dutch oven and bake 1¼ hours. Add sautéed mushrooms; bake 15 minutes longer or until beef is tender. Discard bay leaf before serving. *Makes 6 servings.*

Each serving: About 370 calories, 36 g protein, 13 g carbohydrate, 18 g total fat (6 g saturated), 87 mg cholesterol, 480 mg sodium.

## FOOD EDITOR'S TIP

**Q.** If a recipe calls for wine and I want to make the recipe ahead, will the opened wine still be drinkable at mealtime?

**A.** Yes. The most common myth about wine is that it begins to "turn" soon after it's opened. We found otherwise. In a blind wine tasting, we sampled 3 bottles of identical mid-priced red Cabernet Sauvignon—one opened 48 hours before tasting, one 24 hours before, and one just before. We didn't detect any drop-off in quality at all; in fact, most of us preferred the day-old wine. The reason? According to the California-based Wine Market Council, if you drink a glassful or more from a bottle, allowing the remaining vino to stand gives it a chance to aerate, which helps release its flavors and bouquet. Store leftover wine (at the temperature it's served—white, chilled, and red, at room temperature) for up to 48 hours with the original cork.

# Pasta e Fagioli with Sausage & Spinach

PREP: 15 MINUTES PLUS OVERNIGHT TO SOAK BEANS
COOK: 1¾ HOURS

This chunky, almost stewlike soup is a twist on a classic. To make this soup a last-minute dinner option, use canned beans instead: Substitute three 15- to 19-ounce cans of Great Northern or white kidney beans (cannellini), rinsed and drained. Skip steps 1 and 2. In step 5, omit the salt and simmer soup for 15 minutes before adding beans. Heat to boiling, then simmer 15 minutes longer before adding sausage.

1½ cups dry Great Northern beans
1 pound sweet Italian-sausage links, casings removed
1 tablespoon olive oil

**FAST & SLOW COOKERS**

Pressure cookers and slow cookers make home-made soups and stews easier than ever.

## The Pressure's Off

Sturdy, airtight pressure cookers are major time-savers, able to make traditional slow-cooked favorites in a half hour or less, with tender, flavor-ful results that taste like they simmered for hours. (With its sealed lid, the cooker builds up so much steam that the temperature climbs above 212°F.) And unlike the ones our grandmothers used, today's models have safety mechanisms to prevent bursting.

For soup and stew recipes, cut cooking times by two-thirds and use less liquid (since very little will evaporate): about 1 cup more than you want in the finished dish. (You need at least 1 cup of water or other liquid to produce steam.)

When you buy a pressure cooker, look for some of the following features: an easy-lock lid, low- and high-pressure and quick-release settings, and a heavy bottom for even heat distribution

## Taking It Slow

An electric slow cooker can simmer all day and have dinner ready when you walk in the door. It's as safe as leaving a lamp on. Slow cookers operate at low temperatures and are best for meat stews, chilis, bean soups, and other foods that taste bet-ter the longer they simmer. (For food safety, always cut large pieces of meat and whole poultry into small, uniform chunks so the heat can penetrate them quickly and evenly.)

Some features we look for: heating coils in its side-wall for even heat distribution and a removable, dishwasher-safe ceramic casserole (important for cleanup).

---

2 medium onions, chopped
2 garlic cloves, crushed with garlic press
I can (28 ounces) tomatoes in juice
2 cans (14½ ounces each) chicken broth or
   3½ cups homemade (page 24)
½ teaspoon salt
6 ounces ditalini or tubetti pasta (I rounded cup)
5 ounces prewashed spinach (half 10-ounce bag),
   tough stems removed and leaves cut into I-inch-
   wide strips
Grated Parmesan cheese (optional)

**1** Rinse beans under cold running water and discard any stones or shriveled beans. In large bowl, place dry beans and *8 cups water*. Allow to stand at room tem-perature overnight. (Or, in 4-quart saucepan, heat beans and *8 cups water* to boiling over high heat; cook 2 minutes. Remove from heat; cover and let stand 1 hour.) Drain and rinse beans.

**2** In 4-quart saucepan, heat beans and *enough water to cover* by 2 inches to boiling over high heat. Reduce heat to low; cover and simmer 40 minutes to 1 hour or until beans are tender, stirring occasionally. Drain beans.

**3** Heat 5-quart Dutch oven or saucepot over medi-um-high heat until hot. Add sausages and cook until browned, breaking up meat with spoon. With slotted spoon, transfer sausage meat to bowl.

**4** Reduce heat to medium. To drippings in Dutch oven, add olive oil and onions; cook until tender and golden, about 10 minutes. Add garlic; cook 1 minute. Add tomatoes with their juice, using spoon to break up tomatoes.

**5** Add chicken broth, salt, beans, and *2 cups water*; heat to boiling over high heat. Reduce heat to low; cover and simmer 30 minutes. Add sausage meat; heat through.

**6** Meanwhile, in large saucepot, prepare pasta in *boil-ing water* as label directs, but do not add salt to water. Drain pasta; set aside.

**7** Just before serving, stir spinach and cooked pasta into sausage-bean mixture. Serve with grated Parme-san if you like. ***Makes 12 servings.***

Each serving without Parmesan cheese: About 280 calories,
13 g protein, 28 g carbohydrate, 13 g total fat (4 g saturated),
33 mg cholesterol, 745 mg sodium.

# Hungarian Pork Goulash

PREP: 20 MINUTES ～ BAKE: 1½ HOURS

It's still made with lots of onions and paprika, but we added sauerkraut too.

1 tablespoon vegetable oil
2 large onions, chopped
1 garlic clove, minced
¼ cup paprika (yes, this much)
2 pounds boneless pork shoulder blade roast (fresh pork butt), well trimmed, cut into 1½-inch chunks
1 package (16 ounces) sauerkraut, rinsed and drained
1 can (14½ ounces) diced tomatoes
1 can (14½ ounces) beef broth
½ teaspoon salt
¼ teaspoon coarsely ground black pepper
1 cup light sour cream
Hot cooked egg noodles (optional)

1 In 5-quart Dutch oven or saucepot, heat vegetable oil over medium heat. Add onions; cook 10 minutes. Stir in garlic; cook 5 minutes longer or until onions are very tender, stirring often.

2 Preheat oven to 325°F. Stir paprika into onion mixture; cook 1 minute. Add pork, sauerkraut, tomatoes with their juice, beef broth, salt, and pepper; heat to boiling over high heat. Cover and bake 1½ hours or until meat is fork-tender.

3 Remove stew from oven; stir in sour cream. Heat through on top of range over medium heat (do not boil). Serve over noodles if you like. *Makes 6 servings.*

Each serving without noodles: About 525 calories, 31 g protein, 15 g carbohydrate, 39 g total fat (14 g saturated), 104 mg cholesterol, 920 mg sodium.

# Moroccan Lamb Stew

PREP: 30 MINUTES ～ COOK: 1 HOUR 10 MINUTES

Dried fruit is a common component of North African stews.

2 tablespoons vegetable oil
1½ pounds lamb for stew
2 garlic cloves, minced
1 pound carrots, peeled and cut into 2-inch chunks
3 medium turnips (about 1 pound), peeled and quartered
1 jumbo sweet onion (about 12 ounces), such as Walla Walla, cut into 8 wedges
1 can (14½ to 16 ounces) stewed tomatoes
1 cinnamon stick (3 inches long)
¾ teaspoon salt
¼ teaspoon crushed red pepper
1 cup pitted prunes (about 6 ounces), halved
1 can (15 to 19 ounces) garbanzo beans, rinsed and drained
1 package (10 ounces) couscous (Moroccan pasta)
2 tablespoons chopped fresh parsley leaves

1 In 12-inch skillet, heat 1 tablespoon vegetable oil over high heat until hot. Add half of lamb stew meat and cook, transferring pieces to plate as they brown; repeat with remaining lamb stew meat and remaining 1 tablespoon vegetable oil.

2 Stir garlic into drippings in skillet; cook 30 seconds. Return lamb to skillet. Stir in carrots, turnips, onion, tomatoes, cinnamon stick, salt, crushed red pepper, and *1 cup water*; heat to boiling. Reduce heat to low; cover and simmer 45 minutes, stirring occasionally.

3 Stir in prunes and garbanzo beans. Cook, covered, 15 minutes longer or until lamb and vegetables are fork-tender.

4 Meanwhile, prepare couscous as label directs.

5 Stir parsley into stew. Spoon couscous around stew in skillet. *Makes 6 servings.*

Each serving: About 730 calories, 31 g protein, 84 g carbohydrate, 31 g total fat (11 g saturated), 82 mg cholesterol, 710 mg sodium.

# Veal Stew with Orange Gremolata

PREP: 20 MINUTES ～ BAKE: 1¼ HOURS

A baked stew made with onion, carrots, and tomatoes; just before serving, stir in gremolata, a flavorful garnish of garlic, parsley, and grated citrus peel.

2 tablespoons vegetable oil
2 pounds veal for stew, cut into 1½-inch chunks
4 medium carrots, peeled and cut into 2-inch pieces
1 medium onion, chopped
1 cup chicken broth, canned or homemade (page 24)
1 can (16 ounces) tomatoes in puree
¾ teaspoon salt
¼ teaspoon coarsely ground black pepper
¼ teaspoon dried thyme leaves
2 garlic cloves, minced
2 tablespoons chopped fresh parsley leaves
1 tablespoon grated orange peel

1 Preheat oven to 350°F. In 5-quart Dutch oven, heat 1 tablespoon vegetable oil over medium-high heat until hot. Add veal chunks, half at a time, and cook until browned, transferring veal to bowl as it browns.

2 In same Dutch oven, heat remaining 1 tablespoon vegetable oil over medium heat. Add carrots and onion and cook until browned, about 10 minutes.

3 Add chicken broth, stirring to loosen brown bits from bottom of Dutch oven. Return veal to Dutch oven; add tomatoes with their puree, salt, pepper, and thyme; heat to boiling over high heat. Cover and bake 1¼ hours or until meat and vegetables are tender.

4 In small bowl, combine garlic, parsley, and grated orange peel; stir into stew before serving. *Makes 6 servings.*

Each serving: About 305 calories, 31 g protein, 11 g carbohydrate, 15 g total fat (5 g saturated), 126 mg cholesterol, 640 mg sodium.

# Veal & Mushroom Stew

PREP: 35 MINUTES ～ BAKE: 1 TO 1¼ HOURS

1½ pounds veal for stew, cut into 1½-inch chunks
¾ teaspoon salt
¼ teaspoon coarsely ground black pepper
3 tablespoons olive oil
1 pound medium regular mushrooms, halved
4 ounces shiitake mushrooms, stems discarded
⅓ cup sweet Marsala wine
1 package (10 ounces) frozen peas, thawed

1 Sprinkle veal with salt and pepper. In 5-quart Dutch oven, heat 2 tablespoons olive oil over medium-high heat until hot. Add half of veal chunks and cook until browned on all sides, about 10 minutes; remove veal to bowl. Repeat with remaining veal chunks, without adding additional oil; transfer to bowl.

2 Preheat oven to 350°F. In same Dutch oven, heat remaining 1 tablespoon olive oil over medium-high heat until hot. Add both kinds of mushrooms and cook, stirring occasionally, until lightly browned.

3 Return veal to Dutch oven; stir in Marsala and *½ cup water*, scraping to loosen any brown bits from bottom of Dutch oven. Heat veal mixture to boiling.

4 Cover Dutch oven and bake 1 to 1¼ hours or until veal is tender, stirring occasionally. Stir in peas; heat through. *Makes 6 servings.*

Each serving: About 300 calories, 26 g protein, 13 g carbohydrate, 15 g total fat (4 g saturated), 93 mg cholesterol, 405 mg sodium.

## FOOD EDITOR'S TIP

**Q.** How can I fix a soup or stew if I oversalt it?

**A.** Try this quick trick: Peel and quarter a potato and simmer in the soup or stew for 10 to 15 minutes; remove before serving. The potato's starchy texture should absorb the excess salt—unless you really dumped in a lot, in which case you may be stuck with a salty dish.

# Biscuits & Scones

What could be better to mop up the savory juices from a hearty soup or stew than a homemade biscuit or its British cousin the scone?

## Sweet Potato Biscuits

PREP: 30 MINUTES • BAKE: 15 MINUTES

2 medium sweet potatoes (1 pound),
    peeled and cut into 2-inch chunks
4 cups all-purpose flour
½ cup packed light brown sugar
5 teaspoons baking powder
1 teaspoon salt
10 tablespoons cold margarine or
    butter (1¼ sticks)
⅓ cup milk

1 In 3-quart saucepan, heat sweet-potato chunks and *enough water to cover* to boiling over high heat. Reduce heat to low; cover and simmer 12 to 15 minutes or until potatoes are fork-tender. Drain sweet potatoes; mash and set aside to cool.
2 Preheat oven to 425°F. In large bowl, combine flour, brown sugar, baking powder, and salt. With pastry blender or two knives used scissor-fashion, cut in margarine or butter until mixture resembles coarse crumbs. Stir in milk and cooled mashed sweet potatoes; mix until just combined.
3 On lightly floured surface, pat dough into 8½-inch square. With floured knife, cut dough in half. Cut each half into 10 equal pieces. Place biscuits, 2 inches apart, on 2 ungreased large cookie sheets.
4 Place cookie sheets on 2 oven racks; bake biscuits 12 to 15 minutes or until golden, rotating cookie sheets between upper and lower racks halfway through baking time. Serve biscuits warm. Or, if not serving right away, cool biscuits on wire rack. Store in tightly covered container to use within 1 day or wrap in foil and freeze to use within 2 weeks. Reheat before serving. Makes 20 biscuits.

EACH BISCUIT: ABOUT 200 CALORIES,
3 G PROTEIN, 33 G CARBOHYDRATE,
6 G TOTAL FAT (1 G SATURATED),
1 MG CHOLESTEROL, 280 MG SODIUM.

## Buttermilk Biscuit Duo

PREP: 15 MINUTES • BAKE: 30 MINUTES

6 cups all-purpose flour
⅓ cup sugar
2 tablespoons cream of tartar
1 tablespoon baking soda
1½ teaspoons salt
1 cup shortening
2¼ cups buttermilk
6 ounces Monterey Jack cheese with
    jalapeño chiles, shredded (1½ cups)
4 ounces walnuts, coarsely chopped
3 tablespoons maple syrup

1 In large bowl, mix flour, sugar, cream of tartar, baking soda, and salt. With pastry blender or two knives used scissor-fashion, cut in shortening until mixture resembles coarse crumbs. Stir in buttermilk; mix just until mixture forms soft dough that leaves side of bowl. Turn dough onto floured surface; divide in half; cover lightly with plastic wrap.
2 Preheat oven to 425°F. With floured hands, knead one-half of dough with Monterey Jack, kneading about 6 to 8 strokes to mix thoroughly. With floured rolling pin, roll dough ¾ inch thick. With floured 3-inch round biscuit cutter, cut out biscuits. With pancake turner, place biscuits, about 1 inch apart, on ungreased large cookie sheet. Press trimmings together; roll and cut to make more biscuits (you will have about 9 biscuits). Bake 12 to 15 minutes or until golden. Transfer to wire rack.
3 Knead other half of dough with chopped walnuts, kneading about 6 to 8 strokes to mix thoroughly. Roll and cut dough as above. Brush biscuits with maple syrup; place on same cookie sheet. Bake biscuits 12 to 15 minutes or until golden. Transfer to wire rack.
4 Serve biscuits warm, or cool on wire rack. Reheat if desired. Makes about 18 biscuits.

EACH MONTEREY JACK BISCUIT: ABOUT 360 CALORIES, 10 G PROTEIN, 40 G CARBOHYDRATE, 18 G TOTAL FAT (6 G SATURATED), 21 MG CHOLESTEROL, 565 MG SODIUM.

EACH MAPLE-WALNUT BISCUIT: ABOUT 385 CALORIES, 7 G PROTEIN, 46 G CARBOHYDRATE, 20 G TOTAL FAT (4 G SATURATED), 1 MG CHOLESTEROL, 440 MG SODIUM.

## Smoked Ham & Cheddar Biscuits

PREP: 15 MINUTES • BAKE: 15 MINUTES

2 cups all-purpose flour
1 tablespoon baking powder
1 tablespoon light brown sugar
4 tablespoons cold margarine or butter
    (½ stick)
8 ounces smoked ham, in one piece,
    diced
4 ounces sharp Cheddar cheese,
    shredded (1 cup)
¾ cup milk

1 Preheat heat oven to 450°F.
2 In large bowl, combine flour, baking powder, and brown sugar. With pastry blender or two knives used scissor-fashion, cut in margarine or butter until mixture resembles coarse crumbs. Stir in ham and Cheddar. Stir in milk just until mixture forms soft dough that leaves side of bowl.
3 Turn dough onto lightly floured surface; knead dough 6 to 8 strokes to mix thoroughly. With floured rolling pin, roll dough into 9" by 7" rectangle. With floured knife, cut dough lengthwise into 3 strips, then cut each strip crosswise into 4 pieces. With pancake turner, place biscuits on ungreased cookie sheet, about 1 inch apart. Bake 12 to 15 minutes until golden. Makes 12 biscuits.

EACH BISCUIT: ABOUT 190 CALORIES,
9 G PROTEIN, 19 G CARBOHYDRATE,
9 G TOTAL FAT (3 G SATURATED),
21 MG CHOLESTEROL, 505 MG SODIUM.

## Cheddar Dinner Scones

PREP: 15 MINUTES • BAKE: 25 MINUTES

2 cups all-purpose flour
2 tablespoons sugar
1 tablespoon baking powder
½ teaspoon salt
6 tablespoons cold margarine or butter
    (¾ stick), cut into small pieces
1 large egg
¾ cup milk
4 ounces extrasharp Cheddar cheese,
    shredded (1 cup)

1 Preheat oven to 425°F. Grease large cookie sheet.

**2** In large bowl, combine flour, sugar, baking powder, and salt. With fingertips, blend margarine or butter into mixture until it resembles fine crumbs.

**3** In small bowl, lightly beat egg and milk. Stir egg mixture and Cheddar into flour mixture just until ingredients are blended.

**4** Turn dough onto lightly floured surface (dough will be sticky). Divide dough in half. With lightly floured hands, pat each dough half into 5-inch round, about 1 inch high. Place rounds, about 3 inches apart, on cookie sheet. With floured knife, cut each round into 6 wedges, but do not separate wedges.

**5** Bake scones 20 to 25 minutes or until golden. Serve scones warm or transfer to wire rack to cool completely. Reheat if desired. Makes 12 scones.

EACH SCONE: ABOUT 190 CALORIES, 6 G PROTEIN, 19 G CARBOHYDRATE, 10 G TOTAL FAT (4 G SATURATED), 30 MG CHOLESTEROL, 330 MG SODIUM.

## Lemon-Walnut Scones

PREP: 15 MINUTES • BAKE: 20 MINUTES

*2 tablespoons grated lemon peel (from 2 large lemons)*
*3⅓ cups all-purpose flour*
*2 tablespoons baking powder*
*½ teaspoon salt*
*½ cup plus 1 tablespoon sugar*
*6 tablespoons cold margarine or butter (¾ stick)*
*2 large eggs, beaten*
*1 cup plus 2 tablespoons half-and half or light cream*
*1½ cups walnuts, chopped*

**1** Preheat oven to 400°F. Grease large cookie sheet.

**2** In large bowl, mix lemon peel, flour, baking powder, salt, and ½ cup sugar. With pastry blender or two knives used scissor-fashion, cut in margarine or butter until mixture resembles cornmeal. Stir in eggs, 1 cup half-and-half, and 1 cup chopped walnuts just until ingredients are blended.

**3** Spoon dough onto floured surface (dough will be sticky). With lightly floured hands, pat dough into 9-inch round. Brush remaining 2 tablespoons half-and-half over dough; sprinkle with remaining 1 tablespoon sugar. Top with remaining ½ cup chopped walnuts, pressing them slightly into dough. With floured knife, cut dough into 12 wedges. Place scones, 2 inches apart, on cookie sheet.

**4** Bake scones 15 to 20 minutes or until golden. Serve scones warm or transfer to wire rack to cool completely. Reheat if desired. Makes 12 scones.

EACH SCONE: ABOUT 355 CALORIES, 7 G PROTEIN, 40 G CARBOHYDRATE, 19 G TOTAL FAT (4 G SATURATED), 44 MG CHOLESTEROL, 430 MG SODIUM.

## Corn & Spinach Biscuits

PREP: 15 MINUTES • BAKE: 20 MINUTES

*4 cups all-purpose flour*
*¼ cup sugar*
*1 tablespoon baking powder*
*1½ teaspoons salt*
*½ teaspoon baking soda*
*⅔ cup shortening*
*1 cup buttermilk*
*3 large eggs*
*1 can (11 ounces) white corn, drained*
*1 package (10 ounces) frozen chopped spinach, thawed and squeezed dry*
*4 ounces Cheddar cheese, shredded (1 cup)*

**1** Preheat oven to 425°F.

**2** In large bowl, mix flour, sugar, baking powder, salt, and baking soda. With pastry blender or two knives used scissor-fashion, cut in shortening until mixture resembles coarse crumbs.

**3** In small bowl, beat buttermilk and eggs. Stir buttermilk mixture, corn, spinach, and Cheddar into flour mixture just until mixture forms soft dough that leaves side of bowl.

**4** Turn dough onto floured surface; sprinkle top of dough lightly with flour. With floured hands, gently knead dough, kneading about 6 to 8 strokes to mix thoroughly. With floured rolling pin, roll dough 1 inch thick.

**5** With floured 3-inch round biscuit-cutter, cut out biscuits. Press trimmings together; roll and cut as above. With pancake turner, place biscuits on ungreased large cookie sheet, about 1 inch apart. Bake 15 to 20 minutes or until golden. Serve biscuits warm, or cool on wire rack to serve later. Reheat if desired. Makes about 16 biscuits.

EACH BISCUIT: ABOUT 270 CALORIES, 8 G PROTEIN, 32 G CARBOHYDRATE, 12 G TOTAL FAT (4 G SATURATED), 48 MG CHOLESTEROL, 495 MG SODIUM

## Olive-Parmesan Scones

PREP: 15 MINUTES • BAKE: 20 MINUTES

*3 cups all-purpose flour*
*2 tablespoons sugar*
*2 tablespoons baking powder*
*1 tablespoon chopped fresh parsley leaves*
*½ teaspoon salt*
*⅓ cup plus 2 tablespoons grated Parmesan cheese*
*6 tablespoons cold margarine or butter (¾ stick)*
*2 large eggs, beaten*
*½ cup Kalamata olives, pitted and chopped*
*¾ cup plus 2 teaspoons milk*

**1** Preheat oven to 400°F. Grease cookie sheet.

**2** In large bowl, mix flour, sugar, baking powder, parsley, salt, and ⅓ cup grated Parmesan. With pastry blender or two knives used scissor-fashion, cut in margarine or butter until mixture resembles cornmeal. Stir in eggs, Kalamata olives, and ¾ cup milk just until ingredients are blended.

**3** On lightly floured surface, pat dough into 8-inch square. With floured knife, cut dough lengthwise into 3 strips, then cut each strip crosswise into 3 pieces. With pancake turner, place scones, 1 inch apart, on cookie sheet. Brush scones with remaining 2 teaspoons milk; sprinkle with remaining 2 tablespoons grated Parmesan.

**4** Bake scones 15 to 20 minutes or until golden. Serve scones warm or transfer to wire rack to cool completely. Reheat if desired. Makes 9 scones.

EACH SCONE: ABOUT 310 CALORIES, 8 G PROTEIN, 39 G CARBOHYDRATE, 14 G TOTAL FAT (3 G SATURATED), 53 MG CHOLESTEROL, 780 MG SODIUM.

# Stir-Fries
# & Skillet Dinners

# Vegetarian Stuffed Cabbage

*PREP: 20 MINUTES* ～ *COOK: 50 MINUTES*

1 head savoy cabbage (about 2 pounds)
1 tablespoon vegetable oil
1 medium red pepper, finely chopped
1 medium yellow pepper, finely chopped
1 medium onion, finely chopped
1 tablespoon seasoned rice vinegar
1 tablespoon reduced-sodium soy sauce
2 teaspoons minced, peeled fresh ginger
1 can (16 to 19 ounces) white kidney beans
  (cannellini), rinsed and drained
1 can (8 ounces) sliced water chestnuts, drained
  and finely chopped
2 cans (14½ ounces each) stewed tomatoes
1 teaspoon sugar

1 Discard tough outer leaves from cabbage; with sharp knife, remove core. Fill 8-quart saucepot *three-fourths full with water*; heat to boiling over high heat. Place cabbage in boiling water, cored-side up. Using 2 large spoons or forks, gently separate leaves as outer leaves soften slightly. When about three-fourths of leaves have separated from cabbage, remove remaining head of cabbage from saucepot and set aside. Boil separated cabbage leaves, covered, 10 to 12 minutes or until leaves are very tender. Drain leaves in colander.

2 With knife, trim tough center rib from each cabbage leaf. Reserve 8 large leaves for rolls (if leaves are not very large, you may need to reserve 2 leaves for each roll). Coarsely slice enough of remaining cabbage leaves to make 2 cups for filling, reserving rest of cabbage for use another day.

3 In nonstick 12-inch skillet, heat vegetable oil over medium-high heat until hot. Add peppers and onion and cook until tender and lightly browned, about 8 to 10 minutes. Add sliced cabbage, rice vinegar, soy sauce, and ginger; cook 5 minutes. Stir in kidney beans and water chestnuts. Let cabbage filling cool slightly.

4 On center of each reserved cabbage leaf, place scant ½ cup filling. Fold 2 sides of cabbage leaf over filling, overlapping edges; roll jelly-roll fashion.

5 In same skillet, heat stewed tomatoes and sugar to boiling over high heat, stirring with spoon to break up tomatoes. Add cabbage rolls. Reduce heat to low; cover and simmer 10 to 15 minutes or until cabbage rolls are heated through. *Makes 4 servings.*

Each serving: About 265 calories, 13 g protein, 49 g carbohydrate, 5 g total fat (1 g saturated), 0 mg cholesterol, 950 mg sodium.

# Easy Barbecued Beans & Rice

*PREP: 15 MINUTES* ～ *COOK: 25 MINUTES*

This vegetarian skillet dinner is especially good with a rich, smoky barbecue sauce.

¾ cup regular long-grain rice
1 tablespoon vegetable oil
1 medium green pepper, cut into ½-inch pieces
1 medium red pepper, cut into ½-inch pieces
1 medium onion, chopped
1 can (16 to 19 ounces) black beans, rinsed and
  drained
1 can (15 to 19 ounces) red kidney beans, rinsed
  and drained
1 can (15 to 19 ounces) garbanzo beans, rinsed
  and drained
1 can (15 to 16 ounces) pink beans, rinsed and
  drained
1 can (14½ ounces) no-salt-added stewed
  tomatoes
½ cup bottled barbecue sauce
Parsley sprig for garnish

1 In 2-quart saucepan, prepare rice as label directs.

2 Meanwhile, in 12-inch skillet, heat vegetable oil over medium heat until hot. Add peppers and onion and cook until tender.

3 Add beans, stewed tomatoes, barbecue sauce, and *1 cup water* to pepper mixture; heat to boiling over high heat. Reduce heat to low; cover and simmer 15 minutes.

4 Spoon rice into center of beans and garnish with parsley sprig. Before serving, stir rice into bean mixture. *Makes 6 servings.*

Each serving: About 355 calories, 16 g protein, 61 g carbohydrate, 5 g total fat (1 g saturated), 0 mg cholesterol, 790 mg sodium.

*Easy Barbecued Beans & Rice* ➤

# Spicy Stir-Fried Broccoli & Ziti

PREP: 10 MINUTES ～ COOK: 15 MINUTES

12 ounces ziti or cavatelli pasta

Salt

2 tablespoons olive oil

2 medium bunches broccoli (about 1 pound each),
    cut into 2½" by 1" pieces

2 garlic cloves, minced

½ teaspoon crushed red pepper

½ cup grated Parmesan cheese

½ cup pine nuts (pignoli) or chopped walnuts,
    toasted

**1** In large saucepot, prepare pasta in *boiling salted water* as label directs. Drain ziti, reserving *1 cup pasta cooking water*. Return ziti to saucepot; set aside.

**2** Meanwhile, in nonstick 12-inch skillet, heat olive oil over high heat until hot. Add broccoli and cook, stirring quickly and constantly, until evenly coated with oil. Add garlic, crushed red pepper, ¾ teaspoon salt, and ⅓ cup water. Reduce heat to medium; cover and cook 2 minutes. Uncover and cook, stirring, 5 minutes or until broccoli is tender-crisp.

**3** Toss broccoli mixture and reserved pasta cooking water with ziti over medium-high heat to heat through. Remove saucepot from heat; stir in Parmesan. Sprinkle with pine nuts. *Makes 4 servings.*

Each serving: About 580 calories, 26 g protein, 79 g carbohydrate, 21 g total fat (5 g saturated), 8 mg cholesterol, 980 mg sodium.

## A SKILLET BY ANY OTHER NAME...

What is a skillet? A shallow pan with one long handle. But manufacturers may also call them fry pans, sauté pans, omelet pans, or gourmet pans. The ones with low, sloped sides are best for quick frying and omelets; higher, straight sides are best for deep-frying or cooking dishes with lots of liquid. Skillets come in sizes ranging from 7" to 14". If you want only one, buy an all-purpose size: 10". For a well-rounded kitchen, we suggest three: 8", 10", and 12".

A word about woks: These popular bowl-shaped pans with two handles and high sides are a good alternative to a skillet for stir-frying, deep-frying, or cooking with liquids. Newer models, called stir-fry pans (such the one at right, below), have a single handle and flat bottom that sits securely on the range.

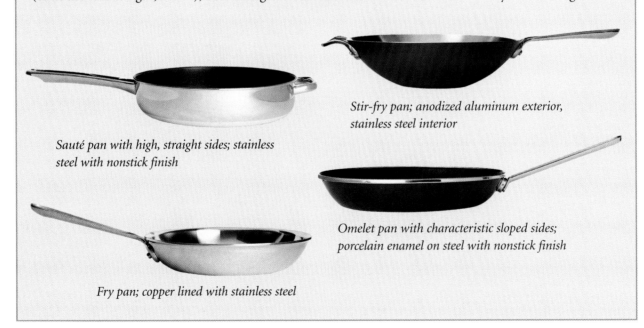

*Stir-fry pan; anodized aluminum exterior, stainless steel interior*

*Sauté pan with high, straight sides; stainless steel with nonstick finish*

*Omelet pan with characteristic sloped sides; porcelain enamel on steel with nonstick finish*

*Fry pan; copper lined with stainless steel*

# Tofu & Vegetable Stir-Fry with Linguine

PREP: 20 MINUTES ～ COOK: 20 MINUTES

1 package (16 ounces) extrafirm tofu
5 tablespoons reduced-sodium teriyaki sauce
2 tablespoons vegetable oil
1 tablespoon cornstarch
1¼ cups chicken broth, canned or homemade (page 24)
12 ounces linguine
1 large red pepper, cut into ¼-inch-wide strips
6 ounces radishes, halved if large
1 large head Napa (Chinese cabbage), about 2 pounds, sliced crosswise into 1-inch-wide slices
4 green onions, cut into ½-inch pieces
2 tablespoons grated, peeled fresh ginger
1 can (15 ounce) Chinese straw mushrooms, rinsed and drained
2 teaspoons Asian sesame oil

1 Drain and blot tofu dry with paper towels. Cut tofu into ¼-inch-thick slices, then 1-inch squares. In bowl, toss tofu with 2 tablespoons teriyaki sauce.

2 In nonstick 5-quart Dutch oven, heat 1 tablespoon vegetable oil over high heat until hot. Add tofu mixture and cook until tofu is golden brown, about 5 minutes, stirring gently. Transfer tofu to plate.

3 Meanwhile, in 2-cup measuring cup, stir cornstarch and 2 tablespoons teriyaki sauce into chicken broth until blended.

4 In large saucepot, prepare pasta in *boiling water* as label directs; do not add salt to water.

5 In same Dutch oven, heat remaining 1 tablespoon vegetable oil over high heat until hot. Add red-pepper strips, radishes, Napa, green onions, and ginger and cook about 5 minutes, stirring quickly and frequently, until vegetables are tender-crisp. Stir in cornstarch mixture; heat to boiling. Boil 1 minute. Add tofu, straw mushrooms, and Asian sesame oil; heat through, stirring gently.

6 Drain linguine; return to saucepot. Stir in remaining 1 tablespoon teriyaki sauce. Spoon linguine onto 4 dinner plates. Serve vegetable mixture over linguine. *Makes 6 servings.*

Each serving: About 410 calories, 21 g protein, 57 g carbohydrate, 12 g total fat (2 g saturated), 0 mg cholesterol, 725 mg sodium.

# Thai Tofu Stir-Fry

PREP: 30 MINUTES ～ COOK: 25 MINUTES

1 package (16 ounces) extrafirm tofu, drained and cut into 1-inch cubes
1 tablespoon curry powder
1 tablespoon grated, peeled fresh ginger
1 tablespoon soy sauce
1 tablespoon Asian fish sauce*
6 teaspoons vegetable oil
1 medium head bok choy (about 1 pound), sliced crosswise into 1-inch slices
1 large zucchini (about 12 ounces), cut into bite-size pieces
3 green onions, cut into 2-inch pieces
8 ounces medium mushrooms, cut into ¼-inch-thick slices
1 medium red pepper, sliced
¼ cup chicken broth, canned or homemade (page 24)
1½ teaspoons cornstarch
½ cup packed fresh basil leaves, chopped

1 In medium bowl, gently toss tofu cubes with curry powder, ginger, soy sauce, and fish sauce.

2 In nonstick 12-inch skillet, heat 2 teaspoons vegetable oil over medium-high heat until hot. Add bok choy, zucchini, and green onions and cook until vegetables are tender-crisp, about 8 minutes. Transfer vegetables to large bowl.

3 With slotted spoon, remove tofu from curry mixture; reserve curry mixture in bowl.

4 In same skillet, heat 2 teaspoons vegetable oil. Add tofu and cook until golden brown, about 5 minutes, gently stirring occasionally. Transfer tofu to bowl with bok choy mixture.

5 In same skillet, heat remaining 2 teaspoons vegetable oil. Add mushrooms and red pepper and cook until pepper is tender-crisp, about 8 minutes.

6 Stir chicken broth and cornstarch into curry mixture. Stir curry-broth mixture into skillet and heat to boiling; boil 1 minute until sauce thickens slightly. Return bok-choy mixture to skillet. Add basil; heat through. *Makes 4 servings.*

*Asian fish sauce is a thin, translucent, salty brown liquid extracted from salted, fermented fish. It can be purchased in the Asian section of some grocery stores.

Each serving: About 295 calories, 24 g protein, 17 g carbohydrate, 18 g total fat (2 g saturated), 2 mg cholesterol, 745 mg sodium.

# Sautéed Cod with Garlic Croutons & Green Beans

PREP: 20 MINUTES ～ COOK: 25 TO 30 MINUTES

To make nonfat garlic croutons, toast the uncubed bread slices in a toaster oven or under the broiler. Rub the toast lightly with a cut garlic clove and cut into cubes.

2 tablespoons plus 2 teaspoons olive oil
1 garlic clove, sliced
4 slices (¾ inch thick) Italian bread, cut into
   ¾-inch cubes
1 pound boneless cod
½ teaspoon salt
Paprika
1 pound green beans, trimmed
1 package (10 ounces) mushrooms, halved
2 tablespoons reduced-sodium soy sauce

1 In nonstick 10-inch skillet, heat 2 teaspoons olive oil over medium-high heat until hot. Add garlic and cook until golden brown; with slotted spoon, remove garlic slices and discard. In oil in same skillet, toast bread cubes until lightly browned. Transfer croutons to small bowl.

2 Sprinkle cod with salt. Cut cod crosswise into 4 pieces. In same skillet, heat 1 tablespoon olive oil over medium-high heat; cook cod until golden brown, about 8 minutes, turning once. Sprinkle cod lightly with paprika. Transfer cod to plate.

3 In same skillet, heat green beans in ¾ *inch boiling water* to boiling over high heat. Reduce heat to low; cover and simmer 5 to 10 minutes or until green beans are tender-crisp; drain. Transfer beans to bowl. Wipe skillet dry.

4 In same skillet, heat remaining 1 tablespoon olive oil over medium-high heat ; cook mushrooms until lightly browned. Return green beans to skillet; continue cooking until vegetables are browned and all liquid evaporates. Stir in soy sauce.

5 Arrange cod on vegetables; heat through. Top with croutons to serve. *Makes 4 servings.*

Each serving: About 310 calories, 27 g protein, 27 g carbohydrate, 11 g total fat (2 g saturated), 49 mg cholesterol, 835 mg sodium.

# Pan-Seared Scallops with Lemon Couscous

PREP: 20 MINUTES ～ COOK: 25 MINUTES

4 teaspoons vegetable oil
1 large red pepper, thinly sliced
1 medium onion, thinly sliced
12 ounces medium mushrooms, quartered
8 ounces sugar snap peas, strings removed
1 medium lemon
1 cup couscous (Moroccan pasta)
¾ teaspoon salt
1 pound sea scallops
2 tablespoons soy sauce
2 bunches arugula (about 8 ounces), stems
   trimmed

1 In nonstick 12-inch skillet, heat 2 teaspoons vegetable oil over medium-high heat until hot. Add red pepper and onion and cook until golden brown. Transfer red-pepper mixture to plate.

2 In same skillet, heat 1 teaspoon vegetable oil until hot; cook mushrooms until golden brown. Transfer mushrooms to plate with red-pepper mixture.

3 Add ¼ *cup water* to same skillet; heat to boiling. Add sugar snap peas and cook 3 to 4 minutes or until tender-crisp. Drain and set aside.

4 Meanwhile, from lemon, grate ½ teaspoon peel and squeeze 1½ teaspoons juice. In 2-quart saucepan, heat lemon juice and *1½ cups water* to boiling over high heat. Stir in couscous and salt. Cover saucepan and remove from heat. Let stand 5 minutes; stir in lemon peel. Keep warm.

5 Wipe skillet dry, add remaining 1 teaspoon vegetable oil, and heat over medium-high heat until hot. Add scallops; cook until they turn opaque throughout, stirring occasionally, about 3 to 4 minutes.

6 Return mushroom-pepper mixture to skillet; stir in soy sauce. Cook mixture over medium-high heat until heated through. Stir in sugar snap peas.

7 Arrange arugula on plates. Top with couscous and scallop mixture. *Makes 6 servings.*

Each serving: About 263 calories, 20 g protein, 36 g carbohydrate, 4 g total fat (1 g saturated), 25 mg cholesterol, 770 mg sodium.

## HOW TO CHOOSE A SKILLET

| Material | Advantages | Disadvantages | Comments |
| --- | --- | --- | --- |
| ALUMINUM | Heats evenly; lightweight; inexpensive | Pits and stains from contact with salt or acidic foods; not harmful to pan or food but may be unappealing. Discolors some foods (cream sauce may turn gray) | The kitchen workhorse: all-purpose and the price is right. Almost always has a nonstick interior finish and often a porcelain-enamel finish on the exterior |
| ANODIZED ALUMINUM | Resistant to sticking, stains, and dents; unlike regular aluminum, won't discolor foods | Expensive | Good choice for serious cooks—top perfor-mance, a professional look (dark gray) |
| STAINLESS STEEL | Very durable; shiny | Poor conductor of heat; can be expensive | All-purpose pans that last forever; your choice if you like your cookware bright and shiny. Almost always has an aluminum or copper bottom or core to help disperse heat |
| COPPER | Beautiful; best conductor of heat; very responsive to change in heat level | Very expensive ($75 to $300); needs special cleansers to maintain shine; tin linings (see Comments) must be replaced when worn | Only for serious cooks with time to keep it clean. Always lined with tin or stainless steel to prevent interaction of copper with food |
| CAST IRON | Inexpensive ($8 to $30); good conductor of heat; retains heat so it's energy efficient; can be source of dietary iron | Can affect color and taste of foods; needs special season-ing and cleaning (see "Cast-Iron Care," page 58) unless it's coated with porcelain enamel; extremely heavy; slow to heat up and cool down | Every cook should have one for browning and deep-frying |
| PORCELAIN ENAMEL ON STEEL | Comes in bright colors; won't interact with food; easy to clean; heavier-weight pans conduct heat well | Lighter-weight pans are poor conductors of heat and develop hot spots | Heavy weights are good performers for cooks who love color in the kitchen. Prices vary depending on weight |

# Gingered Shrimp & Asparagus

PREP: 15 MINUTES ～ COOK: 15 MINUTES

An interesting fusion of Asian and Italian flavors.

1 tablespoon balsamic vinegar
1 tablespoon soy sauce
2 tablespoons olive oil
1¼ pounds asparagus, trimmed and cut into bite-size pieces
1 pound large shrimp, shelled and deveined
1 tablespoon minced, peeled fresh ginger
¼ teaspoon crushed red pepper
1 bunch watercress, tough stems trimmed

1 In cup, mix balsamic vinegar, soy sauce, and *1 tablespoon water*.

2 In nonstick 12-inch skillet, heat olive oil over medium-high heat until hot. Add asparagus and cook until just tender-crisp. Stir in shrimp, ginger, and crushed red pepper, stirring constantly, until shrimp turn opaque throughout. Stir in balsamic-vinegar mixture.

3 Arrange watercress on platter; spoon shrimp mixture over watercress. *Makes 4 servings.*

Each serving: About 190 calories, 23 g protein, 6 g carbohydrate, 9 g total fat (1 g saturated), 140 mg cholesterol, 415 mg sodium.

# Sausage & Seafood Boil

PREP: 20 MINUTES ～ COOK: 40 MINUTES

12 ounces sweet Italian-sausage links
4 medium chicken drumsticks (about 1 pound), skin removed
1 pound large shrimp, shelled and deveined
1 dozen littleneck clams, scrubbed
2 medium ears corn, each cut into 4 pieces
1 large tomato, diced
1 bottle (8 ounces) clam juice
2 tablespoons dry white wine (optional)
1 bay leaf
¼ teaspoon salt

1 In 12-inch skillet, heat sausages and ¼ *cup water* to boiling over medium heat. Cover and cook 5 minutes.

Remove cover; continue cooking until water evaporates. Add chicken to skillet; continue cooking, turning frequently, until chicken and sausages are well browned, 15 to 20 minutes. Transfer sausages and chicken to plate. Cut each sausage diagonally in half.

2 In drippings in skillet, cook shrimp over medium-high heat, stirring frequently, until shrimp turn opaque throughout and are tender; transfer to bowl.

3 In same skillet, heat chicken, clams, corn, tomato, clam juice, white wine, bay leaf, and salt to boiling over high heat. Reduce heat to low; cover and simmer about 10 minutes or until chicken is cooked through, clams open, and corn is tender. Discard any clams that do not open. Discard bay leaf. Stir in sausages and shrimp; heat through. *Makes 6 servings.*

Each serving: About 373 calories, 35 g protein, 9 g carbohydrate, 21 g total fat (7 g saturated), 183 mg cholesterol, 750 mg sodium.

# Paella Pronto

PREP: 10 MINUTES ～ COOK: 25 MINUTES

This favorite Spanish one-dish dinner has been streamlined for busy cooks.

2 hot Italian-sausage links (about 6 ounces), casings removed
1 cup regular long-grain rice
½ teaspoon salt
1 can (14½ to 16 ounces) stewed tomatoes
1 pound large shrimp, shelled and deveined
1 cup frozen peas, thawed

1 Heat nonstick 10-inch skillet over medium-high heat until hot. Add sausages and cook, breaking up sausages with spoon, until browned. With slotted spoon, transfer sausage meat to bowl.

2 Reduce heat to medium. Add rice to skillet and cook 2 minutes. Add salt and *2½ cups water*; heat to boiling. Reduce heat to low; cover and simmer 12 to 15 minutes.

3 Add stewed tomatoes and sausage meat; heat to boiling over high heat. Add shrimp; heat to boiling. Reduce heat to medium; cover and cook 4 minutes. Stir in peas; cover and cook until shrimp turn opaque throughout and peas are heated through. *Makes 4 servings.*

Each serving: About 460 calories, 30 g protein, 51 g carbohydrate, 15 g total fat (4 g saturated), 175 mg cholesterol, 1095 mg sodium.

# Scallop Stir-Fry with Asparagus & Fresh Basil

**PREP: 20 MINUTES  ∾  COOK: 15 MINUTES**

Tossing this dish with chopped basil just before serving adds a touch of fresh flavor. With steamed rice, you have a complete meal!

1 pound sea scallops
1 tablespoon minced, peeled fresh ginger
2 tablespoons reduced-sodium soy sauce
2 tablespoons vegetable oil
2 garlic cloves, sliced
1½ pounds asparagus, trimmed and cut into 2-inch pieces
¼ teaspoon crushed red pepper
½ cup packed fresh basil leaves, chopped
Basil leaves for garnish

**1** In bowl, toss scallops with ginger and 1 tablespoon soy sauce.

**2** In nonstick 12-inch skillet, heat 1 tablespoon vegetable oil over medium-high heat until hot. Add garlic and cook until golden brown, stirring often. With slotted spoon, remove garlic to bowl.

**3** In same skillet, cook asparagus and crushed red pepper about 7 minutes or until asparagus is tender-crisp. Transfer asparagus to bowl with garlic.

**4** Add remaining 1 tablespoon oil to skillet; add scallop mixture and cook, stirring frequently, 3 to 5 minutes or until scallops turn opaque throughout.

**5** Add asparagus, garlic, and remaining 1 tablespoon soy sauce to skillet; heat through. Toss with chopped basil. Spoon mixture onto platter; garnish with basil leaves. *Makes 4 servings.*

Each serving: About 190 calories, 22 g protein, 6 g carbohydrate, 8 g total fat, (1 g saturated), 38 mg cholesterol, 505 mg sodium.

*Scallop Stir-Fry with Asparagus & Fresh Basil*

## Red Snapper Dinner

PREP: 10 MINUTES ∿ COOK: 30 MINUTES

1 tablespoon vegetable oil
4 pieces red snapper fillet (about 4 ounces each)
2½ cups chicken broth, canned or homemade
    (page 24)
½ small head green cabbage (about 1 pound), cut
    into 4 wedges
3 medium carrots, peeled and cut into 1½-inch
    chunks
1 medium onion, cut into ¼-inch-thick slices
1 pound baby red potatoes
¼ teaspoon dried thyme leaves
¼ teaspoon salt
¼ teaspoon ground white pepper

1 In nonstick 12-inch skillet, heat vegetable oil over medium-high heat until hot. Add fish fillets and cook until lightly brown, turning once. Transfer to plate.

2 To same skillet, add broth, cabbage, carrots, onion, whole potatoes, thyme, salt, and pepper. Heat to boiling over high heat. Reduce heat to low; cover and simmer 20 minutes or until vegetables are fork-tender.

3 Arrange snapper over vegetables, skin-side up. Cover skillet and simmer 3 to 4 minutes or until fish flakes easily when tested with a fork. *Makes 4 servings.*

Each serving: About 320 calories, 29 g protein, 36 g carbohydrate, 6 g total fat (1 g saturated), 42 mg cholesterol, 920 mg sodium.

## Scallop & Shrimp Stir-Fry

PREP: 20 MINUTES ∿ COOK: 15 MINUTES

2 tablespoons vegetable oil
1 tablespoon minced, peeled fresh ginger or
    ½ teaspoon ground ginger
1 garlic clove, minced
1 pound asparagus, trimmed and cut into 2-inch
    pieces
12 ounces mushrooms, sliced
3 medium carrots, peeled and cut into ¼-inch-
    thick slices
3 green onions, chopped

¾ pound large shrimp, shelled and deveined
¾ pound sea scallops
2 tablespoons reduced-sodium soy sauce
¼ teaspoon coarsely ground black pepper

1 In 12-inch skillet, heat vegetable oil over medium heat until hot. Add ginger and garlic and cook 1 minute. Add asparagus, mushrooms, carrots, and green onions and cook over high heat until vegetables are tender-crisp. With slotted spoon, transfer vegetable mixture to bowl.

2 In same skillet, cook shrimp and scallops over high heat until shrimp are opaque and scallops are golden. Return vegetable mixture to skillet; add soy sauce, pepper, and ¼ *cup water*, gently tossing to coat well and scraping up any brown bits from bottom of skillet. *Makes 6 servings.*

Each serving: About 190 calories, 23 g protein, 12 g carbohydrate, 6 g total fat (1 g saturated), 89 mg cholesterol, 380 mg sodium.

## Chicken Stir-Fry with Fried Ginger

PREP: 15 MINUTES ∿ COOK: 30 MINUTES

4 small skinless, boneless chicken-breast halves
    (about 1 pound)
3 tablespoons soy sauce
2 tablespoons red wine vinegar
1 tablespoon Asian sesame oil
2 teaspoons sugar
2 teaspoons cornstarch
1 teaspoon sesame seeds
3 tablespoons vegetable oil
1 piece (2 inches long) fresh ginger, about ¾ inch
    in diameter, peeled and cut lengthwise into hair-
    thin strips
1 pound green beans, trimmed

1 With knife held in slanting position, almost parallel to the cutting surface, slice each breast half across width into ⅛-inch-thick slices. In medium bowl, combine chicken, soy sauce, red wine vinegar, sesame oil, sugar, and cornstarch; set aside.

2 In small saucepan, toast sesame seeds over medium-high heat until golden brown, stirring and shaking saucepan frequently; transfer to cup. Wipe saucepan clean.

# SPRING RISOTTO

To make an authentic risotto, you'll need Arborio, or another Italian superfino (best quality) rice that has become widely available. Because it contains more waxy starch than other rices, it can withstand the long, slow cooking necessary to prepare risotto properly, resulting in a deliciously creamy consistency outside while still maintaining an al dente firmness inside. If you can't find Arborio, try substituting American medium-grain rice, sold at health food stores and some supermarkets.

PREP: 30 MINUTES  ~  COOK: 55 MINUTES

*1 can (14½ ounces) vegetable or chicken broth*

*2 tablespoons olive oil*

*3 medium carrots, peeled and diced*

*12 ounces asparagus, trimmed and cut into 2-inch pieces*

*6 ounces sugar snap peas, strings removed and each cut in half*

*¼ teaspoon coarsely ground black pepper*

*1 teaspoon salt*

*1 small onion, chopped*

*2 cups Arborio rice or medium-grain rice*

*½ cup dry white wine*

*½ cup grated Parmesan cheese*

*¼ cup chopped fresh basil or parsley leaves*

**1** In 2-quart saucepan, heat broth and *3½ cups water* to boiling over high heat. Reduce heat to low to maintain simmer; cover.

**2** In 4-quart saucepan, heat 1 tablespoon olive oil over medium heat. Add carrots and cook 10 minutes. Add asparagus, sugar snap peas, pepper, and ¼ tea-

spoon salt; cook, covered, until vegetables are tender-crisp, about 5 minutes. Transfer vegetables to bowl.

**3** In same saucepan, heat remaining 1 tablespoon olive oil until hot; add onion and cook over medium heat until tender, about 7 minutes. Add rice and remaining ¾ teaspoon salt; cook, stirring frequently, until rice grains are opaque. Add wine; cook until absorbed. Add about ½ cup simmering broth to rice, stirring until liquid is absorbed. Continue cooking, adding remaining broth, ½ cup at a time, and stirring after each addition until all liquid is absorbed and rice is tender but still firm, about 25 minutes (risotto should have a creamy consistency). Stir in vegetables, Parmesan, and basil; heat through. Makes 4 servings.

Each serving: About 620 calories, 17 g protein, 106 g carbohydrate, 11 g total fat (3 g saturated), 10 mg cholesterol, 835 mg sodium.

**3** In same saucepan, heat 1 tablespoon vegetable oil over medium-high heat until hot. Add ginger and cook 1 to 2 minutes until lightly browned. With slotted spoon, transfer ginger to paper towels to drain.

**4** In nonstick 12-inch skillet, heat green beans in *½ inch boiling water* to boiling over high heat. Reduce heat to low; cover and simmer 5 to 10 minutes or until green beans are tender-crisp; drain. Wipe skillet dry.

**5** In same skillet, heat 1 tablespoon vegetable oil over high heat until hot. Add green beans and cook, stirring frequently, until beans are browned and tender; remove beans to bowl.

**6** In same skillet, heat remaining 1 tablespoon vegetable oil over high heat until hot. Add chicken mixture and cook, stirring quickly and constantly, until chicken loses its pink color throughout. Return green beans to skillet; heat through. Spoon chicken mixture onto warm platter. Garnish with sesame seeds and fried fresh ginger. *Makes 4 servings.*

Each serving: About 305 calories, 29 g protein, 12 g carbohydrate, 16 g total fat (2 g saturated), 66 mg cholesterol, 850 mg sodium.

# Bistro Chicken with Spinach

PREP: 10 MINUTES ~ COOK: 50 MINUTES

5 medium red potatoes (about 1¼ pounds), quartered
3 tablespoons olive oil
2 medium yellow peppers, cut into ½-inch-wide strips
1 pound medium mushrooms, trimmed
6 large skinless, boneless chicken thighs (about 1¼ pounds), halved
3 garlic cloves, peeled and halved lengthwise
½ teaspoon salt
2 tablespoons brown sugar
3 tablespoons balsamic or red wine vinegar
3 tablespoons reduced-sodium soy sauce
5 ounces prewashed spinach (half 10-ounce bag)

**1** In 3-quart saucepan, heat potatoes with *enough water to cover* to boiling over high heat. Reduce heat to low; cover and simmer 10 to 15 minutes or until potatoes are fork-tender; drain.

**2** Meanwhile, in nonstick 12-inch skillet, heat 1 tablespoon olive oil over high heat until hot. Add pepper strips and cook, stirring frequently, until golden brown and tender-crisp. With slotted spoon, transfer peppers to bowl. In same skillet, heat 1 tablespoon olive oil; cook mushrooms until browned and all liquid evaporates. Transfer to bowl with peppers.

**3** In same skillet, heat remaining 1 tablespoon olive oil over medium-high heat; cook chicken thighs, garlic, and salt until chicken is browned on both sides. Cover skillet and reduce heat to medium; cook 15 minutes longer or until chicken is tender and juices run clear when chicken is pierced with tip of knife.

**4** Meanwhile, in cup, stir brown sugar, balsamic vinegar, and soy sauce. When chicken is done, increase heat to high; stir in potatoes, pepper strips, mushrooms, and vinegar mixture. Then stir in spinach leaves, a little at a time, until spinach just begins to wilt. *Makes 4 servings.*

Each serving: About 455 calories, 35 g protein, 43 g carbohydrate, 17 g total fat (3 g saturated), 118 mg cholesterol, 910 mg sodium.

# Harvest Skillet Chicken Dinner

PREP: 15 MINUTES ~ COOK: 45 MINUTES

For an unusual twist here, try dried cherries in place of the cranberries. The sturdiness of kale works well in this skillet dinner, but if it's hard to find, use spinach instead. Cut the spinach into bite-size pieces and add it for the last 2 to 3 minutes of cooking, just long enough to wilt it.

1 teaspoon vegetable oil
6 large chicken thighs with bones (about 2½ pounds), skin and fat removed
1 medium butternut squash (about 2 pounds), halved lengthwise, peeled, and cut crosswise into ¾-inch-thick slices
1 jumbo onion (about 1 pound), thickly sliced
¾ teaspoon salt
1 can (14½ ounces) chicken broth or 1¾ cups homemade (page 24)
1 tablespoon all-purpose flour
1 pound kale, coarse stems and veins removed, torn into bite-size pieces
¼ cup dried cranberries or raisins

**1** In nonstick 5-quart Dutch oven, heat vegetable oil over medium-high heat until hot. Add chicken thighs and cook until browned on all sides; remove from skillet.

**2** To drippings in Dutch oven, add squash, onion, salt, and *2 tablespoons water*; cook until vegetables are browned.

**3** In bowl, stir together chicken broth and flour. Add chicken-broth mixture, chicken thighs, kale, and dried cranberries to vegetables in Dutch oven; heat to boiling over high heat. Reduce heat to low; cover and simmer 20 minutes or until vegetables are tender and juices run clear when chicken is pierced with tip of knife. *Makes 6 servings.*

Each serving: About 270 calories, 25 g protein, 31 g carbohydrate, 6 g total fat (1 g saturated), 90 mg cholesterol, 710 mg sodium.

◀ *Bistro Chicken with Spinach*

# Turkey & Fennel Piccata

PREP: 20 MINUTES ～ COOK: 20 MINUTES

Turkey is a perfect substitute for veal in a piccata-style dish.

2 tablespoons olive oil
1 large fennel bulb (about 1½ pounds), trimmed
  and cut into ¼-inch-thick slices
3 large carrots, peeled and cut into 3-inch-long
  matchsticks
1 medium onion, diced
1 teaspoon salt
2 medium zucchini (about 8 ounces each)

1¼ pounds turkey cutlets
½ teaspoon coarsely ground black pepper
¼ teaspoon dried thyme leaves
1 large lemon, halved

1 In nonstick 12-inch skillet, heat 1 tablespoon olive oil over medium-high heat until hot. Add fennel, carrots, onion, and ½ teaspoon salt; cook until lightly browned, stirring occasionally. Stir in zucchini; continue cooking until vegetables are tender. Transfer vegetable mixture to bowl.

2 Meanwhile, if turkey cutlets are thick, pound them to ⅛-inch thickness. Cut turkey cutlets into 3" by 2" pieces. Sprinkle cutlets with pepper, thyme, and remaining ½ teaspoon salt.

3 In same skillet, heat remaining 1 tablespoon olive oil over medium-high heat until hot. Add cutlets, a

## SUNDAY-NIGHT VEGETABLE HASH

Hash, the most American of skillet meals, goes perfectly with thick slices of country-style bread.

PREP: 15 MINUTES ～ COOK: 30 MINUTES

1½ pounds all-purpose potatoes (about 4 medium),
  peeled and cut into ½-inch cubes
6 slices bacon, cut into 1-inch pieces
1 large red pepper, cut into ½-inch pieces
¼ teaspoon salt
1 can (15½ to 19 ounces) black beans, rinsed and
  drained
4 large eggs

1 In 3-quart saucepan, heat potatoes and *enough water to cover* to boiling over high heat. Reduce heat to low; cover and simmer 4 minutes or until potatoes are almost tender. Drain well.

2 In nonstick 12-inch skillet, cook bacon, red pepper, potatoes, and salt over medium-high heat until vegetables are tender and browned, about 15 minutes, stirring occasionally. Stir in black beans; heat through.

3 In nonstick 10-inch skillet, heat *1½ inches water* to boiling over high heat. Reduce heat to medium-low. One at a time, break eggs into a custard cup, then, holding cup close to water's surface, slip each egg into simmering water. Cook eggs 3 to 5 minutes or until

of desired doneness. When done, carefully remove eggs from water with a slotted spoon. Drain each egg (still held in spoon) on paper towels. Serve poached eggs on vegetable hash. Makes 4 servings.

Each serving: About 440 calories, 17 g protein, 37 g carbohydrate, 25 g total fat (9 g saturated), 234 mg cholesterol, 720 mg sodium.

few at a time, and cook 2 to 3 minutes or until turkey just loses its pink color throughout. Transfer cutlets to bowl with vegetables.

**4** Squeeze juice from half of lemon; slice remaining half for garnish. Pour lemon juice and *⅓ cup water* into skillet, stirring to loosen brown bits from bottom of skillet.

**5** Return turkey and vegetables to skillet; heat through. Garnish with lemon slices. *Makes 6 servings.*

Each serving: About 205 calories, 26 g protein, 14 g carbohydrate, 6 g total fat (1 g saturated), 59 mg cholesterol, 545 mg sodium.

# Irish Chicken Dinner

PREP: 20 MINUTES ⌒ COOK: 50 MINUTES

Here's an interesting rendition of what New Englanders fondly call a boiled dinner, with chicken standing in for the traditional corned beef.

1 whole chicken (about 3½ pounds), cut up
1 tablespoon vegetable oil
1 small head green cabbage (about 2 pounds), cut
 into 8 wedges
1 large onion, cut into 8 wedges
8 ounces carrots, cut into 2½-inch pieces
2 small turnips (about 8 ounces), peeled and cut
 into 1-inch-wide wedges
10 whole black peppercorns
3 whole cloves
1 large bay leaf
1 cup chicken broth, canned or homemade
 (page 24)
1 cup loosely packed spinach leaves, cut into
 ¼-inch-wide strips

**1** Remove skin and fat from all chicken pieces except wings; cut each chicken breast in half.

**2** In 8-quart Dutch oven, heat oil over medium-high heat until hot. Add cabbage and onion wedges and cook until lightly browned.

**3** Add chicken, carrots, turnips, peppercorns, cloves, bay leaf, chicken broth, and *1 cup water*; heat to boiling over high heat. Reduce heat to low; cover and simmer 40 minutes, gently stirring occasionally, until chicken and vegetables are tender.

**4** With slotted spoon, transfer chicken and vegetables to 4 large soup bowls; top with spinach. Into medium bowl, pour cooking broth through sieve; discard spices and bay leaf. Spoon hot broth over chicken and vegetables in soup bowls. *Makes 4 servings.*

Each serving: About 380 calories, 46 g protein, 27 g carbohydrate, 10 g total fat (2 g saturated), 134 mg cholesterol, 515 mg sodium.

# Turkey-Sausage & Potato Sauté

PREP: 20 MINUTES ⌒ COOK: 30 MINUTES

3 medium red potatoes (about 1 pound),
 quartered
1 pound green beans, trimmed
4 teaspoons vegetable oil
1 pound Italian-style turkey-sausage links
2 large onions, thinly sliced
½ teaspoon salt
¼ teaspoon coarsely ground black pepper
2 medium tomatoes, cut into wedges

**1** In 4-quart saucepan, heat potatoes and *enough hot water to cover* to boiling over high heat. Reduce heat to low; cover and simmer 6 minutes. Stir in green beans, adding *more hot water to cover* if necessary; heat to boiling over high heat. Reduce heat to low; cover and simmer 5 minutes longer; drain.

**2** In nonstick 12-inch skillet, heat 2 teaspoons vegetable oil over medium-high heat until hot. Add sausages and cook until browned. Add onions; continue cooking until onions are browned. Stir in *¼ cup water*; reduce heat to low. Cover; cook until sausages are cooked through. Transfer sausage mixture to bowl.

**3** In same skillet, heat remaining 2 teaspoons vegetable oil; cook potatoes and green beans with salt and pepper until potatoes are golden brown, stirring frequently.

**4** Return sausage mixture to skillet; add tomato wedges and heat through. Spoon onto warm platter. *Makes 4 servings.*

Each serving: About 410 calories, 25 g protein, 43 g carbohydrate, 17 g total fat (4 g saturated), 61 mg cholesterol, 1060 mg sodium.

# Steak & Asparagus Stir-Fry

PREP: 15 MINUTES ～ COOK: 20 MINUTES

If you're in the mood for rice, omit the pasta here and make one of the "Rices for Stir-Fries," below.

6 ounces angel-hair pasta
Salt
¼ cup reduced-sodium soy sauce
2 tablespoons dry sherry
1 tablespoon minced, peeled fresh ginger or
  ¾ teaspoon ground ginger
1 teaspoon cornstarch
2 teaspoons distilled white vinegar
¾ teaspoon sugar
1 garlic clove, minced
1 beef top round steak (12 ounces), thinly sliced
1 tablespoon vegetable oil
1½ pounds asparagus, trimmed and cut into
  2-inch-long pieces
1 small tomato, seeded and diced

1 In large saucepot, prepare pasta in *boiling salted water* as label directs; drain. Return pasta to saucepot; keep warm.

2 Meanwhile, in medium bowl, mix soy sauce, sherry, ginger, cornstarch, white vinegar, sugar, garlic, and ¼ *cup water*; add beef, tossing to coat well; set aside.

3 In nonstick 12-inch skillet, heat vegetable oil over medium-high heat until hot. Add asparagus and cook, stirring frequently, until tender-crisp. Add beef and soy-sauce mixture and cook over medium-high heat, stirring constantly, until beef just loses its pink color and sauce boils and thickens slightly.

4 To serve, arrange beef mixture and angel-hair pasta on 4 warm dinner plates. Sprinkle with diced tomato. *Makes 4 servings.*

Each serving: About 400 calories, 29 g protein, 42 g carbohydrate, 12 g total fat (4 g saturated), 52 mg cholesterol, 795 mg sodium.

## RICES FOR STIR-FRIES

There's no rule that says the rice you serve with a stir-fry has to be plain. With a couple of easy additions, you can transform a plain rice accompaniment into something that complements the stir-fry you are serving. Follow these basic directions to cook up fluffy rice, then stir in the seasonings for one of the 5 options below: Heat *1 cup regular long-grain rice* with *1 cup chicken broth*, *¾ cup water*, and *¼ teaspoon salt* to boiling. Cover and simmer on low heat 18 to 20 minutes or until rice is tender and liquid is absorbed.

**Watercress Rice** After rice has cooked, stir in *1 cup loosely packed watercress leaves*, coarsely chopped. Makes 4 accompaniment servings.

Each serving: About 175 calories, 4 g protein, 37 g carbohydrate, 1 g total fat (0 g saturated), 0 mg cholesterol, 415 mg sodium.

**Orange-Cilantro Rice** After rice has cooked, stir in *2 tablespoons chopped cilantro* and *½ teaspoon grated orange peel*. Makes 4 accompaniment servings.

Each serving: About 175 calories, 4 g protein, 37 g carbohydrate, 1 g total fat (0 g saturated), 3 mg cholesterol, 295 mg sodium.

**Lemon-Parsley Rice** After rice has cooked, stir in *2 tablespoons chopped fresh parsley leaves* and *1 teaspoon grated lemon peel*. Makes 4 accompaniment servings.

Each serving: About 175 calories, 4 g protein, 37 g carbohydrate, 1 g total fat (0 g saturated), 3 mg cholesterol, 295 mg sodium.

**Asian Rice** Omit salt when cooking rice. After rice has cooked, stir in *2 green onions*, chopped, *2 teaspoons soy sauce*, and *¼ teaspoon Asian sesame oil*. Makes 4 accompaniment servings.

Each serving: About 180 calories, 4 g protein, 38 g carbohydrate, 1 g total fat (0 g saturated), 3 mg cholesterol, 380 mg sodium.

**Fluffy Lemon Rice** Grate peel and squeeze juice from *1 large lemon*. Add lemon juice and *¼ teaspoon ground turmeric* to rice as it cooks. When rice is done, stir in grated lemon peel. Makes 4 accompaniment servings.

Each serving: About 180 calories, 4 g protein, 39 g carbohydrate, 1 g total fat (0 g saturated), 0 mg cholesterol, 410 mg sodium.

# Easy Beef Teriyaki Stir-Fry

PREP: 20 MINUTES ∾ COOK: 20 MINUTES

Quickly made with deli roast beef, a great last-minute dinner.

1 cup regular long-grain rice
2 tablespoons vegetable oil
1 garlic clove, crushed with side of chef's knife
1 piece (1" by ¾") fresh ginger, peeled and minced
1 bunch green onions, cut into 1-inch pieces
1 pound carrots, peeled and thinly sliced
8 ounces snow peas, strings removed, halved lengthwise
1 medium red pepper, thinly sliced
½ cup teriyaki sauce
2 teaspoons cornstarch
8 ounces cooked roast beef, in one piece, cut into paper-thin slices (about 3" by 1")
1 can (5 ounces, drained weight) water chestnuts, drained

1 In 2-quart saucepan, prepare rice as label directs.

2 In 10-inch skillet, heat vegetable oil over medium-high heat until hot. Add garlic and cook until golden; discard garlic. Add ginger and green onions; cook until green onions are golden, stirring occasionally. Add carrots; cook 3 minutes, stirring occasionally. Add snow peas and red pepper; cook, stirring occasionally, until vegetables are tender-crisp.

3 In cup, stir together teriyaki sauce and cornstarch. Add teriyaki mixture and ¾ *cup water* to vegetables in skillet. Heat to boiling over high heat. Reduce heat to low; simmer 1 minute or until sauce is thickened slightly. Add beef and water chestnuts; heat through. Serve beef mixture over rice. *Makes 6 servings.*

Each serving: About 500 calories, 24 g protein, 66 g carbohydrate, 15 g total fat (4 g saturated), 47 mg cholesterol, 1465 mg sodium.

# Steak & Mushroom Skillet with Egg Noodles

PREP: 25 MINUTES ∾ COOK: 35 MINUTES

For just a hint of heat, use chili sauce in place of ketchup.

6 ounces egg noodles
Salt
2 tablespoons soy sauce
1 tablespoon ketchup
1½ teaspoons cornstarch
1 beef flank steak (about 1 pound), cut into 1½-inch pieces
2 tablespoons olive oil
3 medium carrots, peeled and thinly sliced
2 medium onions, thinly sliced
1 package (10 ounces) mushrooms, halved

1 In large saucepot, prepare noodles in *boiling salted water* as label directs. Drain and keep warm.

2 Meanwhile, in medium bowl, combine soy sauce, ketchup, and cornstarch. Add flank steak pieces and stir mixture gently until meat pieces are well coated.

3 In nonstick 12-inch skillet, heat 2 teaspoons olive oil over medium-high heat until hot. Add carrots and onions and cook until tender-crisp and lightly browned; with slotted spoon, transfer to another bowl.

4 In same skillet, heat 2 teaspoons olive oil over medium-high heat until hot. Add mushrooms and cook until tender and liquid evaporates; transfer to bowl with carrots and onions.

5 To same skillet, add remaining 2 teaspoons olive oil; cook flank steak mixture about 3 minutes for rare. Gently stir in cooked vegetables and ½ *cup water*; heat mixture through, stirring occasionally.

6 To serve, top noodles with flank steak mixture. *Makes 4 servings.*

Each serving: About 510 calories, 32 g protein, 49 g carbohydrate, 21 g total fat (7 g saturated), 99 mg cholesterol, 820 mg sodium.

## Gingery Beef & Sugar Snaps

PREP: 20 MINUTES ∾ COOK: 25 MINUTES

1 beef flank steak (about 1 pound)
2 tablespoons soy sauce
2 tablespoons dry sherry
2 teaspoons grated, peeled fresh ginger
1 garlic clove, crushed with garlic press
4 teaspoons plus 1 tablespoon vegetable oil
8 ounces medium mushrooms, sliced
1 large red pepper, thinly sliced
8 ounces sugar snap peas or snow peas, strings removed
2 large celery stalks, cut into 1-inch-thick pieces
1 medium onion, thinly sliced
8 ounces bean sprouts*, rinsed and drained
2 teaspoons cornstarch

1 Slice flank steak lengthwise in half. With knife held in slanting position, almost parallel to cutting surface, slice steak crosswise into ⅛-inch-thick slices. In medium bowl, mix steak with soy sauce, sherry, ginger, and garlic; set aside.

2 In nonstick 12-inch skillet, heat 2 teaspoons vegetable oil over medium-high heat until hot. Add mushrooms and red pepper and cook until mushrooms turn golden brown and all liquid evaporates. Transfer mushroom mixture to large bowl.

3 In same skillet, heat 2 teaspoons vegetable oil; cook sugar snap peas, celery, and onion, stirring frequently, until vegetables are tender-crisp. Stir in bean sprouts; cook 2 minutes, stirring constantly. Spoon vegetables into bowl with mushrooms.

4 In small bowl, mix cornstarch and ½ *cup water* until smooth; set aside.

5 In same skillet, heat remaining 1 tablespoon vegetable oil over medium-high heat; cook half of steak mixture until beef loses its pink color, stirring quickly and constantly. Transfer to bowl with mushrooms. Repeat with remaining steak mixture.

6 Return vegetables and meat to skillet. Stir in cornstarch mixture and cook until liquid boils and thickens slightly. *Makes 4 servings.*

*We used soybean sprouts (available at Asian food markets and some supermarkets). Mung bean sprouts, more commonly available, can be substituted.

Each serving: About 430 calories, 34 g protein, 21 g carbohydrate, 24 g total fat (7 g saturated), 59 mg cholesterol, 630 mg sodium.

## Tuscany Veal Shanks

PREP: 10 MINUTES ∾ COOK: 1½ HOURS

You can substitute beef shank cross cuts for the veal in this recipe.

1 tablespoon plus 2 teaspoons olive oil
4 veal shank cross cuts, each 1¼ inches thick (about 2¼ pounds)
¾ teaspoon salt
1 medium carrot, peeled and coarsely chopped
1 medium onion, coarsely chopped
1 medium celery stalk, coarsely chopped
1 can (14½ ounces) diced tomatoes
1 bay leaf
½ teaspoon sugar
1 can (15 ounces) Great Northern beans, rinsed and drained
1 package (10 ounces) frozen Fordhook lima beans

1 In 12-inch skillet, heat 1 tablespoon olive oil over medium-high heat until hot. Add veal shank cross cuts and ½ teaspoon salt and cook until veal shanks are browned on both sides; transfer to plate.

2 In same skillet, heat remaining 2 teaspoons olive oil; cook carrot, onion, and celery until browned. Return veal shanks to skillet. Stir in tomatoes with their juice, bay leaf, sugar, ¼ teaspoon salt, and ¼ *cup water*; heat to boiling. Reduce heat to low; cover and simmer 1 hour, stirring occasionally.

3 Add Great Northern beans and frozen lima beans; heat to boiling over high heat. Reduce heat to low; cover and simmer 30 minutes or until veal is fork-tender. Discard bay leaf. *Makes 4 servings.*

Each serving: About 400 calories, 33 g protein, 47 g carbohydrate, 9 g total fat (2 g saturated), 70 mg cholesterol, 720 mg sodium.

◄ *Gingery Beef & Sugar Snaps*

# Orange Beef & Peppers

PREP: 20 MINUTES ◦ COOK: 20 MINUTES

I beef top round steak, ¾ inch thick (about
   I pound), well trimmed
2 tablespoons soy sauce
3 large oranges
2 tablespoons margarine or butter
I large red pepper, cut into ¼-inch-thick slices
I large yellow pepper, cut into ¼-inch-thick slices
I bunch green onions, cut into 2-inch pieces
I½ teaspoons grated, peeled fresh ginger
¾ teaspoon cornstarch
2 bunches arugula (about 8 ounces), stems
   trimmed

**1** Cut steak lengthwise in half. With knife held in slanting position almost parallel to the cutting surface, slice steak crosswise into ⅛-inch-thick slices. In bowl, toss steak with soy sauce.

**2** With a sharp paring knife, peel 2 oranges; cut the oranges crosswise into ¼-inch-thick slices, then cut each slice in half. Grate 1 teaspoon peel from remaining orange, then squeeze enough juice from the orange to equal ½ cup.

**3** In nonstick 12-inch skillet, melt 2 teaspoons margarine or butter over medium-high heat. Add peppers and cook, stirring frequently, until golden and tender-crisp; transfer to bowl.

**4** In same skillet, melt 1 teaspoon margarine or butter; cook green onions, stirring frequently, until golden and tender-crisp; transfer to bowl with peppers.

**5** In small bowl, mix grated orange peel, orange juice, ginger, and cornstarch until blended; set aside.

**6** In same skillet, melt remaining 1 tablespoon margarine or butter; cook half the beef mixture, stirring quickly and constantly, just until beef loses its pink color; transfer to bowl with vegetables. In drippings in skillet, repeat with remaining beef mixture. Return vegetables and meat to skillet. Stir in orange-juice mixture and sliced oranges; cook until liquid boils and thickens slightly and mixture is heated through.

**7** Serve beef mixture with arugula. *Makes 4 servings.*

Each serving: About 270 calories, 29 g protein, 19 g carbohydrate,
9 g total fat (2 g saturated), 65 mg cholesterol, 625 mg sodium.

# Stove-Top Eye Round with Spring Vegetables

PREP: 25 MINUTES ◦ COOK: 1¼ HOURS

I beef eye round roast (about 2 pounds), well
   trimmed
½ teaspoon coarsely ground black pepper
2 teaspoons olive oil
2 cups beef broth
I garlic clove, halved
I bay leaf
I½ pounds peeled baby carrots
I¾ pounds small red and Yukon Gold potatoes
I½ pounds asparagus, trimmed

**1** Rub roast with pepper.

**2** In nonstick 5-quart Dutch oven, heat olive oil over medium-high heat until hot. Add eye round roast and cook until browned on all sides. Add broth, garlic, bay leaf, and *½ cup water;* heat to boiling. Reduce heat to low; cover and simmer 20 minutes.

**3** Add carrots and unpeeled potatoes to Dutch oven; heat to boiling over high heat. Reduce heat to low; cover and simmer 30 minutes longer or until carrots and potatoes are fork-tender and temperature of roast reaches 135°F. on instant-read meat thermometer when inserted in thickest part of meat. Internal temperature of meat will rise to about 140°F. (medium-rare) upon standing.

**4** When roast is done, place on platter and let stand for 15 minutes for easier slicing; keep warm.

**5** Meanwhile, in 12-inch skillet, cook asparagus in *½ inch boiling water* 3 to 5 minutes or until tender-crisp.

**6** Transfer carrots and potatoes to platter, reserving cooking broth. Discard garlic and bay leaf.

**7** Skim fat from broth. Thinly slice roast. Serve sliced roast, carrots, potatoes, and asparagus in deep dinner plates with broth. *Makes 8 servings.*

Each serving: About 270 calories, 29 g protein, 25 g carbohydrate,
6 g total fat (2 g saturated), 59 mg cholesterol, 345 mg sodium.

*Stove-Top Eye Round with Spring Vegetables*

# Smoked Pork Chop Dinner

PREP: 10 MINUTES ∼ COOK: 1 HOUR

A fruit compote, such as Autumn Fruit Compote (page 220), is the perfect dessert for this hearty German favorite.

1 tablespoon vegetable oil
4 smoked pork loin or rib chops, each ¾ inch thick (about 1¾ pounds), well trimmed
1 medium Granny Smith or Rome Beauty apple
1 pound carrots, peeled and cut into bite-size chunks
1½ pounds sauerkraut, rinsed and drained
1 bottle or can (11 to 12 ounces) beer or nonalcoholic beer

¼ cup packed light or dark brown sugar
2 teaspoons caraway or fennel seeds, crushed

**1** In 12-inch skillet, heat vegetable oil over high heat until hot. Add pork chops and cook until browned on both sides.

**2** Meanwhile, coarsely grate half of unpeeled apple; reserve remaining half to add to skillet in step 4.

**3** To pork chops in skillet, add carrots, grated apple, sauerkraut, beer, brown sugar, caraway seeds, and *½ cup water*; heat to boiling over high heat. Reduce heat to low; cover and simmer 35 minutes.

**4** Cut remaining half apple into wedges; add to mixture in skillet. Cook 10 minutes longer or until carrots and pork chops are fork-tender, occasionally spooning liquid in skillet over pork chops. *Makes 4 servings.*

Each serving: About 380 calories, 32 g protein, 36 g carbohydrate, 12 g total fat (3 g saturated), 82 mg cholesterol, 500 mg sodium.

# Sesame Pork Stir-Fry

PREP TIME: 20 MINUTES ～ COOK TIME: 20 MINUTES

Gingery good and only 375 calories per serving—
rice and all

Watercress Rice (page 52)
1 pork tenderloin (about ¾ pound), thinly sliced
2 tablespoons soy sauce
1 tablespoon minced, peeled fresh ginger
1 teaspoon Asian sesame oil
1 garlic clove, crushed with garlic press
¾ cup chicken broth, canned or homemade
   (page 24)
1¼ teaspoons cornstarch
2 teaspoons olive oil
3 medium carrots, peeled and cut into 2" by ¼"
   sticks
1 medium red pepper, cut into ¼-inch-wide strips
1 medium zucchini (about 8 ounces), cut into
   2" by ¼" sticks

**1** Prepare Watercress Rice; keep warm.

**2** Meanwhile, in medium bowl, toss pork, soy sauce,
ginger, sesame oil, and garlic. In cup, mix chicken
broth and cornstarch.

**3** In nonstick 12-inch skillet, heat 1 teaspoon olive oil
over medium-high heat until hot. Add carrots and red
pepper; cook until lightly browned, about 5 minutes,
stirring frequently. Add *1 tablespoon water* and cook 3
to 5 minutes longer or until tender-crisp. Transfer to
bowl.

**4** In same skillet, heat remaining 1 teaspoon olive oil.
Add zucchini; cook until tender-crisp, about 3 minutes, stirring frequently. Transfer zucchini to bowl
with vegetables.

**5** In same skillet, cook pork mixture, stirring constantly, until pork just loses its pink color. Stir cornstarch mixture; add to pork. Stir in vegetables; heat to
boiling. Boil 1 minute or until sauce thickens. Serve
pork stir-fry with Watercress Rice. *Makes 4 servings.*

Each serving: About 375 calories, 23 g protein, 48 g carbohydrate,
10 g total fat (2 g saturated), 56 mg cholesterol, 975 mg sodium.

# Gingered Pork & Vegetable Stir-Fry

PREP: 15 MINUTES ～ COOK: 12 TO 15 MINUTES

1 pork tenderloin (about ¾ pound), thinly sliced
2 tablespoons grated, peeled fresh ginger
1 cup chicken broth, canned or homemade
   (page 24)
2 tablespoons teriyaki sauce
2 teaspoons cornstarch
2 teaspoons vegetable oil
½ pound snow peas, strings removed
1 medium zucchini (about 8 ounces), halved
   lengthwise and thinly sliced
3 green onions, cut into 3-inch pieces

**1** In medium bowl, toss pork and fresh ginger. In cup,
mix chicken broth, teriyaki sauce, and cornstarch.

## CAST-IRON CARE

Old cast-iron pans are prized for their shiny, jet
black, practically nonstick patina. If you spot
one at a yard sale, grab it—it's a treasure! Or,
buy a new cast-iron skillet and turn it into a
family heirloom. Here's how:

**SEASONING** Pans, new or old, must be seasoned
before using them for the first time. Wash in
hot, soapy water (use bar soap); dry immediately. Using a cloth that has been soaked in oil
or melted solid shortening and wrung out, rub
entire surface, even exterior and lid. Heat upside
down in 350°F. oven for one hour. Turn oven off
and leave pan in place until cool.

**CLEANING** After cooking in cast iron, use hot
soapy water (though many experts avoid soap
unless they'll be reseasoning) and clean the pan
by simply pouring boiling water over it and
wiping it clean with a paper towel. Never use
detergents. Dry at once.

**WHEN TO RESEASON?** When the skillet is rusty
or the surface appears dull, not shiny, or when
food has stuck to the bottom. Scour thoroughly with steel wool, then reseason as explained
above. Store, uncovered, in a dry place.

**2** In nonstick 12-inch skillet, heat 1 teaspoon vegetable oil over medium-high heat until hot. Add snow peas, zucchini, and green onions and cook, stirring frequently, until lightly browned and tender-crisp, about 5 minutes. Transfer to bowl.

**3** In same skillet, heat remaining 1 teaspoon vegetable oil; add pork mixture and cook, stirring quickly and constantly, until pork just loses its pink color. Transfer pork to bowl with vegetables. Stir cornstarch mixture; add to skillet and heat to boiling. Boil 1 minute or until sauce thickens. Stir in pork and vegetables; heat through. *Makes 4 servings.*

Each serving: About 170 calories, 21 g protein, 10 g carbohydrate, 5 g total fat (1 g saturated), 51 mg cholesterol, 550 mg sodium.

# Southwestern-Style Pasta Skillet

PREP: 10 MINUTES ～ COOK: 20 MINUTES

8 ounces wagon wheel or rotelle pasta
4 ounces fully cooked chorizo sausage, thinly sliced
1 large green pepper, diced
1 large onion, diced
1 small zucchini (about 6 ounces), diced
2 cans (14½ to 16 ounces each) no-salt-added stewed tomatoes
1 can (16 ounces) no-salt-added whole-kernel corn, drained
1 can (4 to 4½ ounces) chopped mild green chiles
¼ cup coarsely shredded Monterey Jack cheese

**1** In large saucepot, prepare pasta in *boiling water* as label directs, but do not add salt; drain and keep warm.

**2** Meanwhile, in 12-inch skillet, cook sausage, green pepper, and onion over medium-high heat, stirring frequently until vegetables are tender; discard any fat in skillet.

**3** Stir in zucchini, stewed tomatoes, corn, and chiles with their liquid; heat to boiling. Reduce heat to low; cook 10 minutes to blend flavors.

**4** Stir pasta into sausage mixture; sprinkle with Monterey Jack. *Makes 4 servings.*

Each serving: About 535 calories, 22 g protein, 83 g carbohydrate, 15 g total fat (6 g saturated), 32 mg cholesterol, 620 mg sodium.

# Braised Lamb Shanks with Couscous

PREP: 10 MINUTES ～ COOK: 2¼ HOURS

The preparation for this recipe is minimal—just trim the fat from the shanks, brown quickly in a Dutch oven, add the other ingredients, and let your stove do the rest. Perfect for a Sunday afternoon.

2 teaspoons vegetable oil
4 small lamb shanks (1 pound each), well trimmed
2 medium carrots, peeled and cut into ¼-inch-thick slices
1 large celery stalk, cut into ¼-inch-thick slices
1 medium onion, coarsely chopped
1 can (28 ounces) tomatoes in puree
1 cup beef broth
2 tablespoons chopped fresh rosemary or 2 teaspoons dried rosemary leaves, crushed
2 teaspoons sugar
½ teaspoon salt
1 bay leaf
1 cinnamon stick (3 inches long)
1 can (8 ounces) garbanzo beans, rinsed and drained
¾ cup couscous (Moroccan pasta)

**1** In 8-quart Dutch oven, heat vegetable oil over medium-high heat until hot. Add lamb shanks, 2 at a time, until browned on all sides. Transfer shanks to bowl as they brown.

**2** In same Dutch oven, cook carrots, celery, and onion over medium heat until golden brown. Add tomatoes with their puree, broth, rosemary, sugar, salt, bay leaf, and cinnamon stick; heat to boiling over high heat, stirring with spoon to break up tomatoes. Return shanks to Dutch oven. Reduce heat to low; cover and simmer 2 hours or until lamb shanks are fork-tender, turning meat once.

**3** Discard bay leaf and cinnamon stick; skim fat from sauce. Add garbanzo beans over high heat; heat through.

**4** Meanwhile, prepare couscous as label directs, but do not add margarine or butter.

**5** Serve lamb shanks and their sauce with couscous. *Makes 4 servings.*

Each serving: About 480 calories, 40 g protein, 56 g carbohydrate, 10 g total fat (3 g saturated), 93 mg cholesterol, 1075 mg sodium.

# FRITTATAS & OMELETS

Two different takes on egg skillet dishes. In the Italian-style frittata, beaten eggs serve as the binder for a host of flavorful ingredients. The egg mixture is cooked first on the stovetop and then, usually, finished in the oven or under the broiler. To make an omelet, the eggs are cooked separately, then wrapped around a filling. You can prepare a lighter, more healthful version of either type of egg dish by cutting back on egg yolks (where all of the egg's fat and cholesterol are found). For every whole egg you drop, substitute 2 egg whites. But never replace more than half of the whole eggs called for in the recipe.

## Pepper & Tomato Omelet with Roast Potatoes

PREP: 10 MINUTES • COOK: 30 MINUTES

1½ pounds medium red potatoes, quartered
2 tablespoons plus 2 teaspoons olive oil
1 teaspoon salt
½ teaspoon coarsely ground black pepper
1 large onion, thinly sliced
1 large green pepper, cut into ⅛-inch-wide strips
½ teaspoon dried thyme leaves
3 medium plum tomatoes (about 8 ounces), seeded and coarsely chopped
1 tablespoon chopped fresh parsley leaves
6 large eggs

**1** Preheat oven to 450°F. In medium bowl, mix potatoes, 1 tablespoon olive oil, ½ teaspoon salt, and ¼ teaspoon black pepper. Evenly spread potatoes on 15½" by 10½" jelly-roll pan. Bake potatoes until tender and golden, about 30 minutes, stirring occasionally.
**2** Meanwhile, in nonstick 12-inch skillet, heat 2 teaspoons olive oil over medium-high heat until hot. Stir in onion, green pepper, thyme, ¼ teaspoon salt, and remaining ¼ teaspoon black pepper until coated with oil. Reduce heat to medium-low; cover and cook until

vegetables are tender, stirring occasionally, about 15 minutes. Stir in tomatoes and parsley; heat through. Transfer vegetable mixture to bowl. Wipe skillet clean.
**3** In bowl, beat eggs, remaining ¼ teaspoon salt, and ¼ cup water until blended. In same skillet, heat remaining 1 tablespoon olive oil over medium heat until hot. Pour egg mixture into skillet; cook until set (about 1 minute), gently lifting edge to allow uncooked portion to run under omelet.
**4** When omelet is set but still moist, spoon vegetable mixture on one half of omelet. Tilt skillet and, with spatula, fold omelet in half; slide onto warm platter. Serve with roast potatoes. Makes 4 servings.

EACH SERVING: ABOUT 370 CALORIES, 14 G PROTEIN, 41 G CARBOHYDRATE, 17 G TOTAL FAT (4 G SATURATED), 319 MG CHOLESTEROL, 700 MG SODIUM.

## Red Pepper & Goat Cheese Omelet

PREP: 10 MINUTES • COOK: 15 MINUTES

2 tablespoons margarine or butter
1 medium red pepper, thinly sliced
½ teaspoon salt
1 garlic clove, minced
8 large eggs
2 ounces goat cheese
¼ cup packed torn arugula

**1** In nonstick 10-inch skillet, melt 2 teaspoons margarine or butter over medium-high heat until hot. Add red pepper and ¼ teaspoon salt; cook until tender. Add garlic and cook 1 minute.
**2** In bowl, beat eggs with ¼ cup water and remaining ¼ teaspoon salt.
**3** In nonstick 8-inch skillet, melt 1 teaspoon margarine or butter over medium-high heat. Pour ¼ cup of egg mixture into skillet; cook until set (about 1 minute), gently lifting edge to allow uncooked portion to run under omelet. Spoon one-fourth of pepper mixture,

one-fourth of goat cheese, and 2 tablespoons arugula on half of omelet, fold over other half, and slide onto plate.
**4** Repeat for 3 more omelets. Makes 4 servings.

EACH SERVING: ABOUT 255 CALORIES, 16 G PROTEIN, 3 G CARBOHYDRATE, 20 G TOTAL FAT (7 G SATURATED), 436 MG CHOLESTEROL, 555 MG SODIUM.

## Artichoke & Tomato Frittata

PREP: 5 MINUTES • BAKE: 15 MINUTES

1 package (9 ounces) frozen artichoke hearts
¾ teaspoon salt
1 tablespoon olive oil
1 small onion, diced
8 large eggs
½ teaspoon dried basil leaves
2 plum tomatoes, diced

**1** In 2-quart saucepan, heat frozen artichoke hearts, ¼ teaspoon salt, and ¼ cup water to boiling over high heat. Reduce heat to low; cover and simmer 6 to 8 minutes or until artichokes are tender; drain.
**2** Meanwhile, in nonstick 10-inch skillet with oven-safe handle, heat olive oil over medium heat until hot; cook onion until tender.
**3** Preheat oven to 350°F. In bowl, mix eggs, basil, remaining ½ teaspoon salt, and ¼ cup water. Pour egg mixture over onion in skillet; sprinkle with artichokes and tomatoes. Cook over medium heat until edge begins to set, about 3 to 4 minutes.
**4** Place frittata in oven; bake 15 minutes or until set. Makes 4 servings.

EACH SERVING: ABOUT 220 CALORIES, 15 G PROTEIN, 10 G CARBOHYDRATE, 14 G TOTAL FAT (4 G SATURATED), 425 MG CHOLESTEROL, 595 MG SODIUM.

## Asparagus & Pasta Frittata

PREP: 20 MINUTES • BAKE: 10 MINUTES

4 ounces penne pasta or elbow
    macaroni (about 1½ cups penne or
    1 cup macaroni)
Salt
4 teaspoons margarine or butter
12 ounces asparagus, trimmed and cut
    into 1-inch pieces
4 ounces mushrooms, sliced
1 medium onion, diced
1 medium red pepper, diced
¼ teaspoon coarsely ground black
    pepper
8 large eggs
2 tablespoons grated Parmesan cheese
1 tablespoon all-purpose flour
2 tablespoons chopped fresh basil or
    1 teaspoon dried basil leaves
Nonstick cooking spray

**1** In large saucepot, prepare pasta in *boiling salted water* as label directs; drain. Set aside.
**2** Meanwhile, in nonstick 10-inch skillet with oven-safe handle, melt 2 teaspoons margarine or butter over medium-high heat. Add asparagus and cook, stirring occasionally, until tender-crisp. With slotted spoon, transfer asparagus to bowl.
**3** Preheat oven to 375°F. In same skillet, heat remaining 2 teaspoons margarine or butter; cook mushrooms, onion, red pepper, black pepper, and ¼ teaspoon salt until vegetables are golden and tender, stirring frequently. Transfer vegetables to bowl with asparagus; wipe skillet clean.
**4** In large bowl, mix eggs, grated Parmesan, flour, basil, ¼ teaspoon salt, and ¼ *cup water* until blended; stir in vegetable mixture and cooked pasta.
**5** Spray skillet with nonstick cooking spray. Pour egg mixture into skillet and cook over medium-high heat 1 to 2 minutes until egg mixture begins to set around edge; remove skillet from heat. Place skillet in oven and bake frittata 10 minutes. If you like, when frittata is done, broil 1 to 2 minutes to brown top slightly.

*Chive & Goat Cheese Frittata*

**6** To serve, slide frittata onto warm large platter. Cut into wedges. Makes 4 servings.

EACH SERVING: ABOUT 355 CALORIES, 21 G PROTEIN, 33 G CARBOHYDRATE, 16 G TOTAL FAT (4 G SATURATED), 427 MG CHOLESTEROL, 610 MG SODIUM.

## Apple, Ham & Cheese Omelet

PREP: 5 MINUTES • COOK: 15 MINUTES

2 tablespoons margarine or butter
2 Golden Delicious apples, peeled,
    cored, and cut into ¼-inch wedges
8 large eggs
¼ teaspoon salt
½ cup shredded Gruyère or Jarlsberg
    cheese (2 ounces)
4 ounces sliced ham, cut into thin strips

**1** In nonstick 10-inch skillet, melt 2 teaspoons margarine or butter over medium-high heat. Add apples and cook until golden and tender.
**2** In bowl, beat eggs with ¼ *cup water* and salt.
**3** In nonstick 8-inch skillet, melt 1 teaspoon margarine or butter over medium-high heat. Pour ¼ cup of egg mixture into skillet; cook until set (about 1 minute), gently lifting edge to allow uncooked portion to run under omelet.

Spoon one-fourth of apples, one-fourth of Gruyère or Jarlsberg, and one-fourth of ham on one half of omelet, fold over other half, and slide onto plate.
**4** Repeat for 3 more omelets. Makes 4 servings.

EACH SERVING: ABOUT 345 CALORIES, 22 G PROTEIN, 12 G CARBOHYDRATE, 24 G TOTAL FAT (8 G SATURATED), 457 MG CHOLESTEROL, 755 MG SODIUM.

## Chive & Goat Cheese Frittata

PREP: 10 MINUTES • BAKE: 10 MINUTES

8 large eggs
½ cup milk
½ teaspoon salt
⅛ teaspoon coarsely ground black
    pepper
1 medium tomato, diced
2 tablespoons chopped fresh chives
2 teaspoons margarine or butter
3 ounces mild goat cheese or shredded
    Fontina cheese

**1** Preheat oven to 375°F. In bowl, mix eggs, milk, salt, and pepper. Stir in tomato and chives.
**2** In nonstick 10-inch skillet with oven-safe handle, melt margarine or butter over medium heat. Pour in egg mixture; drop spoonfuls of goat cheese on top of egg mixture. Cook 3 to 4 minutes or until frittata begins to set around the edge. Remove skillet from heat.
**3** Place skillet in oven. Bake 9 to 10 minutes or until frittata begins to set and knife inserted in center comes out clean. Makes 4 servings.

EACH SERVING: ABOUT 240 CALORIES, 17 G PROTEIN, 4 G CARBOHYDRATE, 17 G TOTAL FAT (7 G SATURATED), 440 MG CHOLESTEROL, 505 MG SODIUM.

## Spinach, Cheddar & Bacon Omelet

PREP: 5 MINUTES • COOK: 15 MINUTES

*1 large bunch spinach (10 to 12
 ounces), tough stems discarded,
 rinsed*
*8 large eggs*
*¼ teaspoon salt*
*4 teaspoons margarine or butter*
*4 slices bacon, cooked and crumbled*
*1 cup shredded Cheddar cheese
 (4 ounces)*

**1** In 3-quart saucepan, cook spinach over high heat just until wilted; drain. Press out excess liquid from spinach; coarsely chop.
**2** In bowl, beat eggs with *¼ cup water* and salt.
**3** In nonstick 8-inch skillet, melt 1 teaspoon margarine or butter over medium-high heat. Pour ¼ cup of egg mixture into skillet; cook until set (about 1 minute), gently lifting edge to allow uncooked portion to run under omelet. Spoon one-fourth of spinach, one-fourth of bacon, and one-fourth of Cheddar on one half of omelet, fold over other half, and slide onto plate.
**4** Repeat for 3 more omelets. Makes 4 servings.

EACH SERVING: ABOUT 345 CALORIES,
23 G PROTEIN, 4 G CARBOHYDRATE,
27 G TOTAL FAT (11 G SATURATED),
460 MG CHOLESTEROL, 635 MG SODIUM.

## Black Bean & Salsa Omelet

PREP: 5 MINUTES • COOK: 15 MINUTES

*1 cup canned black beans, rinsed and
 drained*
*1 cup medium-hot salsa*
*8 large eggs*
*¼ teaspoon salt*
*4 teaspoons margarine or butter*
*1 medium avocado, peeled and diced*
*¼ cup sour cream*

**1** In nonstick 10-inch skillet, heat black beans and salsa over medium-high heat until all liquid evaporates, stirring often.
**2** In bowl, beat eggs with *¼ cup water* and salt.
**3** In nonstick 8-inch skillet, melt 1

*Spinach, Cheddar & Bacon Omelet*

teaspoon margarine or butter over medium-high heat. Pour ¼ cup of egg mixture into skillet; cook until set (about 1 minute), gently lifting edge to allow uncooked portion to run under omelet. Spoon one-fourth of black bean mixture, one-fourth of avocado, and 1 tablespoon sour cream on half of omelet, fold over other half, and slide onto plate.
**4** Repeat for 3 more omelets. Makes 4 servings.

EACH SERVING: ABOUT 360 CALORIES,
17 G PROTEIN, 17 G CARBOHYDRATE,
25 G TOTAL FAT (7 G SATURATED),
431 MG CHOLESTEROL, 1095 MG SODIUM.

## Potato Frittata

PREP: 10 MINUTES • COOK: 30 MINUTES

*2 tablespoons olive oil*
*1¼ pounds all-purpose potatoes,
 peeled and very thinly sliced*
*1 medium red pepper, diced*
*1 medium green pepper, diced*
*1 medium onion, halved lengthwise and
 thinly sliced crosswise*
*¾ teaspoon salt*
*5 large eggs*
*2 tablespoons grated Parmesan cheese*
*2 tablespoons chopped fresh parsley
 leaves*
*½ teaspoon coarsely ground black
 pepper*

**1** In nonstick 10-inch skillet, heat 1 tablespoon olive oil over medium heat until hot. Add potatoes, red and green

peppers, onion, and ½ teaspoon salt and cook until vegetables begin to brown slightly.
**2** Reduce heat to low; cover and cook, turning vegetables occasionally, until vegetables are fork-tender, about 15 minutes. Transfer potato mixture to medium bowl to cool slightly. Wipe skillet clean.
**3** In bowl, beat eggs, grated Parmesan, parsley, black pepper, and remaining ¼ teaspoon salt until blended. Stir in potato mixture.
**4** In same skillet, heat 2 teaspoons olive oil over medium-low heat, tilting skillet to grease side. Pour potato-egg mixture into skillet; cook until set around edge.
**5** With spatula, gently lift edge as it sets, tilting skillet to allow uncooked portion to run under frittata. Shake skillet occasionally to keep frittata moving freely in pan. When frittata is set but still moist on top, increase heat slightly to brown bottom of frittata.
**6** Turn frittata: Be sure mixture is loosened from bottom of skillet. Invert large plate over skillet; flip frittata onto plate; wipe skillet clean. Over medium heat, heat remaining 1 teaspoon olive oil in skillet. Slide frittata back into skillet, browned-side up. Cook, shaking pan occasionally to prevent sticking, until bottom of frittata is golden brown, about 5 minutes; invert frittata onto warm large platter.
**7** To serve, cut frittata into wedges. Makes 4 servings.

EACH SERVING: ABOUT 275 CALORIES,
12 G PROTEIN, 26 G CARBOHYDRATE,
14 G TOTAL FAT (3 G SATURATED),
268 MG CHOLESTEROL, 570 MG SODIUM.

## Individual Egg-White Frittatas with Sautéed Vegetables

PREP: 20 MINUTES • BAKE: 15 MINUTES

*1 tablespoon olive oil*
*1 medium red pepper, diced*
*1 medium onion, diced*
*4 ounces mushrooms, diced*
*¼ teaspoon dried oregano leaves*
*⅛ teaspoon coarsely ground black
 pepper*
*½ teaspoon salt*

3 tablespoons grated Parmesan cheese
8 large egg whites

**1** Preheat oven to 375°F.
**2** In nonstick 10-inch skillet, heat olive oil over medium-high heat until hot. Add red pepper, onion, mushrooms, oregano, black pepper, and salt and cook until vegetables are tender and browned. Remove skillet from heat; stir in Parmesan cheese.
**3** Meanwhile, in large bowl, with mixer at high speed, beat egg whites until stiff peaks form.
**4** Gently fold half of beaten egg whites into vegetable mixture in skillet. Then, fold mixture into remaining beaten egg whites in bowl. Do not overmix. Spoon mixture into two 2-cup shallow baking dishes or ramekins.
**5** Bake frittatas 15 minutes or until cooked through and golden brown on top. Serve immediately. Makes 2 servings.

EACH SERVING: ABOUT 218 CALORIES, 20 G PROTEIN, 14 G CARBOHYDRATE, 9 G TOTAL FAT (2 G SATURATED), 6 MG CHOLESTEROL, 945 MG SODIUM.

## Creamy Mushroom Omelet

PREP: 5 MINUTES • COOK: 20 MINUTES

1 tablespoon plus 4 teaspoons
 margarine or butter
1 medium onion, minced
8 ounces mushrooms, thinly sliced
½ teaspoon salt
⅛ teaspoon coarsely ground black
 pepper
¼ cup heavy or whipping cream
2 tablespoons chopped fresh parsley
 leaves
8 large eggs

**1** In nonstick 10-inch skillet, heat 1 tablespoon margarine or butter over medium-high heat. Add onion and cook 5 minutes. Stir in mushrooms, ¼ teaspoon salt, and pepper and cook until liquid evaporates.
**2** Stir in heavy cream; boil 3 minutes. Stir in parsley.
**3** In bowl, beat eggs with ¼ cup water and remaining ¼ teaspoon salt.
**4** In nonstick 8-inch skillet, melt 1 tea-

spoon margarine or butter over medium-high heat. Pour ¼ cup of egg mixture into skillet; cook until set (about 1 minute), gently lifting edge. Spoon one-fourth of mushroom mixture on half of omelet, fold over other half, and slide onto plate.
**5** Repeat for 3 more omelets. Makes 4 servings.

EACH SERVING: ABOUT 290 CALORIES, 15 G PROTEIN, 8 G CARBOHYDRATE, 23 G TOTAL FAT (8 G SATURATED), 445 MG CHOLESTEROL, 505 MG SODIUM.

## Garden Vegetable Omelet

PREP: 5 MINUTES • COOK: 15 MINUTES

1 tablespoon olive oil
1 small onion, chopped
1 small zucchini (6 ounces), chopped
1 small yellow pepper, chopped
½ teaspoon salt
⅛ teaspoon coarsely ground black
 pepper
2 plum tomatoes, chopped
¼ cup chopped fresh basil leaves
8 large eggs
4 teaspoons margarine or butter

**1** In nonstick 10-inch skillet, heat olive oil over medium-high heat until hot. Add onion, zucchini, yellow pepper, ¼ teaspoon salt, and black pepper and cook until tender.
**2** Add tomatoes and basil and heat through.
**3** In bowl, beat eggs with ¼ cup water and remaining ¼ teaspoon salt.
**4** In nonstick 8-inch skillet, melt 1 teaspoon margarine or butter over medium-high heat. Pour ¼ cup of egg mixture into skillet; cook until set (about 1 minute), gently lifting edge to allow uncooked portion to run under omelet. Spoon one-fourth of vegetable mixture on half of omelet, fold over other half, and slide onto plate.
**5** Repeat for 3 more omelets. Makes 4 servings.

EACH SERVING: ABOUT 240 CALORIES, 14 G PROTEIN, 7 G CARBOHYDRATE, 17 G TOTAL FAT (4 G SATURATED), 425 MG CHOLESTEROL, 465 MG SODIUM.

## Smoked Turkey Frittata

PREP: 15 MINUTES • BAKE: 25 MINUTES

1 tablespoon olive oil
8 ounces mushrooms, sliced
1 medium onion, diced
6 large eggs
4 ounces Jarlsberg or Swiss cheese,
 coarsely shredded (1 cup)
4 ounces sliced smoked turkey, slivered
1 cup milk
⅓ cup buttermilk baking mix
¼ cup hot pepper rings, chopped
¼ teaspoon salt
1 small tomato, diced

**1** In nonstick 10-inch skillet, heat olive oil over medium-high heat until hot. Add mushrooms and onion and cook until mushrooms are lightly browned, all liquid has evaporated, and onion is tender.
**2** Preheat oven to 375°F. Grease 10-inch quiche dish or 9" by 9" glass baking dish. In bowl, beat eggs, Jarlsberg or Swiss cheese, smoked turkey, milk, buttermilk baking mix, hot pepper rings, salt, and mushroom mixture until well mixed; pour into quiche dish.
**3** Bake frittata 20 to 25 minutes or until egg mixture is set. Top with diced tomato. Makes 6 servings.

EACH SERVING: ABOUT 265 CALORIES, 18 G PROTEIN, 13 G CARBOHYDRATE, 16 G TOTAL FAT (3 G SATURATED), 240 MG CHOLESTEROL, 550 MG SODIUM.

*Garden Vegetable Omelet*

# Casseroles
# & Oven Dinners

# Caesar-Salad-Style Stuffed Artichokes

PREP: 1 HOUR ～ BAKE: 15 TO 20 MINUTES

A simple bread stuffing is seasoned, like the salad, with garlic, anchovies, and Parmesan cheese.

4 large artichokes
4 slices white bread, torn into ¼-inch pieces
2 tablespoons olive oil
1 large garlic clove, finely chopped
4 anchovy fillets, chopped
½ cup pine nuts (pignoli) or chopped walnuts, lightly toasted
⅓ cup grated Parmesan cheese
2 tablespoons chopped fresh parsley leaves
1 tablespoon fresh lemon juice
¼ teaspoon salt
¾ cup chicken broth, canned or homemade (page 24)

**1** Prepare and cook artichokes (see "Artichoke Know-How," page 68).

**2** Meanwhile, preheat oven to 400°F. Spread bread in jelly-roll pan and bake about 5 minutes or until golden.

**3** In 1-quart saucepan, heat olive oil over medium heat. Add garlic; cook 1 minute. Add anchovies; cook until garlic is golden and anchovies almost dissolve, stirring constantly.

**4** Dice artichoke stems. In medium bowl, mix stems, bread, pine nuts, Parmesan, parsley, lemon juice, salt, garlic mixture, and ¼ cup chicken broth.

**5** Pour remaining ½ cup chicken broth into shallow baking dish large enough to hold artichokes (about 13" by 9"); arrange artichokes in dish. Spoon bread mixture between artichoke leaves and into center cavities. Bake 15 to 20 minutes or until stuffing is golden and artichokes are heated through. *Makes 4 servings.*

Each serving: About 310 calories, 15 g protein, 29 g carbohydrate, 18 g total fat (4 g saturated), 12 mg cholesterol, 805 mg sodium.

# Baked Rigatoni with Smoked Ham & Fontina

PREP: 30 MINUTES ～ BAKE: 30 MINUTES

In Italian, *rigate* means ridged, and many pastas come in plain and rigate forms (for example, there is plain ziti—sometimes called *lisce*, or "smooth"—and ziti rigate). When the ending -*oni* is appended to a pasta name, it means the pasta is large. So rigatoni are large, ridged pastas.

1 pound rigatoni or ziti rigate pasta
Salt
2 tablespoons vegetable oil
1 small onion, chopped
⅓ cup all-purpose flour
1 quart low-fat (1%) milk
⅛ teaspoon ground white pepper
6 ounces Fontina cheese, shredded (1½ cups)
1 package (10 ounces) frozen peas
6 ounces smoked ham, diced

**1** Preheat oven to 350°F. In large saucepot, prepare pasta in *boiling salted water* as label directs. Drain pasta; return to saucepot.

**2** Meanwhile, in 2-quart saucepan, heat vegetable oil over medium heat until hot. Add onion and cook until tender but not browned. Stir in flour; cook 1 minute. With wire whisk or fork, gradually stir in milk, ¼ teaspoon salt, and white pepper until smooth; heat to boiling over high heat, stirring constantly. Remove saucepan from heat; stir in half of Fontina.

**3** Stir cheese sauce, frozen peas, and diced ham into pasta. Spoon pasta mixture into shallow 3-quart casserole or 13" by 9" glass baking dish. Top with remaining Fontina

**4** Bake pasta 25 to 30 minutes or until mixture is hot and bubbly and cheese melts and browns slightly. *Makes 6 servings.*

Each serving: About 590 calories, 30 g protein, 76 g carbohydrate, 18 g total fat (8 g saturated), 51 mg cholesterol, 1105 mg sodium.

*Baked Rigatoni with Smoked Ham & Fontina* ➤

# Couscous-Stuffed Artichokes

PREP: 1 HOUR ～ BAKE: 15 TO 20 MINUTES

4 large artichokes
2 tablespoons olive oil
2 medium carrots, peeled and diced
2 garlic cloves, minced
¼ cup chopped fresh mint leaves
3 tablespoons chopped fresh parsley leaves
1 cup couscous (Moroccan pasta)
1½ cups chicken broth, canned or homemade
   (page 24)
½ teaspoon salt
¼ teaspoon coarsely ground black pepper
1 lemon, cut into wedges

**1** Prepare and cook artichokes (see below).

**2** Meanwhile, preheat oven to 400°F. In nonstick 10-inch skillet, heat 1 tablespoon olive oil over medium heat. Add carrots and cook until tender, about 10 minutes. Stir in garlic; cook 1 minute longer. Transfer to medium bowl. Dice artichoke stems; add to carrot mixture with mint and parsley.

**3** Prepare couscous as label directs, but use 1 cup chicken broth in place of water. When couscous is done, stir in salt, pepper, carrot mixture, and remaining 1 tablespoon olive oil.

**4** Pour remaining ½ cup broth into shallow baking dish large enough to hold artichokes (about 13" by 9"); arrange artichokes in dish. Spoon couscous mixture between artichoke leaves and into center cavities. Bake 15 to 20 minutes or until artichokes are heated through. Serve with lemon wedges. *Makes 4 servings.*

Each serving: About 345 calories, 13 g protein, 61 g carbohydrate, 8 g total fat (1 g saturated), 0 mg cholesterol, 855 mg sodium.

## ARTICHOKE KNOW-HOW

Look for artichokes that are compact, firm, and heavy for their size. They're at their peak in April and May. In spring and summer, choose those with an even green color. In fall and winter, it's okay to buy artichokes with touches of light brown or bronze on the outer leaves, caused by frost (which doesn't affect the flavor). Artichokes range in size from baby (2 to 3 ounces) to jumbo (15 to 20 ounces), but size is not a sign of maturity; they're all fully grown when picked. Cooked or raw, they keep for a week in the refrigerator.

**TO PREPARE ARTICHOKES FOR COOKING** With sharp knife, cut 1 inch straight across the top (photo 1). Cut off the stem so the artichoke can stand upright. Peel stem. Pull outer dark green leaves from artichoke bottom. With kitchen shears, trim thorny tips of leaves (photo 2). Spread artichoke open and carefully cut around choke with small knife, then scrape out center petals and fuzzy center portion with a teaspoon (photo 3) and discard. Rinse artichoke well. (You can remove the choke *after* cooking, but you have to wait till the artichoke cools a bit.)

**TO COOK** In 5-quart saucepot, heat *1 tablespoon lemon juice* and *1 inch water* to boiling over high heat. Place artichoke on stem end in boiling water, along with stem; heat to boiling. Reduce heat to low; cover and simmer 30 to 40 minutes or until knife inserted in center goes through bottom easily. Drain.

# Chicken-Enchilada Casserole

This is a great recipe for leftover turkey, as well as chicken. Try this with turkey drumstick meat, which tends to be moister and more flavorful than white-meat turkey.

I can (15¼ to 19 ounces) red kidney beans, rinsed and drained
I small bunch spinach (about 8 ounces), finely chopped
1½ cups shredded Monterey Jack cheese, (6 ounces)
I large tomato, seeded and chopped
I pound cooked chicken breast, torn into shreds
I tablespoon olive oil
I tablespoon all-purpose flour
1¼ cups milk
½ teaspoon salt
¼ teaspoon ground red pepper (cayenne)
¼ teaspoon ground cumin
6 (9-inch diameter) flour tortillas

1 In small bowl, reserve ¼ cup kidney beans, ¼ cup chopped spinach, ½ cup Monterey Jack, and ¼ cup chopped tomato; set aside.

2 In medium bowl, mash remaining kidney beans slightly. Stir in chicken, half of remaining spinach, ½ cup Monterey Jack, and remaining tomato.

3 Preheat oven to 400°F. In 2-quart saucepan, heat olive oil over medium heat until hot. Stir in flour and cook 1 minute, stirring constantly. Stir in milk, salt, ground red pepper, and cumin; cook, stirring, until sauce boils and thickens slightly. Stir in the remaining ½ cup Monterey Jack and spinach.

4 Onto center of each tortilla, spoon about ¾ cup chicken mixture; fold sides of tortilla over to enclose filling. Arrange enchiladas, seam-side down, in 13" by 9" glass baking dish.

5 Pour sauce over enchiladas in baking dish; sprinkle with reserved kidney beans, spinach, cheese, and tomato. Bake enchiladas, uncovered, 15 minutes or until cheese is melted and enchiladas are heated. *Makes 6 servings.*

Each serving: About 505 calories, 42 g protein, 41 g carbohydrate, 19 g total fat (8 g saturated), 101 mg cholesterol, 775 mg sodium.

# Louisiana Shrimp Casserole

8 ounces hot Italian-sausage links
2 medium celery stalks, cut into ½-inch pieces
I large red pepper, cut into ½-inch pieces
I large green pepper, cut into ½-inch pieces
I medium onion, diced
I package (16 ounces) regular long-grain rice
I can (14½ ounces) chicken broth
I can (14½ to 16 ounces) stewed tomatoes
I bay leaf
½ teaspoon hot pepper sauce
¼ teaspoon dried thyme leaves
I pound monkfish or scrod fillets, cut into 1½-inch pieces
12 ounces large shrimp, shelled and deveined
12 ounces sea scallops
2 tablespoons chopped fresh parsley leaves

1 In 8-quart Dutch oven, cook hot Italian sausage links over medium-high heat until browned on all sides; drain sausages on paper towels. When sausages are cool enough to handle, cut into ½-inch-thick diagonal slices.

2 In drippings in Dutch oven, cook celery, peppers, and onion over medium-high heat, stirring occasionally, until tender and golden.

3 Preheat oven to 350°F. Stir rice into vegetable mixture. Cook, stirring, until rice is opaque. Add chicken broth, *1¾ cups water*, stewed tomatoes, bay leaf, hot pepper sauce, thyme, and cooked sausages; heat to boiling over high heat. Cover Dutch oven and bake 25 minutes.

4 Stir seafood into rice mixture. Cover and bake 20 to 25 minutes longer, stirring occasionally, until rice is tender and seafood is opaque throughout. Stir in parsley. Discard bay leaf to serve. *Makes 8 servings.*

Each serving: About 460 calories, 31 g protein, 55 g carbohydrate, 11 g total fat (4 g saturated), 102 mg cholesterol, 720 mg sodium.

# Eggplant & Potato Moussaka

2 small eggplants (about 1¼ pounds each), cut
   crosswise into ½-inch-thick slices
1½ teaspoons salt
4 tablespoons olive oil
1 large onion, chopped
1 can (28 ounces) tomatoes in juice
1 teaspoon sugar
¼ teaspoon dried oregano leaves
6 medium potatoes (about 2 pounds), peeled and
   cut into ¾-inch-thick slices
2 tablespoons tomato paste
⅓ cup grated Parmesan cheese
¼ cup all-purpose flour
3 cups low-fat (1%) milk
⅛ teaspoon ground nutmeg
1 large egg

1 Preheat broiler if manufacturer directs. In large
bowl, toss eggplant slices with 4 teaspoons olive oil
and ½ teaspoon salt. Arrange eggplant slices in single
layer on rack in broiling pan. With oven rack at closest
position to source of heat, broil eggplant 15 minutes
or until tender and browned, turning slices once
halfway through broiling. When eggplant slices are
done, turn oven control to 375°F.

2 Meanwhile, prepare potato layer: In nonstick 4-
quart saucepan, heat 2 teaspoons olive oil over medium-high heat until hot. Add onion and cook 10 minutes or until tender and golden.

3 Add tomatoes with their juice, sugar, oregano, and
½ teaspoon salt to onion, stirring with spoon to break
up tomatoes. Add potato slices; heat to boiling over
high heat. Reduce heat to low; cover and simmer 20 to
25 minutes or until potatoes are tender.

4 With slotted spoon, transfer potatoes to large bowl.
Stir tomato paste into liquid remaining in saucepan;
heat to boiling over high heat. Reduce heat to low;
simmer, uncovered, 5 minutes or until liquid thickens
slightly. Add tomato mixture and ¼ cup Parmesan to
potatoes; toss.

5 In 2-quart saucepan, heat remaining 2 tablespoons
olive oil over medium heat until hot. Stir in flour and
cook until bubbly but not browned; stir in milk, nutmeg, and remaining ½ teaspoon salt. Cook over medium heat until sauce boils and thickens, stirring fre-

quently; boil 1 minute. Remove saucepan from heat.
In small bowl, beat egg. Stir small amount of hot
sauce into beaten egg; stir egg mixture back into sauce
in saucepan.

6 In 13" by 9" glass or ceramic baking dish, arrange
half of eggplant slices. Top with potato mixture, then
remaining eggplant slices. Pour sauce evenly over top;
sprinkle with remaining Parmesan.

7 Bake moussaka 30 minutes or until hot and Parmesan on top is lightly browned. *Makes 8 servings.*

Each serving: About 280 calories, 10 g protein, 40 g carbohydrate,
10 g total fat (2 g saturated), 33 mg cholesterol, 685 mg sodium.

# "Fish & Chips"

A baked dish that respects the spirit of fish & chips
but eliminates the hassle (and fat) of deep-frying.

4 large red potatoes (about 1½ pounds), thinly
   sliced
1 fennel bulb (about 1¼ pounds), trimmed and
   thinly sliced
1 garlic clove, minced
2 tablespoons olive oil
¾ teaspoon plus ⅛ teaspoon salt
½ teaspoon coarsely ground black pepper
1¼ pounds scrod, cut into 4 pieces
1 medium tomato, seeded and diced
Feathery fennel tops for garnish

1 Preheat oven to 425°F. In shallow 2½-quart casserole, toss potatoes, fennel, garlic, olive oil, ¾ teaspoon
salt, and ¼ teaspoon pepper. Bake, uncovered, 45 minutes or until vegetables are fork-tender and lightly
browned, stirring once.

2 Sprinkle scrod with remaining ¼ teaspoon pepper
and remaining ⅛ teaspoon salt. Arrange scrod on top
of potato mixture; bake 10 to 15 minutes longer or
until scrod flakes easily when tested with a fork. Sprinkle with diced tomato; garnish with fennel tops.
*Makes 4 servings.*

Each serving: About 320 calories, 30 g protein, 33 g carbohydrate,
8 g total fat (1 g saturated), 61 mg cholesterol, 580 mg sodium.

*"Fish & Chips"* ➤

# Turkey & Polenta Casserole

**PREP: 45 MINUTES ⌒ BAKE: 20 MINUTES**

2 tablespoons olive oil

2 medium zucchini (about 8 ounces each), diced

1½ pounds ground turkey

1 large onion, chopped

1¼ teaspoons salt

1 can (14½ ounces) stewed tomatoes

1 can (8 ounces) tomato sauce

½ cup (about 1 ounce) sun-dried tomatoes (not oil-packed), chopped

2½ cups low-fat (1%) milk

2 cups yellow cornmeal

2 cups shredded part-skim mozzarella cheese (8 ounces)

**1** In nonstick 12-inch skillet, heat 1 tablespoon olive oil over medium-high heat until hot. Add zucchini until lightly browned and tender; transfer to bowl.

**2** In same skillet, heat remaining 1 tablespoon olive oil; cook ground turkey, onion, and ½ teaspoon salt until turkey is browned and onion is tender.

**3** Stir stewed tomatoes, tomato sauce, sun-dried tomatoes, and *½ cup water* into turkey mixture; heat to boiling over high heat. Reduce heat to low; cover and simmer 5 minutes to blend flavors, stirring occasionally. Remove skillet from heat; stir in sautéed zucchini.

**4** Preheat oven to 450°F. In 3-quart saucepan, heat milk, remaining ¾ teaspoon salt, and *3½ cups water* to boiling over high heat. With wire whisk or fork, gradually stir in cornmeal, stirring constantly to prevent lumping. Reduce heat to low; simmer 10 minutes, stirring constantly, until polenta is very thick.

---

## A MAKEOVER FOR AN AMERICAN FAVORITE

They'll never know we sneaked out 10 grams of fat per serving because this macaroni and cheese is as good as—even better than—the old favorite.

### Reduced-Fat Macaroni & Cheese

**PREP: 15 MINUTES ⌒ BAKE: 20 MINUTES**

*8 ounces elbow macaroni twists*

*Nonstick cooking spray*

*1 container (16 ounces) low-fat (1%) cottage cheese*

*2 tablespoons all-purpose flour*

*2 cups skim milk*

*1 cup shredded sharp Cheddar cheese (4 ounces)*

*1 teaspoon salt*

*¼ teaspoon coarsely ground black pepper*

*¼ teaspoon ground nutmeg*

*¼ cup grated Parmesan cheese*

**1** In large saucepot, prepare pasta in *boiling water* as label directs, but do not add salt to water; drain.

**2** Preheat oven to 375°F. Spray shallow, broiler-safe, 2½-quart casserole with nonstick cooking spray.

**3** In food processor, with knife blade attached, blend cottage cheese until smooth. (Or, in blender, at high speed, blend cottage cheese with ¼ cup of the milk called for in step 4, for easier blending.)

**4** In 2-quart saucepan, mix flour with ¼ cup milk until smooth. Slowly stir in remaining 1¾ cups milk until blended. Cook over medium heat until mixture just boils and thickens slightly, stirring frequently. Remove saucepan from heat; stir in cottage cheese, Cheddar, salt, pepper, and nutmeg.

**5** Place elbow macaroni in casserole; cover with cheese sauce. Bake, uncovered, 20 minutes. Remove casserole from oven. Turn oven control to broil. Sprinkle Parmesan on top of macaroni mixture.

**6** Place casserole in broiler at closest position to source of heat; broil 2 to 3 minutes or until top is golden brown. Makes 6 servings.

Each serving: About 320 calories, 23 g protein, 37 g carbohydrate, 8 g total fat (5 g saturated), 26 mg cholesterol, 690 mg sodium.

**5** Grease 13" by 9" glass baking dish. Spread half of polenta in baking dish; top with half of turkey mixture, then half of mozzarella. Repeat layering. Bake casserole 20 minutes or until cheese on top is lightly browned. *Makes 8 servings.*

Each serving: About 435 calories, 30 g protein, 43 g carbohydrate, 16 g total fat (6 g saturated), 82 mg cholesterol, 920 mg sodium.

# Roasted Chicken & Vegetables

PREP: 10 MINUTES ∽ BAKE: 1 HOUR

1 pound small Yukon Gold potatoes, halved
2 large carrots, peeled and cut into 3-inch pieces
1 jumbo onion (1 pound), cut into **8** wedges
12 garlic cloves, unpeeled
2 tablespoons olive oil
¾ teaspoon salt
½ teaspoon coarsely ground black pepper
8 medium chicken thighs with bones (about 2 pounds), skin removed
1 medium red pepper, cut into 6 wedges
1 medium yellow pepper, cut into 6 wedges
¾ teaspoon dried tarragon leaves

**1** Preheat oven to 425°F. In 15½" by 10½" roasting pan or 15" by 10" glass baking dish, toss potatoes, carrots, onion, and garlic with olive oil, ½ teaspoon salt, and ¼ teaspoon black pepper. Cover and roast vegetables 20 minutes.

**2** Remove pan from oven; uncover. Add chicken thighs and red and yellow pepper wedges; toss with tarragon, remaining ¼ teaspoon salt, and remaining ¼ teaspoon black pepper. Roast, uncovered, 25 minutes; stir vegetables and chicken to brown evenly.

**3** Roast 25 minutes longer or until vegetables are golden and juices run clear when chicken is pierced with tip of knife. Add *½ cup hot water*, stirring to loosen brown bits from bottom of casserole. Spoon sauce over chicken and vegetables to serve. *Makes 4 servings.*

Each serving: About 405 calories, 33 g protein, 41 g carbohydrate, 13 g total fat (2 g saturated), 114 mg cholesterol, 540 mg sodium.

# Chicken Marianne

PREP: 15 MINUTES ∽ BAKE: 45 TO 50 MINUTES

8 medium chicken thighs with bones (about 2 pounds), skin removed
½ teaspoon coarsely ground black pepper
½ teaspoon dried oregano leaves
¾ teaspoon salt
1 medium onion, thinly sliced
3 small plum tomatoes, cut crosswise into ¼-inch-thick slices
3 strips (3" by 1" each) lemon peel
2 tablespoons margarine or butter
1¼ pounds carrots, peeled and cut into 2-inch pieces
1¼ pounds parsnips, peeled and cut into 2-inch pieces

**1** Preheat oven to 400°F. Place chicken thighs in 13" by 9" metal baking pan. Sprinkle chicken with pepper, oregano, and ½ teaspoon salt. Arrange onion, tomatoes, and lemon peel in pan with chicken.

**2** Place margarine in 15½" by 10½" jelly-roll pan. Place pan in oven just long enough to melt margarine. Toss carrots, parsnips, and remaining ¼ teaspoon salt with melted margarine in jelly-roll pan.

**3** Place chicken and vegetables on 2 oven racks. Bake 45 to 50 minutes, switching pans halfway through cooking time. Baste chicken occasionally with pan juices and turn vegetables twice, with pancake turner, until juices run clear when chicken is pierced with tip of knife and vegetables are fork-tender and nicely browned.

**4** Arrange chicken and vegetables on large platter. Spoon tomato mixture from pan over chicken. *Makes 4 servings.*

Each serving: About 380 calories, 29 g protein, 40 g carbohydrate, 12 g total fat (2 g saturated), 107 mg cholesterol, 675 mg sodium.

# Roasted Chicken, Fennel & Potatoes

PREP: 20 MINUTES ～ BAKE: 50 MINUTES

A tempting one-dish meal—with fennel, potatoes, and onion—that's ready in just over an hour.

I whole chicken (3 pounds), cut up and skin
   removed
I pound all-purpose potatoes, cut into 2-inch
   chunks
I fennel bulb (about 1½ pounds), trimmed and cut
   into 8 wedges
I large red onion, cut into 8 wedges
2 tablespoons olive oil
I tablespoon chopped fresh thyme or I teaspoon
   dried thyme leaves
1¼ teaspoons salt
½ teaspoon coarsely ground black pepper
Thyme sprigs for garnish

1 Preheat oven to 450° F. In 17" by 11½" roasting pan, toss chicken, potatoes, fennel, and onion with olive oil; sprinkle with thyme, salt, and pepper.

2 Roast 20 minutes; baste chicken and vegetables with any drippings in roasting pan. Roast 20 minutes longer, basting once, until juices run clear when chicken breasts are pierced with tip of knife. Transfer chicken breasts to platter; cover and keep warm.

3 Continue roasting 10 minutes longer or until juices run clear when remaining chicken pieces are pierced with tip of knife and vegetables are tender. Transfer chicken and vegetables to platter with breasts.

4 To drippings, add ⅓ *cup hot water*, stirring to loosen brown bits from bottom of pan. Spoon drippings over chicken and vegetables. Garnish with thyme sprigs. *Makes 4 servings.*

Each serving: About 395 calories, 40 g protein, 33 g carbohydrate, 12 g total fat (2 g saturated), 114 mg cholesterol, 875 mg sodium.

# Summer Chicken Dinner

PREP: 10 MINUTES ～ BAKE: 45 MINUTES

To add a touch of color, use one yellow summer squash and one zucchini in place of the two zucchini called for.

4 medium chicken-breast halves with bones (about
   2½ pounds)
½ teaspoon dried oregano leaves
¾ teaspoon salt
4 medium ears of corn, shucked and cut crosswise
   into 3 pieces
2 large zucchini (about 10 ounces each), cut into
   3-inch chunks
4 large plum tomatoes, halved lengthwise
3 tablespoons fresh lemon juice
I tablespoon extravirgin olive oil
2 tablespoons chopped fresh basil or I teaspoon
   dried basil leaves
½ teaspoon sugar
¼ teaspoon crushed red pepper

1 Preheat oven to 400°F. Place chicken breasts in 17" by 11½" roasting pan; sprinkle with oregano and ½ teaspoon salt. Arrange corn and zucchini around chicken. Bake chicken and vegetables 30 minutes.

2 Add tomatoes to chicken and vegetables and bake 15 minutes longer or until juices run clear when chicken is pierced with tip of knife.

3 Meanwhile, in cup, mix lemon juice, olive oil, chopped basil, sugar, crushed red pepper, and remaining ¼ teaspoon salt.

4 Arrange chicken and vegetables on large platter. Drizzle chicken and vegetables with lemon mixture. (Remove skin from chicken before eating if you like.) *Makes 4 servings.*

Each serving: About 535 calories, 52 g protein, 25 g carbohydrate, 26 g total fat (7 g saturated), 145 mg cholesterol, 600 mg sodium.

◄ *Roasted Chicken, Fennel & Potatoes*

# Chicken with Roasted Garlic & Vegetables

PREP: 40 MINUTES ～ BAKE: I HOUR

1 large whole head garlic, separated into cloves
1 whole chicken (about 3½ pounds), cut up
4 medium red potatoes, halved
3 medium zucchini (about 8 ounces each), halved crosswise
2 medium yellow peppers, cut lengthwise into thirds
1 medium red pepper, cut lengthwise into thirds
6 jumbo mushrooms, halved
2 tablespoons olive oil
1 tablespoon chopped fresh rosemary or 1½ teaspoons dried rosemary leaves, crushed
1 teaspoon salt
½ teaspoon coarsely ground black pepper
1 large artichoke

1 Preheat oven to 425°F. In 17" by 11½" roasting pan, place garlic cloves and chicken pieces, skin-side up. Bake, uncovered, 15 minutes.

2 Meanwhile, in bowl, combine potatoes, zucchini, yellow and red peppers, mushrooms, oil, rosemary, salt, and black pepper; toss.

3 After chicken has baked 15 minutes, arrange vegetables around chicken pieces. Bake 40 minutes, basting with drippings often.

4 Meanwhile, prepare artichoke: With sharp knife, cut 1 inch straight across the top. Cut off the stem and discard. Pull outer dark green leaves from artichoke bottom. With kitchen shears, trim thorny tips of leaves. Pull off any loose leaves from around the bottom. Cut artichoke into 6 wedges; cut out fuzzy choke from center of wedges. In 2-quart saucepan, heat artichoke wedges in *1 inch boiling water* to boiling over high heat. Reduce heat to low; cover and simmer 15 minutes or until a leaf can be pulled off easily. Drain.

5 After chicken and vegetable mixture has baked 40 minutes, add artichoke wedges to roasting pan, basting artichoke with pan drippings and bake 5 minutes longer or until vegetables are tender and brown and juice runs clear when chicken is pierced with tip of knife.

6 To serve, arrange vegetables and chicken on large platter. Skim fat from drippings. Into juice remaining in roasting pan, stir *½ cup water;* heat to boiling over medium heat. With spoon, stir to loosen any brown bits from bottom of pan. Pour juice over chicken and vegetables on platter. Let each person cut through skin of each garlic clove and spread some soft, sweet-tasting garlic on chicken and vegetables. *Makes 6 servings.*

Each serving: About 555 calories, 38 g protein, 35 g carbohydrate, 30 g total fat (8 g saturated), 110 mg cholesterol, 525 mg sodium.

# Chicken & Leek Casserole

PREP: 40 MINUTES ～ BAKE: I¼ HOURS

1 tablespoon vegetable oil
6 large chicken legs (about 4½ pounds), skin removed
1 tablespoon all-purpose flour
6 medium leeks (about 2½ pounds), rinsed and cut crosswise into 2-inch pieces
1½ pounds medium red potatoes, quartered
1 pound carrots, peeled and cut into 2½" by ½" pieces
1 can (14½ ounces) chicken broth or 1¾ cups homemade (page 24)
¾ teaspoon salt

1 Preheat oven to 375°F. In 8-quart Dutch oven, heat vegetable oil over medium-high heat until hot. Add 3 chicken legs and cook until golden on all sides; transfer to plate. In drippings, brown remaining chicken legs.

2 In cup, stir flour and *½ cup water*. Return chicken to Dutch oven; stir in leeks, potatoes, carrots, chicken broth, salt, and flour mixture. Heat to boiling over high heat. Cover Dutch oven and bake 1¼ hours or until juices run clear when chicken is pierced with tip of knife.

3 Into 2-cup measuring cup, spoon 1½ cups vegetables and ¼ cup liquid from Dutch oven. In covered blender (with center part of blender cover removed), at low speed, blend vegetables and liquid until very smooth. Stir pureed vegetables into Dutch oven. *Makes 6 servings.*

Each serving: About 440 calories, 44 g protein, 41 g carbohydrate, 11 g total fat (2 g saturated), 156 mg cholesterol, 810 mg sodium.

## HOW TO CHOOSE A CASSEROLE

| Material | Advantages | Disadvantages | Comments |
|---|---|---|---|
| Uncoated Cast Iron | Inexpensive; very durable; conduct and retain heat exceptionally well; good for stove-top browning; can be a source of dietary iron | Extremely heavy; can affect color and taste of foods; needs special seasoning and cleaning (see "Cast-Iron Care," page 58) | Look for a one-piece pan with handles formed from the iron itself; with proper care, a cast-iron casserole or Dutch oven can last for generations |
| Enameled Cast Iron | Good heat conductors; won't interact with food | Extremely heavy; requires careful handling to avoid chipping of enamel; will rust if it gets chipped; does not brown food well | Choose a pot with steel handles; if the handles are of another material, it should be ovenproof to 425°F |
| Stainless Steel | Durable; easy to clean; pots with an aluminum or copper core or bottom will conduct heat well and be good for browning | All-steel pans do not conduct heat well | Pots for oven use must be of heavy-gauge steel; also, see comment on handles, above |
| Porcelain Enamel on Steel | Come in bright colors; won't react with food; easy to clean; heavyweight pans conduct heat well | Not good for browning; lightweight pans do not conduct heat well and are not suitable for oven use | These attractive pots are particularly suitable for oven-to-table use |
| Aluminum | Lightweight; heat quickly and evenly | Pit and stain from contact with salt or acidic foods; may discolor some foods (cream sauce may turn gray) | Only heavy cast aluminum or aluminum alloy is suitable for oven use |
| Anodized Aluminum | Resistant to sticking, stains, and dents; unlike regular aluminum, won't discolor foods; lighter than cast iron | Expensive | Good choice for serious cooks—top performance, a professional look (dark gray) |
| Pottery (Stoneware, Earthenware) | Attractive for oven-to-table use; retains heat well; if glazed, easy to clean | Not for stove-top use, so food cannot be browned before baking; fragile; unglazed ware is hard to clean | Buy pottery from a reliable source; cheap tourist wares may have a dangerous lead content (see "Lead Check," page 90) |
| Ovenproof Glass | Retains heat very well; won't react with food; can go from freezer to oven to table | Not for stove-top use, so food cannot be browned before baking; relatively fragile | Come in clear and opaque versions; reduce oven temperature by 25° when baking in glass |

# Indian Chicken & Rice Casserole

PREP: 30 MINUTES  BAKE: 35 MINUTES

This elaborate feast dish is usually made with lamb; our lighter recipe calls for skinless, boneless chicken breast.

1 can (14½ ounces) chicken broth or 1¾ cups homemade (page 24)
1 cup basmati rice
3 garlic cloves, peeled
1 piece (1" by ½") fresh ginger, peeled and coarsely chopped
¼ cup sweetened flaked coconut
1 large onion, cut lengthwise in half and thinly sliced
3 teaspoons vegetable oil
1 small red pepper, cut into ½-inch pieces
1 pound skinless, boneless chicken-breast halves, cut into ½-inch pieces
¾ teaspoon ground cumin
¾ teaspoon ground coriander
½ teaspoon salt
⅛ teaspoon ground red pepper (cayenne)

2 cups cauliflower flowerets (about ½ medium head), cut into ½-inch pieces
1 package (10 ounces) frozen peas and carrots
1 can (14½ ounces) diced tomatoes
1 container (8 ounces) plain nonfat yogurt
Raisins, toasted sliced almonds, and toasted sweetened flaked coconut for garnish (optional)

1 Preheat oven to 350°F. In 2-cup measuring cup, add *enough water* to chicken broth to equal 2 cups liquid. In 2-quart saucepan, heat chicken-broth mixture to boiling over high heat. Place rice in shallow 2½-quart casserole; stir in boiling broth mixture. Cover casserole tightly and bake 20 minutes or until rice is tender and all liquid is absorbed. Remove casserole from oven; set aside.

2 Meanwhile, in food processor, with knife blade attached, or in blender, at medium speed, blend garlic, ginger, coconut, and half of onion slices until a paste forms; set aside.

3 In nonstick 12-inch skillet, heat 2 teaspoons vegetable oil over medium heat. Add red pepper and remaining onion slices, and cook until golden, about 10 minutes. With slotted spoon, transfer vegetables to large bowl.

4 Add garlic mixture to same skillet and cook 8 to 10 minutes or until golden. Add chicken pieces and remaining 1 teaspoon oil and cook, stirring occasionally, until chicken is lightly browned on the outside and loses its pink color on the inside. Add cumin, coriander, salt, and ground red pepper and cook 2 minutes longer. Transfer chicken mixture to bowl with vegetables.

5 To same skillet, add cauliflower and *¾ cup water*; heat to boiling over high heat. Reduce heat to low; cover and simmer 6 minutes. Add frozen peas and carrots, and tomatoes with their juice; heat to boiling over high heat. Reduce heat to low; uncover and cook 2 minutes longer or until cauliflower is tender and peas and carrots are heated through. Transfer cauliflower mixture to bowl with chicken. Stir in yogurt until well mixed.

6 With fork, fluff rice. Top cooked rice with chicken mixture. Bake, uncovered, 15 minutes longer or until heated through. Serve garnished with raisins, toasted almonds, and toasted coconut if you like. *Makes 6 servings.*

Each serving without garnishes: About 335 calories, 28 g protein, 45 g carbohydrate, 6 g total fat (2 g saturated), 45 mg cholesterol, 760 mg sodium.

## RICE IS NICE

Rice has come a long way since our grandmothers' day. In older cookbooks, a recipe merely called for rice. Now a cook needs to be on the lookout for the shape of the rice grain—long, short, or medium—as well as the variety, such as Arborio (an Italian short-grain rice used to make risotto, see page 47). One category of rice that has been an especially nice addition to the American pantry is the aromatics, which are rices with a nutlike aroma and flavor. The first of these rices to capture our attention was basmati from India (try it in our biryani-style casserole, Indian Chicken & Rice, above). But now there is a wealth of other aromatics available, from Thai jasmine rice to a whole range of domestic aromatics, such as Texmati—a basmati rice from Texas—wehani, pecan rice, and popcorn rice from Louisiana.

*Indian Chicken & Rice Casserole* ➤

# Southwest Tortilla Casserole

PREP: 20 MINUTES  ∽  BAKE: 30 TO 35 MINUTES

1 can (15¼ to 16 ounces) whole-kernel corn,
    drained
1 can (14½ ounces) stewed tomatoes
1 can (4 to 4½ ounces) chopped mild green chiles
2 tablespoons vegetable oil
3 tablespoons all-purpose flour
2½ cups milk
12 ounces cooked chicken breast, cut into ½-inch
    cubes (2½ cups)
1 can (15 to 19 ounces) black beans, rinsed and
    drained
¼ cup chopped fresh cilantro or parsley leaves
4 ounces Monterey Jack cheese with jalapeño
    chiles, shredded (1 cup)
8 (6-inch diameter) corn tortillas, each cut in half
Chopped cilantro or parsley for garnish

1 Preheat oven to 375°F. In bowl, combine corn, stewed tomatoes, and green chiles with their liquid. Spoon half of corn mixture into bottom of 13" by 9" glass baking dish.

2 Prepare white sauce: In 2-quart saucepan, heat vegetable oil over medium heat until hot. Stir in flour until blended; cook 1 minute. Gradually stir in milk; cook, stirring constantly, until mixture boils and thickens.

3 Into corn mixture in bowl, stir chicken, black beans, cilantro, ½ cup Monterey Jack, and half the white sauce.

4 Arrange half of tortillas over corn mixture in baking dish; top with chicken mixture. Arrange remaining tortillas over chicken mixture; top with remaining white sauce, then remaining Monterey Jack.

5 Bake casserole 30 to 35 minutes or until hot in the center and bubbling around the edges. Let stand 15 minutes for easier serving. Garnish with cilantro. *Makes 8 servings.*

Each serving: About 325 calories, 21 g protein, 35 g carbohydrate, 12 g total fat (5 g saturated), 50 mg cholesterol, 600 mg sodium.

# Chicken Bouillabaisse

PREP: 1 HOUR  ∽  BAKE: 30 MINUTES

Don't miss this tasty non-seafood version of the Mediterranean favorite.

1 tablespoon olive oil
8 medium chicken thighs with bones (about
    2½ pounds), skin removed
2 large carrots, peeled and diced
1 medium onion, diced
1 medium fennel bulb (1¼ pounds), sliced
3 garlic cloves, minced
1 can (14½ ounces) diced tomatoes
1 can (14½ ounces) chicken broth or
    1¾ cups homemade (page 24)
½ cup dry white wine
2 tablespoons anise-flavor liquor (optional)
½ teaspoon salt
¼ teaspoon dried thyme leaves
⅛ teaspoon ground red pepper (cayenne)
1 bay leaf
Pinch saffron threads
Thyme sprigs for garnish

1 In 5-quart Dutch oven, heat olive oil over medium-high heat. Add chicken thighs, half at a time, and cook until browned on both sides, about 12 minutes per batch; transfer to bowl.

2 In same Dutch oven, cook carrots and onion over medium heat until tender and golden, about 10 minutes, stirring occasionally; transfer to bowl with chicken thighs.

3 Preheat oven to 350°F. Add fennel and ½ *cup water* to Dutch oven, stirring to loosen brown bits. Cook, stirring occasionally, about 7 minutes or until fennel is tender and browned; add garlic and cook 3 minutes longer.

4 Return chicken and carrot mixture to Dutch oven; add tomatoes with their juice, chicken broth, white wine, anise liquor, salt, thyme, ground red pepper, bay leaf, and saffron. Heat to boiling over high heat. Cover and bake 30 minutes or until juices run clear when thickest part of chicken is pierced with tip of knife. Discard bay leaf before serving. Garnish with thyme sprigs. *Makes 4 servings.*

Each serving: About 310 calories, 32 g protein, 24 g carbohydrate, 10 g total fat (2 g saturated), 119 mg cholesterol, 935 mg sodium.

*Chicken Bouillabaisse* ➤

# Country Captain Casserole

~~~~~~~~~~~~~~~~~~~~~~~~~~~~~~~~~~~~~~

PREP: 50 MINUTES ～ BAKE: 1 HOUR

2 tablespoons plus 1 teaspoon vegetable oil
2 whole chickens (3½ pounds each), cut up and
   skin removed
2 medium onions, chopped

1 large Granny Smith apple, peeled and diced
1 large green pepper, diced
3 large garlic cloves, minced
1 tablespoon grated, peeled fresh ginger
3 tablespoons curry powder
½ teaspoon coarsely ground black pepper
¼ teaspoon ground cumin
1 can (28 ounces) tomatoes in puree
1 can (14½ ounces) chicken broth or
   1¾ cups homemade (page 24)
½ cup dark seedless raisins
1 teaspoon salt

---

## BAKED-POTATO DINNERS

Start with 4 big (around 12-ounce) baking potatoes, pierced with a fork. Bake in preheated 450°F. oven 45 minutes, or place on a paper towel and cook on High (100% power) in a microwave for 13 to 18 minutes, turning halfway through, until fork-tender. Slash top, spoon on one of these toppings, and serve with a tossed green salad. An easy supper for 4!

**Chunky Vegetable Potatoes** Cut *1 small eggplant, 1 medium zucchini,* and *1 large red pepper* into ½-inch pieces. In nonstick 12-inch skillet, cook vegetables in *1 tablespoon olive oil* over medium-high heat 15 minutes. Stir in *one 14½-ounce can stewed tomatoes, ¼ cup water, 1 tablespoon balsamic vinegar,* and *½ teaspoon salt;* heat. [Each serving: About 345 calories, 10 g protein, 71 g carbohydrate, 4 g total fat (1 g saturated), 0 mg cholesterol, 80 mg sodium.]

**Broccoli Welsh Rabbit Potatoes** Steam *6 cups broccoli flowerets* until tender, 8 minutes. In saucepan, heat *¾ cup beer, 1¾ teaspoons cornstarch, ½ teaspoon Dijon mustard,* and *⅛ teaspoon ground red pepper* to boiling over medium-high heat; boil 1 minute. Reduce heat to low; stir in *2 cups shredded Cheddar cheese* (8 ounces). Serve with broccoli. [Each serving: About 565 calories, 28 g protein, 70 g carbohydrate, 20 g total fat (12 g saturated), 60 mg cholesterol, 475 mg sodium.]

**Spinach & Feta Potatoes** In saucepan, melt *2 tablespoons margarine or butter* over medium heat; stir in *2 tablespoons flour.* Add *1⅔ cups milk;* heat to boiling. Stir in *one 10-ounce package frozen chopped spinach,* thawed, *¼ teaspoon dillweed* and *¼ teaspoon coarsely ground black pepper,* and *2 ounces crumbled feta cheese;* heat through. Top with another *2 ounces crumbled feta.* [Each serving: About 470 calories, 17 g protein, 68 g carbohydrate, 16 g total fat (7 g saturated), 40 mg cholesterol, 510 mg sodium.]

**BLT Potatoes** In 12-inch skillet, cook *4 slices bacon* over medium heat until browned. Drain on paper towels; crumble. In bowl, mix *⅔ cup reduced-fat mayonnaise, ⅓ cup milk,* and *¼ teaspoon coarsely ground black pepper.* Cut *2 medium tomatoes* and *½ small head iceberg lettuce* into ½-inch chunks; toss with bacon and dressing. [Each serving: About 430 calories, 11 g protein, 70 g carbohydrate, 13 g total fat (3 g saturated), 8 mg cholesterol, 465 mg sodium.]

**Ham & Eggs Potatoes** In nonstick 12-inch skillet, heat *2 tablespoons margarine or butter* over medium heat. Add *1 medium green pepper,* diced, and *1 medium onion,* diced; cook until tender and browned. Stir in *4 ounces cooked ham,* diced, and *6 large eggs,* beaten with *¼ cup water* and *¼ teaspoon salt* and *¼ teaspoon coarsely ground black pepper,* until eggs are cooked. [Each serving: About 485 calories, 24 g protein, 62 g carbohydrate, 16 g total fat (4 g saturated), 336 mg cholesterol, 755 mg sodium.]

**Chili Potatoes** In nonstick 12-inch skillet, cook *12 ounces lean ground beef* and *1 small onion,* chopped, over medium-high heat until meat is browned and onion is tender. Stir in *3 tablespoons chili powder;* cook 1 minute. Add *one 14½-ounce can chopped tomatoes, ¾ cup water,* and *1 teaspoon sugar;* cook 1 minute. [Each serving: About 530 calories, 25 g protein, 67 g carbohydrate, 19 g total fat (7 g saturated), 64 mg cholesterol, 310 mg sodium.]

1 In 8-quart Dutch oven, heat 2 tablespoons vegetable oil over medium-high heat until hot. Brown chicken in batches, removing pieces to bowl as they brown.

2 Preheat oven to 350°F. In same Dutch oven, heat remaining 1 teaspoon oil over medium-high heat; cook onions, apple, green pepper, garlic, and ginger 2 minutes, stirring frequently. Reduce heat to medium; cover and cook 5 minutes.

3 Stir in curry powder, black pepper, and cumin; cook 1 minute. Add tomatoes with their puree, chicken broth, raisins, salt, and chicken pieces; heat to boiling over high heat; boil 1 minute.

4 Cover Dutch oven and bake 1 hour or until juices run clear when chicken is pierced with tip of knife. *Makes 8 servings.*

Each serving: About 325 calories, 39 g protein, 21 g carbohydrate, 10 g total fat (2 g saturated), 122 mg cholesterol, 710 mg sodium.

# Chicken & Black Bean Casserole

PREP: 15 MINUTES ⮂ BAKE: 45 MINUTES

You could also prepare this with the cooked chicken that you get when you make your own chicken broth (see "Taking Stock," page 24).

1 roasted whole chicken, (about 2¼ pounds), from deli or meat department
2 tablespoons chopped fresh cilantro or parsley leaves
2 medium plum tomatoes, seeded and diced
1 can (15 to 19 ounces) black beans, rinsed and drained
1¼ cups bottled medium salsa (about 10 ounces)
6 ounces Monterey Jack cheese, shredded (1½ cups)
4 (8-inch diameter) flour tortillas

1 Discard skin and bones from chicken, pull meat into shreds.

2 Preheat oven to 400°F. Reserve 1 teaspoon chopped cilantro. In large bowl, stir together chicken, tomatoes, black beans, salsa, 1 cup Monterey Jack, and remaining cilantro until blended. Spoon mixture into shallow 2½-quart casserole.

3 Cut each tortilla into quarters. Arrange tortilla quarters, slightly overlapping, over chicken mixture. Cover with foil; bake 45 minutes or until filling is hot and bubbly.

4 Remove casserole from oven; turn oven control to broil. Remove foil from casserole and sprinkle with remaining ½ cup cheese and reserved cilantro. Broil casserole 3 minutes or until top is crisp and golden. *Makes 6 servings.*

Each serving: About 415 calories, 39 g protein, 24 g carbohydrate, 17 g total fat (7 g saturated), 112 mg cholesterol, 950 mg sodium.

# No-Fuss Country Chicken & Potato Bake

PREP: 20 MINUTES ⮂ BAKE: 1 HOUR

6 medium all-purpose potatoes (2 pounds), cut into 1½-inch chunks
1 medium onion, finely chopped
2 whole chickens (3 pounds each), cut up
1¼ teaspoons salt
2 tablespoons chopped fresh rosemary or 2 teaspoons dried rosemary leaves, crushed
½ teaspoon coarsely ground black pepper

1 Preheat oven to 425°F. In 17" by 11½" roasting pan, toss potatoes and onion with chicken, salt, rosemary, and pepper. Arrange the chicken pieces, skin-side up; bake, uncovered, 1 hour or until potatoes are tender and browned and juices run clear when chicken is pierced with tip of knife, basting with pan drippings occasionally.

2 Skim and discard any fat from pan drippings. Serve chicken and vegetables with pan juices. *Makes 8 servings.*

Each serving: About 535 calories, 44 g protein, 21 g carbohydrate, 30 g total fat (9 g saturated), 140 mg cholesterol, 495 mg sodium.

# Chicken & Winter Squash Casserole

PREP: 30 MINUTES ∼ BAKE: 1¼ HOURS

Acorn squash has a lovely deep orange color and sweet flavor. However, because of its ridged shape, it can be a bit of a chore to peel. You can either leave the peel on (though this won't appeal to everyone), or use butternut squash instead. One medium butternut squash at 1½ pounds should do it here.

2 small acorn squash (about 12 ounces each), halved, peeled, and cut into 2-inch chunks
4 garlic cloves, unpeeled
1 teaspoon vegetable oil
4 medium chicken legs (2½ pounds)
¼ cup packed light brown sugar
1 teaspoon salt
1 teaspoon dried rosemary leaves, crushed
1 can (16 ounces) sliced cling peaches in juice

1 Preheat oven to 400°F. In shallow 3-quart casserole or 13" by 9" ceramic or glass baking dish, toss squash chunks and garlic cloves with vegetable oil.

2 Cut each chicken leg at joint to separate drumstick and thigh. Arrange chicken pieces in casserole with squash and garlic cloves. Sprinkle with brown sugar, salt, and rosemary. Bake casserole, uncovered, 1 hour, basting the chicken and squash occasionally with drippings.

3 Remove casserole from oven; skim fat from drippings and spoon any pan juices over chicken and squash. Add peaches with their juice to casserole. Bake 15 minutes longer or until chicken and squash are fork-tender and peaches are heated through.

4 To serve, let each person cut through garlic skin and spread some soft, sweet-tasting garlic onto chicken and squash. *Makes 4 servings.*

Each serving: About 550 calories, 38 g protein, 41 g carbohydrate, 27 g total fat (7 g saturated), 134 mg cholesterol, 720 mg sodium.

# Baked Honey-Mustard Chicken & Vegetables

PREP: 10 MINUTES ∼ BAKE: 50 MINUTES

It all cooks in the oven at the same time. Delicious with steamed fresh green beans.

1½ pounds small red potatoes, quartered
1 jumbo onion (1 pound), cut into eighths
6 teaspoons olive oil
¾ teaspoon salt
¼ teaspoon coarsely ground black pepper
4 medium chicken-breast halves with bones (about 2½ pounds), skin removed
2 tablespoons honey mustard

1 Preheat oven to 450°F. In 13" by 9" metal baking pan, toss potatoes and onion with 4 teaspoons olive oil, salt, and pepper; bake 25 minutes on middle oven rack.

2 Meanwhile, place chicken-breast halves in small roasting pan; coat chicken with 1 teaspoon oil. In cup, mix remaining 1 teaspoon oil with honey mustard; set aside.

3 After vegetables have baked 25 minutes, remove pan from oven and carefully turn vegetables with metal spatula. Return vegetables to oven, placing pan on lower oven rack. Place chicken on upper rack.

4 After chicken has baked 10 minutes, remove from oven; brush with honey-mustard mixture. Bake chicken and vegetables 12 to 15 minutes longer or until juices run clear when thickest part of chicken is pierced with tip of knife and vegetables are golden. Serve chicken with vegetables. *Makes 4 servings.*

Each serving: About 380 calories, 31 g protein, 44 g carbohydrate, 10 g total fat (1 g saturated), 66 mg cholesterol, 630 mg sodium.

*Baked Honey-Mustard Chicken & Vegetables* ➤

# Beef Paprikash Casserole

~~~~~~~~~~~~~~~~~~~~~~~~~~~~~~~~~~~~~

PREP: 25 MINUTES ~ BAKE: 1¼ HOURS

Paprika—a mainstay seasoning in Hungarian cooking and the reason for the title of this Hungarian-style casserole—is finely ground red peppers. Although hotter, more pungent paprikas are can be found, the most commonly available paprikas are sweet and mild. This recipe calls for the sweet type.

1 tablespoon plus 2 teaspoons vegetable oil
1½ pounds beef for stew, cut into 1½-inch chunks
2 large onions, thinly sliced
12 ounces mushrooms, halved if large

2 tablespoons paprika
1 tablespoon all-purpose flour
¾ teaspoon salt
½ cup reduced-fat sour cream
1 cup brown rice
2 tablespoons chopped fresh parsley leaves

1 Preheat oven to 350°F. In 4- to 5-quart Dutch oven, heat 1 tablespoon vegetable oil over medium-high heat until hot. Add beef chunks, half at a time, until meat is well browned, transferring them to bowl as they brown.

2 In drippings in Dutch oven, heat remaining 2 teaspoons vegetable oil; cook onions and mushrooms until lightly browned. Stir in paprika; cook 1 minute.

3 In cup, mix flour and *1½ cups water*; stir into onion mixture with salt. Return meat to Dutch oven; heat to boiling over high heat. Cover Dutch oven and bake in 350°F. oven 1¼ hours or until meat is fork-tender,

---

## POTATO & ARTICHOKE RÖSTI

Just 4 ingredients—a very satisfying weeknight dish.

PREP: 15 MINUTES ~ COOK: 45 MINUTES

*2½ pounds baking potatoes (about 4 large)*
*¾ teaspoon salt*
*¼ teaspoon coarsely ground black pepper*
*2 tablespoons olive oil*
*1 cup shredded Fontina or mozzarella cheese (4 ounces)*
*1 jar (8¼ ounces) marinated artichoke hearts, rinsed, well drained, and sliced*

1 Preheat oven to 400°F. Peel and coarsely shred potatoes; pat dry with paper towels. In large bowl, toss potatoes with salt and pepper.

2 In nonstick 10-inch skillet, with oven-safe handle (or wrap handle with a double thickness of foil), heat 1 tablespoon olive oil over medium heat. Working quickly, add half the potatoes, gently patting with rubber spatula to cover bottom of skillet. Leaving a ½-inch border, top potatoes with half the Fontina, all the artichokes, then remaining cheese. Cover with remaining potatoes, gently patting to edge of skillet. Cook 10 minutes or until browned, gently shaking skillet from time to time to keep pancake from sticking.

3 Carefully invert potato pancake onto large, flat plate. Add remaining 1 tablespoon oil to skillet, then slide pancake back into skillet. Cook 10 minutes longer, gently shaking skillet from time to time.

4 Place skillet, uncovered, in oven and bake 20 to 25 minutes or until potatoes are tender throughout. Makes 4 servings.

Each serving: About 410 calories, 14 g protein, 50 g carbohydrate, 18 g total fat (6 g saturated), 33 mg cholesterol, 760 mg sodium.

stirring once halfway through baking time. When meat is done, stir in sour cream.

**4** During last 50 minutes of cooking paprikash, prepare brown rice as label directs. Toss rice with chopped fresh parsley leaves. Serve paprikash over rice. *Makes 6 servings.*

Each serving: About 525 calories, 26 g protein, 37 g carbohydrate, 31 g total fat (11 g saturated), 88 mg cholesterol, 385 mg sodium.

# Oven-Braised Short Rib Dinner

PREP: 25 MINUTES ⌢ BAKE: 2½ HOURS

The chopped parsley and grated lemon peel added at the end contribute a wonderful fresh flavor to this hearty oven braise.

1 tablespoon vegetable oil
4 pounds beef chuck short ribs
1 pound carrots, peeled and cut into 1-inch pieces
2 large onions, sliced
2 tablespoons all-purpose flour
1 can (14½ ounces) stewed tomatoes
¾ teaspoon salt
2 cans (16 to 19 ounces each) Great Northern or
    small white beans, rinsed and drained
Chopped fresh parsley leaves and grated lemon
    peel for garnish

**1** Preheat oven to 350°F. In 5-quart Dutch oven, heat vegetable oil over medium-high heat until hot. Add short ribs, half at a time, and cook until browned on all sides; transfer to bowl as they brown. In drippings in Dutch oven, cook carrots and onions until lightly browned, stirring vegetables occasionally.

**2** In cup, stir flour with *1 cup water.* Return short ribs to Dutch oven; stir in flour mixture, stewed tomatoes, and salt. Heat to boiling over high heat. Cover Dutch oven and bake 2 hours, stirring occasionally.

**3** Stir in Great Northern beans; bake 30 minutes longer or until short ribs are fork-tender. Skim fat from sauce. Garnish with chopped fresh parsley leaves and grated lemon peel if you like. *Makes 8 servings.*

Each serving: About 790 calories, 30 g protein, 27 g carbohydrate, 63 g total fat (26 g saturated), 126 mg cholesterol, 650 mg sodium.

# Spiced Beef Casserole

PREP: 30 MINUTES ⌢ BAKE: 1 HOUR 40 MINUTES

1 tablespoon ground cinnamon
¾ teaspoon salt
½ teaspoon coarsely ground black pepper
5 tablespoons all-purpose flour
2 pounds beef for stew, cut into 2-inch chunks
2 tablespoons plus 2 teaspoons vegetable oil
1 medium onion, chopped
1 large celery stalk, chopped
3¼ cups reduced-sodium beef broth
1 garlic clove, minced
½ teaspoon dried thyme leaves
3 medium carrots, peeled and cut into 2-inch
    chunks
1 large zucchini (about 10 ounces), cut into 2-inch
    chunks
1 large yellow straightneck squash (about 10
    ounces), cut into 2-inch chunks
1 cup frozen peas, thawed

**1** In large plastic bag, mix cinnamon, salt, pepper, and 2 tablespoons flour. Add beef chunks and shake to coat with flour mixture.

**2** In 5-quart Dutch oven, heat 2 tablespoons vegetable oil over medium-high heat until hot. Add beef cubes, half at a time, until meat is well browned, transferring them to bowl as they brown.

**3** Preheat oven to 350°F. In drippings in Dutch oven, heat remaining 2 teaspoons oil; cook onion and celery until tender.

**4** Return beef to Dutch oven. Add beef broth, garlic, and thyme; heat to boiling over high heat. Cover Dutch oven and bake 1 hour.

**5** Add carrots, zucchini, and yellow squash to Dutch oven; cover and bake 30 minutes longer or until meat and vegetables are fork-tender, stirring occasionally.

**6** Skim fat from liquid in Dutch oven. In cup, mix remaining 3 tablespoons flour with ¼ cup water. Stir flour mixture and peas into simmering beef mixture and bake, covered, until mixture thickens slightly. *Makes 8 servings.*

Each serving: About 345 calories, 25 g protein, 14 g carbohydrate, 21 g total fat (7 g saturated), 78 mg cholesterol, 590 mg sodium.

# Baked Brisket & Vegetables

PREP: 30 MINUTES ∿ BAKE: 2½ HOURS

1 fresh beef brisket (about 3 pounds)
½ teaspoon coarsely ground black pepper
1 teaspoon salt
3 large carrots, peeled and cut into 2½-inch-long
   pieces
3 large celery stalks, cut into 2½-inch-long pieces
1 large onion, sliced
1 large tomato, cut into 1½-inch chunks
½ bunch fresh parsley
2 tablespoons all-purpose flour
6 medium red potatoes (about 1¼ pounds),
   quartered

**1** Preheat oven to 325°F. Sprinkle brisket with pepper and ½ teaspoon salt. In 10-inch skillet, brown brisket fat-side down first over high heat; turn and brown other side; set skillet aside.

**2** Place brisket in shallow 3½-quart casserole. Arrange carrots, celery, onion, tomato, and half of parsley sprigs around brisket.

**3** In 1-cup measuring cup, mix flour, ¼ teaspoon salt, and *1 cup water*. Pour liquid mixture into skillet, stirring to loosen any brown bits from bottom of skillet.

**4** Pour skillet juices over brisket and vegetables. Cover tightly and bake 2 hours.

**5** Add potatoes to casserole, sprinkle with remaining ¼ teaspoon salt, and bake, covered, 30 minutes longer or until potatoes and brisket are fork-tender. Garnish with remaining parsley. *Makes 9 servings.*

Each serving: About 565 calories, 28 g protein, 20 g carbohydrate, 41 g total fat (16 g saturated), 111 mg cholesterol, 390 mg sodium.

*Caribbean Pork Casserole*

# Caribbean Pork Casserole

PREP: 25 MINUTES PLUS 30 MINUTES TO MARINATE
BAKE: 45 MINUTES

4 green onions
2 pork tenderloins (about 12 ounces each), cut
 into 1-inch-thick slices
2 tablespoons minced, peeled fresh ginger
2 tablespoons soy sauce
2 tablespoons Worcestershire sauce
1 tablespoon fresh thyme, chopped, or ½ teaspoon
 dried thyme leaves
½ teaspoon ground red pepper (cayenne)
½ teaspoon ground allspice
3 medium sweet potatoes (1½ pounds), peeled
 and cut into ½-inch-thick slices
1 large red pepper, cut into bite-size pieces
2 tablespoons vegetable oil
1 can (15¼ to 16 ounces) pineapple chunks in
 their own juice

1 Preheat oven to 425°F. Mince 2 green onions. Cut remaining green onions into 2-inch pieces; set aside. In bowl, toss minced green onions with pork slices, ginger, soy sauce, Worcestershire sauce, thyme, ground red pepper, and allspice. Cover pork and marinate 30 minutes.

2 In shallow 6-quart casserole, toss sweet potatoes, red pepper, green-onion pieces, and 1 tablespoon vegetable oil. Bake, uncovered, 15 minutes.

3 Meanwhile, in 10-inch skillet, heat remaining 1 tablespoon vegetable oil over medium-high heat until hot. Add half of pork (reserving marinade) and cook until browned. Transfer pork to bowl; repeat with remaining pork.

4 Pour pineapple chunks with their juice into same skillet, scraping to loosen any brown bits from bottom of skillet. Pour pineapple mixture, pork slices, and any remaining marinade over vegetables.

5 Bake casserole, uncovered, 30 minutes longer or until pork and vegetables are tender, stirring occasionally. *Makes 6 servings.*

Each serving: About 330 calories, 28 g protein, 34 g carbohydrate, 9 g total fat (2 g saturated), 60 mg cholesterol, 480 mg sodium.

# Spanish Beef Casserole

PREP: 40 MINUTES    BAKE: 1 HOUR

Toasting brings out the flavor of the almonds. You can toast them in an ungreased skillet on the stove top or in a toaster oven. (Watch them closely; they burn easily!)

2 tablespoons olive oil
1 large onion, chopped
1 small red pepper, diced
1 small green pepper, diced
2 pounds beef for stew, cut into ½-inch chunks
2 tablespoons all-purpose flour
2 tablespoons chili powder
1 teaspoon salt
1 can (16 ounces) tomatoes in puree
1 medium tomato, diced
1 jar (3 ounces) small pimiento-stuffed olives
½ cup dark seedless raisins
¼ cup sliced almonds, toasted

1 In 5-quart Dutch oven, heat 1 tablespoon olive oil over medium-high heat until hot. Add onion and peppers and cook until tender and golden. With slotted spoon, transfer vegetables to bowl.

2 In large bowl, toss beef with flour, chili powder, and salt.

3 Preheat oven to 400°F. In same Dutch oven, heat remaining 1 tablespoon olive oil. Add half of seasoned beef chunks and cook until browned; with slotted spoon, transfer to bowl with vegetables. Repeat with remaining beef.

4 Return beef-vegetable mixture to Dutch oven; add tomatoes with their puree and ¾ *cup water*, stirring to loosen brown bits from bottom of pan. Heat to boiling over high heat. Cover Dutch oven; bake 45 minutes or until meat is almost tender.

5 Stir diced fresh tomato, olives, and raisins into Dutch oven. Cover and bake 15 minutes longer or until meat is tender. To serve, skim fat from liquid in casserole; sprinkle beef casserole with toasted almonds. *Makes 8 servings.*

Each serving: About 360 calories, 23 g protein, 18 g carbohydrate, 22 g total fat (7 g saturated), 78 mg cholesterol, 740 mg sodium.

# Polenta & Sausage Casserole

~~~~~~~~~~~~~~~~~~~~~~~~~~~~~~~~~~~~~~~~

PREP: 40 MINUTES ∼ BAKE: 35 MINUTES

8 ounces sweet Italian-sausage links, casings
   removed
8 ounces hot Italian-sausage links, casings removed
1 large onion, chopped
1 large celery stalk, chopped
1 medium carrot, peeled and chopped
1 can (28 ounces) tomatoes in puree
2 cups yellow cornmeal
1 cup chicken broth, canned or homemade
   (page 24)
½ teaspoon salt
½ cup grated Parmesan cheese
8 ounces Fontina or mozzarella cheese, shredded
   (2 cups)

**1** In 5-quart Dutch oven, cook sausages over medium-high heat until browned, stirring with spoon to break them up. Transfer sausages to bowl. Pour off all but 1 tablespoon fat from pan.

**2** In drippings in Dutch oven, cook onion, celery, and carrot until browned. Stir in sausages and tomatoes with their puree; heat to boiling over high heat. Reduce heat to low; cover and simmer 10 minutes. Remove cover and simmer 10 minutes longer, stirring with spoon to break up tomatoes.

**3** Preheat oven to 350°F. In 4-quart saucepan, with wire whisk, mix cornmeal, chicken broth, and salt. Over medium-high heat, gradually add *5 cups boiling water*, whisking constantly, until mixture thickens (about 5 minutes); whisk in Parmesan cheese.

**4** Grease 13" by 9" glass baking dish. Spread half of polenta in baking dish; top with half of tomato-sausage sauce, then half of Fontina. Repeat with remaining polenta and sauce.

**5** Bake casserole, uncovered, 15 minutes. Sprinkle with remaining cheese; bake about 20 minutes longer or until mixture is hot and bubbling. Let stand 15 minutes for easier serving. *Makes 8 servings.*

Each serving: About 455 calories, 22 g protein, 38 g carbohydrate, 24 g total fat (11 g saturated), 70 mg cholesterol, 1145 mg sodium.

## GH INSTITUTE REPORT

### LEAD CHECK

If your ceramic ovenware is old, imported, handcrafted, or highly decorated, it may contain lead that can leach into food and cause health problems over time. Although most reputable manufacturers now use lead-free glazes and paints, we conducted personal research. Staff members checked their own ceramic casseroles with do-it-yourself test kits available at pharmacies, home centers, and hardware stores. (You rub a chemically treated swab on the dish for 30 seconds; if the tip turns pink, lead is present.) We were relieved to find that only one casserole—a white one from the 1960s—contained lead; fortunately, it had been left on a cabinet shelf, unused, for years. Note: If a favorite ceramic casserole tests positive, use it for decorative purposes only; don't cook or store food in it, especially if ingredients have a high acid content (like vinegar or tomatoes), which can cause lead to leach out.

# Country Chicken & Beef Casserole

~~~~~~~~~~~~~~~~~~~~~~~~~~~~~~~~~~~~~~~~

PREP: 35 MINUTES ∼ BAKE: 2½ HOURS

12 ounces small white onions
3 medium chicken legs (1¾ pounds)
1 tablespoon olive oil
1 fresh beef brisket (1½ pounds)
1 bay leaf
6 medium red potatoes (about 1¼ pounds), halved
3 medium carrots, peeled and quartered
2 medium leeks (about 4 ounces each), split and
   rinsed
½ medium head green cabbage (about
   1½ pounds), cut into 6 wedges
1 teaspoon salt
¼ teaspoon ground white pepper

**1** Peel onions, leaving some of root end on so that onions remain whole while cooking. Cut each chicken leg at joint to separate drumstick and thigh. Remove skin and fat from chicken pieces.

2 In 8-quart Dutch oven, heat olive oil over medium-high heat until hot. Add onions, turning them occasionally, until golden. With slotted spoon, transfer onions to bowl. In oil in Dutch oven, cook chicken pieces over medium-high heat until golden brown on all sides, transferring pieces to bowl with onions as they brown. Cover bowl and refrigerate.

3 In drippings in Dutch oven, cook brisket over medium-high heat until browned on all sides. Add bay leaf and *4 cups water*; heat to boiling over high heat. Cover Dutch oven and bake in 375°F. oven 1 hour.

4 Add potatoes, carrots, leeks, cabbage, browned chicken pieces, onions, salt, and pepper. Cover Dutch oven and bake 1½ hours longer, stirring occasionally, or until meat and vegetables are tender.

5 To serve, discard bay leaf. Transfer brisket to cutting board; thinly slice. Place brisket, chicken, vegetables, and broth in 6 large soup bowls. *Makes 6 servings.*

Each serving: About 630 calories, 39 g protein, 37 g carbohydrate, 36 g total fat (13 g saturated), 143 mg cholesterol, 580 mg sodium.

2 In nonstick 12-inch skillet, heat vegetable oil over medium-high heat until hot. Add pork chops and cook until brown on both sides. Transfer pork chops to plate.

3 In same skillet, cook onions and ¼ teaspoon salt until onions are golden brown, about 10 minutes.

4 Meanwhile, arrange potatoes in bottom of shallow 2½-quart casserole or 13" by 9" glass baking dish. Sprinkle potatoes with remaining ¼ teaspoon salt. In 1-cup measuring cup, mix apple-cranberry juice with remaining 1 tablespoon flour.

5 To skillet, add apple-cranberry juice mixture, stirring to loosen any brown bits from bottom of skillet. Spoon onions and liquid over potatoes in casserole. Tuck pork chops and apple slices into onions in casserole.

6 Cover casserole with foil and bake 1 hour. Uncover casserole and brush pork chops with apple jelly; bake, covered, 30 minutes longer until pork chops are fork-tender. Garnish with dried cranberries. *Makes 4 servings.*

Each serving: About 615 calories, 31 g protein, 77 g carbohydrate, 21 g total fat (6 g saturated), 84 mg cholesterol, 525 mg sodium.

## *Apple-Cranberry Pork Chops*

PREP: 30 MINUTES  ⌇  BAKE: 1½ HOURS

3 tablespoons all-purpose flour
¾ teaspoon salt
4 pork loin chops, ½ inch thick (about 6 ounces each)
1 tablespoon vegetable oil
2 jumbo onions (1 pound each), cut into ½-inch-thick slices
5 small potatoes (about 12 ounces)
¾ cup apple-cranberry juice
2 red cooking apples, cut into ¼-inch-thick slices
¼ cup apple jelly, melted
¼ cup dried cranberries for garnish

1 Preheat oven to 350°F. On waxed paper, mix 2 tablespoons flour and ¼ teaspoon salt. Coat pork chops with flour mixture.

## CASSEROLE SIZE GUIDE

Here, some common casserole/baking dish equivalents:

| CASSEROLE CAPACITY* | BAKING-DISH SIZE |
| --- | --- |
| 1½ quarts | 8" by 8" by 1½" |
| 2 quarts | 9" by 9" by 1½" |
| 1½ quarts | 9½" by 1½" deep-dish pie plate |
| 2 quarts | 11" by 7" by 1½" |
| 3½ to 4 quarts | 13" by 9" by 2" |
| 5 quarts | 15" by 10" by 2" |

* If you substitute a casserole for one of the baking-dish sizes listed, be sure it is shallow (2" high or less); if it is deeper, ingredients may not cook properly.

# Smoked Pork & Navy Bean Casserole

~~~~~~~~~~~~~~~~~~~~~~~~~~~~~~

PREP: 40 MINUTES PLUS 1 HOUR TO SOAK BEANS
BAKE: 2 HOURS

1 package (16 ounces) dry navy (pea) beans
1 tablespoon olive oil
1 pound pork tenderloin, cut into 1-inch cubes
½ teaspoon salt
¼ teaspoon coarsely ground black pepper
2 large celery stalks, diced
2 medium onions, chopped
1 garlic clove, crushed with side of chef's knife
6 whole cloves
1 teaspoon dried thyme leaves
1 bay leaf

1 smoked pork shoulder roll (about 1½ pounds)
1 package (16 ounces) peeled baby carrots
2 tablespoons chopped fresh parsley leaves

**1** Rinse beans under cold running water and discard any stones or shriveled beans. In 4-quart saucepan, heat beans and *8 cups water* to boiling over high heat; cook 3 minutes. Remove saucepan from heat; cover and let stand 1 hour.

**2** Preheat oven to 350°F. In 5-quart Dutch oven, heat olive oil over medium-high heat until hot. Add pork cubes, salt, and pepper and cook until meat is browned. Transfer meat to bowl. In drippings in Dutch oven, cook celery and onions over medium heat until tender and golden.

**3** Meanwhile, prepare spice bag: Cut double thickness of 5-inch-square cheesecloth. On cheesecloth, place garlic, whole cloves, thyme, and bay leaf. Form small bag and tie with undyed cotton string.

## TURKEY & LENTIL CLAY POT CASSEROLE

Clay pot casseroles provide an easy way of cooking food slowly and evenly. All clay pots need to be soaked before use; be sure to consult the directions that came with the pot. If you do not have a clay pot, this can be made in a 5-quart Dutch oven.

PREP: 20 MINUTES PLUS SOAKING TIME
BAKE: 1½ HOURS

*1 tablespoon plus 1 teaspoon vegetable oil*
*4 turkey drumsticks (about 3 pounds)*
*1½ cups dry lentils, rinsed*
*4 medium carrots, peeled and cut into 1-inch chunks*
*1 large onion, sliced*
*1 can (35 ounces) Italian plum tomatoes*
*1 tablespoon sugar*
*½ teaspoon salt*
*2 medium zucchini (about 8 ounces each), halved lengthwise, then cut crosswise into ½-inch-thick slices*
*1 can (15 to 19 ounces) garbanzo beans, rinsed and drained*

**1** Soak 4- to 4½-quart clay pot as manufacturer directs. Note that clay pots start out in a cold oven

**2** In nonstick 12-inch skillet, heat 1 tablespoon vegetable oil over medium-high heat until hot. Add turkey drumsticks and cook until drumsticks are browned on all sides; transfer to clay pot. Add lentils to turkey in clay pot.

**3** In same skillet, heat remaining 1 teaspoon vegetable oil; cook carrots and onion until they are lightly browned. Stir in tomatoes with their juice, sugar, and salt. Heat to boiling over high heat. Stir in *1 cup water* (adding boiling liquid to clay pot may cause it to break; adding 1 cup water to boiling tomato mixture cools it slightly). Add tomato mixture to drumsticks and lentils. Cover and bake in a 375°F oven for 1½ hours.

**4** Stir zucchini and garbanzo beans into clay pot. Cover and bake 30 minutes longer or until lentils and turkey are tender. Makes 4 servings.

*Each serving: About 900 calories, 85 g protein, 82 g carbohydrate, 27 g total fat (7 g saturated), 201 mg cholesterol, 1075 mg sodium.*

**4** Remove stockinette casing from pork shoulder roll. Cut off as much fat as possible; cut meat into bite-size chunks.

**5** Drain and rinse beans; add to Dutch oven with spice bag, smoked-pork chunks, and *3 cups water*; heat to boiling over high heat. Cover Dutch oven and bake 1 hour, stirring occasionally. Add pork cubes and carrots; bake 1 hour longer or until meat and beans are fork-tender, stirring occasionally.

**6** To serve, discard spice bag; sprinkle with parsley. *Makes 10 servings.*

Each serving: About 400 calories, 29 g protein, 37 g carbohydrate, 16 g total fat (5 g saturated), 62 mg cholesterol, 630 mg sodium.

# Baked Greek-Style Lamb Shanks

PREP: 30 MINUTES  ∾  BAKE: 2¾ HOURS

1 tablespoon vegetable oil
1 teaspoon salt
4 small lamb shanks (1 pound each)
2 medium onions, diced
1 large carrot, peeled and diced
2 garlic cloves, minced
1 can (14½ ounces) diced tomatoes
1 cup chicken broth, canned or homemade (page 24)
4 medium all-purpose potatoes (about 1¾ pounds), quartered
12 ounces green beans, trimmed and cut into 2-inch pieces
2 medium lemons
2 tablespoons chopped fresh dill
2 tablespoons chopped fresh parsley leaves

**1** In 8-quart Dutch oven, heat vegetable oil over medium-high heat until hot. Sprinkle ¼ teaspoon salt on lamb shanks. Cook lamb shanks, 2 at a time, until browned on all sides. Transfer shanks to bowl as they brown.

**2** Preheat oven to 350°F. In drippings in Dutch oven, cook onions and carrot until tender, about 10 minutes. Add garlic; cook 2 minutes.

**3** Return lamb shanks to Dutch oven. Add tomatoes with their juice, chicken broth, and remaining ¾ teaspoon salt; heat to boiling over high heat. Cover Dutch oven and bake 1½ hours. Turn lamb shanks

over; add potatoes and green beans. Cover and bake 1¼ hours or until lamb and potatoes are tender.

**4** Meanwhile, from lemons, grate 1 tablespoon peel and squeeze 2 tablespoons juice.

**5** When lamb shanks are done, skim fat from sauce. Stir in lemon peel, lemon juice, dill, and parsley. *Makes 4 servings.*

Each serving: About 625 calories, 50 g protein, 53 g carbohydrate, 24 g total fat (9 g saturated), 159 mg cholesterol, 995 mg sodium.

# Sweet & Sour Pork Casserole

PREP: 25 MINUTES  ∾  BAKE: 1 TO 1¼ HOURS

1 small head green cabbage (about 1½ pounds), cut into 6 wedges
8 small red potatoes (about 1 pound)
1 tablespoon vegetable oil
3 large onions, quartered
6 smoked pork loin chops, each ½ inch thick
½ cup apple juice
¼ cup cider vinegar
½ teaspoon coarsely ground black pepper
1 package (11 ounces) mixed dried fruit

**1** Preheat oven to 375°F. Arrange cabbage and potatoes in shallow 15½" by 10½" casserole or roasting pan.

**2** In nonstick 12-inch skillet, heat vegetable oil over medium-high heat until hot. Add onions and cook until golden brown. Transfer onions to casserole with cabbage.

**3** In same skillet, cook pork chops, 3 at a time, until lightly browned. Tuck pork chops among vegetables in casserole.

**4** In same skillet, heat apple juice, cider vinegar, pepper, and dried fruit over high heat, stirring to loosen any brown bits from bottom.

**5** Pour apple juice mixture over pork chops and vegetables. Cover casserole and bake 1 to 1¼ hours or until pork chops and vegetables are fork-tender, basting meat and vegetables with liquid in casserole several times during baking. *Makes 6 servings.*

Each serving: About 465 calories, 24 g protein, 69 g carbohydrate, 14 g total fat (3 g saturated), 60 mg cholesterol, 1760 mg sodium.

# Lamb & White Bean Casserole

PREP: 30 MINUTES ～ BAKE: 1½ HOURS

4 small lamb shanks (1 pound each)
2 tablespoons all-purpose flour
1 tablespoon vegetable oil
1 large celery stalk, diced
1 medium onion, diced
1 can (14½ ounces) no-salt-added stewed tomatoes
1 can (14½ ounces) beef broth
1 garlic clove, minced
1 bay leaf
½ teaspoon dried thyme leaves
¼ teaspoon salt
¼ teaspoon coarsely ground black pepper
1 can (16 to 19 ounces) white kidney beans (cannellini), rinsed and drained
1 teaspoon chopped fresh parsley leaves
1 teaspoon grated lemon peel

1 Preheat oven to 350°F. Coat lamb shanks with flour. In 5-quart Dutch oven, heat vegetable oil over medium-high heat until hot. Add lamb shanks and cook until browned on all sides. Transfer shanks to bowl.

2 In drippings in Dutch oven, cook celery and onion over medium heat until well browned. Return shanks to Dutch oven; add stewed tomatoes, beef broth, garlic, bay leaf, thyme, salt, and pepper; heat to boiling over high heat.

3 Cover Dutch oven and bake 1½ hours or until lamb shanks are fork-tender, turning meat once.

4 When lamb shanks are done, skim fat from liquid in Dutch oven. Stir in white kidney beans; heat through. Discard bay leaf. Sprinkle with parsley and lemon peel to serve. *Makes 4 servings.*

Each serving: About 415 calories, 50 g protein, 29 g carbohydrate, 11 g total fat (3 g saturated), 128 mg cholesterol, 1015 mg sodium.

# Eggplant & Lamb Casserole

PREP: 1 HOUR ～ BAKE: 35 TO 40 MINUTES

Nonstick cooking spray
2 medium eggplants (about 1¼ pounds each), cut lengthwise into ½-inch-thick slices
3 tablespoons olive oil

## GH's Very First Casserole Recipe

Even 113 years ago, in our first year of publication, our editors considered casserole cooking an efficient, economical, and appealing way to feed a family.

This Stewed Chicken dish was the first casserole recipe to appear on our pages. And while we've come a long way since singeing a chicken's feathers was a required step, we still think a casserole with chicken, onion, and tomato is a great idea (see Country Captain Casserole, page 82).

*Stewed Chicken* Use a fowl about a year old and weighing about five pounds. After singeing it and wiping it, cut it into handsome joints. Wash carefully and dredge well with salt, pepper, and flour. Cut into bits a piece of chicken fat about the size of an egg and cook it in a frying pan until there are about four tablespoons of liquid fat; then remove any remaining solid particles from the frying pan and put in the pieces of chicken. Cook until they are brown on both sides, and then put them into a stewpan. When all the meat has been browned, cut an onion fine and cook it slowly for five minutes in the fat remaining in the frying pan. Add three tablespoonfuls of flour and stir until brown; then add three pints of water and stir until it boils. Next, add half a cupful of stewed tomato, and enough salt and pepper to season highly. Strain this liquor over the chicken. Put the heart, liver, and gizzard into the stewpan and, after putting on the cover, set the stewpan in a hot place on the stove. When the stew begins to boil, skim it, and set the stewpan back where its contents will simply simmer for two hours. The dish should never be allowed to boil hard.—September 19, 1885

2 pounds ground lamb or ground beef
1 large onion, chopped
2 garlic cloves, minced
1 teaspoon ground cumin
½ teaspoon ground cinnamon
1¼ teaspoons salt
½ teaspoon coarsely ground black pepper
1 can (28 ounces) tomatoes in puree
⅓ cup all-purpose flour
3 cups reduced-fat (2%) milk
4 large eggs, lightly beaten
¼ teaspoon ground nutmeg

1 Preheat oven to 450°F. Spray 2 cookie sheets with nonstick cooking spray. Place eggplant slices on cookie sheets; brush with 2 tablespoons olive oil. Bake eggplant 20 minutes, until soft and browned, rotating cookie sheets between upper and lower racks halfway through baking time. Remove eggplant from oven; turn oven control to 375°F.

2 Meanwhile, heat nonstick 12-inch skillet (at least 2 inches deep) over medium-high heat. Add ground lamb, onion, and garlic and cook until browned, about 15 minutes. Stir in cumin, cinnamon, ¾ teaspoon salt, and ¼ teaspoon pepper; cook 1 minute longer. Remove skillet from heat; add tomatoes with their puree, stirring with spoon to break them up.

3 In 3-quart saucepan, heat remaining 1 tablespoon olive oil over medium heat until hot. Stir in flour and cook 1 minute (mixture will appear dry and crumbly). With wire whisk, gradually beat in milk; cook until mixture boils and thickens, about 15 minutes. Remove saucepan from heat. Gradually beat small amount of hot milk mixture into eggs. Return egg mixture to saucepan, beating to combine. Stir in nutmeg, remaining ½ teaspoon salt, and remaining ¼ teaspoon pepper.

4 In shallow 3½- to 4-quart casserole or 13" by 9" glass or ceramic baking dish, arrange half of eggplant slices, overlapping slices to fit if necessary; top with half of meat mixture. Repeat layering with remaining eggplant slices and remaining meat mixture; pour egg mixture over top. Bake casserole 35 to 40 minutes or until top is puffed and golden and casserole is heated through. *Makes 10 servings.*

Each serving: About 435 calories, 23 g protein, 21 g carbohydrate, 29 g total fat (11 g saturated), 157 mg cholesterol, 535 mg sodium.

# Veal & Basil Spaetzle Casserole

PREP: 45 MINUTES ～ BAKE: 1¾ TO 2 HOURS

2 tablespoons olive oil
2 large celery stalks, cut into ½-inch pieces
4 medium carrots, peeled and cut into ½-inch pieces
1 large onion, cut into ½-inch pieces
4 veal shank cross cuts, 2 inches thick (about 1 pound each)
1 can (14½ to 16 ounces) tomatoes in juice
½ cup dry white wine
¼ teaspoon coarsely ground black pepper
¼ teaspoon dried oregano leaves
1 teaspoon salt
1½ cups all-purpose flour
½ cup finely chopped fresh basil leaves
2 large eggs

1 Preheat oven to 375°F. In 8-quart Dutch oven, heat olive oil over medium-high heat until hot. Add celery, carrots, and onion and cook, stirring occasionally, until vegetables are golden and tender-crisp; with slotted spoon, transfer to bowl.

2 In oil in Dutch oven, cook veal shanks over medium-high heat until browned on all sides.

3 Return vegetables to Dutch oven. Add tomatoes with their juice, white wine, pepper, oregano, and ½ teaspoon salt, stirring with spoon to break up tomatoes; heat to boiling over high heat. Cover Dutch oven and bake 1¾ to 2 hours or until veal is very tender.

4 When veal is done, prepare basil spaetzle: In 5-quart saucepot, heat *4 quarts water* to boiling over high heat. In medium bowl, with spoon, beat flour, basil, eggs, remaining ½ teaspoon salt, and *⅓ cup water* until smooth.

5 Reduce heat to medium. Into simmering water, drop dough by measuring teaspoons, stirring water gently so spaetzle pieces do not stick together. Cook 2 to 3 minutes or until tender but firm; drain.

6 To serve, skim fat from liquid in Dutch oven. Gently stir in spaetzle. *Makes 4 servings.*

Each serving: About 535 calories, 44 g protein, 55 g carbohydrate, 15 g total fat (4 g saturated), 230 mg cholesterol, 940 mg sodium.

# LAZY-DAY CASSEROLES

As hands-off as a casserole is to cook, it does require a certain amount of preparation before you can stick it in the oven. Here's a collection of recipes that take advantage of some prepared foods to help speed up the process. For example, refrigerated bread twists can be used for a clever topping (see Sunburst Chili Pie, opposite page), canned refried beans (nonfat brands are readily available) enrich Tex-Mex casseroles, instant soup mix makes the gravy for a pot roast casserole, and a variety of packaged corn breads (frozen muffins and muffin mix) can be used to make quick crusts.

## Baked Chili with Corn Bread Topping

PREP: 20 MINUTES • BAKE: 55 MINUTES

2 tablespoons vegetable oil
1 beef top round steak (2 pounds),
    well trimmed, cut into ½-inch cubes
2 medium onions, diced
1 large red pepper, diced
1 large green pepper, diced
3 tablespoons chili powder
¾ teaspoon salt
½ teaspoon ground cumin
1 can (12 ounces) whole-kernel corn,
    drained
1 can (15¼ to 19 ounces) red kidney
    beans, rinsed and drained
1 can (14½ to 16 ounces) tomatoes
    in juice
½ cup bottled mild chunky salsa
1 teaspoon hot pepper sauce
1 package (12 ounces) corn-muffin
    mix
¼ cup milk
1 large egg

1 Preheat oven to 400°F. In 5-quart Dutch oven, heat vegetable oil over high heat until hot. Add meat, one-third at a time, and cook, stirring often, until browned on all sides; transfer to bowl as it browns.
2 In drippings in Dutch oven, cook onions and red and green peppers over medium heat until tender, stirring occasionally. Stir in chili powder, salt, and cumin; cook 1 minute.

3 Reserve ½ cup corn for corn bread topping. Return meat to Dutch oven; add kidney beans, tomatoes with their juice, salsa, hot pepper sauce, and remaining corn. Heat to boiling over high heat; reduce to low, cover, and simmer 30 minutes, stirring occasionally.
4 In 2-cup measure, mix 1 cup water with ¼ cup corn-muffin mix until smooth; add to chili mixture in Dutch oven. Heat to boiling over high heat; boil 1 minute.
5 In medium bowl, mix milk, egg, remaining corn-muffin mix, and reserved corn until blended (mixture will be lumpy).
6 Spoon corn bread batter over chili mixture around edge of Dutch oven. Bake, uncovered, 20 to 25 minutes or until corn bread is golden, covering with foil during last 5 minutes of baking. Makes 10 servings.

EACH SERVING: ABOUT 425 CALORIES, 27 G PROTEIN, 42 G CARBOHYDRATE, 17 G TOTAL FAT (5 G SATURATED), 78 MG CHOLESTEROL, 925 MG SODIUM.

## Pot Roast Casserole

PREP: 15 MINUTES
BAKE: 3 TO 3½ HOURS

1 boneless beef round rump roast
    (3½ pounds)
1 container (5.6 ounces) hearty beef
    stew soup mix
1 medium rutabaga (about 1¾
    pounds), peeled and cut into
    1½-inch chunks
1 bag (16 ounces) peeled baby carrots
1 pound green beans, trimmed

1 Preheat oven to 375°F. In 8-quart Dutch oven, cook beef, fat-side down first, over medium-high heat until browned on all sides. Discard fat in Dutch oven.
2 Add soup mix and 5½ cups water to Dutch oven; heat to boiling over high heat. Cover Dutch oven and bake 1½ hours.

3 With slotted spoon, transfer 2 cups soup-mix vegetables to blender; cover (with center part of blender cover removed) and blend at low speed until mixture is smooth. Stir into liquid remaining in Dutch oven.
4 Add rutabaga and carrots to Dutch oven; cover and bake 1 hour. Add green beans; cover and bake 30 to 60 minutes longer until meat and vegetables are fork-tender. Makes 10 servings.

EACH SERVING: ABOUT 380 CALORIES, 32 G PROTEIN, 25 G CARBOHYDRATE, 17 G TOTAL FAT (6 G SATURATED), 95 MG CHOLESTEROL, 670 MG SODIUM.

## Individual Harvest Casseroles

PREP: 25 MINUTES • BAKE: 20 MINUTES

2 tablespoons vegetable oil
1 large onion, thickly sliced
1 medium bunch broccoli, cut into
    2" by 1" pieces
½ large head cauliflower, cut into 2" by
    1" pieces
¼ teaspoon salt
12 ounces medium mushrooms, halved
1 large red pepper, cut into ¾-inch-
    wide strips
1 can (19 ounces) minestrone soup
2 teaspoons all-purpose flour
1 package (8 ounces) refrigerated
    crescent rolls

1 In nonstick 12-inch skillet, heat 1 tablespoon vegetable oil over medium-high heat until hot. Add onion and cook until tender and lightly browned. With slotted spoon, transfer onion to large bowl.
2 In oil in skillet, stir broccoli and cauliflower until evenly coated; add ¼ cup water and ¼ teaspoon salt. Reduce heat to medium; cover skillet and cook vegetables 5 to 10 minutes, stirring occasionally, until vegetables are tender-crisp. Transfer broccoli mixture to bowl with onion.
3 In same skillet, heat remaining 1 tablespoon vegetable oil over medium-high heat. Add mushrooms, red pepper,

and remaining ¼ teaspoon salt and cook until vegetables are lightly browned and tender.

**4** Preheat oven to 375°F. Return vegetables in bowl to skillet; stir in minestrone soup; heat to boiling. In cup, mix flour with ½ cup water; stir into liquid in skillet; boil 1 minute.

**5** Meanwhile, open package of crescent rolls, but do not unroll cylinder of dough. Cut cylinder crosswise into 16 slices. Cut each slice in half.

**6** Spoon hot vegetable mixture into four 16-ounce casseroles or ramekins. (Or use oven-safe bowls.) Arrange crescent-roll slices around edge of casseroles. Place casseroles on jelly-roll pan for easier handling. Bake, uncovered, 20 minutes or until crescent dough is crisp and brown and vegetable mixture is hot. Makes 4 servings.

EACH SERVING: ABOUT 440 CALORIES, 17 G PROTEIN, 56 G CARBOHYDRATE, 21 G TOTAL FAT (4 G SATURATED), 0 MG CHOLESTEROL, 1095 MG SODIUM.

## Sunburst Chili Pie

PREP: 30 MINUTES • BAKE: 20 MINUTES

1 tablespoon vegetable oil
1½ pounds lean ground beef (90%)
1 large onion, chopped
¼ cup chili powder
1 teaspoon ground cumin
1 can (28 ounces) tomatoes in puree
1 can (16 ounces) hominy* or whole-
    kernel corn, drained
1 can (15¼ to 19 ounces) red kidney
    beans, drained
1 can (8 ounces) tomato sauce
1 can (4 to 4½ ounces) chopped mild
    green chiles, drained
1 teaspoon sugar
¼ teaspoon salt
1 package (11½ ounces) refrigerated
    corn bread twists

**1** In nonstick 12-inch skillet (at least 2 inches deep), with oven-safe handle, heat vegetable oil over medium-high heat until hot. Add ground beef and onion, and cook, stirring frequently, until all pan juices evaporate, beef is well browned, and onion is tender, about 15 minutes.

**2** Stir in chili powder and cumin; cook 1 minute. Add tomatoes with their puree, hominy, kidney beans, tomato sauce, chopped chiles, sugar, salt, and ½ cup water; heat to boiling over high heat. Reduce heat to low; simmer 5 minutes.

**3** Preheat oven to 350°F. Separate corn bread twist dough into 16 pieces as label directs; cut each piece crosswise in half. Place corn-bread pieces on top of chili around outer edge of skillet, placing every other piece slightly over edge of skillet. Place sheet of foil underneath skillet; crimp edges, forming a rim, to catch any drips during baking. Bake 20 minutes or until corn bread is golden. Makes 8 servings.

*Hominy is dried corn kernels from which the hull and germ have been removed. It is sold in cans ready-to-eat, or in dried form, which must be reconstituted before using. When ground, hominy is called grits.

EACH SERVING: ABOUT 450 CALORIES, 26 G PROTEIN, 47 G CARBOHYDRATE, 18 G TOTAL FAT (5 G SATURATED), 53 MG CHOLESTEROL, 1105 MG SODIUM.

*Sunburst Chili Pie*

## Chicken & Stuffing Casserole

PREP: 20 MINUTES • BAKE: 50 MINUTES

2 chickens (3 pounds each), cut up
2 small red apples, diced
6 slices rye bread without seeds, cut
    into 1-inch pieces
1 package (8 ounces) corn-bread
    stuffing
1 bag (12 ounces) frozen Italian green
    beans
½ cup dark seedless raisins
2 medium celery stalks, sliced
1 large red pepper, diced
1 medium onion, chopped
½ teaspoon salt

**1** In nonstick 12-inch skillet, cook half of chicken pieces, skin-side down, over medium-low heat until some fat is rendered. Increase heat to medium-high and cook until chicken is golden; transfer to medium bowl. In drippings in same skillet, brown remaining chicken; transfer to bowl.

**2** Meanwhile, in very large bowl, mix apples, rye bread, corn-bread stuffing, frozen green beans, and raisins.

**3** Preheat oven to 375°F. Pour off all but 1 tablespoon fat from skillet. Add celery, red pepper, and onion and cook over medium heat until tender and lightly browned. Stir in 2 cups water; heat to boiling over high heat. Pour hot mixture into stuffing mixture; toss to mix.

**4** Spoon stuffing mixture into 15" by 10" glass baking dish or small roasting pan; tuck in chicken pieces. Sprinkle with salt. Pour any juices from chicken remaining in bowl over casserole. Cover baking dish with foil and bake 50 minutes or until juices run clear when chicken is pierced with tip of knife. Makes 8 servings.

EACH SERVING: ABOUT 615 CALORIES, 48 G PROTEIN, 51 G CARBOHYDRATE, 24 G TOTAL FAT (6 G SATURATED), 133 MG CHOLESTEROL, 755 MG SODIUM.

## Filet-of-Sole Casserole

PREP: 20 MINUTES • BAKE: 55 MINUTES

1 package (5.6 ounces) seasoned
    risotto mix, preferably "primavera"
Margarine or butter
4 small sole or flounder fillets (about
    6 ounces each)
¼ teaspoon salt
¼ teaspoon paprika
1 medium zucchini (about 8 ounces),
    thinly sliced
2 medium plum tomatoes, each cut
    into 6 wedges

1 Preheat oven to 350°F. In shallow
2-quart casserole or 11" by 7" glass
baking dish, stir risotto mix with amount
of margarine or butter and *water* called
for on label for range-top method.
Cover loosely with foil and bake 25
minutes, stirring twice.
2 Meanwhile, sprinkle sole fillets with
salt and paprika.
3 Remove casserole from oven; remove
foil and stir in zucchini and tomatoes.
Fold each sole fillet in half and tuck fillets
slightly into risotto mixture, making sure
that zucchini slices are in the liquid.
Loosely cover and return casserole to
oven; bake 30 minutes longer or until
sole flakes easily when tested with a
fork and all liquid is absorbed. Makes 4
servings.

EACH SERVING: ABOUT 410 CALORIES,
52 G PROTEIN, 33 G CARBOHYDRATE,
7 G TOTAL FAT (1 G SATURATED),
123 MG CHOLESTEROL, 910 MG SODIUM.

## Beef "Tamale" Bake

PREP: 15 MINUTES • BAKE: 25 MINUTES

1 pound lean ground beef (90%)
6 ounces Monterey Jack cheese with
    jalapeño chiles, shredded (1½ cups)
1 package (10 to 11½ ounces) frozen
    corn muffins
1 can (16 ounces) nonfat refried
    beans
2 large tomatoes, cut into ¼-inch-thick
    slices

*Louisiana Gumbo Casserole*

1 In nonstick 10-inch skillet, cook
ground beef over medium-high heat,
stirring frequently, until all pan juices
evaporate and beef is well browned;
remove skillet from heat.
2 Stir 1 cup Monterey Jack into ground
beef. Preheat oven to 350°F.
3 Slice corn muffins ¼ inch thick. Layer
sliced corn muffins in bottom of shallow
2-quart casserole; spread refried beans
on top of corn muffins.
4 Arrange half of tomato slices over
refried beans; spoon meat mixture over
tomatoes. Arrange remaining tomatoes,
overlapping slightly, around edge of
casserole; top with remaining Monterey
Jack. Bake, covered, 15 minutes; uncover
and bake 10 minutes longer or until
cheese melts and casserole is heated
through. Makes 6 servings.

EACH SERVING: ABOUT 470 CALORIES,
30 G PROTEIN, 41 G CARBOHYDRATE,
21 G TOTAL FAT (9 G SATURATED),
77 MG CHOLESTEROL, 750 MG SODIUM.

## Louisiana Gumbo Casserole

PREP: 45 MINUTES • BAKE: 45 MINUTES

3 hot Italian-sausage links (about
    8 ounces), casings removed
1 medium onion, chopped
8 ounces skinless, boneless chicken
    breast, cut into ½-inch strips
1 pound large shrimp, shelled and
    deveined
1 package (10 ounces) frozen whole
    okra, thawed
1 tablespoon vegetable oil
3 tablespoons all-purpose flour
¼ teaspoon salt
1 bottle (8 ounces) clam juice
1 can (14½ ounces) stewed tomatoes
1 package (12 ounces) corn-muffin mix
½ cup milk
1 large egg

1 In nonstick 10-inch skillet, cook
sausage meat over medium heat until
browned, stirring frequently. Transfer
sausage meat to medium bowl.
2 In drippings in skillet, cook onion 10
minutes. Add chicken and cook 2 to 3
minutes longer or until chicken is lightly
browned; transfer to deep 3-quart
casserole. Add shrimp and okra to
casserole.
3 Preheat oven to 400°F. In same skillet,
heat vegetable oil over low heat. Stir in
flour and salt; cook 1 minute. Gradually
stir in clam juice until blended; stir in
stewed tomatoes and cook, stirring
frequently, until mixture boils and
thickens slightly. Pour into casserole.
4 Stir corn-muffin mix, milk, and egg into
sausage meat just until mixed. Spoon
corn-bread batter over seafood mixture
around edge of casserole, leaving center
open.
5 Bake casserole, uncovered, 20
minutes or until corn bread is nicely
browned. Cover casserole loosely with
foil to prevent overbrowning; bake 20 to
25 minutes longer or until mixture is hot
and bubbly and shrimp turn opaque
throughout. Let stand 10 minutes before
serving. Makes 8 servings.

EACH SERVING: ABOUT 430 CALORIES,
26 G PROTEIN, 41 G CARBOHYDRATE,
18 G TOTAL FAT (5 G SATURATED),
137 MG CHOLESTEROL, 1015 MG SODIUM.

## Vegetable Burrito Casserole

PREP: 25 MINUTES • BAKE: 30 MINUTES

⅔ cup regular long-grain rice
2 teaspoons vegetable oil
1 large green pepper, diced
1 medium onion, chopped
1 can (8¾ ounces) whole-kernel corn, drained
½ cup medium bottled salsa
4 ounces queso blanco or Monterey Jack cheese, shredded (1 cup)
8 (8-inch diameter) flour tortillas
1 can (16 ounces) nonfat refried beans
1 can (8 ounces) no-salt-added tomato sauce
⅛ teaspoon ground red pepper (cayenne)
½ cup sour cream
1 tablespoon chopped fresh cilantro or parsley leaves

1 In small saucepan, prepare rice as label directs but do not add salt.
2 Meanwhile, in nonstick 10-inch skillet, heat vegetable oil over medium heat until hot. Add green pepper and onion and cook until vegetables are tender. Remove skillet from heat; stir in corn and salsa.
3 Preheat oven to 400°F. When rice is done, stir into vegetable mixture along with cheese.
4 Spread each tortilla with a scant ¼ cup refried beans. Spoon one-eighth of rice mixture (about ½ cup) along center of each tortilla. Roll up tortillas to enclose filling and arrange, seam-side down, in 13" by 9" glass or ceramic baking dish. In small bowl, stir tomato sauce and ground red pepper together. Spoon sauce along center of rolled tortillas; spoon sour cream over sauce. Cover baking dish with foil and bake casserole 30 minutes or until hot.
5 To serve, sprinkle with cilantro. Makes 4 servings.

EACH SERVING: ABOUT 690 CALORIES, 23 G PROTEIN, 101 G CARBOHYDRATE, 22 G TOTAL FAT (10 G SATURATED), 38 MG CHOLESTEROL, 1425 MG SODIUM.

## Easy Ravioli Casserole

PREP: 30 MINUTES • BAKE: 30 MINUTES

2 tablespoons olive oil
1 small eggplant (about 1 pound), diced
1 medium celery stalk, finely chopped
1 medium carrot, peeled and finely chopped
1 small onion, finely chopped
1 can (28 ounces) tomatoes in juice
½ teaspoon sugar
Salt
2 package (13 ounces each) frozen large spinach-filled ravioli
2 cups shredded part-skim mozzarella cheese (8 ounces)

1 In 4-quart saucepan, heat olive oil over medium heat until hot. Add eggplant, celery, carrot, and onion; cover and cook 8 to 10 minutes, stirring occasionally, until vegetables are almost tender. Stir in tomatoes with their juice, sugar, and ½ teaspoon salt; heat to boiling over high heat. Reduce heat to low; cover and simmer 15 minutes, stirring occasionally with spoon to break up tomatoes.
2 Preheat oven to 375°F. Meanwhile, in large saucepot, prepare ravioli in *boiling salted water* as label directs; drain. Into 13" by 9" glass baking dish, spoon 1½ cups of the tomato sauce. Top with half of ravioli, half of remaining sauce, and half of mozzarella. Repeat layering.
3 Bake, uncovered, 30 minutes or until bubbly and cheese on top is golden. Makes 6 servings.

EACH SERVING: ABOUT 580 CALORIES, 32 G PROTEIN, 51 G CARBOHYDRATE, 29 G TOTAL FAT (5 G SATURATED), 123 MG CHOLESTEROL, 1235 MG SODIUM.

## Bread Pudding Casserole

PREP: 20 MINUTES • BAKE: 1 HOUR

1 loaf (16 ounces) very thinly sliced white bread
1 package (8 ounces) sliced turkey ham, coarsely chopped
1 package (10 ounces) frozen chopped spinach, thawed and squeezed dry
4 ounces Jarlsberg or Swiss cheese, shredded (1 cup)
2 medium tomatoes, cut into ¼-inch-thick slices
3½ cups milk
½ teaspoon salt
¼ teaspoon coarsely ground black pepper
5 large eggs

1 Preheat oven to 350°F. Grease 3-quart shallow casserole or 13" by 9" baking dish.
2 Line casserole with one-third of bread slices, overlapping bread if necessary. Sprinkle turkey ham over bread; top with one-third more bread slices. Top with all the spinach and half the Jarlsberg, then with remaining bread slices. Arrange tomatoes, overlapping slices slightly, on top; sprinkle with remaining Jarlsberg.
3 In bowl, mix milk, salt, pepper, and eggs. Pour egg mixture over casserole, pressing top gently with pancake turner so top bread layer absorbs some egg mixture.
4 Bake, uncovered, 55 to 60 minutes or until knife inserted in center of pudding comes out clean. Remove casserole from oven; let stand 10 minutes for easier serving. Makes 8 servings.

EACH SERVING: ABOUT 370 CALORIES, 22 G PROTEIN, 37 G CARBOHYDRATE, 14 G TOTAL FAT (4 G SATURATED), 175 MG CHOLESTEROL, 920 MG SODIUM.

# Main-Dish Salads

# Southwestern "Succotash" Salad in Corn Husks

PREP: 35 MINUTES ᓚ COOK: 15 MINUTES

4 small ears corn with husks
¼ cup apricot preserves
3 tablespoons fresh lime juice
1 tablespoon vegetable oil
½ teaspoon salt
½ teaspoon coarsely ground black pepper
½ teaspoon chili powder
2 cups loosely packed thinly sliced iceberg lettuce
   (about ½ small head)
1 medium red pepper, diced
1 can (15 to 19 ounces) black beans, rinsed and
   drained
1 package (10 ounces) frozen baby lima beans,
   thawed
1 jalapeño chile, finely chopped
1 tablespoon chopped fresh cilantro leaves
Tortilla chips, cilantro sprigs, and jalapeño chiles for
   garnish

1 Prepare corn and corn husks: Pull husk back from each ear of corn, making sure to leave husk attached to the corn stem. Break off ears of corn from husks and discard corn silk. In 5-quart saucepot, heat corn and corn husks in *3 inches boiling water* to boiling over high heat. Reduce heat to low; cover and simmer 5 minutes. Drain corn and husks. When corn is cool enough to handle, cut off kernels.

2 In large bowl, mix apricot preserves, lime juice, vegetable oil, salt, black pepper, and chili powder. Add corn kernels, lettuce, red pepper, black beans, lima beans, chopped jalapeño chile, and cilantro; toss gently.

3 Tie leafy ends of each corn husk with a thin strip of husk or string; spread corn husk open to form pocket. Fill pockets with corn salad. If not serving right away, place filled corn husks on large platter; cover and refrigerate.

4 To serve, arrange filled husks on 4 dinner plates; garnish with tortilla chips, cilantro sprigs, and whole jalapeño chiles. *Makes 4 servings.*

Each serving without garnish: About 330 calories, 14 g protein, 62 g carbohydrate, 6 g total fat (1 g saturated), 0 mg cholesterol, 555 mg sodium.

# Tortellini Salad

PREP: 10 MINUTES ᓚ COOK: 20 MINUTES

Tortellini come with a wide variety of fillings. Plain cheese tortellini work well in this salad, but feel free to use other types. If you can find them, try pumpkin-filled tortellini—a typical Italian filling that often has a hint of sweetness in it.

2 packages (9 ounces each) refrigerated or
   1 package (16 ounces) frozen cheese tortellini
¼ cup white wine vinegar
3 tablespoons extravirgin olive oil
1 teaspoon sugar
½ teaspoon salt
¼ teaspoon coarsely ground black pepper
1 medium red pepper, cut into thin strips
1 medium yellow pepper, cut into thin strips
1 medium tomato, seeded and diced
1 jar (6 ounces) marinated artichoke hearts,
   drained and halved
2 bunches arugula or watercress (about 3 cups
   lightly packed), stems trimmed

1 Prepare tortellini as label directs; drain.

2 In large bowl, mix white wine vinegar, olive oil, sugar, salt, and black pepper. Add red and yellow peppers, tomato, artichokes, and tortellini; toss to coat. Cover and refrigerate if not serving right away.

3 Just before serving, set aside a few whole arugula leaves for garnish. Tear remaining arugula into bite-size pieces; toss with tortellini mixture. Garnish with reserved whole arugula leaves. *Makes 6 servings.*

Each serving: About 360 calories, 14 g protein, 46 g carbohydrate, 14 g total fat, (3 g saturated), 40 mg cholesterol, 555 mg sodium.

*Tortellini Salad* ➤

# Szechwan Peanut-Noodle Salad

PREP: 20 MINUTES   COOK: 15 MINUTES

Serve warm or refrigerate to serve cold later. If noodles become too sticky upon standing, toss with a little hot water until of desired consistency.

1 package (16 ounces) linguine or spaghetti
Salt
¼ pound snow peas, strings removed
¾ cup creamy peanut butter
3 tablespoons reduced-sodium soy sauce
1 tablespoon hot Asian sesame oil
1 tablespoon cider vinegar
2 teaspoons grated, peeled fresh ginger
1 medium red pepper, thinly sliced
Dry roasted peanuts and chopped green onion for
   garnish

1 In large saucepot, prepare pasta in *boiling salted water* as label directs.

2 Meanwhile, in 3-quart saucepan, heat snow peas in *1 inch boiling water* to boiling over high heat. Reduce heat to low and simmer 2 minutes or until snow peas are tender-crisp. Rinse snow peas under cold running water to stop the cooking; drain. Cut snow peas into matchstick-thin strips.

3 Drain linguine, reserving *1 cup pasta cooking water*. In large bowl, beat together peanut butter, soy sauce, sesame oil, cider vinegar, ginger, and reserved pasta cooking water until smooth.

4 Add linguine, snow peas, and red pepper to peanut-butter mixture; toss to coat well. Sprinkle with peanuts and green onion if you like. *Makes 4 servings.*

Each serving without garnish: About 760 calories, 30 g protein, 97 g carbohydrate, 30 g total fat (5 g saturated), 0 mg cholesterol, 1075 mg sodium.

# Nutty Couscous Salad

PREP: 15 MINUTES   COOK: 15 MINUTES

1 package (10 ounces) couscous (Moroccan pasta)
1 large navel orange
2 tablespoons vegetable oil
2 tablespoons cider vinegar
½ teaspoon sugar
¼ teaspoon salt
½ cup pitted dates, cut into thirds
3 tablespoons chopped fresh parsley leaves
1 cup dried currants or dark seedless raisins
2 tablespoons coarsely chopped crystallized ginger
4 ounces salted cashews, chopped

1 Prepare couscous as label directs, but do not add margarine or butter.

2 Meanwhile, grate peel and squeeze juice from orange. In large bowl, mix orange peel, orange juice, vegetable oil, cider vinegar, sugar, and salt.

3 Add couscous, dates, parsley, currants, ginger, and chopped cashews to bowl with dressing. Toss to mix well. Cover and refrigerate if not serving right away. *Makes 4 servings.*

Each serving: About 710 calories, 16 g protein, 122 g carbohydrate, 21 g total fat (4 g saturated), 0 mg cholesterol, 345 mg sodium.

## FOOD EDITOR'S TIP

**Q.** What is crystallized ginger? I have found many recipes that call for it and cannot find it in our local store.

**A.** Crystallized or candied ginger has been cooked in a sugar mixture, dried, then coated with sugar. It can be eaten as a confection and is especially good added to desserts, breads, relishes, and chutneys. It also lends a sweet-spicy note to stuffings or grain-based dishes, such as Nutty Couscous Salad (above). Look for it in the baking section of your supermarket where spices are sold.

# Grilled Vegetable & Cracked Wheat Salad

PREP: 15 MINUTES ～ BROIL: 20 TO 30 MINUTES

1 can (14½ ounces) chicken broth or 1¾ cups
    homemade (page 24)
1¼ teaspoons dried thyme leaves
1 cup bulgur (cracked wheat)
Nonstick cooking spray
2 tablespoons olive oil
½ teaspoon salt
½ teaspoon coarsely ground black pepper
1 medium yellow pepper, cut into ¾-inch-wide
    slices
1 medium zucchini (about 8 ounces), halved
    lengthwise and cut crosswise into ¾-inch
    chunks
8 ounces medium mushrooms, halved
1 small eggplant (about 12 ounces), cut lengthwise
    into quarters, then crosswise into ¾-inch-wide
    slices
1 cup frozen peas, thawed
1 small tomato, cut into ½-inch chunks

**1** In 2-cup glass measuring cup, combine chicken broth and *enough water* to equal 2 cups.

**2** In 2-quart saucepan, heat broth mixture and ¼ teaspoon thyme to boiling over high heat. Add bulgur; reduce heat to medium-low. Cover and simmer 10 to 15 minutes or until liquid is absorbed.

**3** Meanwhile, preheat broiler if manufacturer directs. Spray rack in broiling pan with nonstick cooking spray. In medium bowl, mix 1 tablespoon olive oil, ¼ teaspoon salt, ½ teaspoon thyme, and ¼ teaspoon black pepper; add yellow pepper, zucchini, and mushrooms, tossing to coat. Arrange vegetables on rack in broiling pan. Place pan in broiler 5 to 7 inches from source of heat; broil vegetables 10 to 15 minutes or until tender and browned, stirring them occasionally and removing them to large bowl as they are done. Keep vegetables warm.

**4** In same medium bowl, mix remaining 1 tablespoon olive oil, remaining ¼ teaspoon salt, remaining ½ teaspoon thyme, and remaining ¼ teaspoon black pepper; add eggplant, tossing to coat. Arrange eggplant on rack in broiling pan; broil eggplant 10 to 15 minutes or until tender and browned, stirring occasionally. Transfer to large bowl with other vegetables.

**5** Place peas in strainer and run under *very hot tap water* to warm through. Add peas, bulgur, and tomato chunks to bowl with vegetables; toss to mix well. *Makes 4 servings.*

Each serving: About 275 calories, 10 g protein, 44 g carbohydrate, 9 g total fat (1 g saturated), 0 mg cholesterol, 795 mg sodium.

# Panzanella

PREP: 10 TO 15 MINUTES

Panzanella, a rustic bread and vegetable salad, is served with a robust caper and basil dressing. Though it takes only minutes to assemble, you should let the salad stand for a bit before serving so the bread can absorb the dressing.

½ cup olive oil
¼ cup red wine vinegar
¼ cup lightly packed fresh basil leaves, chopped
2 tablespoons capers, drained
½ teaspoon salt
¼ teaspoon coarsely ground black pepper
1 garlic clove, minced
4 medium tomatoes, cut into bite-size pieces
2 medium cucumbers (about 10 ounces each), cut
    into bite-size pieces
1 large yellow pepper, cut into bite-size pieces
1 medium red onion, cut into bite-size pieces
1 loaf (12 ounces) Italian bread, cut into 1-inch
    chunks
½ cup Kalamata olives, pitted and slivered
Fresh basil sprigs for garnish

**1** In large bowl, mix olive oil, red wine vinegar, basil, capers, salt, black pepper, and garlic.

**2** Add tomatoes, cucumbers, yellow pepper, and onion to dressing and toss to coat.

**3** Add bread to vegetable mixture; toss gently to coat with dressing. Top salad with olives. Garnish with basil sprig. *Makes 6 servings.*

Each serving: About 405 calories, 8 g protein, 44 g carbohydrate, 24 g total fat (3 g saturated), 0 mg cholesterol, 870 mg sodium.

# Couscous Salad with Orange-Balsamic Vinaigrette

PREP: 15 MINUTES ∾ COOK: 15 MINUTES

1 cup couscous (Moroccan pasta)
1 can (14½ ounces) chicken broth or 1¾ cups homemade (page 24)
¼ cup olive oil
¼ cup frozen orange-juice concentrate, thawed
¼ cup balsamic vinegar
1 tablespoon Dijon mustard
¼ teaspoon salt
¼ teaspoon coarsely ground black pepper
1 can (15 to 19 ounces) garbanzo beans, rinsed and drained
3 green onions, chopped
½ cup pitted prunes, chopped
1 small bunch spinach (about 8 ounces), tough stems removed
2 large navel oranges
¼ cup sliced almonds, toasted

1 Prepare couscous as label directs, but use broth plus *water* to equal amount of water called for on label and do not add margarine or salt.

2 In large bowl, mix olive oil, orange-juice concentrate, balsamic vinegar, mustard, salt, pepper, and *2 tablespoons water*. Stir in couscous, garbanzo beans, green onions, and prunes; toss well.

3 Reserve several small spinach leaves for garnish. Tear remaining leaves into bite-size pieces and stir into couscous mixture. Cut peel and pith from both oranges. Cut 1 orange into slices; cut each slice in half. Cut remaining orange into bite-size chunks. Stir orange chunks into couscous mixture.

4 Spoon couscous salad into large serving bowl. Garnish with orange slices and reserved spinach leaves. Sprinkle almonds on top. *Makes 6 servings.*

Each serving: About 375 calories, 12 g protein, 53 g carbohydrate, 14 g total fat (2 g saturated), 3 mg cholesterol, 730 mg sodium.

# Couscous with Sun-Dried Tomatoes & Spinach

PREP: 20 MINUTES ∾ COOK: 15 MINUTES

10 sun-dried tomatoes, about 1 ounce (not oil-packed)
1 package (10 ounces) couscous (Moroccan pasta)
2 tablespoons olive oil
2 tablespoons red wine vinegar
½ teaspoon salt
½ teaspoon sugar
1 teaspoon prepared mustard
¼ teaspoon coarsely ground black pepper
1 cup golden raisins
1 large tomato, diced
1 bunch spinach (about 1 pound), tough stems removed and coarsely chopped

1 Place sun-dried tomatoes in small heatproof bowl; pour *1 cup boiling water* over tomatoes. Let stand 5 minutes to soften; drain and chop.

2 Prepare couscous as label directs, but do not add margarine or butter.

3 In medium bowl, mix olive oil, red wine vinegar, salt, sugar, mustard, and pepper. Add raisins, diced fresh tomato, chopped sun-dried tomatoes, spinach, and couscous; toss to mix well. *Makes 4 servings.*

Each serving: About 490 calories, 15 g protein, 94 g carbohydrate, 8 g total fat (1 g saturated), 0 mg cholesterol, 395 mg sodium.

◄ *Couscous Salad with Orange-Balsamic Vinaigrette*

# Fennel & Carrot Salad with Crostini

PREP: 25 MINUTES ～ BROIL: 10 MINUTES

1 jar (7 ounces) roasted red peppers, drained
3 tablespoons olive oil
2 tablespoons white wine vinegar
½ teaspoon salt
¾ teaspoon sugar
½ small head romaine lettuce
1 fennel bulb (about 1 pound), trimmed and cut into thin matchsticks
3 medium carrots, peeled and cut into thin matchsticks
2 medium pears, cut into thin matchsticks
2 cups loosely packed torn frisée or hearts of chicory
8 slices (½ inch thick) Italian bread

1 tablespoon oil from jar of oil-packed sun-dried tomatoes
1 package (8 ounces) part-skim mozzarella cheese, cut into 8 slices
½ teaspoon coarsely ground black pepper
¼ cup slivered oil-packed sun-dried tomatoes

1 For dressing, in blender, at high speed, or in food processor, with knife blade attached, blend roasted red peppers, olive oil, white wine vinegar, salt, and sugar until pureed.

2 Coarsely chop enough romaine leaves to measure 2 cups packed leaves. Line large platter with remaining leaves.

3 In large bowl, toss fennel, carrots, pears, chopped romaine, and frisée with red-pepper dressing.

4 Prepare crostini: Preheat broiler if manufacturer directs. Brush slices of Italian bread with oil from sun-dried tomatoes. Arrange bread on small un-greased cookie sheet; broil until golden on both sides, turning bread once. Place 1 slice of mozzarella on

*Quesadilla Salad*

each slice of bread; sprinkle with black pepper. Broil until mozzarella melts slightly; top with sun-dried tomatoes.

**5** Spoon salad onto lettuce-lined platter; arrange crostini around salad. ***Makes 4 servings.***

Each serving: About 605 calories, 25 g protein, 69 g carbohydrate, 28 g total fat (8 g saturated), 33 mg cholesterol, 1060 mg sodium.

## Quesadilla Salad

PREP: 30 MINUTES ～ COOK: 10 MINUTES

Monterey Jack with jalapeño chiles "heats up" the quesadillas.

2 medium limes
¾ teaspoon chili powder
½ teaspoon ground coriander
½ teaspoon sugar
½ teaspoon salt
4 teaspoons olive oil
1 head romaine lettuce, leaves cut crosswise into ¾-inch-wide strips
1 pint (12 ounces) cherry tomatoes, halved or quartered if large
1 small avocado (about 8 ounces), cut into ½-inch wedges
2 green onions, thinly sliced
8 (6-inch diameter) flour tortillas
6 ounces Monterey Jack cheese with jalapeño chiles, shredded (1½ cups)
Green onions for garnish

**1** From limes, grate ¼ teaspoon peel and squeeze 3 tablespoons juice. In large bowl, mix lime peel, lime juice, chili powder, coriander, sugar, and salt. Whisk in oil until blended.

**2** To large bowl, add lettuce, tomatoes, avocado, and green onions; toss well.

**3** Heat nonstick 10-inch skillet over medium heat until hot. Place 1 tortilla in skillet. Sprinkle with one-fourth of Monterey Jack; top with second tortilla, pressing lightly. Cook quesadilla about 1 minute or until lightly toasted. Turn quesadilla and cook 1 minute longer or until cheese melts. Repeat with remaining tortillas and Monterey Jack.

**4** Cut quesadillas into wedges and serve with salad. Garnish with whole green onions if you like. ***Makes 4 servings.***

Each serving: About 505 calories, 19 g protein, 44 g carbohydrate, 30 g total fat (10 g saturated), 46 mg cholesterol, 850 mg sodium.

## Warm Salmon Salad with Oranges

PREP: 20 MINUTES ～ COOK: 15 MINUTES

1 piece skinless salmon fillet (1 pound)
4 large oranges
2 tablespoons balsamic vinegar
2 tablespoons reduced-sodium soy sauce
2 teaspoons brown sugar
1 tablespoon margarine or butter
1 bunch green onions, cut into 1-inch pieces
2 heads Boston lettuce, separated into leaves
2 small plum tomatoes, diced

**1** With tweezers, remove any small bones from salmon fillet. With knife held in slanting position, almost parallel to cutting surface, slice salmon crosswise into ¼-inch-thick slices.

**2** Cut peel from 3 oranges. Set small strainer over 2-cup measuring cup to catch juices. Holding oranges over strainer, cut segments from oranges between membranes; drop segments into strainer. Set orange segments aside. Squeeze juice from membranes into measuring cup. Squeeze enough juice from remaining orange into measuring cup to equal ¾ cup juice in all. Stir in balsamic vinegar, soy sauce, and brown sugar.

**3** In nonstick 12-inch skillet, heat margarine over medium-high heat until hot; cook salmon slices until golden, carefully turning once during cooking, 1 to 2 minutes; transfer to plate. In drippings in same skillet, cook green onions, stirring frequently, until golden; stir in orange-juice mixture; heat to boiling; boil 1 minute.

**4** Arrange lettuce, orange segments, and salmon on 4 dinner plates. Spoon warm green-onion mixture over salmon. Top with diced tomatoes. ***Makes 4 servings.***

Each serving: About 350 calories, 26 g protein, 28 g carbohydrate, 16 g total fat (3 g saturated), 67 mg cholesterol, 410 mg sodium.

# Crab & Avocado Salad

1 cup chicken broth, canned or homemade (page 24)
⅔ cup couscous (Moroccan pasta)
1 small cucumber, halved lengthwise, seeded, and diced
1 medium tomato, seeded and diced
1 container (16 ounces) lump crabmeat, picked over to remove any cartilage
1 tablespoon plus 1 teaspoon vegetable oil
1 small onion, minced
2 tablespoons dry white wine
2 tablespoons light mayonnaise
1 tablespoon chopped fresh parsley leaves
⅛ teaspoon coarsely ground black pepper
½ teaspoon salt
1 medium avocado, peeled and cut lengthwise into thin slices
8 ounces mixed baby greens or mixed salad greens
2 teaspoons white wine vinegar

1 In 1-quart saucepan, heat chicken broth to boiling over high heat. Stir in couscous; cover and remove saucepan from heat. Let couscous stand 5 minutes. Remove cover; let couscous cool slightly.

2 In medium bowl, combine couscous with cucumber and tomato. Place crabmeat in another bowl

3 In nonstick small skillet, heat 1 teaspoon vegetable oil over medium-high heat until hot. Add onion and cook until tender and very lightly browned; stir in white wine. Cool slightly. Gently stir onion mixture, mayonnaise, parsley, pepper, and ¼ teaspoon salt into crabmeat in bowl.

4 Assemble salads: Mound one-fourth of couscous mixture in center of a dinner plate. Top each mound of couscous with one-fourth of avocado slices, then one-fourth of crab mixture. Repeat with remaining couscous mixture, avocado, and crab mixture for 3 more salads.

5 Place mixed baby greens in large bowl; toss with white wine vinegar, remaining 1 tablespoon vegetable oil, and remaining ¼ teaspoon salt. Arrange greens around crab salads. *Makes 4 servings.*

Each serving: About 425 calories, 30 g protein, 37 g carbohydrate, 17 g total fat (3 g saturated), 113 mg cholesterol, 955 mg sodium.

# Grilled Portobello & Prosciutto Salad

Grilling (or broiling) brings out the hearty flavor of the thick, meaty mushrooms, served on a bed of arugula with a balsamic vinegar dressing. To make the Parmesan curls, start with a small wedge of Parmesan. Draw a vegetable peeler along one side of the wedge to shave off thin curls of cheese.

2 bunches arugula (about 8 ounces), tough stems removed
2 tablespoons balsamic vinegar
2 tablespoons olive oil
2 tablespoons minced shallots
2 tablespoons chopped fresh parsley leaves
¼ teaspoon salt
¼ teaspoon coarsely ground black pepper
4 portobello mushrooms (about 1½ pounds), stems discarded
8 ounces thinly sliced prosciutto
½ cup Parmesan curls (1 ounce)

1 Prepare outdoor grill for barbecuing. Arrange arugula on platter.

2 In small bowl, mix balsamic vinegar, olive oil, shallots, parsley, salt, and pepper until blended.

---

### ▮ FOOD EDITOR'S TIP ▮

**Q.** What are portobello mushrooms? What's the best way to cook them?

**A.** Portobellos (or portabellas) are large brown Italian mushrooms, called cremini. With caps that measure up to 6 inches in diameter, they're prized for their delicious, almost meaty flesh and rich flavor. Sold whole, as caps only, or sliced and packaged, they're best grilled or roasted whole (brush with olive oil and broil 4 to 5 minutes each side) or sautéed in a little olive oil.

Look for portobellos with a smooth, fresh appearance and dry surface; refrigerate and use within several days. To keep them longer, place in a brown paper bag in the refrigerator or, if packaged, leave them in their tray but remove the plastic wrap and rewrap with paper towels. Before using whole portobellos, trim off the tough end of their stems.

**3** Place mushrooms, top side up, on grill over medium heat. Brush mushroom tops with 1 tablespoon dressing. Grill 4 minutes. Turn mushrooms and brush with 2 tablespoons dressing. Grill 5 minutes longer or until tender.

**4** Thickly slice mushrooms and arrange on arugula. Spoon remaining dressing over salad. Arrange prosciutto on platter with salad. Top with Parmesan curls. *Makes 4 servings.*

TO BROIL: Preheat broiler if manufacturer directs. Follow recipe step 2. Place mushrooms, top side up, on rack in broiling pan. Brush mushroom tops with 1 tablespoon dressing. Place pan in broiler at closest position to source of heat; broil mushrooms 4 minutes. Turn mushrooms over; brush with 2 more tablespoons dressing and broil 5 minutes longer or until tender. Complete recipe step 4.

Each serving: About 200 calories, 18 g protein, 11 g carbohydrate, 11 g total fat (3 g saturated), 38 mg cholesterol, 885 mg sodium.

# *Warm Shrimp & Bulgur Salad with Artichokes*

PREP: 45 MINUTES ～ COOK: 50 MINUTES

2 large artichokes (about 12 ounces each)
¼ cup fresh lemon juice
1 cup chicken broth, canned or homemade
  (page 24)
¾ cup bulgur (cracked wheat)
4 sun-dried tomatoes (not oil-packed)
1 pound large shrimp, shelled and deveined
3 teaspoons margarine or butter
⅛ teaspoon plus ¼ teaspoon salt
1 cup frozen peas, thawed
1 medium tomato, diced
1 green onion, thinly sliced
8 ounces mixed baby greens or mixed salad greens
  (about 6 cups loosely packed)
2 tablespoons seasoned rice vinegar

**1** With sharp knife, cut 1 inch across tops of artichokes. Cut off and discard stems. Pull outer dark outer leaves from artichoke bottoms. With kitchen shears, trim thorny tips of leaves. Rinse artichokes well under cold running water.

**2** In 5-quart saucepot, heat 2 tablespoons lemon juice and *1 inch water* to boiling over high heat. Place artichokes on stem ends in boiling water; heat to boiling. Reduce heat to low; cover and simmer 30 to 40 minutes or until knife inserted in center goes through bottom easily.

**3** Meanwhile, in 2-quart saucepan, heat chicken broth and *½ cup water* to boiling over high heat; add bulgur. Reduce heat to low; cover and simmer 15 minutes or until bulgur is tender and liquid is absorbed. Transfer bulgur to large bowl.

**4** Place sun-dried tomatoes in small heatproof bowl; pour *1 cup boiling water* over tomatoes; let stand 15 minutes to soften. Drain dried tomatoes; chop and set aside.

**5** Set aside 8 shrimp for garnish; cut remaining shrimp into ½-inch pieces. In nonstick 10-inch skillet, heat 1 teaspoon margarine or butter over medium-high heat until hot. Add whole shrimp and ⅛ teaspoon salt and cook, stirring frequently, until shrimp are golden and turn opaque throughout; transfer to a plate and set aside.

**6** In same skillet, heat remaining 2 teaspoons margarine until hot; cook shrimp pieces and remaining ¼ teaspoon salt, stirring frequently, until shrimp are golden and turn opaque throughout; transfer to bowl with bulgur. Add peas, fresh tomato, chopped dried tomatoes, green onion, and remaining 2 tablespoons lemon juice; stir to mix well.

**7** In medium bowl, toss mixed baby greens with rice vinegar. When artichokes are done, cut each lengthwise in half. With spoon, scoop out fuzzy choke from center of each half; discard. Arrange mixed baby greens and artichoke halves on 4 dinner plates. Spoon bulgur mixture onto artichoke halves. Garnish each plate with 2 whole shrimp. *Makes 4 servings.*

Each serving: About 320 calories, 28 g protein, 41 g carbohydrate, 6 g total fat (1 g saturated), 140 mg cholesterol, 930 mg sodium.

# Salmon Salad with Caper-Dill Dressing

PREP: 20 MINUTES ~ COOK: 40 MINUTES

Chunks of salmon, potato, and hard-cooked eggs, coated with a tangy caper, mustard, and dill dressing. For easy serving, this springtime salad can be prepared ahead and assembled at the last minute, but it's best when cooked, mixed, and served right away.

Caper-Dill Dressing (at right)
1 piece skinless salmon fillet (1 pound)
1 teaspoon whole black peppercorns
1 pound small red potatoes
1 pound asparagus, trimmed and cut into 2-inch
    pieces
1 medium head green-leaf lettuce, torn into bite-
    size pieces
2 large hard-cooked eggs, shelled and each cut into
    quarters

1 Prepare Caper-Dill Dressing; set aside.

2 With tweezers, remove any small bones from salmon fillet. In 10-inch skillet, heat *1 inch water* to boiling over high heat. Add salmon fillet and peppercorns; heat to boiling. Reduce heat to low; cover and simmer 8 to 10 minutes or until salmon turns opaque throughout. Drain salmon; refrigerate until ready to assemble salad.

3 Meanwhile, in 3-quart saucepan, heat unpeeled potatoes and *enough water to cover* to boiling over high heat. Reduce heat to low; cover and simmer until potatoes are fork-tender, 15 to 20 minutes. Drain; cut each potato into quarters. While potatoes are still warm, toss with ¼ cup Caper-Dill Dressing.

4 In 2-quart saucepan, heat asparagus and *1 inch water* to boiling. Reduce heat to low; simmer, uncovered, 5 minutes or until asparagus is tender-crisp. Drain; refrigerate until ready to assemble salad.

5 To serve, pour ¼ cup Caper-Dill Dressing into medium bowl. Add potatoes and asparagus; toss to coat. Divide lettuce among 4 dinner plates; top with potato mixture, egg quarters, and chunks of salmon. Drizzle any remaining dressing over salads. *Makes 4 servings.*

CAPER-DILL DRESSING: From *2 large lemons*, grate 1 teaspoon peel and squeeze ⅓ cup juice. In small bowl, combine lemon juice and lemon peel with *2 tablespoons chopped capers, 2 tablespoons Dijon mustard with seeds, 2 tablespoons chopped fresh dill, 1 teaspoon sugar, ½ teaspoon salt*, and *¼ teaspoon coarsely ground black pepper*. With wire whisk, slowly beat in *¼ cup olive oil* until mixture thickens slightly.

Each serving: About 515 calories, 32 g protein, 30 g carbohydrate, 29 g total fat (5 g saturated), 173 mg cholesterol, 780 mg sodium.

# Shrimp, Orange & Jicama Salad

PREP: 45 MINUTES ~ COOK: 1 TO 2 MINUTES

Jicama, a crisp, slightly sweet root vegetable, is commonly used in Mexican cooking. Substituting for it is difficult since its particular combination of texture and flavor aren't easily matched.

1 pound large shrimp, shelled and deveined, cut
    horizontally in half
¾ teaspoon salt
2 medium navel oranges
1 medium jicama (about 1¼ pounds), peeled and
    cut into 1½" by ¼" sticks
2 bunches watercress (about 8 ounces), tough
    stems removed
1 large lime
1 cup loosely packed fresh cilantro leaves
¼ cup light mayonnaise
1 teaspoon sugar
¼ teaspoon ground red pepper (cayenne)
½ cup plain low-fat yogurt

1 In 3-quart saucepan, heat *3 inches water* to boiling over high heat. Add shrimp and ½ teaspoon salt; heat to boiling. Cook 1 minute or until shrimp turn opaque throughout. Drain shrimp, rinse with cold running water to cool slightly, and drain well. Refrigerate until ready to use.

**2** Cut peel and pith from oranges. Cut out segments between membranes. Place segments (do not add juice) in large salad bowl with jicama and watercress; set aside.

**3** From lime, grate 1 teaspoon peel and squeeze 2 tablespoons juice. In food processor, with knife blade attached, or in blender, at medium speed, blend lime peel, lime juice, cilantro leaves, mayonnaise, sugar, ground red pepper, and remaining ¼ teaspoon salt until blended, about 30 seconds. Add yogurt, pulsing just until blended.

**4** Add shrimp to bowl with jicama mixture; toss with yogurt dressing. *Makes 4 servings.*

Each serving: About 250 calories, 23 g protein, 28 g carbohydrate, 5 g total fat (1 g saturated), 141 mg cholesterol, 485 mg sodium.

# Spicy Garlic-Sautéed Shrimp Salad

**PREP: 25 MINUTES ∿ COOK: 8 TO 10 MINUTES**

One of the most labor-intensive tasks of any shrimp dish is shelling and deveining. You can buy already-cleaned shrimp (for a price), or you can trim prep time by starting with larger—and thus *fewer*— shrimp. If you use large or jumbo shrimp, just halve the shrimp horizontally (and then halve again crosswise, if necessary) to approximate the size of medium shrimp.

3 tablespoons vegetable oil
1 pound medium shrimp, shelled and deveined
1 garlic clove, minced
¼ teaspoon ground red pepper (cayenne)
½ teaspoon salt
2 tablespoons fresh lemon juice
1 teaspoon prepared mustard
¾ teaspoon sugar
¾ pound mixed baby greens or mixed salad greens
¼ cup loosely packed fresh cilantro leaves

**1** In nonstick 12-inch skillet, heat 1 tablespoon vegetable oil over medium-high heat until hot. Add shrimp, garlic, ground red pepper, and ¼ teaspoon salt, stirring occasionally until shrimp turn opaque throughout.

**2** In large bowl, combine lemon juice, mustard, sugar, and remaining ¼ teaspoon salt. Slowly beat in remaining 2 tablespoons vegetable oil until mixture thickens slightly. Add baby greens and cilantro leaves; toss to coat.

**3** Divide salad among 4 dinner plates; top with shrimp. *Makes 4 servings.*

Each serving: About 220 calories, 20 g protein, 6 g carbohydrate, 12 g total fat (2 g saturated), 140 mg cholesterol, 460 mg sodium.

# Sicilian-Style Swordfish with Pasta

PREP: 15 MINUTES PLUS 30 MINUTES TO MARINATE
GRILL: 8 TO 10 MINUTES

Chunks of grilled fish tossed with pasta in a light vinaigrette made with fresh mint and tomato.

3 medium tomatoes, cut into ½-inch chunks
   (about 2½ cups)
¼ cup chopped fresh mint
1 tablespoon red wine vinegar
1 small garlic clove, minced
3 tablespoons olive oil
Salt
½ teaspoon coarsely ground black pepper
1 teaspoon grated orange peel
1 swordfish steak, 1 inch thick (about 1 pound)
1 pound penne or bow-tie pasta

1 In large bowl, combine tomatoes, mint, vinegar, garlic, 2 tablespoons olive oil, ½ teaspoon salt, and ¼ teaspoon pepper. Cover and let stand 30 minutes.

2 In cup, combine orange peel, remaining 1 tablespoon olive oil, ¼ teaspoon salt, and remaining ¼ teaspoon pepper; brush on both sides of swordfish.

3 Place swordfish on grill over medium heat; cook 8 to 10 minutes or until just opaque throughout, turning once. Transfer swordfish to cutting board and cut into ¾-inch pieces.

4 Meanwhile, prepare pasta in *boiling salted water* as label directs. Drain.

5 Add swordfish and pasta to tomato mixture; toss. *Makes 6 servings.*

Each serving: About 440 calories, 25 g protein, 60 g carbohydrate, 11 g total fat (2 g saturated), 29 mg cholesterol, 340 mg sodium.

# Tuna & White Beans with Smoked Gouda

PREP: 15 MINUTES

Try another smoked cheese here in place of Gouda, but choose one of slicing consistency, such as smoked Cheddar or Jarlsberg.

1 large lemon
1 can (12 ounces) tuna in oil
2 tablespoons olive oil
1 tablespoon mustard
1 teaspoon coarsely ground black pepper
1 head romaine lettuce, separated into
   leaves
1 bunch arugula (about 4 ounces), stems trimmed
2 cans (16 to 19 ounces each) white kidney beans
   (cannellini), rinsed and drained
3 small tomatoes, cut into thin wedges
½ small red onion, thinly sliced
3 ounces smoked Gouda cheese, thinly sliced and
   then slivered

1 Grate peel from lemon; reserve for garnish. Squeeze ¼ cup juice. Drain oil from tuna into large bowl; add lemon juice, olive oil, mustard, and pepper and beat until blended.

2 Arrange romaine lettuce and arugula on platter; drizzle with half of lemon-juice mixture. To lemon-juice mixture remaining in bowl, add tuna, white kidney beans, tomatoes, and onion; toss to coat.

3 Arrange tuna mixture over lettuce and arugula on platter. Top with slivered Gouda. Garnish with grated lemon peel. *Makes 6 servings.*

Each serving: About 415 calories, 29 g protein, 25 g carbohydrate, 22 g total fat (5 g saturated), 54 mg cholesterol, 900 mg sodium.

# CAESAR SALAD

The Caesar Salad—created in 1924 by Italian chef Caesar Cardini in Tijuana, Mexico—has weathered the storms of food fashion and remains one of the most popular salads on restaurant menus. It has been altered over the years to reflect modern concerns with the use of uncooked eggs (the original recipe called for a coddled egg; later incarnations of the recipe used a raw egg yolk in the dressing). Caesar Salad has also been dressed up with all manner of other ingredients that push it into the category of main-dish salad. What follows is a standard recipe for a Caesar Salad with suggestions for what you can add to it to make it a main dish.

PREP: 10 MINUTES

*3 tablespoons olive oil*
*2 tablespoons mayonnaise*
*1 tablespoon Dijon mustard*
*1 tablespoon fresh lemon juice*
*½ teaspoon anchovy paste*
*1 garlic clove, finely minced*
*⅓ cup coarsely grated Parmesan cheese*
*1 medium head romaine lettuce*
*1 medium head red-leaf lettuce*
*1 medium cucumber*

1 In large bowl, mix olive oil, mayonnaise, mustard, lemon juice, anchovy paste, garlic, and 2 tablespoons Parmesan.

2 Into dressing in large bowl, tear romaine and red-leaf lettuces into bite-size pieces. With vegetable peeler, remove several strips of skin from cucumber, leaving some green for attractive look. Thinly slice cucumber. Add cucumber slices to bowl; gently toss to mix.

3 To serve, arrange salad on 4 dinner plates. Sprinkle salad with remaining Parmesan. Makes 4 servings.

**Beef Caesar Salad** Preheat broiler if manufacturer directs. Place *1 beef flank steak (about 1 pound)* on rack in broiling pan; sprinkle with *¼ teaspoon salt* and *½ teaspoon coarsely ground black pepper.* With broiling pan at closest position to source of heat, broil steak 10 to 12 minutes for rare or until of desired doneness, turning steak once. Transfer

*Beef Caesar Salad*

steak to cutting board. Cut steak into strips and place on top of dressed salad.

Each serving with beef: About 405 calories, 28 g protein, 8 g carbohydrate, 29 g total fat (8 g saturated), 66 mg cholesterol, 515 mg sodium.

**Chicken Caesar Salad** Preheat broiler if manufacturer directs. Arrange *1 pound chicken cutlets* on rack in broiling pan. Place pan in broiler at closest position to source of heat; broil chicken, without turning, 5 to 7 minutes or until it loses its pink color throughout. Slice chicken and place on top of dressed salad.

Each serving with chicken: About 360 calories, 33 g protein, 8 g carbohydrate, 21 g total fat (4 g saturated), 82 mg cholesterol, 370 mg sodium.

**Shrimp Caesar Salad** Shell and devein *1 pound medium shrimp.* In 4-quart saucepan, heat *2 inches water* to boiling over high heat. Add shrimp and *1 teaspoon salt;* cook 1 minute or until shrimp turn opaque throughout. Drain shrimp. Serve warm on the dressed salad or rinse under cold running water to cool and drain again before placing on salad.

Each serving with shrimp: About 315 calories, 25 g protein, 9 g carbohydrate, 20 g total fat (4 g saturated), 149 mg cholesterol, 585 mg sodium.

## Grilled Chicken &
## Mango Salad

PREP: 15 MINUTES ∼ GRILL: 5 TO 7 MINUTES

If mangoes are out of season, use 4 medium
nectarines instead. Cut them into thin wedges.

1 large lemon
¼ cup apricot preserves
¼ cup olive oil
½ teaspoon salt
1 pound chicken cutlets
½ teaspoon coarsely ground black pepper
2 medium mangoes (about 10 ounces each), peeled
   and cut into thin strips
2 large celery stalks, thinly sliced
1 bunch spinach, tough stems removed

1 From lemon, grate ½ teaspoon peel and squeeze
¼ cup juice. In large bowl, stir lemon juice, apricot
preserves, olive oil, and salt until blended. Transfer
2 tablespoons lemon-juice mixture to medium bowl.

---

## FOR THE FRESHEST SALAD GREENS

If you pick greens carefully, then store them properly, most will keep fresh and crisp in the fridge for
up to four days (delicate greens, such as butterhead
lettuce, arugula, and mâche, are best used within a
day or two). For the tastiest salad:

**SHOPPING** Look for fresh, crisp greens. Pass up any
with withered leaves, brown or yellow edges, or
slimy spots. Salad greens are highly perishable, so
buy at a market that keeps them under refrigera-
tion. With bagged greens, check the "sell by" date
for optimum freshness.

**CLEANING** Greens that come wrapped in cello-
phane should be stored in the wrapper, then
cleaned when you're ready to use them. Otherwise,
clean before storing, discarding any bruised, dis-
colored, or wilted leaves. *Iceberg lettuce:* Hit stem
end on counter; twist and lift out core. Rinse core
end with running cold water, then invert head and
let drain. *Leaf lettuce, romaine, Boston, Bibb, curly
endive*: Cut off bottom core and wash leaves under
running cold water. *Spinach, watercress, arugula*
(and other greens with small leaves): Swish leaves
around in a large bowl of cold water to remove any
dirt or sand; let the debris settle in the bottom of
the bowl and lift out the greens carefully. Repeat
until no debris collects in bowl. Break off and discard tough stems. Hydroponic greens and others
sold attached to their roots keep best refrigerated, with the roots immersed in a glass of water or
wrapped in damp paper towels and covered with a
plastic bag.

**DRYING** Excess moisture dilutes the salad dressing
if you're serving greens right away, and will speed
deterioration if you're storing them. Place washed

greens on a clean towel and gently pat dry. Or
use a salad spinner—easier, quicker, and just as
thorough.

**STORAGE** Wrap dry greens in a damp cloth towel
or between layers of damp paper towels, and place
in a plastic bag or in an airtight container in the
refrigerator crisper.

**PREPARATION** Tear delicate greens by hand (don't
cut with a knife) to avoid bruising. Other greens
are also best torn, but can be cut as long as you use
a knife with a stainless steel blade (carbon steel can
cause "rusty" discoloration and alter the flavor).
Toss with dressing just before serving and use only
enough to lightly coat the leaves.

**2** Add chicken cutlets, lemon peel, and pepper to medium bowl with lemon-juice mixture; toss to coat.

**3** Prepare outdoor grill for barbecuing.

**4** Place chicken cutlets on grill over medium heat; grill about 5 minutes or until chicken is fork-tender and loses its pink color throughout, turning chicken occasionally.

**5** Cut each chicken cutlet into several pieces. Add chicken, mangoes, celery, and spinach to large bowl with lemon-juice mixture; toss to coat. *Makes 4 servings.*

TO BROIL: Complete steps 1 and 2 as above. Preheat broiler if manufacturer directs. Arrange chicken cutlets on rack in broiling pan. Place pan in broiler at closest position to source of heat; broil chicken, without turning, 5 to 7 minutes or until it loses its pink color throughout. Cut chicken and toss with other ingredients as above in step 5.

Each serving: About 380 calories, 29 g protein, 34 g carbohydrate, 15 g total fat (2 g saturated), 66 mg cholesterol, 440 mg sodium.

# Tuna & Artichoke Salad with Feta Cheese

PREP: 15 MINUTES ⌒ COOK: 20 MINUTES

Mild goat cheese would make a nice substitute for the feta.

8 ounces wagon wheels or rotelle pasta
2 jars (6 ounces each) marinated artichoke hearts
2 tablespoons white wine vinegar
2 medium tomatoes, cut into wedges
½ cup Kalamata olives, pitted and coarsely chopped
1 can (12 ounces) tuna in water, drained and separated into chunks
1 bag (10 ounces) prewashed spinach
4 ounces feta cheese, crumbled (1 cup)
¼ teaspoon coarsely ground black pepper

**1** In large saucepot, prepare pasta in *boiling water* as label directs, but do not add salt to water. Drain pasta and rinse with cold water; transfer to large bowl.

**2** Drain artichoke hearts, reserving ¼ cup marinade. Stir white wine vinegar into reserved marinade.

**3** To bowl with pasta, add tomatoes, olives, artichokes, reserved marinade mixture, and tuna. Toss gently.

**4** Arrange spinach leaves on 4 dinner plates. Spoon pasta salad onto spinach leaves. Top with feta cheese and sprinkle with pepper. *Makes 4 servings.*

Each serving: About 550 calories, 39 g protein, 58 g carbohydrate, 19 g total fat (6 g saturated), 58 mg cholesterol, 1400 mg sodium.

# Smoked Turkey & Potato Salad

PREP: 10 MINUTES ⌒ COOK: 25 MINUTES

1 pound small red potatoes
⅓ cup light mayonnaise
⅓ cup light sour cream
¼ cup milk
2 tablespoons Dijon mustard
¼ teaspoon salt
2 green onions, chopped
12 ounces smoked turkey, in one piece, cut into bite-size chunks
2 medium celery stalks, thinly sliced
1 small red pepper, cut into 1-inch pieces

**1** In 2-quart saucepan, heat potatoes and *enough water to cover* to boiling over high heat. Reduce heat to low; cover and simmer 15 minutes or until potatoes are fork-tender, drain.

**2** Meanwhile, in large bowl, mix mayonnaise, sour cream, milk, mustard, salt, and green onions until blended. Stir in turkey, celery, and red pepper.

**3** When potatoes are cool enough to handle, cut unpeeled potatoes into bite-size pieces; gently stir into turkey mixture. *Makes 6 servings.*

Each serving: About 200 calories, 14 g protein, 20 g carbohydrate, 7 g total fat (2 g saturated), 35 mg cholesterol, 925 mg sodium.

# Tuscan Tuna Salad

PREP: 25 MINUTES ~ COOK: 10 MINUTES

Homemade garlic croutons and crunchy green beans give new style to this Italian favorite.

1 tablespoon plus ¼ cup olive oil
4 ounces (half 8-ounce long loaf) Italian bread, cut into 1-inch cubes
2 large garlic cloves, crushed with side of chef's knife
8 ounces green beans, trimmed
¼ cup red-wine vinegar
2 tablespoons capers, drained and chopped
1 teaspoon sugar
1 teaspoon Dijon mustard
½ teaspoon salt
¼ teaspoon coarsely ground black pepper
1 can (12 ounces) solid white tuna in water, drained and broken into large pieces
1 can (16 to 19 ounces) white kidney beans (cannellini), rinsed and drained
2 tomatoes, each cut into 8 wedges
1 head green-leaf lettuce, torn into 2-inch pieces
½ small head chicory, torn into 2-inch pieces
1 small red onion, cut in half and thinly sliced

1 In nonstick 12-inch skillet, heat 1 tablespoon olive oil over medium heat. Add bread cubes and garlic and cook, stirring occasionally, until bread is lightly browned. Remove skillet from heat; discard garlic.

2 In 2-quart saucepan, heat green beans in *1 inch boiling water* to boiling over high heat. Reduce heat to low; simmer 5 to 10 minutes or until beans are tender-crisp. Drain and rinse beans under cold running water to cool slightly.

3 In large salad bowl, mix red wine vinegar, capers, sugar, mustard, salt, pepper, and remaining ¼ cup olive oil until blended.

4 To dressing in bowl, add tuna, white kidney beans, tomatoes, lettuce, chicory, red onion, green beans, and croutons; toss to serve. *Makes 4 servings.*

Each serving: About 520 calories, 35 g protein, 50 g carbohydrate, 21 g total fat (3 g saturated), 33 mg cholesterol, 1035 mg sodium.

# Chicken & Roasted Potato Salad

PREP: 20 MINUTES ~ COOK: 25 MINUTES

10 small red potatoes (about 1¼ pounds), halved
3 tablespoons olive oil
Salt
1½ cups penne or corkscrew pasta (4 ounces)
4 large skinless, boneless chicken-breast halves (about 1½ pounds), cut into 1-inch-wide strips
½ teaspoon coarsely ground black pepper
1 medium lemon
½ teaspoon sugar
3 medium plum tomatoes, each cut into 8 wedges
½ cup coarsely chopped watercress
½ cup Kalamata olives, pitted and sliced
4 ounces feta cheese, crumbled (1 cup)

1 Preheat oven to 450°F. In 9" by 9" metal baking pan, toss potatoes with 1 tablespoon olive oil and ¼ teaspoon salt. Roast potatoes 25 minutes or until golden and tender, turning potatoes with pancake turner.

2 Meanwhile, in large saucepot, prepare pasta in *boiling salted water* as label directs; drain.

3 In nonstick 10-inch skillet, heat 1 tablespoon olive oil over medium-high heat until hot. Add chicken and ¼ teaspoon pepper, stirring occasionally, until chicken is tender and loses its pink color throughout.

4 From lemon, grate peel and squeeze 2 tablespoons juice. In large bowl, mix lemon peel, lemon juice, sugar, remaining 1 tablespoon olive oil, ½ teaspoon salt, and remaining ¼ teaspoon pepper.

5 To bowl with lemon dressing, add roasted potatoes, pasta, chicken, tomatoes, watercress, olives, and feta; toss to coat well.

6 To serve, arrange chicken salad on platter. *Makes 6 servings.*

Each serving: About 425 calories, 33 g protein, 35 g carbohydrate, 16 g total fat (5 g saturated), 83 mg cholesterol, 855 mg sodium.

◄ *Tuscan Tuna Salad*

# Smoked Turkey & Raspberry Salad

PREP: 20 MINUTES

3 large navel oranges
1 large bunch spinach (about 1¼ pounds), tough
   stems trimmed, torn into bite-size pieces
1 small red onion, thinly sliced
12 ounces smoked turkey breast, in one piece, cut
   into bite-size chunks
½ pint raspberries
2 tablespoons raspberry vinegar or red wine
   vinegar
2 tablespoons orange marmalade
2 teaspoons Dijon mustard
¼ teaspoon salt
¼ teaspoon coarsely ground black pepper
2 tablespoons olive oil

1 Grate peel from 1 orange; squeeze juice to measure 2 tablespoons. Peel and section remaining oranges.

2 In large bowl, toss spinach with onion. Top with turkey chunks, orange sections, and raspberries.

3 In small bowl, combine orange peel, orange juice, raspberry vinegar, marmalade, mustard, salt, and pepper. Slowly beat in olive oil until dressing thickens slightly. Drizzle dressing over salad. *Makes 4 servings.*

Each serving: About 285 calories, 22 g protein, 29 g carbohydrate, 10 g total fat (2 g saturated), 36 mg cholesterol, 1090 mg sodium.

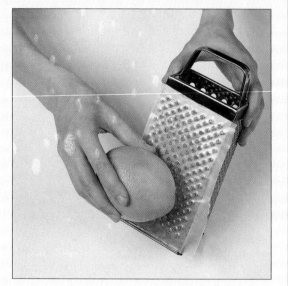

## GRATING ORANGE PEEL

*To grate orange (and lemon) peel without messy scraping and jammed grater holes, press a piece of waxed paper or plastic wrap over the fine side of grater first. When you're finished, the peel will come right off with the paper.*

# Ginger-Fried Chicken Salad

PREP: 10 MINUTES  ~  COOK: 15 MINUTES

8 ounces bean sprouts
2 tablespoons vegetable oil
1 piece (2" by ½") fresh ginger, peeled and cut into
   2-inch-long slivers
1 large green onion, cut into 2-inch-long slivers
4 large skinless, boneless chicken thighs (about
   1½ pounds), cut into 1-inch pieces
½ teaspoon salt
3 tablespoons seasoned rice vinegar
1 tablespoon soy sauce
¼ teaspoon crushed red pepper
1 large head romaine lettuce, torn into bite-size
   pieces
1 large red pepper, cut into 2" by ¼" strips
1 bunch radishes, each cut into quarters

1 In 3-quart saucepan, heat *1 quart water* to boiling over high heat. Stir in bean sprouts and cook 1 minute; drain.

2 Meanwhile, in nonstick 12-inch skillet, heat 1 tablespoon vegetable oil over medium-high heat until hot. Add ginger and green onion and cook until lightly browned. With slotted spoon, transfer green-onion mixture to bowl.

3 In oil in same skillet, cook chicken and salt over medium-high heat until chicken loses its pink color throughout, stirring often.

4 While chicken is cooking, in small bowl, mix rice vinegar, soy sauce, crushed red pepper, and remaining 1 tablespoon vegetable oil. Set dressing aside.

5 Place lettuce in large serving bowl. Top lettuce with bean sprouts, red pepper, radishes, then chicken; sprinkle with green-onion mixture.

6 To serve, pour dressing over salad; toss to coat well. *Makes 4 servings.*

Each serving: About 330 calories, 39 g protein, 13 g carbohydrate, 14 g total fat (3 g saturated), 141 mg cholesterol, 935 mg sodium.

# Smoked Chicken, Nectarine & Wheatberry Salad

PREP: 20 MINUTES PLUS OVERNIGHT FOR SOAKING
COOK: 1 HOUR

Wheatberries, also known as whole-grain wheat, can be found in health food stores or in some supermarkets. Note that they must be soaked overnight before using, so plan accordingly.

1½ cups wheatberries
2 tablespoons soy sauce
2 tablespoons fresh lemon juice
2 tablespoons peach or apricot preserves
1 boneless smoked chicken breast (about
    12 ounces), skinned and cut into ½-inch-thick
    slices
¾ cup coarsely chopped watercress leaves
2 medium nectarines, cut into ½-inch chunks
1 medium celery stalk, thinly sliced

1 In large bowl, place wheatberries and *enough water to cover* by 2 inches. Soak wheatberries overnight.

2 Drain wheatberries. In 4-quart saucepan, heat wheatberries and *7 cups water* to boiling over high heat. Reduce heat to low; cover and simmer 1 hour or until wheatberries are just tender but still firm to the bite. Drain wheatberries; rinse with cold water; set aside.

3 In large bowl, stir soy sauce, lemon juice, and peach preserves until blended. Add wheatberries, smoked chicken, watercress, nectarines, and celery; toss to coat. If not serving salad right away, cover and refrigerate. *Makes 4 servings.*

Each serving: About 415 calories, 24 g protein, 67 g carbohydrate, 9 g total fat (2 g saturated), 48 mg cholesterol, 875 mg sodium.

# Warm Chicken-Breast, Potato & Arugula Salad

PREP: 15 MINUTES  ∽  COOK: 25 MINUTES

2 bunches arugula or watercress (about 8 ounces),
    stems trimmed
1 pound small red potatoes, halved
2 tablespoons olive oil
1 large red pepper, cut into ½-inch-wide strips
1 large yellow pepper, cut into ½-inch-wide strips
¾ teaspoon salt
4 medium skinless, boneless chicken-breast halves
    (about 1¼ pounds), cut crosswise into ½-inch-
    wide strips
3 tablespoons red wine vinegar
1 teaspoon Dijon mustard
¾ teaspoon sugar
¼ teaspoon coarsely ground black pepper

1 Use 1 bunch arugula to line platter; set remaining bunch aside.

2 In 3-quart saucepan, heat potatoes and *enough water to cover* to boiling over high heat. Reduce heat to low; cover and simmer 8 to 10 minutes or until potatoes are fork-tender; drain.

3 Meanwhile, in nonstick 12-inch skillet, heat 1 tablespoon olive oil over medium-high heat until hot. Add red and yellow peppers and ¼ teaspoon salt and cook, stirring frequently, until tender-crisp. With slotted spoon, transfer pepper strips to bowl.

4 To oil in same skillet, add chicken and ¼ teaspoon salt and cook, stirring frequently, until chicken begins to brown and loses its pink color throughout.

5 In small bowl, mix red wine vinegar, mustard, sugar, black pepper, remaining 1 tablespoon olive oil, and remaining ¼ teaspoon salt until blended.

6 Return pepper strips to skillet with chicken. Add vinegar mixture, potatoes, and reserved arugula, tossing to coat; heat through. To serve, spoon warm chicken salad over leaves on platter. *Makes 4 servings.*

Each serving: About 335 calories, 36 g protein, 26 g carbohydrate, 9 g total fat (1 g saturated), 82 mg cholesterol, 575 mg sodium.

## Black & White Bean Salad with Lemon-Basil Vinaigrette

PREP: 15 MINUTES

Lemon-Basil Vinaigrette (below)
1 small head green-leaf lettuce, torn into bite-size pieces
1 small head red-leaf lettuce, torn into bite-size pieces
12 ounces cooked chicken breast, cut into bite-size chunks
2 small green peppers, cut into ¼-inch-wide strips
2 small tomatoes, cut into ½-inch-wide wedges
1 can (16 to 19 ounces) white kidney beans (cannellini), rinsed and drained
1 can (15 to 19 ounces) black beans, rinsed and drained
¼ cup whole Niçoise or pitted and quartered Kalamata olives
1 tablespoon capers (optional)

1 Prepare Lemon-Basil Vinaigrette. Cover and refrigerate until ready to serve.

2 Line platter with lettuces. Spoon chicken onto center of lettuce.

3 Arrange green peppers, tomato wedges, white kidney beans, and black beans on platter with chicken.

4 Spoon Lemon-Basil Vinaigrette over chicken and vegetables. Top with Niçoise olives and capers if you like. *Makes 6 servings.*

LEMON-BASIL VINAIGRETTE: In small bowl, with wire whisk or fork, mix *2 tablespoons extravirgin olive oil* or olive oil, *2 tablespoons fresh lemon juice, 1 tablespoon minced fresh basil, 2 teaspoons Dijon mustard, ½ teaspoon sugar, ½ teaspoon salt,* and *¼ teaspoon coarsely ground black pepper* until blended.

Each serving: About 295 calories, 25 g protein, 22 g carbohydrate, 12 g total fat (2 g saturated), 48 mg cholesterol, 580 mg sodium.

## Winter Chicken Salad

PREP: 15 MINUTES ∽ COOK: 20 MINUTES

1 package (16 ounces) bow-tie or corkscrew pasta
Salt
1 roasted whole chicken (about 2½ pounds), from deli or meat department
1 bag (10 ounces) prewashed spinach
1 pound seedless red grapes, halved if large
¼ cup grated Parmesan cheese
3 tablespoons extravirgin olive oil or olive oil
2 tablespoons red wine vinegar
¾ teaspoon salt
1 teaspoon coarsely ground black pepper

1 In large saucepot, prepare pasta in *boiling salted water* as label directs; drain. Rinse pasta with cold running water to cool; drain.

2 Meanwhile, remove and discard skin and bones from chicken; tear meat into bite-size pieces.

3 In large bowl, toss pasta with chicken, spinach, grapes, Parmesan, olive oil, red wine vinegar, ¾ teaspoon salt, and pepper; mix well. *Makes 6 servings.*

Each serving: About 615 calories, 43 g protein, 72 g carbohydrate, 17 g total fat (4 g saturated), 94 mg cholesterol, 745 mg sodium.

## Warm Pasta Salad with Asian Vegetables & Chicken

PREP: 10 MINUTES ∽ COOK: 20 MINUTES

The chicken and snow peas are cut into strips to complement the shape of the pasta. If you'd like to use a nonstrand-type pasta, such as shells or corkscrews, cut the ingredients into chunkier pieces.

1 package (8 ounces) linguine
2 tablespoons vegetable oil
1 garlic clove, crushed with side of chef's knife
2 large skinless, boneless chicken-breast halves (about 1 pound), cut into ½-inch-wide strips

# 3 Low-Fat Dressings

These dressings will coat one 16-ounce package of shredded cabbage for coleslaw, one 10-ounce bag prewashed salad greens, or 2 large cucumbers, sliced.

PREP: 5 MINUTES

***Buttermilk-Chive Dressing*** In small bowl, with wire whisk or fork, mix *½ cup reduced-fat (1.5%) buttermilk, 2 tablespoons distilled white vinegar, 2 tablespoons chopped fresh chives, 1 tablespoon low-fat mayonnaise dressing, ¼ teaspoon salt, and ¼ teaspoon coarsely ground black pepper.* Makes ¾ cup.

Each tablespoon: About 6 calories, 0 g protein, 1 g carbohydrate, 0 g total fat (0 g saturated), 0 mg cholesterol, 65 mg sodium.

***Tomato-Orange Vinaigrette*** In small bowl, with wire whisk or fork, mix *½ cup tomato juice, 1 tablespoon balsamic vinegar, ¼ teaspoon grated orange peel, ¼ teaspoon sugar, and ⅛ teaspoon coarsely ground black pepper.* Makes about ¼ cup.

Each tablespoon: About 5 calories, 0 g protein, 1 g carbohydrate, 0 g total fat (0 g saturated), 0 mg cholesterol, 55 mg sodium.

***Honey-Lime Vinaigrette*** In small bowl, with wire whisk or fork, mix *⅓ cup fresh lime juice, 4 teaspoons honey, 1 tablespoon rice vinegar, and ⅛ teaspoon salt.* Makes about ½ cup.

Each tablespoon: About 15 calories, 0 g protein, 4 g carbohydrate, 0 g total fat (0 g saturated), 0 mg cholesterol, 35 mg sodium.

---

8 ounces snow peas, strings removed and cut lengthwise into thin strips

8 ounces bean sprouts

3 tablespoons soy sauce

3 tablespoons distilled white vinegar

1 tablespoon prepared mustard

1 teaspoon sugar

1 medium head Belgian endive, cut lengthwise into thin strips

1 small head radicchio, cut lengthwise into thin strips

1 bunch watercress, tough stems trimmed

**1** In large saucepot, prepare pasta in *boiling water* as label directs, but do not add salt to water; drain.

**2** Meanwhile, in nonstick 12-inch skillet, heat 1 tablespoon vegetable oil over medium heat. Add garlic and cook until golden brown. Discard garlic.

**3** In oil in same skillet, cook chicken strips over medium-high heat until chicken just loses its pink color throughout. With slotted spoon, transfer chicken to plate. To drippings in skillet, add snow peas and bean sprouts and cook until vegetables are tender-crisp and lightly browned. Transfer vegetables to plate with chicken.

**4** In cup, mix soy sauce, white vinegar, mustard, sugar, and remaining 1 tablespoon vegetable oil until blended.

**5** To serve, arrange endive, radicchio, and watercress around rim of 6 dinner plates. Place linguine and snow-pea mixture in center; top with chicken. Drizzle with mustard vinaigrette; toss to serve. ***Makes 6 servings.***

Each serving: About 310 calories, 26 g protein, 37 g carbohydrate, 6 g total fat (1 g saturated), 44 mg cholesterol, 620 mg sodium.

# Taverna Chicken Salad

PREP: 15 MINUTES ∾ COOK: 45 MINUTES

2 large chicken-breast halves with bones (about
  1½ pounds)
5 whole cloves
1 teaspoon salt
8 ounces green beans, trimmed
4 small red potatoes (about 8 ounces), cut into
  ¼-inch-thick slices
2 tablespoons extravirgin olive oil or olive oil
4 teaspoons fresh lemon juice
2 teaspoons Dijon mustard
1 teaspoon coarsely ground black pepper
½ teaspoon dried oregano leaves
1 pint cherry tomatoes, halved
½ cup Kalamata olives, pitted and coarsely
  chopped
1 bunch arugula (about 4 ounces), stems trimmed

**1** In 3-quart saucepan, heat chicken, cloves, ½ teaspoon salt, and *3 cups water* to boiling. Reduce heat to low; cover and simmer 20 minutes. Remove chicken from liquid; set aside to cool. When chicken is cool enough to handle, discard skin and bones; tear meat into bite-size pieces. Discard cooking liquid.

## FOOD EDITOR'S TIP

**Q.** What is balsamic vinegar?

**A.** Its name comes from balm (since it was originally used as a medicine), and it's made in Italy from white grape juice that is cooked down and concentrated before it's fermented. Balsamic vinegar is sweeter and more mellow than regular vinegar and lends rich fat-free flavor to today's cooking. The best of the balsamics are artisan-made and cost from $40 to $100-plus per bottle; they're produced in the provinces of Modena or Reggio by cooking freshly pressed grape juice and aging it for at least 12 years in wooden casks. These vinegars have a full-bodied, complex flavor and are sipped like fine liqueurs or drizzled on fresh fruit or cooked foods (like grilled meat or vegetables). Commercial balsamics, also made in Italy, are blends that are more plentiful and affordable (about $5 to $10 per bottle), meant to be used in cooking, and vary from mellow to acidic. Their aging period is considerably shorter and depending on the brand, they may contain wine vinegar and caramel.

**2** Meanwhile, in 2-quart saucepan, heat green beans in *2 inches boiling water* to boiling over high heat. Reduce heat to low; simmer 3 minutes or until tender-crisp. With slotted spoon, transfer to colander; rinse with cold water. In saucepan, in same 2 inches boiling water, heat potato slices to boiling; simmer 2 to 3 minutes or just until tender. Drain in colander with beans; rinse with cold water.

**3** In medium bowl, mix olive oil with lemon juice, mustard, pepper, remaining ½ teaspoon salt, and oregano. Add chicken, green beans, potatoes, tomatoes, and olives; toss to coat. Serve over arugula on 4 dinner plates. ***Makes 4 servings.***

Each serving: About 295 calories, 22 g protein, 20 g carbohydrate, 14 g total fat (2 g saturated), 52 mg cholesterol, 790 mg sodium.

# Sesame Noodle & Chicken Salad

PREP: 25 MINUTES ∾ COOK: 12 TO 15 MINUTES

A great dish to make when you have leftover chicken. No leftovers? Buy it, roasted or rotisseried, at your market or deli.

12 ounces linguine or spaghetti
Salt
6 ounces snow peas, strings removed and cut
  crosswise into thirds
¼ cup creamy peanut butter
3 tablespoons seasoned rice vinegar
3 tablespoons soy sauce
1 tablespoon light brown sugar
1 tablespoon minced, peeled fresh ginger
1 tablespoon Asian sesame oil
¼ teaspoon ground red pepper (cayenne)
1 small garlic clove, crushed with garlic press
2 medium carrots, peeled and shredded
3 cups thinly sliced red cabbage (½ small head)
12 ounces boneless, roasted chicken, pulled into
  thin strips

**1** In large saucepot, prepare pasta in *boiling salted water* as label directs. During last minute of cooking, add snow peas. Drain linguine and snow peas; rinse under cold running water to cool; drain again and set aside.

**2** In small bowl, mix peanut butter, rice vinegar, soy sauce, brown sugar, ginger, sesame oil, ground red pepper, garlic, and ¾ *cup very hot tap water* until blended.

**3** In large bowl, toss pasta, snow peas, carrots, red cabbage, and chicken with peanut-butter sauce. *Makes 6 servings.*

Each serving: About 460 calories, 28 g protein, 58 g carbohydrate, 13 g total fat (3 g saturated), 51 mg cholesterol, 880 mg sodium.

# Spinach & Garbanzo Salad with Smoked Turkey

### PREP: 25 MINUTES

A unique and delicious turkey salad with nectarines, and a cumin-spiced vinaigrette.

¼ cup fresh lemon juice (1 large lemon)
3 tablespoons olive oil
½ teaspoon salt
½ teaspoon sugar
½ teaspoon ground cumin
¼ teaspoon coarsely ground black pepper
1 small garlic clove, crushed with garlic press
1 large bunch spinach (1 pound), tough stems
    removed and leaves torn into 2-inch pieces
1 can (15 to 19 ounces) garbanzo beans, rinsed
    and drained
8 ounces sliced smoked turkey, cut into 2" by ½"
    strips
3 medium nectarines, cut into ¼-inch wedges

**1** In large salad bowl, mix lemon juice, olive oil, salt, sugar, cumin, pepper, and garlic until blended.

**2** To dressing in bowl, add spinach, garbanzo beans, smoked turkey, and nectarines; toss to mix well. *Makes 4 servings.*

Each serving: About 365 calories, 22 g protein, 42 g carbohydrate, 14 g total fat (2 g saturated), 23 mg cholesterol, 1065 mg sodium.

# Steak Salad with Buttermilk Dressing

### PREP: 20 MINUTES ⌒ COOK: 5 MINUTES
### GRILL: 8 TO 10 MINUTES

1 beef top round steak, ¾ inch thick (12 ounces),
    well trimmed
1 tablespoon plus 2 teaspoons Worcestershire
    sauce
⅔ cup reduced-fat (1.5%) buttermilk
3 tablespoons Dijon mustard with seeds
1 teaspoon prepared white horseradish
½ teaspoon sugar
1 medium cucumber
¼ pound sugar snap peas or snow peas, strings
    removed
2 medium heads Boston lettuce, separated into
    leaves
1 can (15 to 19 ounces) garbanzo beans, rinsed
    and drained
2 small tomatoes, cut into ½-inch wedges
Coarsely ground black pepper for garnish

**1** Place steak and 1 tablespoon Worcestershire sauce in 11" by 7" glass baking dish or on large plate; turn to coat; set aside.

**2** Preheat broiler if manufacturer directs. Prepare dressing: In small bowl, mix buttermilk, mustard, horseradish, sugar, and remaining 2 teaspoons Worcestershire.

**3** Peel several strips of skin from cucumber, leaving some green for an attractive look. Cut cucumber into ¼-inch-thick diagonal slices.

**4** In 2-quart saucepan, heat *2 cups water* to boiling over high heat. Add sugar snap peas; heat to boiling. Reduce heat to medium-low; simmer 3 to 5 minutes or until sugar snap peas are tender-crisp; drain.

**5** Place steak on rack in broiling pan; brush with Worcestershire remaining in baking dish. Broil steak 8 to 10 minutes for rare, or until of desired doneness, turning steak once. Thinly slice steak.

**6** Arrange lettuce leaves, garbanzo beans, sugar snap peas, tomatoes, cucumber, and steak on 4 dinner plates; drizzle with dressing. Sprinkle with black pepper if you like. *Makes 4 servings.*

Each serving: About 285 calories, 29 g protein, 26 g carbohydrate, 6 g total fat (2 g saturated), 56 mg cholesterol, 550 mg sodium.

# Warm Pork Tenderloin Salad with Dijon Dressing

PREP: 20 MINUTES ∽ COOK: 5 MINUTES

1 pork tenderloin (12 ounces), well trimmed
2 tablespoons dry sherry
1 tablespoon plus 1½ teaspoons soy sauce
2 teaspoons grated, peeled fresh ginger
2 tablespoons light mayonnaise
2 tablespoons balsamic vinegar
1 tablespoon Dijon mustard with seeds
1 teaspoon sugar
¼ teaspoon coarsely ground black pepper
2 large heads Belgian endive, cut crosswise into
  1-inch-thick slices
1 small head radicchio, thinly sliced

2 bunches arugula (8 ounces), stems trimmed
Nonstick cooking spray
1 package (10 ounces) frozen peas, thawed

1 With knife held in slanting position, almost parallel to the cutting surface, slice pork crosswise into very thin slices. In bowl, mix pork, sherry, soy sauce, and ginger; set aside.

2 In large bowl, stir mayonnaise, vinegar, mustard, sugar, pepper, and *1 tablespoon water* until blended. Add endive, radicchio, and arugula; toss well.

3 Spray nonstick 12-inch skillet lightly with nonstick cooking spray. In hot skillet, cook pork mixture over medium-high heat, stirring quickly and constantly, 2 minutes or until pork just loses its pink color.

4 Add pork and peas to salad; toss well. *Makes 4 servings.*

Each serving: About 230 calories, 24 g protein, 17 g carbohydrate, 7 g total fat (2 g saturated), 45 mg cholesterol, 270 mg sodium.

## NOT GUILTY!

Concerned about taking salads made with mayonnaise on a picnic because the mayo might spoil? You're blaming the wrong ingredient: Mayo has a clean record. The rumors began decades ago with homemade mayonnaise, which contains raw eggs; commercial brands, made with pasteurized eggs, have a high acid content (they contain vinegar and lemon juice) that actually prevents the growth of food-poisoning bacteria. The real culprits? Low-acid salad ingredients, such as tuna, ham, chicken, eggs, potatoes, and macaroni. When mishandled (left unrefrigerated too long, or prepared with hands or utensils that have not been washed properly), they can encourage bacterial growth, even if dressed with mayo.

### Safety tips
• Practice good kitchen hygiene.
• Always begin with clean, fresh ingredients.
• Once a salad is made, keep it cold until serving.
• Don't let food stand outdoors longer than 1 hour.

# Mexican Steak Salad

PREP: 15 MINUTES ∽ COOK: 35 MINUTES

¾ cup regular long-grain rice
1 cup canned black beans, rinsed and drained
1 can (4 to 4½ ounces) chopped mild green chiles,
  drained
½ medium head iceberg lettuce, coarsely chopped
3 medium tomatoes (1 pound), seeded and diced
¼ cup plain nonfat yogurt
2 tablespoons nonfat mayonnaise dressing
1 teaspoon Worcestershire sauce
1 teaspoon fresh lemon juice
½ teaspoon fennel seeds, crushed
½ teaspoon chili powder
¼ teaspoon salt
¼ teaspoon cracked black pepper
1 beef top round steak, ¾ inch thick (about
  12 ounces), well trimmed

1 Prepare rice as label directs. Set aside to cool.

2 Meanwhile, place beans, chiles, lettuce, and tomatoes in large bowl. In small bowl, mix yogurt, mayonnaise, Worcestershire sauce, and lemon juice.

3 Preheat broiler if manufacturer directs. In small bowl, mix fennel seeds, chili powder, salt, and cracked pepper. Rub steak with fennel-seed mixture. Place

steak on rack in broiling pan; with broiling pan at closest position to source of heat, broil steak about 8 minutes for medium-rare or until of desired doneness, turning steak once.

4 To serve, add cooked rice and yogurt mixture to black-bean mixture. Arrange salad on 4 dinner plates. Thinly slice steak and arrange on top of salad. *Makes 4 servings.*

Each serving: About 360 calories, 27 g protein, 47 g carbohydrate, 7 g total fat (2 g saturated), 52 mg cholesterol, 590 mg sodium.

# Steak Salad with Warm Mushroom Dressing

PREP: 30 MINUTES ～ COOK: 25 MINUTES

12 cups packed assorted salad greens, torn into bite-size pieces
1 beef top round steak, 1 inch thick (about 1½ pounds), well trimmed
½ teaspoon coarsely ground black pepper
4 tablespoons olive oil
8 ounces medium shiitake mushrooms, stems discarded and caps left whole
8 ounces medium white mushrooms, sliced
¾ teaspoon salt
¼ cup balsamic or red wine vinegar
1 tablespoon Dijon mustard
½ teaspoon sugar

1 Place salad greens in large bowl.

2 Sprinkle top round steak with pepper. In 12-inch skillet, heat 1 tablespoon olive oil over high heat until hot. Add steak and cook until browned on both sides, about 5 minutes. Reduce heat to medium and continue cooking 8 to 10 minutes longer for rare or until of desired doneness. Remove steak to cutting board; let rest 10 minutes for easier slicing.

3 Meanwhile, in the same skillet, heat 1 tablespoon olive oil over medium-high heat until hot. Add both kinds of mushrooms and ¼ teaspoon salt and cook until mushrooms are golden brown and all the liquid has evaporated, stirring frequently.

4 In small bowl, mix balsamic vinegar, mustard, sugar, remaining 2 tablespoons olive oil, remaining ½ teaspoon salt, and ⅓ cup water. Stir vinegar mixture into skillet with mushrooms. Remove skillet from heat.

5 With knife held in slanting position, almost parallel to cutting board, cut steak across its width into ⅛-inch-thick slices. Add sliced steak and mushroom mixture to salad greens; toss well. Spoon onto large platter to serve. *Makes 6 servings.*

Each serving: About 315 calories, 30 g protein, 15 g carbohydrate, 13 g total fat (3 g saturated), 65 mg cholesterol, 465 mg sodium.

# Porterhouse Steak with Grilled Salad

PREP: 10 MINUTES ～ GRILL: 30 TO 40 MINUTES

¼ cup chili sauce
¼ cup balsamic vinegar
¾ teaspoon salt
1 garlic clove, crushed with side of chef's knife
1 beef loin porterhouse steak, 2 inches thick (about 2¼ pounds), well trimmed
Grilled Salad (below)

1 Prepare outdoor grill for barbecuing. In a pie plate or deep dish, mix chili sauce, balsamic vinegar, salt, and garlic. Add steak to chili-sauce mixture to coat.

2 Prepare Grilled Salad; keep warm.

3 Place steak on grill over medium heat and brush with half chili-sauce mixture remaining in pie plate. Cook steak 20 to 30 minutes for medium-rare or until of desired doneness, turning steak occasionally and brushing with chili-sauce mixture remaining in plate halfway through grilling. Serve with Grilled Salad. *Makes 6 servings.*

GRILLED SALAD: Cut *1 large head radicchio* into 6 wedges. Cut each of *3 medium heads Belgian endive* lengthwise in half. In small bowl, mix *3 tablespoons olive oil, 1 tablespoon chopped fresh rosemary leaves* or 1 teaspoon dried rosemary leaves, crushed, and ½ *teaspoon salt*. Place radicchio and endive on grill over medium heat; brush with olive-oil mixture. Cook 5 to 10 minutes, turning them occasionally, until vegetables are tender-crisp.

Each serving with salad: About 335 calories, 33 g protein, 7 g carbohydrate, 19 g fat (6 g saturated), 91 mg cholesterol, 540 mg sodium.

# Thai Beef Salad

PREP: 45 MINUTES ∿ COOK: 10 MINUTES

The distinctive flavor comes from a dressing of cilantro, mint, garlic, ginger, and Asian fish sauce.

2 large bunches cilantro
2 large bunches mint
1 head Boston lettuce
¼ cup seasoned rice vinegar
2 tablespoons vegetable oil
4 teaspoons Asian fish sauce*
4 teaspoons grated, peeled fresh ginger
1 jalapeño chile, seeded and minced
⅛ teaspoon plus ¼ teaspoon salt
1 large carrot, cut into 2-inch-long matchstick-thin strips
1 medium red pepper, cut into 2-inch-long matchstick-thin strips
2 large green onions, cut into 2-inch-long matchstick-thin strips
1 pound lean ground beef (90%)
1 garlic clove, crushed with garlic press

1 From cilantro, remove enough leaves to equal ½ cup loosely packed; chop enough remaining leaves to equal ¼ cup. Repeat with mint to get ½ cup loosely packed mint leaves and ¼ cup chopped mint. Separate Boston lettuce into leaves. Tear very large leaves into bite-size pieces.

2 In medium bowl, combine chopped cilantro, chopped mint, vinegar, oil, fish sauce, ginger, jalapeño, and ⅛ teaspoon salt. Spoon half of dressing into large bowl; set aside. To dressing remaining in medium bowl, add carrot, red pepper, and green onions.

3 In nonstick 10-inch skillet, cook ground beef over medium-high heat until browned, stirring to break up beef with spoon. Spoon off fat from beef; add garlic and remaining ¼ teaspoon salt and cook 1 minute, stirring. Toss hot beef mixture with carrot mixture.

4 To large bowl with dressing, add Boston lettuce, cilantro leaves, and mint leaves; toss well. Spoon lettuce mixture onto 4 dinner plates; top with beef mixture. *Makes 4 servings.*

*Asian fish sauce is a thin, translucent, salty brown liquid extracted from salted, fermented fish. This condiment is used predominantly in Thai and Vietnamese cooking. It can be purchased in the Asian section of some grocery stores.

Each serving: About 425 calories, 25 g protein, 15 g carbohydrate, 29 g total fat (8 g saturated), 72 mg cholesterol, 1105 mg sodium.

# Mandarin Lamb Salad

PREP: 15 MINUTES

A great use for leftover leg of lamb. If you'd like to make this salad without using leftovers, start with 1 pound well-trimmed boneless loin lamb chops. Broil until medium to medium rare. Cool slightly and cut into cubes. Save any lamb juices from the broiler pan to add to the dressing.

2 tablespoons olive oil
1 tablespoon orange juice
1 tablespoon cider vinegar
2 tablespoons light sour cream
½ teaspoon salt
⅛ teaspoon ground red pepper (cayenne)
12 ounces cooked lamb, cut into bite-size pieces
½ cup sliced celery
½ cup finely chopped green pepper
1 teaspoon grated onion
1 can (11 ounces) mandarin orange sections, drained
⅓ cup slivered almonds, toasted

1 In large bowl, mix olive oil, orange juice, cider vinegar, sour cream, salt, and ground red pepper.

2 Add lamb, celery, green pepper, and onion; toss to mix well. Cover and refrigerate.

3 Garnish salad with mandarin oranges and toasted almonds. *Makes 4 servings.*

Each serving: About 445 calories, 24 g protein, 18 g carbohydrate, 32 g total fat (10 g saturated), 85 mg cholesterol, 375 mg sodium.

◄ *Thai Beef Salad*

# Side Salads

Most one-dish meals are better off when paired with a good side salad. It can be as simple as tossed greens with a vinaigrette (see page 123 for a collection of good low-fat dressings). Or, you can up the ante a bit and try Spinach & Tangerine Salad (at right). And if company's coming, go all out with Fennel, Fresh Pear & Endive Salad (see overleaf).

## Asparagus with Parmesan Vinaigrette

PREP: 30 MINUTES PLUS 2 HOURS
STANDING TIME • COOK: 5 TO 7 MINUTES

3 pounds asparagus, trimmed
⅓ cup olive oil
3 tablespoons red wine vinegar
1 tablespoon Dijon mustard
3 tablespoons grated Parmesan cheese
¼ cup minced prosciutto or cooked
   ham, about 2 ounces (optional)

1 In 12-inch skillet, heat asparagus in ½ inch boiling water to boiling over high heat. Reduce heat to low; cover and simmer 5 minutes or until asparagus is tender-crisp; drain well.
2 In 13" by 9" glass baking dish, prepare vinaigrette: Mix olive oil, red wine vinegar, mustard, and 2 tablespoons Parmesan. Add asparagus to vinaigrette, turning to coat well. Cover with plastic wrap and refrigerate at least 2 hours to blend flavors, turning asparagus occasionally.
3 To serve, spoon asparagus and vinaigrette onto platter. Sprinkle prosciutto and remaining 1 tablespoon Parmesan over asparagus. Makes 8 accompaniment servings.

EACH SERVING WITHOUT PROSCIUTTO: ABOUT 120 CALORIES, 5 G PROTEIN, 5 G CARBOHYDRATE, 10 G TOTAL FAT (2 G SATURATED), 2 MG CHOLESTEROL, 85 MG SODIUM.

*Spinach & Tangerine Salad*

## Vegetables with Sesame Vinaigrette

PREP: 15 MINUTES • COOK: 15 MINUTES

1 medium bunch broccoli (1½
   pounds), cut into 2½-inch-long
   pieces
2 teaspoons vegetable oil
2 large zucchini (about 10 ounces
   each), cut into 1½-inch chunks
1 bunch green onions, cut into 1-inch
   pieces
½ teaspoon salt
1 pound asparagus, trimmed and cut
   into 2-inch pieces
8 ounces sugar snap peas or snow
   peas, strings removed
3 tablespoons seasoned rice vinegar
1 tablespoon Asian sesame oil
½ teaspoon sugar

1 In 3-quart saucepan, heat broccoli in 1 inch boiling water to boiling over high heat. Reduce heat to low; cover and simmer 4 to 5 minutes or until broccoli is just tender-crisp. Drain.
2 In nonstick 12-inch skillet, heat 1 teaspoon vegetable oil over medium-high heat until hot. Add zucchini, green onions, and ¼ teaspoon salt, stirring frequently, until vegetables are tender-crisp; with slotted spoon, transfer to bowl.
3 To same skillet, add remaining 1 teaspoon vegetable oil, asparagus, sugar snap peas, and remaining ¼ teaspoon salt; cook, stirring frequently, until vegetables are tender-crisp.
4 In cup, mix rice vinegar, sesame oil, and sugar. Add zucchini, green onions, and broccoli to vegetables in skillet; stir in sesame vinaigrette, tossing to coat vegetables well; heat through. Serve vegetables warm. Or, cover and refrigerate to serve cold later. Makes 10 accompaniment servings.

EACH SERVING: ABOUT 75 CALORIES, 5 G PROTEIN, 10 G CARBOHYDRATE, 3 G TOTAL FAT (0 G SATURATED), 0 MG CHOLESTEROL, 230 MG SODIUM.

## Spinach & Tangerine Salad

PREP: 30 MINUTES

4 medium tangerines or small oranges
3 tablespoons extravirgin olive oil
3 tablespoons cider vinegar
1 teaspoon sugar
1 teaspoon Dijon mustard
⅛ teaspoon salt
⅛ teaspoon coarsely ground black
   pepper
1 large bunch spinach (about
   1 pound), stems trimmed, torn into
   bite-size pieces
2 small heads Bibb lettuce (about
   8 ounces), torn into bite-size pieces

1 Grate peel from 1 tangerine. Cut remaining peel and pith from all tangerines; discard. Cut each tangerine in half, then cut each half crosswise into ¼-inch-thick slices.
2 In large bowl, mix olive oil, vinegar, sugar, mustard, salt, pepper, and tangerine peel. Add spinach, lettuce, and tangerine slices; toss well. Makes 8 accompaniment servings.

EACH SERVING: ABOUT 80 CALORIES, 2 G PROTEIN, 8 G CARBOHYDRATE, 5 G TOTAL FAT (1 G SATURATED), 0 MG CHOLESTEROL, 95 MG SODIUM.

## Tomato & Cucumber Salad with Avocado Dressing

PREP: 15 MINUTES

1 medium avocado
1 tablespoon milk
1 tablespoon fresh lemon juice
¾ teaspoon salt
1 bunch watercress, tough stems trimmed
4 medium tomatoes, each cut into 8 wedges
3 medium cucumbers (about 2 pounds), peeled, halved lengthwise, and cut into bite-size chunks

1 Prepare avocado dressing: Cut avocado lengthwise in half; remove and discard seed. With spoon, scoop avocado into a blender or food processor, with knife blade attached. Add milk, lemon juice, salt, and ½ cup loosely packed watercress and blend at medium speed until smooth. Spoon into large bowl.
2 Place tomatoes and cucumbers in bowl with avocado dressing; gently toss to coat.
3 To serve, line platter with remaining watercress; top with tomato-cucumber salad. Makes 10 accompaniment servings.

EACH SERVING: ABOUT 55 CALORIES, 2 G PROTEIN, 7 G CARBOHYDRATE, 3 G TOTAL FAT (1 G SATURATED), 0 MG CHOLESTEROL, 195 MG SODIUM.

## Tomato & Melon Salad

PREP: 15 MINUTES

1 pint cherry tomatoes
1 large honeydew melon (about 4½ pounds)
1 large cantaloupe (about 3 pounds)
¼ cup red currant or apple jelly
½ teaspoon salt
1 teaspoon coarsely ground black pepper
1 bunch spinach

1 In 5-quart saucepot, heat 3 quarts water to boiling over high heat. Cut small "x" in stem end of each cherry tomato. Add tomatoes to boiling water; cook 5 seconds. Drain; cool under cold running water.
2 With fingers, slip cherry tomatoes from their skins, one at a time; place in colander to drain off excess liquid. Cut each melon in half; discard seeds. With melon baller, scoop melons into balls; reserve any remaining melon for use another day. Place melon balls in bowl with cherry tomatoes. Cover and refrigerate melon-tomato mixture if not serving right away.
3 To serve, in another large bowl, stir jelly, salt, and pepper until jelly is smooth. Mince enough spinach to equal ¼ cup. Drain liquid from the melon-tomato mixture. Add melon-tomato mixture and chopped spinach to bowl with jelly mixture; toss to coat. Arrange remaining spinach leaves on platter; spoon melon-tomato mixture over spinach leaves. Toss to serve. Makes 8 accompaniment servings.

EACH SERVING: ABOUT 110 CALORIES, 2 G PROTEIN, 27 G CARBOHYDRATE, 1 G TOTAL FAT (0 G SATURATED), 0 MG CHOLESTEROL, 190 MG SODIUM.

## Green Bean Salad with Lemon-Pepper Dressing

PREP: 25 MINUTES • COOK: 10 MINUTES

2 pounds green beans, trimmed
⅓ cup light mayonnaise
¼ teaspoon salt
½ teaspoon coarsely ground black pepper
½ teaspoon grated lemon peel
3 small tomatoes, cut into thin wedges
1 small red onion, slivered

1 In 12-inch skillet, heat green beans in ½ inch boiling water to boiling over high heat. Reduce heat to low; cover and simmer 10 minutes or until beans are tender; drain well.
2 In large bowl, stir together mayonnaise, salt, pepper, and lemon peel.
3 Add green beans and tomatoes to mayonnaise mixture; toss to coat. Spoon salad onto large platter and sprinkle with red onion. Serve warm or cover and refrigerate to serve cold later. Makes 10 accompaniment servings.

EACH SERVING: ABOUT 55 CALORIES, 2 G PROTEIN, 10 G CARBOHYDRATE, 2 G TOTAL FAT (0 G SATURATED), 0 MG CHOLESTEROL, 130 MG SODIUM.

## Warm Peas & Carrots Salad

PREP: 10 MINUTES • COOK: 10 MINUTES

1 cup frozen peas
1 tablespoon vegetable oil
3 medium carrots, peeled and thinly sliced
1 small onion, thinly sliced
½ teaspoon salt
1 tablespoon fresh lemon juice
4 cups loosely packed shredded romaine lettuce

1 In small bowl, place frozen peas; cover with boiling water and let stand 5 minutes.
2 Meanwhile, in nonstick 10-inch skillet, heat vegetable oil over medium-high heat until hot. Add carrots, onion, and salt and cook until vegetables are tender and lightly browned.
3 Drain peas; stir into vegetable mixture with lemon juice. Remove skillet from heat.
4 In large bowl, toss lettuce with carrot mixture to mix well. Makes 4 accompaniment servings.

EACH SERVING: ABOUT 115 CALORIES, 4 G PROTEIN, 18 G CARBOHYDRATE, 4 G TOTAL FAT (1 G SATURATED), 0 MG CHOLESTEROL, 365 MG SODIUM.

## Baby Greens Salad with Grapefruit Vinaigrette

PREP: 30 MINUTES

*2 medium grapefruits*
*1 tablespoon balsamic vinegar*
*1 tablespoon Dijon mustard*
*2 teaspoons capers, drained*
*½ teaspoon sugar*
*½ teaspoon salt*
*¼ cup olive oil*
*1 pound mixed baby greens or mixed salad greens (about 12 cups loosely packed)*
*2 medium heads Belgian endive, cut lengthwise into matchstick-thin strips*

**1** With knife, cut peel from grapefruits. Holding grapefruits over small bowl to catch juice, cut sections from grapefruits between membranes. Set aside.
**2** In large bowl, combine balsamic vinegar, mustard, capers, sugar, salt, and 2 tablespoons grapefruit juice (reserve any remaining grapefruit juice for another use). Slowly beat in olive oil until mixture thickens slightly.
**3** Add baby greens, grapefruit sections, and endive to dressing; toss to coat. Makes 12 accompaniment servings.

EACH SERVING: ABOUT 65 CALORIES, 1 G PROTEIN, 5 G CARBOHYDRATE, 5 G TOTAL FAT (1 G SATURATED), 0 MG CHOLESTEROL, 155 MG SODIUM.

## Sweet & Sour Broccoli Slaw

PREP: 15 MINUTES

*⅓ cup light mayonnaise*
*¼ cup cider vinegar*
*4 teaspoons sugar*
*2 teaspoons celery seeds*
*1 bunch watercress, tough stems removed*
*1 package (15 to 16 ounces) broccoli coleslaw or shredded cabbage mix for coleslaw*

**1** In large bowl, mix mayonnaise, cider vinegar, sugar, and celery seeds.
**2** Add watercress and broccoli slaw to dressing; toss well to coat. Makes 4 accompaniment servings.

EACH SERVING: ABOUT 125 CALORIES, 5 G PROTEIN, 16 G CARBOHYDRATE, 5 G TOTAL FAT (1 G SATURATED), 0 MG CHOLESTEROL, 205 MG SODIUM.

## Green Bean, Walnut & Radicchio Salad

PREP: 10 MINUTES • COOK: 20 MINUTES

*2 pounds green beans, trimmed*
*2 tablespoons olive oil*
*1 large onion, diced*
*½ cup walnuts, chopped*
*1 small lemon*
*1 large head radicchio, cut into ½-inch-wide slices*
*1 tablespoon Dijon mustard*
*¾ teaspoon salt*

**1** In 5-quart Dutch oven or saucepot, heat green beans and *enough water to cover* to boiling over high heat. Reduce heat to medium-low; simmer, uncovered, 10 minutes or until green beans are tender. Drain and rinse green beans under cold running water to cool; drain.
**2** Meanwhile, in 10-inch skillet, heat olive oil over medium-high heat until hot. Add onion and cook until tender, stirring occasionally. Add walnuts and cook until walnuts and onion are golden.
**3** From lemon, grate ½ teaspoon peel and squeeze 1 tablespoon juice. In large bowl, combine green beans, onion mixture, radicchio, lemon peel, lemon juice, mustard, and salt; toss to coat. Spoon salad onto large platter to serve. Makes 8 accompaniment servings.

EACH SERVING: ABOUT 125 CALORIES, 4 G PROTEIN, 12 G CARBOHYDRATE, 8 G TOTAL FAT (1 G SATURATED), 0 MG CHOLESTEROL, 275 MG SODIUM.

## Fennel, Fresh Pear & Endive Salad

PREP: 45 MINUTES

*¼ cup extravirgin olive oil*
*¼ cup tarragon vinegar*
*1 tablespoon Dijon mustard*
*¾ teaspoon salt*
*¼ teaspoon coarsely ground black pepper*
*5 medium Bartlett pears (about 2 pounds)*
*2 large fennel bulbs (about 1 pound each)*
*4 medium heads Belgian endive*
*½ cup walnuts, toasted and coarsely chopped*

**1** In small bowl, prepare dressing: Mix olive oil, tarragon vinegar, mustard, salt, and pepper; set aside. (If you like, combine dressing ingredients in jar with tight-fitting lid; refrigerate overnight.)
**2** Remove core and slice each pear into 12 wedges, leaving skin on. Place pear wedges in large bowl. Trim top and bottom from each fennel bulb. Slice each bulb lengthwise in half; remove core. Slice halves crosswise into paper-thin slices; place in bowl with pear wedges.
**3** Cut 2 endives crosswise into ⅛-inch-thick slices; toss with fennel mixture. Separate leaves from remaining heads of endive.
**4** Toss dressing with fennel mixture. Arrange remaining endive leaves around edge of large shallow bowl or platter; top with fennel salad. Sprinkle with toasted walnuts. Makes 8 accompaniment servings.

EACH SERVING: ABOUT 210 CALORIES, 3 G PROTEIN, 26 G CARBOHYDRATE, 13 G TOTAL FAT (2 G SATURATED), 0 MG CHOLESTEROL, 310 MG SODIUM.

## Warm Carrot & Apple Salad

PREP: 10 MINUTES
COOK: 3 TO 5 MINUTES

1 medium red pepper, thinly sliced
¼ cup dark seedless or golden raisins
2 tablespoons cider vinegar
1 tablespoon brown sugar
¼ cup light mayonnaise
1 tablespoon Dijon mustard
⅛ teaspoon coarsely ground black
   pepper
1 medium McIntosh or Red Delicious
   apple, thinly sliced
2 packages (8 ounces each) shredded
   carrots

1 In 1-quart saucepan, heat red pepper, raisins, cider vinegar, and brown sugar to boiling over high heat. Reduce heat to low and simmer, uncovered, 3 to 5 minutes or until red pepper is tender. Remove saucepan from heat and let mixture cool slightly. Stir in mayonnaise, Dijon mustard, and black pepper.
2 Add apple and shredded carrots to red-pepper mixture; toss to mix well. Makes 6 accompaniment servings.

EACH SERVING: ABOUT 105 CALORIES,
1 G PROTEIN, 21 G CARBOHYDRATE,
2 G TOTAL FAT (0 G SATURATED),
0 MG CHOLESTEROL, 170 MG SODIUM.

## Fruited Barley Salad

PREP: 30 MINUTES
COOK: 35 TO 45 MINUTES

1 package (16 ounces) barley
2 teaspoons salt
4 medium limes
⅓ cup olive oil
1 tablespoon sugar
¾ teaspoon coarsely ground black
   pepper
1½ pounds nectarines (about
   4 medium), cut into ½-inch pieces
1 pound tomatoes (about 2 large),
   seeded and cut into ½-inch pieces
4 green onions, thinly sliced
½ cup chopped fresh mint leaves

1 In 4-quart saucepan, heat 6 cups water to boiling over high heat. Add barley and 1 teaspoon salt; heat to boiling. Reduce heat to low; cover and simmer 35 to 45 minutes or until barley is tender and liquid is absorbed (barley will have a creamy consistency).
2 Meanwhile, from limes, grate 1 tablespoon peel and squeeze ½ cup juice. In large bowl, mix lime peel, lime juice, olive oil, sugar, pepper, and remaining 1 teaspoon salt.
3 Rinse barley under cold running water; drain well. Add barley, nectarines, tomatoes, green onions, and mint to lime dressing; with rubber spatula, stir gently to coat. If not serving right away, cover and refrigerate. Makes 16 accompaniment servings.

EACH SERVING: ABOUT 170 CALORIES,
4 G PROTEIN, 28 G CARBOHYDRATE,
5 G TOTAL FAT (1 G SATURATED),
0 MG CHOLESTEROL, 267 MG SODIUM.

## Asian Coleslaw

PREP: 15 MINUTES

⅓ cup seasoned rice vinegar
2 tablespoons vegetable oil
2 teaspoons Asian sesame oil
¾ teaspoon salt
1 large head savoy cabbage (about 2½
   pounds), thinly sliced and tough ribs
   discarded
1 pound carrots, peeled and shredded
4 green onions, thinly sliced
½ cup chopped fresh cilantro leaves

1 In large bowl, mix rice vinegar, vegetable oil, sesame oil, and salt.
2 Add cabbage, carrots, green onions, and cilantro; toss well. If not serving right away, cover and refrigerate. Makes 8 accompaniment servings.

EACH SERVING: ABOUT 110 CALORIES,
4 G PROTEIN, 18 G CARBOHYDRATE,
4 G TOTAL FAT (0 G SATURATED),
0 MG CHOLESTEROL, 520 MG SODIUM.

## Cherry Tomato Salad

PREP: 15 MINUTES

2 medium lemons
2 pints red cherry tomatoes (about 12
   ounces each pint), each cut in half
1 pint yellow cherry tomatoes (about
   12 ounces), each cut in half
1 tablespoon sugar
2 tablespoons chopped fresh chives
2 tablespoons extravirgin olive oil
¾ teaspoon salt
½ teaspoon coarsely ground black
   pepper

1 Cut peel and pith from lemons. Cut lemons crosswise into slightly less than ¼-inch-thick slices.
2 In medium bowl, toss lemon slices, tomatoes, sugar, chives, olive oil, salt, and pepper. Makes 8 accompaniment servings.

EACH SERVING: ABOUT 65 CALORIES,
1 G PROTEIN, 9 G CARBOHYDRATE,
4 G TOTAL FAT (1 G SATURATED),
0 MG CHOLESTEROL, 210 MG SODIUM.

*Cherry Tomato Salad*

# Pasta

# Bow Ties with Cannellini & Spinach

PREP: 10 MINUTES ～ COOK: 15 MINUTES

12 ounces bow-tie pasta
Salt
1 tablespoon olive oil
1 jumbo onion (about 1 pound), thinly sliced
¾ cup chicken broth, canned or homemade (page 24)
1 teaspoon cornstarch
¼ teaspoon crushed red pepper
1 can (15 to 19 ounces) white kidney beans (cannellini), rinsed and drained
2 bags (10 ounces each) prewashed spinach
2 tablespoons grated Romano or Parmesan cheese

1 In large saucepot, prepare pasta in *boiling salted water* as label directs.

2 Meanwhile, in nonstick 12-inch skillet, heat olive oil over medium-high heat until hot. Add onion and cook until golden brown, about 10 to 12 minutes.

3 In 1-cup glass measuring cup, mix chicken broth, cornstarch, crushed red pepper, and ½ teaspoon salt. Add to same skillet along with beans and cook over medium-high heat until sauce boils and thickens slightly, about 1 minute.

4 Just before draining pasta, stir spinach into water in saucepot; leave in only until it wilts. Drain pasta and spinach; return to saucepot. Add sauce; toss to mix well. Sprinkle with Romano to serve. *Makes 4 servings.*

Each serving: About 545 calories, 24 g protein, 99 g carbohydrate, 7 g total fat (1 g saturated), 5 mg cholesterol, 925 mg sodium.

# Late-Summer Pasta

PREP: 15 MINUTES ～ COOK: 30 MINUTES

A pasta dish that takes advantage of the bounty from the garden in late summer or early autumn.

2 tablespoons olive oil
2 medium zucchini (about 8 ounces each), cut into 1½-inch chunks
Salt
1 medium eggplant (1½ pounds), cut into 1-inch pieces
1 medium onion, diced
2 large yellow peppers, cut into 1-inch pieces
1 can (14½ ounces) stewed tomatoes
½ teaspoon coarsely ground black pepper
¼ cup chopped fresh basil leaves
1 package (16 ounces) corkscrew or penne pasta
¼ cup grated Parmesan cheese

1 In nonstick 12-inch skillet, heat 2 teaspoons olive oil over medium-high heat until hot. Add zucchini with ¼ teaspoon salt until zucchini is tender-crisp; transfer zucchini to bowl.

2 In same skillet, heat 1 tablespoon olive oil; cook eggplant, onion, and ¼ teaspoon salt, stirring occasionally, until eggplant begins to brown slightly. Add yellow peppers and remaining 1 teaspoon olive oil and cook, stirring occasionally, until vegetables are golden.

3 Stir in stewed tomatoes, black pepper, and ¼ teaspoon salt; heat to boiling. Reduce heat to low; cover and simmer 15 minutes, stirring occasionally, until vegetables are tender. Stir in zucchini and basil; heat through.

4 Meanwhile, in large saucepot, prepare pasta in *boiling salted water* as label directs; drain. To serve, toss pasta with vegetable mixture and Parmesan cheese. *Makes 6 servings.*

Each serving: About 415 calories, 15 g protein, 75 g carbohydrate, 7 g total fat (2 g saturated), 3 mg cholesterol, 800 mg sodium.

# Penne with Spinach & Almonds

PREP: 10 MINUTES ～ COOK: 20 MINUTES

8 ounces penne, ziti, or corkscrew pasta
Salt
2 tablespoons sliced almonds
1 teaspoon olive oil
1 garlic clove, minced
1 large bunch spinach (about 1 pound), coarsely
    chopped
3 tablespoons golden raisins
2 medium plum tomatoes, peeled, seeded, and
    diced
3 tablespoons grated Parmesan cheese

1 In large saucepot, prepare pasta in *boiling salted water* as label directs; drain and return to saucepot; keep warm.

2 Meanwhile, in nonstick 12-inch skillet, cook almonds over medium heat until golden, stirring and shaking skillet frequently; remove toasted almonds from skillet.

3 In same skillet, heat olive oil over medium heat until hot; cook garlic until golden. Increase heat to medium-high; add spinach, raisins, and ½ teaspoon salt, cooking until spinach just wilts.

4 To pasta in saucepot, add spinach mixture and tomatoes; heat through. Add 2 tablespoons Parmesan; toss. Spoon penne mixture into 4 pasta bowls; sprinkle penne with toasted almonds and remaining 1 tablespoon Parmesan to serve. *Makes 4 first-course servings.*

Each serving: About 305 calories, 13 g protein, 54 g carbohydrate, 5 g total fat (1 g saturated), 3 mg cholesterol, 650 mg sodium.

# Tortellini Primavera

PREP: 15 MINUTES ～ COOK: 30 MINUTES

2 packages (9 ounces each) refrigerated cheese-
    and-basil or cheese-filled tortellini
Salt
2 tablespoons olive oil
5 medium carrots, peeled and cut into 3" by ¼"
    sticks
1 large red pepper, cut into ¼-inch-wide strips
2 medium zucchini (about 8 ounces each), cut into
    3" by ¼" sticks
4 green onions, cut into 3-inch pieces
8 ounces sugar snap peas or snow peas, strings
    removed
¼ teaspoon coarsely ground black pepper
⅓ cup loosely packed basil leaves (optional), cut
    into thin strips

1 In large saucepot, prepare tortellini in *boiling salted water* as label directs. Drain tortellini; set aside.

2 Meanwhile, in nonstick 12-inch skillet, heat 2 teaspoons olive oil over medium-high heat until hot. Add carrots and cook 2 minutes, stirring frequently. Add red pepper and ¼ teaspoon salt; cook until carrots and red pepper are tender-crisp; transfer to bowl.

3 To same skillet, add 2 teaspoons olive oil, zucchini, and ¼ teaspoon salt; cook, stirring frequently, until zucchini is tender-crisp; transfer to bowl with carrot mixture.

4 To same skillet, add remaining 2 teaspoons olive oil and green onions; cook, stirring frequently, until golden. Add sugar snap peas and ¼ teaspoon salt; cook until sugar snap peas are tender-crisp.

5 Return carrot mixture to skillet. Stir in cooked tortellini and black pepper; heat through. Pile basil strips on top of tortellini mixture if you like; toss before serving. *Makes 6 servings.*

Each serving: About 360 calories, 14 g protein, 54 g carbohydrate, 11 g total fat (3 g saturated), 35 mg cholesterol, 800 mg sodium.

# Try Our Easy Homemade Pasta!

Just follow the easy steps outlined below to make our tender, delicious pasta. First we tell how to make a basic pasta dough, or a flavored variation. Then we explain how to roll and cut the pasta—it should take about 20 minutes. Finally we outline the quick and simple cooking instructions.

## To Prepare Homemade Pasta Dough

*About 2¼ cups all-purpose flour*
*1 tablespoon olive oil*
*1 teaspoon salt*
*2 large eggs*

**1** In large bowl, stir 2¼ cups flour with olive oil, salt, eggs, and *¼ cup water* to make a stiff dough.

**2** On well-floured surface, knead dough until smooth and not sticky, about 20 times. Cover dough with plastic wrap and let rest 30 minutes for easier rolling. (Or, in food processor with knife blade attached, blend all ingredients 10 to 15 seconds to form a smooth ball. Do not knead dough; cover and let dough rest for 30 minutes.) Makes about 1 pound pasta, enough for 8 accompaniment or 4 main-dish servings.

Each main-dish serving: About 325 calories, 10 g protein, 54 g carbohydrate, 7 g total fat (1 g saturated), 107 mg cholesterol, 565 mg sodium.

**Tomato** Prepare Homemade Pasta Dough as above, but do not add water, use only 1 large egg, and add *one 6-ounce can tomato paste* to mixture.

**Lemon-Pepper** Prepare Homemade Pasta Dough as above, but add *½ teaspoon coarsely ground black pepper* and *1 tablespoon finely grated lemon peel* to mixture.

**Arugula** Remove tough stems from *2 bunches arugula* (about 8 cups loosely packed). In 3-quart saucepan, blanch arugula leaves in *enough boiling water to cover*, about 30 seconds. Drain arugula; squeeze dry and coarsely chop. Prepare Homemade Pasta Dough as above, but use only *2 tablespoons water* and add arugula to mixture.

**Herb** Prepare Homemade Pasta Dough as above, but add small pieces of parsley or other herbs such as dill, chervil, or tarragon to dough as it is rolled. This pasta is beautiful when served in clear soup or tossed with olive oil and grated cheese.

## To Cut Pasta

THIS CAN BE DONE UP TO 1 DAY AHEAD.

**Fettuccine** Prepare Homemade Pasta Dough (any variation). Cut dough in half. Follow instructions with pasta machine. Or, place half of dough on lightly floured surface and keep remaining dough in plastic wrap. With floured rolling pin, roll dough into 16" by 12" rectangle (dough should be about ¹⁄₁₆ inch thick). Fold dough in half into 16" by 6" rectangle, then fold in half again into 16" by 3" rectangle. With pastry wheel or knife, cut folded dough crosswise into strips about ¼ inch wide. Unfold strips. Sprinkle strips with flour to prevent them from sticking. Roll strips into "nests" and place on lightly floured jelly-roll pan. Repeat with remaining dough. Follow To Cook Pasta (below) or cover pan with plastic wrap and refrigerate until ready to cook.

**Pappardelle** Prepare Homemade Pasta Dough (any variation). Cut dough in half. Follow directions with pasta machine. Or, place half of dough on lightly floured surface and keep remaining dough in plastic wrap. With floured rolling pin, roll dough into 12" by 12" square. With pastry wheel or knife, cut dough crosswise into twelve 1-inch-wide strips. Sprinkle strips with flour to prevent them from sticking. Place strips on lightly floured jelly-roll pan. Place plastic wrap between layers of pasta strips. Repeat with remaining dough. Follow To Cook Pasta (below) or cover pan with plastic wrap and refrigerate until ready to cook.

## To Cook Pasta

In 8-quart saucepot, cook pasta in *6 quarts boiling water*. Add 2 teaspoons salt, if desired. Gently stir to separate pasta; cook 3 to 5 minutes or until tender but firm. Drain and serve with desired sauce.

## Fusilli with Stir-Fried Vegetables

PREP: 15 MINUTES ∿ COOK: 25 MINUTES

This is great with fresh shiitake mushrooms. Discard the stems and cut the caps into thick slices.

12 ounces fusilli or corkscrew pasta
1 tablespoon olive oil
2 large onions, diced
2 garlic cloves, minced
2 medium red peppers, cut into 1-inch pieces
1 large bunch broccoli (1¼ pounds)
1 tablespoon minced, peeled fresh ginger
½ teaspoon salt
1 pound medium mushrooms, halved if large
3 tablespoons soy sauce
1 tablespoon Asian sesame oil

1 In large saucepot, prepare pasta in *boiling water* as label directs, but do not add salt to water.

2 Meanwhile, in nonstick 5-quart Dutch oven, heat olive oil over medium-high heat until hot. Add onions, garlic, red peppers, broccoli, ginger, and salt and cook 5 minutes, stirring often. Add mushrooms and cook 5 to 10 minutes longer or until red pepper and broccoli are tender-crisp, stirring occasionally.

3 Drain pasta; return to saucepot. Add vegetable mixture, soy sauce, and sesame oil; toss well. *Makes 6 servings.*

Each serving: About 340 calories, 13 g protein, 60 g carbohydrate, 6 g total fat (1 g saturated), 0 mg cholesterol, 745 mg sodium.

## Sesame Noodles & Vegetables

PREP: 10 MINUTES ∿ COOK: 20 MINUTES

If you have access to Asian ingredients, try this with fresh Chinese noodles. Cook the broccoli and carrots in the boiling water first, then add the fresh noodles for the last minute or so of cooking. They should cook in the time it takes the water to come back to boiling once they are added.

1 package (16 ounces) linguine or spaghetti
1 package (7 to 8 ounces) broccoli flowerets
3 medium carrots, peeled and shredded
½ cup reduced-fat smooth peanut butter
3 tablespoons seasoned rice vinegar
3 tablespoons soy sauce
1 tablespoon Asian sesame oil
2 teaspoons sugar
2 ounces sliced cooked ham, cut into thin slivers
2 green onions, thinly sliced

1 In large saucepot, prepare linguine in *boiling water* as label directs, but do not add salt to water. After linguine has cooked 4 minutes, add broccoli and carrots. Continue cooking 5 to 10 minutes longer or until linguine is al dente and vegetables are tender-crisp. Drain linguine mixture; return to saucepot.

2 Meanwhile, in medium bowl, mix peanut butter, rice vinegar, soy sauce, sesame oil, sugar, and *1 cup hot tap water* until smooth.

3 Add ham and peanut sauce to linguine mixture; toss well. Spoon into large bowl; sprinkle with sliced green onions. *Makes 6 servings.*

Each serving: About 490 calories, 19 g protein, 76 g carbohydrate, 13 g total fat (2 g saturated), 6 mg cholesterol, 930 mg sodium.

## Penne with Tomatoes & Pesto

PREP: 10 MINUTES ∿ COOK: 20 MINUTES

1 package (16 ounces) penne or ziti pasta
Salt
1 teaspoon olive oil
1 medium onion, coarsely chopped
1 package (10 ounces) medium mushrooms, coarsely chopped
2 medium tomatoes, seeded and diced
1 cup pesto, homemade (opposite page) or store-bought

1 In large saucepot, prepare pasta in *boiling salted water* as label directs; drain. Return pasta to saucepot; keep warm.

2 Meanwhile, in nonstick 10-inch skillet, heat olive oil over medium-high heat until hot. Add onion and mushrooms and cook with ½ teaspoon salt until mix-

ture is lightly browned. Stir in ¼ *cup water;* reduce heat to medium; cover and continue cooking, stirring often, until onion is tender.

**3** Stir tomatoes and pesto into mushroom mixture; heat through. Pour mixture over penne; toss gently. Spoon mixture onto warm platter. *Makes 4 servings.*

Each serving: About 720 calories, 23 g protein, 99 g carbohydrate, 27 g total fat (5 g saturated), 5 mg cholesterol, 1210 mg sodium.

# Sicilian Linguine

PREP: 10 MINUTES ⌒ COOK: 25 MINUTES

If your supermarket doesn't carry broccoli rabe, you can make this with regular broccoli. Cut the tops into very small flowerets and the stems into thick matchsticks.

1 package (16 ounces) linguine or spaghetti
Salt
2 tablespoons olive oil
3 garlic cloves, crushed with side of chef's knife
2 bunches broccoli rabe (about 1 pound each),
    tough stems removed
¼ teaspoon crushed red pepper
½ cup golden raisins
1 can (2 ounces) anchovy fillets

**1** In large saucepot, prepare linguine in *boiling salted water* as label directs. Drain linguine, reserving *½ cup pasta cooking water.*

**2** Meanwhile, in 5-quart Dutch oven, heat olive oil over medium heat until hot. Add garlic and cook until golden. Increase heat to medium-high. Add broccoli rabe, crushed red pepper, and ¼ teaspoon salt; cook, stirring occasionally, until broccoli rabe wilts. Add raisins and continue cooking, stirring, until broccoli rabe is tender.

**3** In pasta cooking pot, cook anchovies with their oil over medium heat, stirring, until anchovies just begin to dissolve. Transfer from heat; add linguine, tossing to coat.

**4** Add linguine mixture and reserved pasta cooking water to broccoli rabe mixture, tossing to combine well. *Makes 4 servings.*

Each serving: About 620 calories, 23 g protein, 106 g carbohydrate, 13 g total fat (2 g saturated), 6 mg cholesterol, 985 mg sodium.

# HOMEMADE PESTO

Pesto is an extremely forgiving recipe. Feel free to experiment with it according to taste and availability of ingredients.

PREP: 10 MINUTES

*2 cups loosely packed fresh basil leaves*
*¼ cup olive oil*
*¼ cup grated Parmesan cheese*
*2 tablespoons pine nuts (pignoli)*
*½ teaspoon salt*

In food processor, with knife blade attached, or in blender, at medium speed, blend basil, olive oil, Parmesan, pine nuts, salt, and *¼ cup hot tap water* until smooth. Makes about ¾ cup (enough to serve over 1 pound pasta).

Each tablespoon: About 60 calories, 2 g protein, 1 g carbohydrate, 6 g total fat (1 g saturated), 1 mg cholesterol, 130 mg sodium.

## Some Pesto Variables

• For a more traditional, Genovese-style pesto, add 1 or 2 cloves of garlic. To tame the garlic's pungency, cook the cloves in boiling water for about 1 minute before adding them to the food processor or blender.

• For a much lighter version of pesto, try reducing the olive oil to only 2 tablespoons and adding chicken broth or water in its place.

• Although the pine nuts are a traditional pesto ingredient, you can either leave them out altogether or use another type of nut: walnuts or almonds work well.

• For a greener, less basil-y flavor, substitute torn baby spinach leaves for about one-third of the basil.

# Hearty Meatless Pasta & Vegetables

PREP: 15 MINUTES ∾ COOK: 35 MINUTES

Textured soy protein (TSP) comes in forms that mimic meat or poultry. For instance, one form resembles ground beef; another looks like chicken strips. This recipe calls for the ground-beef type. We've added a bit more seasoning than would be called for in a beef-based casserole to make up for TSP's milder flavor.

1¼ cups textured soy protein (ground-beef type)
2 teaspoons vegetable oil
2 medium carrots, peeled and thinly sliced
1 medium onion, diced
1 small green pepper, diced
2 garlic cloves, crushed with garlic press
1 can (28 ounces) crushed tomatoes
1 teaspoon sugar
¼ teaspoon coarsely ground black pepper
Salt
1 package (16 ounces) corkscrew or rotelle pasta
Grated Parmesan cheese (optional)

1 Rehydrate textured soy protein: In 2-quart saucepan, heat *1¼ cups water* to boiling over high heat. Remove saucepan from heat; stir in textured soy protein; set aside.

2 In nonstick 12-inch skillet, heat vegetable oil over medium heat until hot. Add carrots, onion, green pepper, garlic, and *2 tablespoons water*; cook, stirring frequently, until vegetables are tender and golden, about 15 minutes.

3 Stir in rehydrated textured soy protein, tomatoes, sugar, black pepper, ½ teaspoon salt, and *½ cup water*; heat to boiling over high heat. Reduce heat to low; simmer, covered, 20 minutes.

4 Meanwhile, in large saucepot, prepare pasta in *boiling salted water* as label directs.

5 Drain pasta; return to saucepot. Add sauce; toss to mix well. Serve with Parmesan if you like. *Makes 4 servings.*

Each serving without Parmesan: About 630 calories, 34 g protein, 117 g carbohydrate, 5 g total fat (.5 g saturated), 0 mg cholesterol, 780 mg sodium.

# Orzo "Risotto" with Mushrooms

PREP: 10 MINUTES ∾ COOK: 20 MINUTES

1 package (16 ounces) orzo (rice-shaped pasta)
Salt
1 tablespoon olive oil
1 medium onion, chopped
8 ounces medium shiitake mushrooms, stems discarded and caps cut into ¼-inch-thick slices
8 ounces medium regular mushrooms, cut into ¼-inch-thick slices
¼ cup dry white wine
2 tablespoons cornstarch
2½ cups low-fat (1%) milk
⅓ cup grated Parmesan cheese
3 tablespoons chopped fresh parsley leaves
1 tablespoon margarine or butter

1 In 5-quart saucepot, prepare orzo in *boiling salted water* as label directs; drain orzo.

2 Meanwhile, in nonstick 12-inch skillet, heat olive oil over medium heat until hot. Add onion and cook 5 minutes. Increase heat to medium-high. Add both kinds of mushrooms and ¼ teaspoon salt; cook, stirring frequently, until mushrooms are tender and golden. Remove skillet from heat; stir in white wine.

3 In small bowl, mix cornstarch with milk. Add cornstarch mixture to same 5-quart saucepot. Heat to boiling over medium heat. Reduce heat to low; simmer 1 minute. Stir in orzo, mushroom mixture, grated Parmesan, parsley, margarine or butter, and ¼ teaspoon salt; heat through. Serve "risotto" immediately while still creamy. *Makes 6 servings.*

Each serving: About 425 calories, 17 g protein, 70 g carbohydrate, 8 g total fat (2 g saturated), 8 mg cholesterol, 615 mg sodium.

◄ *Orzo "Risotto" with Mushrooms*

# Quick Vegetarian Cincinnati Chili

PREP: 15 MINUTES  ⌒  COOK: 15 MINUTES

Low in fat and a snap to put together.

12 ounces spaghetti
Salt
2 teaspoons vegetable oil
1 medium onion, chopped
1 tablespoon chili powder
¼ teaspoon ground cinnamon
1 can (15 to 16 ounces) pink beans, rinsed and
    drained
1 can (14½ ounces) diced tomatoes
1 tablespoon tomato paste
½ teaspoon sugar
Toppings: ¼ cup shredded reduced-fat Cheddar
    cheese, 2 tablespoons nonfat sour cream, 3
    green onions, chopped

**1** In large saucepot, prepare spaghetti in *boiling salted water* as label directs; drain and keep warm.

**2** Meanwhile, in nonstick 10-inch skillet, heat vegetable oil over medium heat until hot. Add onion and *3 tablespoons water*; cook until onion is tender and golden, about 10 minutes. Add chili powder and cinnamon; cook, stirring, 1 minute.

**3** Stir in pink beans, tomatoes with their juice, tomato paste, sugar, ¼ teaspoon salt, and ½ *cup water*; heat to boiling over high heat. Reduce heat to low; simmer, uncovered, 5 minutes.

**4** To serve, divide spaghetti evenly among 4 warm dinner plates. Spoon chili over spaghetti; serve with toppings. *Makes 4 servings.*

Each serving with toppings: About 475 calories, 20 g protein, 86 g carbohydrate, 6 g total fat (1 g saturated), 6 mg cholesterol, 900 mg sodium.

# Cantonese Noodle Pancake

PREP: 10 MINUTES  ⌒  COOK: 45 MINUTES

1 package (16 ounces) spaghetti
1 pork tenderloin (about 12 ounces), thinly sliced
2 tablespoons dry sherry
¼ cup soy sauce
2 teaspoons cornstarch
3 tablespoons vegetable oil
4 large green onions, cut into 1-inch pieces
1 large red pepper, cut into 1-inch pieces
1 small head bok choy (about 12 ounces), cut
    crosswise into 2-inch pieces
4 ounces snow peas, strings removed
2 tablespoons minced, peeled fresh ginger
1 can (15 ounces) Chinese straw mushrooms,
    drained

**1** In large saucepot, prepare spaghetti in *boiling water* as label directs, but do not add salt to water. Drain spaghetti.

**2** In 11" by 7" glass baking dish, mix pork, sherry, and 2 tablespoons soy sauce. In cup, mix cornstarch, *1 cup water*, and remaining 2 tablespoons soy sauce. Set aside.

**3** In nonstick 12-inch skillet, heat 1 tablespoon vegetable oil over medium heat until hot. Arrange cooked spaghetti in skillet to form a 12-inch round pancake. Cook 5 to 8 minutes or until spaghetti pancake is golden on bottom. Carefully invert pancake onto 12-inch plate. Carefully slide pancake back into skillet; cook 5 to 8 minutes longer or until golden on the other side. Transfer pancake to large platter; keep warm.

**4** While pancake is cooking, in nonstick 5-quart Dutch oven or saucepot, heat 2 teaspoons vegetable oil over medium-high heat until hot. Add green onions and red pepper and cook until tender-crisp; transfer to bowl.

**5** In same Dutch oven, heat 2 teaspoons vegetable oil; cook bok choy and snow peas until vegetables are tender-crisp; transfer to bowl with pepper mixture.

**6** In same Dutch oven, heat remaining 2 teaspoons vegetable oil; cook pork mixture and ginger until pork loses its pink color.

**7** Return vegetable mixture to Dutch oven. Stir cornstarch mixture; stir into vegetable mixture with straw mushrooms. Heat over medium-high heat until mixture boils and thickens slightly.

**8** Spoon pork mixture onto noodle pancake. Cut into wedges to serve. *Makes 6 servings.*

Each serving: About 455 calories, 25 g protein, 65 g carbohydrate, 10 g total fat (1 g saturated), 32 mg cholesterol, 975 mg sodium.

## Egg Noodles Florentine

PREP: 5 MINUTES ∿ COOK: 20 MINUTES

1 package (16 ounces) curly wide egg noodles
Salt
2 tablespoons pine nuts (pignoli) or 2 tablespoons
    chopped walnuts
2 tablespoons olive oil
1 medium onion, chopped
2 tablespoons all-purpose flour
⅛ teaspoon coarsely ground black pepper
2½ cups reduced-fat (2%) milk
1 package (10 ounces) frozen chopped spinach,
    thawed and squeezed dry
⅓ cup grated Parmesan cheese

**1** In large saucepot, prepare noodles in *boiling salted water* as label directs. Drain noodles, reserving *¼ cup pasta cooking water.*

**2** Meanwhile, in 10-inch skillet, toast pine nuts over medium heat, shaking skillet frequently, until nuts are golden; transfer to plate.

**3** In same skillet, heat olive oil over medium heat until hot. Add onion and cook until very tender but not brown. Stir in flour, pepper, and ½ teaspoon salt; cook 1 minute. Gradually add milk and cook, stirring, until mixture thickens and is smooth. Stir in spinach, Parmesan, and reserved pasta cooking water. Stir in noodles; heat through. Sprinkle with pine nuts. *Makes 6 servings.*

Each serving: About 445 calories, 19 g protein, 66 g carbohydrate, 13 g total fat (4 g saturated), 83 mg cholesterol, 635 mg sodium.

## Pasta with Sun-Dried Tomatoes & Olives

PREP: 5 MINUTES ∿ COOK: 25 MINUTES

1 package (16 ounces) radiatore pasta
1 tablespoon olive oil
3 garlic cloves, minced
⅓ cup chopped sun-dried tomatoes
1 can (14½ ounces) chicken broth or
    1¾ cups homemade (page 24)
½ cup Kalamata olives, pitted and chopped
¼ cup chopped fresh parsley leaves
2 ounces mild goat cheese, crumbled

**1** In large saucepot, prepare pasta in *boiling water* as label directs, but do not add salt to water.

**2** Meanwhile, in a nonstick 10-inch skillet, heat olive oil over medium-high heat until hot. Add garlic and cook over medium heat 30 seconds. Add sun-dried tomatoes and chicken broth and simmer 10 minutes.

**3** Add olives and parsley. Drain pasta and toss with dried-tomato sauce. Served topped with goat cheese. *Makes 4 servings.*

Each serving: About 585 calories, 20 g protein, 93 g carbohydrate, 15 g total fat (4 g saturated), 11 mg cholesterol, 840 mg sodium.

### FOOD EDITOR'S TIP

**Q.** My supermarket sells packages of dry sun-dried tomatoes that cost much less than the oil-packed kind. How do I use them?

**A.** It's easy. If the tomatoes are to be cooked in a soup or a sauce (such as for Pasta with Sun-Dried Tomatoes & Olives, above), you can add them straight to the liquid. However, if you are adding them as a seasoning to pasta or a salad, or using them in a salad dressing, for example, they need to be rehydrated. To rehydrate the tomatoes (which can be stored dry in an airtight container for up to a year), cover them with boiling water and let stand for about 5 minutes. For storage once they've been rehydrated, drain and squeeze out excess water. Then pack loosely in a jar, cover with olive oil, and add dried herbs if you like. Store in the refrigerator for up to 6 months.

# Tuscan Bow Ties

〰〰〰〰〰〰〰〰

PREP: 10 MINUTES 〰 COOK: 30 MINUTES

Potatoes and pasta seasoned with the earthy flavors of mushrooms and rosemary make this dish a Tuscan treat.

1 pound red potatoes, unpeeled and cut into
    ¾-inch chunks
Salt
12 ounces bow-tie or farfalle pasta
1 tablespoon olive oil
12 ounces shiitake mushrooms, stems discarded
    and caps cut into ½-inch-thick slices, or 12
    ounces regular mushrooms, sliced
2 garlic cloves, crushed with side of chef's knife
1½ teaspoons chopped fresh rosemary or
    ¾ teaspoon dried rosemary leaves, crushed
1¼ cups chicken broth, canned or homemade
    (page 24)
1½ teaspoons cornstarch
¼ cup dry vermouth, dry white wine, or chicken
    broth
2 ounces thinly sliced prosciutto, cut crosswise
    into ½-inch-wide strips

1 In 4-quart saucepan, heat *3 quarts water* and 1 tablespoon salt to boiling over high heat. Add potatoes; heat to boiling. Cook potatoes 5 to 10 minutes or until tender. With slotted spoon, transfer potatoes to bowl; cover and keep warm.

2 Return water in saucepan to boiling. Add bow ties and cook until tender; drain and return to saucepan.

3 Meanwhile, in nonstick 12-inch skillet, heat olive oil over medium-high heat until hot. Add mushrooms, garlic, and rosemary and cook until mushrooms are tender and golden.

4 In small bowl, mix chicken broth and cornstarch until smooth. Add chicken-broth mixture and vermouth to mushrooms. Heat to boiling over high heat; boil 1 minute. Add bow ties and potatoes; heat through.

5 Spoon bow-tie mixture into large serving bowl; toss with prosciutto. *Makes 6 servings.*

Each serving: About 325 calories, 13 g protein, 59 g carbohydrate, 4 g total fat (1 g saturated), 8 mg cholesterol, 425 mg sodium.

# Pumpkin-Potato Gnocchi with Fresh Tomato-Sage Sauce

〰〰〰〰〰〰〰〰〰〰

PREP: 20 MINUTES 〰 COOK: 40 MINUTES

1 pound all-purpose potatoes, peeled and cut into
    2-inch chunks
1 cup canned solid-pack pumpkin
1 teaspoon salt
⅛ teaspoon ground nutmeg
1¾ cups all-purpose flour
Fresh Tomato-Sage Sauce (opposite page) or
    melted butter
Sage leaves for garnish

1 In 2-quart saucepan, heat potatoes and *enough water to cover* to boiling over high heat. Reduce heat to low; cover and simmer 15 to 20 minutes or until potatoes are very tender. Drain potatoes very well.

2 In large bowl, with potato masher, mash potatoes until very smooth. Add pumpkin, salt, and nutmeg; mash until blended. With wooden spoon, stir in flour until dough almost comes together. With hands, gently press dough into a ball. Divide dough in half.

3 On floured surface, with floured hands, gently knead each dough half to a smooth, soft dough. Divide each half into 6 pieces. Working with 1 piece of dough at a time, roll into a rope, about ¾ inch in diameter. Then, cut rope crosswise into 1-inch pieces (gnocchi). Place gnocchi on lightly floured jelly-roll pan. Repeat rolling, cutting, and placing gnocchi on jelly-roll pan with remaining pieces of dough.

4 In 5-quart saucepot, heat *4 quarts water* to boiling over high heat. Using pancake turner, transfer gnocchi, one-third at a time, to boiling water. As soon as gnocchi float, with slotted spoon, carefully lift gnocchi from water, blotting bottom of slotted spoon with paper towels to remove excess water; place on warm platter. Repeat with remaining gnocchi.

5 Serve gnocchi with Fresh Tomato-Sage Sauce or melted butter. Garnish with sage leaves if you like. *Makes 6 servings.*

Each serving of gnocchi without sauce or butter: About 195 calories, 6 g protein, 42 g carbohydrate, 1 g total fat (0 g saturated), 0 mg cholesterol, 360 mg sodium.

# Fresh Tomato-Sage Sauce

PREP: 5 MINUTES ～ COOK: 20 MINUTES

1 tablespoon olive oil
1 small onion, finely chopped
½ teaspoon salt
2 pounds plum tomatoes, peeled and coarsely
   chopped
3 tablespoons butter or olive oil
1 tablespoon chopped fresh sage

1 In 10-inch skillet, heat olive oil over medium heat until hot. Add onion and cook until golden. Add salt and tomatoes with their juice; heat to boiling over high heat. Reduce heat to low; cover and simmer 15 minutes, stirring and mashing tomatoes with spoon occasionally.

2 Stir in butter and sage. *Makes about 3½ cups sauce, 6 servings.*

Each serving: About 105 calories, 2 g protein, 8 g carbohydrate, 9 g total fat (4 g saturated), 15 mg cholesterol, 250 mg sodium.

*Pumpkin-Potato Gnocchi with Fresh Tomato-Sage Sauce*

# Bow-Tie Pasta with Baby Artichokes & Basil

PREP: 20 MINUTES ～ COOK: 25 MINUTES

If baby artichokes are not available, use two regular artichokes and simply trim and remove chokes, cut each artichoke into eighths and follow the recipe as written for baby artichokes.

12 baby artichokes (about 1½ pounds)
2 teaspoons olive oil
1 small onion, chopped
2 garlic cloves, minced
1¾ cups chicken broth, canned or homemade
   (page 24)
½ cup dry white wine
¼ teaspoon crushed red pepper
Salt
1 package (16 ounces) bow-tie or farfalle pasta
½ teaspoon cornstarch
⅓ cup loosely packed fresh basil leaves, cut into
   thin strips

1 Trim baby artichokes: Bend back outer green leaves and snap them off at base until leaves are half green (at the top) and half yellow (at the bottom). Cut off stems and across top of each artichoke at point where yellow meets green. Cut each artichoke lengthwise in half.

2 In nonstick 12-inch skillet, heat olive oil over medium heat. Add onion and cook 7 minutes; add garlic and cook 3 minutes longer.

3 Add 1½ cups chicken broth, white wine, crushed red pepper, and ½ teaspoon salt; heat to boiling over high heat. Add artichokes; heat to boiling. Reduce heat to medium-low; cover and simmer just until artichokes are tender, about 15 minutes, or until knife inserted in bottom of artichoke goes through easily.

4 Meanwhile, in large saucepot, prepare pasta in *boiling salted water* as label directs.

5 In cup, mix cornstarch with remaining ¼ cup chicken broth; stir into artichoke mixture; heat to boiling over high heat. Boil 1 minute.

6 Drain pasta and place in large serving bowl; toss with artichoke mixture and basil. *Makes 4 servings.*

Each serving: About 515 calories, 19 g protein, 99 g carbohydrate, 5 g total fat (1 g saturated), 5 mg cholesterol, 655 mg sodium.

# Shells with Peas & Cream

1 package (16 ounces) medium shell pasta
Salt
1 tablespoon olive oil
1 medium onion, chopped
2 cans (14½ ounces each) diced tomatoes
1 package (10 ounces) frozen peas, thawed
¼ cup packed fresh basil leaves, chopped
¼ cup heavy or whipping cream
¼ teaspoon crushed red pepper

1 In large saucepot, prepare pasta in *boiling salted water* as label directs.

2 Meanwhile, in a 10-inch skillet, heat olive oil over medium-high heat until hot. Add onion and cook until tender.

3 Add diced tomatoes, peas, basil, cream, crushed red pepper, and ¼ teaspoon salt to skillet. Cook until slightly thickened and heated through.

4 Drain pasta and toss with sauce. *Makes 4 servings.*

Each serving: About 635 calories, 22 g protein, 113 g carbohydrate, 12 g total fat (4 g saturated), 20 mg cholesterol, 965 mg sodium.

# Farfalle with Light Alfredo Sauce

1 package (16 ounces) farfalle or bow-tie pasta
Salt
1 pound broccoli flowerets
2 teaspoons vegetable oil
1 small onion, diced

## THE 4 TOP GRATING CHEESES

Sit down to a plate of steaming pasta and your first move is usually to reach for the grated cheese. Most have been aged a year or more, which accounts for their deliciously intense flavor and crumbly texture. (Italians take their grating cheeses so seriously that production of many of them is government-controlled to guarantee quality.) You may think grated cheese means Parmesan, but there are many delicious alternatives. Our favorites:

***Parmigiano-Reggiano*** The best Parmesan cheese, and one of the most expensive. Produced in the Emilia-Romagna region of northern Italy (to be sure you're getting the real thing, look for the name stenciled on the rind of the cheese), it's made from skim or part-skim cow's milk and has pale to deep yellow coloring and a slightly sweet, nutty taste.

***Grana Padano*** Country cousin of Parmigiano-Reggiano. This straw-colored cheese is similar to the best but has a slightly softer texture, is not as sweet, and is less expensive. The flavor: mellow, rich, and slightly salty.

***Pecorino Romano*** Pecorino Romano is made from sheep's milk. It is straw-white in color and has a sharper flavor than the other cheeses listed here.

Although it is sometimes referred to as "Locatelli," Locatelli is a brand name of Pecorino Romano.

***Asiago*** Made from whole or part-skim cow's milk, Asiago has a nutty, slightly sharp, salty flavor. Because it is not as well-known as the other cheeses, it may be harder to find.

**SHOPPING TIPS** Ask for a wedge to be cut from a large wheel of cheese, or look for pieces that are tightly sealed in plastic wrap with no white spots (a sign that the cheese is drying out).

**KEEP-FRESH STORAGE** To prevent moisture from escaping, wrap the cheese in foil and place in a resealable plastic bag. Store it in the cheese or dairy drawer of your refrigerator where it is not as cold and the cheese will be less likely to dry out. Never freeze grated cheese—it will dry out quickly. Since the flavor fades once the cheese is grated, grate it as you need it, never ahead. You'll notice the difference.

**GH TIP** Don't throw away the rinds of grating cheeses. For a terrific flavor booster, toss them into the pot while you're simmering tomato sauce or minestrone or lentil soup.

1 garlic clove, minced
2 cups skim milk
1 cup chicken broth, canned or homemade
   (page 24)
3 tablespoons all-purpose flour
¼ teaspoon coarsely ground black pepper
½ cup grated Parmesan cheese

1 In large saucepot, prepare pasta in *boiling salted water* as label directs. After pasta has cooked 9 minutes, add the broccoli and cook until tender-crisp.

2 Meanwhile, in a 10-inch skillet, heat the vegetable oil over medium-high heat until hot. Add onion and garlic and cook until golden.

3 In bowl, mix milk, chicken broth, flour, ¼ teaspoon salt, and pepper. Stir into onion mixture and cook, stirring, until thickened. Stir in Parmesan.

4 Drain pasta and broccoli and toss with sauce. *Makes 4 servings.*

Each serving: About 600 calories, 28 g protein, 104 g carbohydrate, 8 g total fat (3 g saturated), 10 mg cholesterol, 1100 mg sodium.

## Fettuccine with Asparagus & Shrimp

PREP: 20 MINUTES ∾ COOK: 20 MINUTES

1 large lemon
1 pound large shrimp, shelled and deveined
¼ to ½ teaspoon crushed red pepper
Salt
1 package (8 ounces) fettuccine or linguine
2 tablespoons vegetable oil
1 medium onion, diced
2 medium yellow peppers, cut into ¼-inch-thick
   strips
1 pound asparagus, trimmed and cut diagonally into
   3-inch pieces
1 tablespoon soy sauce

1 From lemon, grate peel and squeeze juice. In bowl, mix shrimp with lemon juice, crushed red pepper, and ¼ teaspoon salt.

2 In large saucepot, prepare fettuccine in *boiling salted water* as label directs; drain and return pasta to saucepot; keep warm.

3 Meanwhile, in nonstick 12-inch skillet, heat 1 tablespoon vegetable oil over medium-high heat until hot. Add onion, yellow-pepper strips, and ¼ teaspoon salt and cook until peppers are tender-crisp; transfer to bowl.

4 In same skillet, heat remaining 1 tablespoon vegetable oil; add asparagus and shrimp mixture and cook until asparagus are tender-crisp and shrimp turn opaque throughout, about 3 minutes. Stir in yellow-pepper mixture and *½ cup water*; heat through.

5 To serve, toss fettuccine with shrimp mixture and soy sauce. Sprinkle with grated lemon peel. *Makes 4 servings.*

Each serving: About 420 calories, 30 g protein, 54 g carbohydrate, 10 g total fat (1 g saturated), 140 mg cholesterol, 740 mg sodium.

## Ziti with Spinach, Garbanzos & Raisins

PREP: 10 MINUTES ∾ COOK: 20 MINUTES

1 package (16 ounces) ziti or penne pasta
Salt
2 tablespoons olive oil
4 garlic cloves, crushed with garlic press
1 bag (10 ounces) prewashed spinach, stems
   removed
1 can (19 ounces) garbanzo beans, rinsed and
   drained
¼ cup golden raisins
¼ teaspoon crushed red pepper
½ cup chicken broth, canned or homemade
   (page 24)

1 In large saucepot, prepare pasta in *boiling salted water* as label directs.

2 Meanwhile, in a nonstick 10-inch skillet, heat olive oil over medium-high heat until hot. Add garlic and cook until golden.

3 Increase the heat to high and stir in the spinach, garbanzo beans, raisins, crushed red pepper, and ¼ teaspoon salt. Cook until spinach wilts. Stir in chicken broth.

4 Drain pasta and toss with sauce. *Makes 4 servings.*

Each serving: About 620 calories, 21 g protein, 108 g carbohydrate, 11 g total fat (1 g saturated), 0 mg cholesterol, 860 mg sodium.

# Penne with Gorgonzola & Walnuts

PREP: 5 MINUTES ～ COOK: 20 MINUTES

1 package (16 ounces) penne pasta
Salt
1 cup half-and-half or light cream
¾ cup chicken broth, canned or homemade
  (page 24)
4 ounces Gorgonzola or blue cheese, crumbled
¼ teaspoon coarsely ground black pepper
½ cup chopped walnuts, toasted

1 In large saucepot, prepare pasta in *boiling salted water* as label directs; drain.

2 Meanwhile, in 2-quart saucepan, heat half-and-half and chicken broth to boiling over medium-high heat. Reduce heat to medium; cook 5 minutes. Add Gorgonzola and pepper, whisking constantly, until melted and smooth.

3 In large serving bowl, toss pasta with sauce. Sprinkle with walnuts to serve. *Makes 6 servings.*

Each serving: About 460 calories, 17 g protein, 61 g carbohydrate, 17 g total fat (7 g saturated), 28 mg cholesterol, 455 mg sodium.

# Ravioli with Light Cream Sauce

PREP: 5 MINUTES ～ COOK: 20 MINUTES

1 package (13 ounces) frozen large cheese ravioli
1 tablespoon olive oil
1 small onion, minced
1½ teaspoons all-purpose flour
1 cup low-fat (1%) milk
2 tablespoons grated Parmesan cheese
¼ cup finely chopped prosciutto or cooked ham
  (about 1 ounce)
Fresh parsley leaves for garnish

1 In large saucepot, prepare ravioli in *boiling water* as label directs, but do not add salt to water; drain. Keep warm.

2 Meanwhile, in 3-quart saucepan, heat olive oil over medium heat until hot. Add onion and cook until tender but not browned. Stir in flour; cook 1 minute. Gradually stir in milk and cook over medium-high heat, stirring constantly, until mixture boils and thickens slightly. Remove from heat; stir in Parmesan .

3 To serve, spoon sauce onto 3 dinner plates; arrange ravioli in sauce. Sprinkle with prosciutto. Garnish with parsley leaves. *Makes 3 servings.*

Each serving: About 540 calories, 27 g protein, 58 g carbohydrate, 22 g total fat (9 g saturated), 120 mg cholesterol, 745 mg sodium.

# Angel Hair Pasta with Shrimp & Escarole

PREP: 20 MINUTES ～ COOK: 15 MINUTES

Watch the pot closely as angel hair pasta (or capellini) cooks in a very few minutes.

12 ounces angel hair pasta or capellini
2 cans (14½ ounces each) chicken broth or
  3½ cups homemade (page 24)
1½ cups spicy hot vegetable juice
1 cup sun-dried tomatoes, about 1½ ounces (not
  oil-packed), thinly sliced
1 pound large shrimp, shelled and deveined, sliced
  horizontally in half
4 cups loosely packed sliced escarole (about
  ½ small head)
1 medium tomato, seeded and chopped

1 In large saucepot, prepare angel hair pasta in *boiling water* as label directs, but do not add salt to water. Drain pasta; return to saucepot.

2 Meanwhile, in 3-quart saucepan, heat chicken broth, spicy hot vegetable juice, sun-dried tomatoes, and *1½ cups water* to boiling over high heat. Add shrimp; heat to boiling. Cook 1 minute or until shrimp turn opaque throughout.

3 Add escarole to shrimp mixture; cook just until escarole wilts.

4 Add shrimp mixture to pasta; toss well. Spoon pasta into large bowl; sprinkle with chopped tomato. *Makes 6 servings.*

Each serving: About 335 calories, 23 g protein, 53 g carbohydrate, 3 g total fat (1 g saturated), 93 mg cholesterol, 885 mg sodium.

# Farfalle with Smoked Salmon & Dill Cream

~~~~~~~~~~~~~~~~~~~~~~~

PREP: 10 MINUTES ～ COOK: 20 MINUTES

12 ounces farfalle or bow-tie pasta
1 large carrot, peeled and grated (about 1 cup)
⅓ cup dry vermouth or dry white wine
1 cup half-and-half or light cream
½ teaspoon salt
¼ teaspoon coarsely ground black pepper
½ pound sliced smoked salmon, cut into 2-inch
  pieces
1 tablespoon chopped fresh dill

1 In large saucepot, prepare pasta in *boiling water* as label directs, but do not add salt to water; drain.

2 Meanwhile, in nonstick 10-inch skillet, cook grated carrot and *½ cup water* over medium-high heat until tender, about 5 minutes. Add vermouth and heat to boiling; cook 1 minute. Stir in half-and-half, salt, and pepper; heat to boiling. Cook 1 minute. Remove skillet from heat; stir in salmon pieces and dill.

3 To serve, toss salmon mixture with pasta. *Makes 4 servings.*

Each serving: About 590 calories, 23 g protein, 71 g carbohydrate, 22 g total fat (12 g saturated), 79 mg cholesterol, 755 mg sodium.

## ▇ FOOD EDITOR'S TIP ▇

**Q.** My supermarket doesn't even carry saffron, and my local gourmet store charges way too much for it. Is there any other spice I can use that will do the same job as saffron?

**A.** Yes and no. There isn't really anything that can take the place of the subtle flavor that saffron brings to a dish. But you can reproduce the deep golden color of saffron by substituting ground turmeric. This spice—used in curries and other Indian dishes—is far less expensive, and much more available, than saffron. Start out with the same amount of turmeric as saffron called for in the recipe, but if the color does not look rich enough, add a pinch more turmeric.

# Capellini with Shrimp & Saffron Cream Sauce

~~~~~~~~~~~~~~~~~~~~~~~

PREP: 10 MINUTES ～ COOK: 20 MINUTES

1 tablespoon plus 2 teaspoons vegetable oil
1 pound large shrimp, shelled and deveined
Salt
1 large shallot or ½ small onion, finely chopped
1 can (14½ ounces) chicken broth or
  1¾ cups homemade (page 24)
¼ cup dry white wine (optional)
1 cup frozen peas
¼ teaspoon saffron threads, crushed
¾ cup half-and-half or light cream
2 teaspoons finely chopped fresh parsley leaves
12 ounces capellini or angel hair pasta or thin
  spaghetti

1 In nonstick 12-inch skillet, heat 1 tablespoon vegetable oil over medium-high heat until hot. Add shrimp and ⅛ teaspoon salt and cook, stirring frequently, until shrimp turn opaque throughout and are tender; transfer to bowl.

2 In same skillet, heat remaining 2 teaspoons vegetable oil over medium heat until hot. Add shallot and cook until golden. Add chicken broth, wine, frozen peas, and saffron threads; heat to boiling. Reduce heat to low; cover and simmer 5 minutes. Add shrimp and half-and-half; heat over medium-high heat just to simmering (but do not boil or mixture may curdle). Stir in parsley.

3 Meanwhile, in large saucepot, prepare capellini in *boiling salted water* as label directs. Drain pasta and place in large serving bowl. Pour shrimp mixture over pasta. Toss before serving. *Makes 4 servings.*

Each serving: About 565 calories, 34 g protein, 74 g carbohydrate, 14 g total fat (4 g saturated), 162 mg cholesterol, 690 mg sodium.

## Spaghettini with Pesto, Shrimp & Vegetables

12 ounces spaghettini or capellini
2 tablespoons olive oil
1 medium red pepper, cut into thin strips
1 medium yellow pepper, cut into thin strips
¾ teaspoon salt
1 large zucchini (about 12 ounces), halved
    crosswise, then cut into julienne strips
1 package (10 ounces) frozen peas
12 ounces large shrimp, shelled and deveined
¾ cup pesto, homemade (page 141) or store-
    bought

1 In large saucepot, prepare spaghetti in *boiling water* as label directs, but do not add salt to water.

2 Meanwhile, in nonstick 12-inch skillet, heat 1 tablespoon olive oil over medium-high heat until hot. Add peppers and ½ teaspoon salt and cook until the pep-

pers are lightly browned; add zucchini and frozen peas and cook until zucchini is tender-crisp and peas are heated through. Transfer vegetables to large bowl.

3 In same skillet, heat remaining 1 tablespoon olive oil over medium-high heat. Add shrimp and remaining ¼ teaspoon salt and cook, stirring constantly, until shrimp turn opaque throughout and are lightly browned. Add shrimp to vegetables.

4 Drain pasta and add to vegetable mixture. Add pesto and toss to mix well. *Makes 6 servings.*

Each serving: About 470 calories, 23 g protein, 55 g carbohydrate, 18 g total fat (3 g saturated), 72 mg cholesterol, 870 mg sodium.

## Radiatore with Shrimp Fra Diavolo

If ¼ teaspoon crushed red pepper isn't enough "diavolo" for you, make this more devilish with a cautious pinch of ground red pepper (cayenne).

1 package (16 ounces) radiatore pasta
Salt
2 tablespoons olive oil
2 garlic cloves, minced
¼ teaspoon crushed red pepper
1 can (28 ounces) tomatoes in puree
¾ pound medium shrimp, shelled and deveined

1 In large saucepot, prepare pasta in *boiling salted water* as label directs.

2 Meanwhile, in a 10-inch skillet, heat olive oil, garlic, crushed red pepper, and ¼ teaspoon salt over medium heat for 30 seconds.

3 Add tomatoes with their puree; heat to boiling. Cook 5 minutes. Stir in shrimp; cook 2 minutes or until shrimp turn opaque throughout.

4 Drain pasta and toss with sauce. *Makes 4 servings.*

Each serving: About 610 calories, 30 g protein, 98 g carbohydrate, 10 g total fat (1 g saturated), 105 mg cholesterol, 955 mg sodium.

### FUN SHAPES

Move over, spaghetti. Pasta now comes in a variety of shapes—such as the leaves and baseball paraphernalia shown here—colors, and even flavors. In addition to such standards as spinach and tomato pasta, we've also

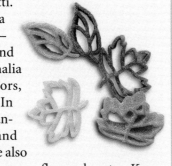

tasted garlic- and pepper-flavored pastas. Keep an eye out for special shapes in your local specialty food shops, and even in supermarkets. Sometimes pasta companies will issue special shapes to commemorate a holiday, such as July 4th (we once saw pasta in the shape of the Statue of Liberty).

# Bow Ties with Curry-Spiced Chicken

PREP: 15 MINUTES ∾ COOK: 30 MINUTES

Fresh ginger underscores the curry spices in this pasta-and-chicken dish.

1½ cups farfalle or bow-tie pasta (about 3 ounces)
2 tablespoons margarine or butter
4 small skinless, boneless chicken-breast halves (about 1 pound), cut crosswise into 2 or 3 pieces
¾ teaspoon salt
3 large carrots, peeled and cut into 1½" by ¼" sticks
1 medium onion, chopped
1½ teaspoons curry powder
1 teaspoon grated, peeled fresh ginger
1 can (14½ ounces) diced tomatoes
1 cup frozen peas, thawed
½ teaspoon sugar

1 In 2-quart saucepan, heat *4 cups water* to boiling over high heat. Add bow-tie pasta and cook until almost tender; drain and set aside.

2 In nonstick 12-inch skillet, heat 1 tablespoon margarine or butter over medium-high heat. Add chicken and ¼ teaspoon salt and cook until chicken is browned and juices run clear when chicken is pierced with tip of knife; transfer to plate.

3 In same skillet, heat remaining 1 tablespoon margarine until hot; cook carrots and onion until browned. Reduce heat to medium. Add *3 tablespoons water*; cover and cook until vegetables are tender, about 5 minutes longer.

4 Stir curry powder and ginger into vegetable mixture; cook 1 minute. Stir in pasta, chicken, tomatoes with their juice, peas, sugar, remaining ½ teaspoon salt, and *½ cup water*; heat to boiling over high heat. Reduce heat to low; simmer, uncovered, until pasta is tender and mixture heats through, about 3 minutes. *Makes 4 servings.*

Each serving: About 355 calories, 33 g protein, 38 g carbohydrate, 8 g total fat (1 g saturated), 66 mg cholesterol, 815 mg sodium.

# Noodles Paprikash

PREP: 10 MINUTES ∾ COOK: 20 MINUTES

Peppers and chicken in a rosy cream sauce.

2 tablespoons vegetable oil
2 medium red peppers, cut into 1-inch pieces
1 medium green pepper, cut into 1-inch pieces
1 jumbo onion (1 pound), cut in half and thinly sliced
12 ounces extrawide curly egg noodles
Salt
2 tablespoons paprika
1 tablespoon all-purpose flour
5 large skinless, boneless chicken thighs (about 1 pound), cut into 2-inch chunks
1 cup chicken broth, canned or homemade (page 24)
1 cup reduced-fat sour cream

1 In nonstick 12-inch skillet, heat 1 tablespoon vegetable oil over medium-high heat until hot. Add peppers and onion and cook until tender and golden, about 15 minutes, stirring occasionally. Transfer pepper mixture to bowl.

2 Meanwhile, in large saucepot, prepare noodles in *boiling salted water* as label directs. Drain noodles.

3 On waxed paper, combine paprika and flour; use to coat chicken. In same skillet, heat remaining 1 tablespoon vegetable oil over medium-high heat until hot. Add chicken and cook until just beginning to brown, about 2 to 3 minutes. Add broth and ¾ teaspoon salt; heat to boiling. Reduce heat to low; cover and simmer until chicken loses its pink color throughout, about 8 to 10 minutes.

4 Stir in sour cream and sautéed pepper mixture; heat through (but do not allow to boil or mixture may curdle). Serve paprikash mixture over noodles. *Makes 6 servings.*

Each serving: About 425 calories, 26 g protein, 54 g carbohydrate, 12 g total fat (2 g saturated), 123 mg cholesterol, 605 mg sodium.

# Shells with Asian Chicken & Green Beans

PREP: 15 MINUTES ～ COOK: ABOUT 15 MINUTES

Toss sliced chicken breast and fresh green beans with an aromatic combination of ginger, garlic, cilantro, and coconut milk.

1 package (16 ounces) large shell pasta or fusilli
Salt
¾ pound green beans, trimmed
1 tablespoon olive oil
1 pound skinless, boneless chicken-breast halves, thinly sliced
2 tablespoons grated, peeled fresh ginger
2 garlic cloves, crushed with garlic press
⅛ to ¼ teaspoon crushed red pepper
1 can (14 ounces) light coconut milk (not cream of coconut)*
2 tablespoons fresh lime juice
¼ cup chopped fresh cilantro leaves

**1** In large saucepot, prepare pasta in *boiling salted water* as label directs. After pasta has cooked 5 minutes, add green beans to pasta cooking water and continue cooking until pasta and beans are done.

**2** Meanwhile, in nonstick 12-inch skillet, heat olive oil over medium-high heat until hot. Add chicken and cook, stirring often, about 2 minutes or until chicken just loses its pink color. Add ginger, garlic, crushed red pepper, and ¾ teaspoon salt, stirring constantly, about 30 seconds. Stir in coconut milk and lime juice; heat to boiling.

**3** Drain pasta and beans; return to saucepot. Add coconut milk-chicken mixture and cilantro; toss well. *Makes 6 servings.*

*Coconut milk is made by processing equal amounts of coconut meat and water to a paste and straining out the milky liquid; light coconut milk has a higher water content, so it's lower in fat. Cream of coconut, a sweeter, thicker version of coconut milk, contains sugar and stabilizers. Coconut cream, available in Asian and Hispanic specialty stores, is pressed and rehydrated coconut meat; it resembles vegetable shortening.

Each serving: About 465 calories, 29 g protein, 63 g carbohydrate, 10 g total fat (4 g saturated), 44 mg cholesterol, 420 mg sodium.

## GH MARINARA SAUCE

So many people—from friends to talk-radio hosts—have raved about mail-order spaghetti sauces that we decided to blind-taste a sampling of marinaras, putting them up against each other and a sauce made from our own GH recipe. We mail-ordered sauces from top Italian restaurants and mail-order food companies across the country, and our Food Department's expert tasters tried them alone and tossed with cooked spaghetti. Their decision was unanimous: Homemade is best! Some panelists' comments on the mail-order contestants: "tasted of musty dried oregano," and "not horrid but not great." The sauce from Rao's, a famous New York City restaurant, got the most positive comments ("good tomato flavor," "spicy hot"), but our GH sauce got rave reviews ("fresh flavor," "nice big chunks of tomato," "coats pasta well"). And when we considered the price of the mail-order sauces—$8 to $10 for a 32-ounce jar—the time it took to cook our sauce (10 minutes for preparation, 20 for simmering) became a minor issue.

PREP: 10 MINUTES   COOK: 20 MINUTES

*2 tablespoons olive oil*
*1 small onion, chopped*
*1 garlic clove, minced*
*1 can (29 to 35 ounces) tomatoes in juice*
*1 can (6 ounces) tomato paste*
*½ teaspoon salt*
*2 tablespoons chopped fresh basil or parsley (optional)*

**1** In a 3-quart saucepan, heat oil over over medium heat until hot. Add onion and garlic and cook until tender.

**2** Stir in tomatoes with their liquid, tomato paste, salt, and basil (if you like); heat to boiling, stirring with spoon to break up tomatoes. Reduce heat to low; partially cover pan and simmer 20 minutes, stirring occasionally. Serve over pasta or use in your favorite recipe. Makes 4 cups.

Each ½ cup: About 75 calories, 2 g protein, 10 g carbohydrate, 4 g total fat (1 g saturated), 0 mg cholesterol, 500 mg sodium.

# Thai Curry Chicken & Noodles

PREP: 15 MINUTES ～ COOK: 30 MINUTES

8 ounces flat dried rice noodles* or linguine
1 stalk fresh lemongrass (optional)
4 large green onions
1 tablespoon vegetable oil
1 package (10 ounces) mushrooms, sliced
1 tablespoon minced, peeled fresh ginger
2 teaspoons red curry paste*
2 large skinless, boneless chicken-breast halves
   (about 1 pound), cut into 1-inch-wide strips
2 tablespoons soy sauce
1 can (10 to 14 ounces) light or regular coconut
   milk*
1 medium red pepper
2 tablespoons chopped fresh cilantro leaves

1 Prepare noodles as label directs; drain and keep warm. (If package has no directions, prepare as you would regular pasta but cook only until just tender, about 5 minutes.)

2 Meanwhile, remove outer leaf from stalk of lemongrass if using. From bulb end, trim and cut a 6-inch-long piece; discard top. Cut lemongrass stalk lengthwise in half.

3 Slice 2 green onions into 1-inch pieces; reserve remaining 2 for garnish.

4 In nonstick 12-inch skillet, heat vegetable oil over medium-high heat until hot. Add mushrooms and cut green onions and cook until vegetables are golden brown. Transfer to small bowl.

5 To same skillet, add ginger and red curry paste; cook, stirring, 1 minute. Add lemongrass, chicken, soy sauce, coconut milk, and *1 cup water*; heat to boiling. Reduce heat to low; cover and simmer 10 minutes or until chicken just loses its pink color throughout.

6 While chicken is cooking, cut red pepper and remaining green onions into 3-inch-long paper-thin strips.

7 Remove lemongrass from chicken mixture and discard. Stir in mushroom mixture and cilantro; heat through. Arrange noodles in large bowl; top with chicken mixture. Garnish with red-pepper and green-onion strips. *Makes 4 servings.*

*Curry paste, coconut milk, and wide rice noodles can be purchased in the Asian section of some grocery stores. Red curry paste, used in Thai cooking, is a pungent blend of herbs and spices pulverized into paste form. Coconut milk is made by processing equal amounts of coconut meat and water to a paste and straining out the milky liquid; light coconut milk has a higher water content, so it's lower in fat. Cream of coconut, a sweeter, thicker version of coconut milk, contains sugar and stabilizers. Coconut cream, available in Asian and Hispanic specialty stores, is pressed and rehydrated coconut meat; it resembles vegetable shortening.

Each serving: About 475 calories, 36 g protein, 52 g carbohydrate, 14 g total fat (8 g saturated), 66 mg cholesterol, 650 mg sodium.

# Linguine with Spicy Sausage Sauce

PREP: 10 MINUTES ～ COOK: 25 MINUTES

1 package (16 ounces) linguine or spaghetti
12 ounces hot Italian-sausage links, casings
   removed
1 medium onion, diced
1 can (28 ounces) tomatoes in juice
¾ teaspoon sugar
¼ teaspoon salt
¼ cup chopped fresh basil leaves or 2 tablespoons
   chopped fresh parsley leaves plus 2 teaspoons
   dried basil leaves

1 In large saucepot, prepare linguine in *boiling water* as label directs, but do not add salt; drain pasta; keep warm.

2 Meanwhile, in nonstick 12-inch skillet, cook sausage and onion over medium-high heat until browned, stirring frequently with spoon to break up sausage. Discard fat in skillet.

3 Add tomatoes with their juice, sugar, and salt; heat to boiling over high heat. Reduce heat to low; cover and simmer 15 minutes. Stir in basil. Spoon linguine into large bowl. Pour sausage sauce over linguine. *Makes 4 servings.*

Each serving: About 680 calories, 29 g protein, 99 g carbohydrate, 18 g total fat (6 g saturated), 49 mg cholesterol, 1050 mg sodium.

# Spaghetti with Mini-Meatball Sauce

~~~~~~~~~~~~~~~~~~~~~~~~~~~~~~~~

PREP: 35 MINUTES ~ COOK: 1 HOUR

1 tablespoon plus 1 teaspoon olive oil
1 medium onion, finely chopped
1 large egg
1 pound lean ground beef (90%)
2 tablespoons seasoned dried bread crumbs
½ teaspoon salt
¼ teaspoon coarsely ground black pepper
1 large carrot, peeled and diced
1 small garlic clove, minced
1 can (28 ounces) tomatoes in juice
2½ teaspoons sugar
¾ teaspoon dried basil leaves
¼ teaspoon crushed red pepper (optional)
12 ounces spaghetti or spaghettini
2 tablespoons chopped fresh parsley leaves

1 In nonstick 1-quart saucepan, heat 1 teaspoon olive oil over medium-high heat until hot. Add half of onion and cook, stirring occasionally, until tender and golden.

2 In medium bowl, mix cooked onion, egg, ground beef, bread crumbs, salt, and pepper just until blended. With hands, shape ground-beef mixture into ¾-inch balls.

3 In nonstick 12-inch skillet, heat remaining 1 tablespoon olive oil over medium-high heat until hot. Add meatballs and cook until browned on all sides, removing them to plate as they brown.

4 In drippings in skillet, cook carrot and remaining onion, stirring occasionally, until onion is golden and carrot is tender-crisp. Add garlic and cook, stirring, just until garlic begins to brown.

5 Add tomatoes with their juice, sugar, dried basil, and crushed red pepper to skillet, breaking tomatoes up with spoon; heat to boiling over high heat. Reduce heat to medium-low and cook, uncovered, 20 minutes, stirring occasionally.

6 Meanwhile, in large saucepot, prepare spaghetti in *boiling water* as label directs, but do not add salt to water.

7 Return meatballs to skillet and cook, uncovered, 10 minutes longer or until meatballs are cooked through.

8 Drain spaghetti. Stir parsley into sauce. Spoon sauce over spaghetti; toss to serve. **Makes 4 servings.**

Each serving: About 660 calories, 39 g protein, 84 g carbohydrate, 19 g total fat (6 g saturated), 124 mg cholesterol, 825 mg sodium.

# Rigatoni with Fennel-Beef Sauce

~~~~~~~~~~~~~~~~~~~~~~~~~~~~~~~~

PREP: 5 MINUTES ~ COOK: 25 MINUTES

Extralean ground beef flavored with crushed fennel seeds makes a delicious and low-fat stand-in for Italian sausage.

12 ounces rigatoni or ziti pasta
Salt
12 ounces extralean ground beef
1 medium onion, diced
1 teaspoon fennel seeds, crushed
¼ teaspoon crushed red pepper
2 cans (14½ ounces each) Italian-style stewed tomatoes
Chopped fresh parsley leaves for garnish

1 In large saucepot, prepare rigatoni in *boiling salted water* as label directs; drain and keep warm.

2 Meanwhile, in nonstick 12-inch skillet, cook ground beef, onion, fennel seeds, crushed red pepper, and ½ teaspoon salt over medium-high heat, stirring occasionally, until all pan juices evaporate and meat is well browned.

3 Stir in stewed tomatoes; heat to boiling over high heat. Reduce heat to low; cover and simmer 10 minutes. Spoon sauce over rigatoni; sprinkle with parsley. **Makes 4 servings.**

Each serving: About 585 calories, 29 g protein, 79 g carbohydrate, 16 g total fat (6 g saturated), 57 mg cholesterol, 975 mg sodium.

*Rigatoni with Fennel-Beef Sauce* ➤

# Ziti with Cremini Mushrooms

~~~~~~~~~~~~~~~~~~~~

PREP: 10 MINUTES ～ COOK: 20 MINUTES

1 package (16 ounces) ziti pasta
Salt
4 ounces sweet Italian-sausage links, casings
   removed
2 garlic cloves, minced
1 pound medium cremini mushrooms, sliced
1 can (28 ounces) tomatoes in juice
1 teaspoon sugar

1 In large saucepot, prepare ziti in *boiling salted water* as label directs.

2 Meanwhile, in 10-inch skillet, brown sausage with garlic over medium-high heat; stirring frequently with spoon to break up sausage. Increase heat to high, add mushrooms, and cook until browned.

3 Stir in tomatoes with their juice and sugar. Simmer on low, uncovered, 5 to 8 minutes.

4 Drain pasta and toss with sauce. *Makes 4 servings.*

Each serving: About 595 calories, 23 g protein, 100 g carbohydrate, 12 g total fat (4 g saturated), 22 mg cholesterol, 835 mg sodium.

# Pasta with Sausage & Butternut Squash

~~~~~~~~~~~~~~~~~~~~

PREP: 15 MINUTES ～ COOK: 20 MINUTES

Our food editor sampled this in Italy—now it's our favorite 5-ingredient pasta.

12 ounces sweet Italian-sausage links, casings
   removed
1 package (16 ounces) corkscrew pasta
Salt
1 medium butternut squash (about 1¾ pounds),
   peeled and cut into ½-inch chunks
¼ teaspoon coarsely ground black pepper
⅓ cup packed fresh basil leaves, chopped, plus
   additional basil for garnish
¼ cup grated Parmesan cheese

1 In nonstick 12-inch skillet, cook sausage over medium-high heat until browned, about 7 minutes, stirring frequently with spoon to break up sausage. With slotted spoon, transfer sausage meat to bowl; discard all but 2 tablespoons drippings from skillet.

2 Meanwhile, in large saucepot, prepare pasta in *boiling salted water* as label directs.

3 To drippings in same skillet, add butternut squash, pepper, and ¼ teaspoon salt. Cook, covered, over medium heat, about 10 minutes or until squash is tender, stirring occasionally.

4 Drain pasta, reserving ¾ *cup pasta cooking water.* Return pasta to saucepot; toss with sausage, butternut squash, basil, Parmesan, and reserved pasta cooking water. Garnish with basil. *Makes 6 servings.*

Each serving: About 505 calories, 20 g protein, 66 g carbohydrate, 17 g total fat (6 g saturated), 40 mg cholesterol, 645 mg sodium.

# Sausage & Eggplant Pasta

~~~~~~~~~~~~~~~~~~~~

PREP: 10 MINUTES ～ COOK: 45 MINUTES

Here's a dish the whole family will devour: marinara sauce, dressed up with sausage and eggplant, to spoon over ziti and top with ricotta.

8 ounces hot Italian-sausage links
8 ounces sweet Italian-sausage links
1 small eggplant (about 1¼ pounds), cut into
   ½-inch chunks
GH Marinara Sauce (page 154) or 1 jar (32
   ounces) spaghetti sauce
1 package (16 ounces) ziti or penne pasta
1 container (8 ounces) part-skim ricotta cheese
¼ teaspoon cracked black pepper
Coarsely shredded Parmesan cheese for garnish

1 In 12-inch skillet, heat sausages and ¼ *cup water* over medium-high heat to boiling. Reduce heat to low; cover and simmer 5 minutes. Remove cover and cook until sausages are browned, about 15 minutes. Transfer sausages to cutting board. When cool enough to handle, cut diagonally into ¼-inch-thick slices.

2 In drippings in same skillet, cook eggplant and *2 tablespoons water* over medium heat until eggplant is tender, about 15 minutes, stirring often and adding *additional water* if necessary to keep eggplant from

sticking. Add Marinara Sauce and sausages; heat to boiling over high heat. Reduce heat to low; cover and simmer 5 minutes.

3 Meanwhile, in large saucepot, prepare ziti in *boiling water* as label directs, but do not add salt to water. Drain ziti; return to saucepot. Add sausage mixture; heat through over medium heat.

4 To serve, spoon ziti into 8 individual pasta bowls or dinner plates; top each serving with some ricotta and cracked pepper. Sprinkle with Parmesan if you like. *Makes 8 servings.*

Each serving without Parmesan: About 540 calories, 21 g protein, 59 g carbohydrate, 25 g total fat (8 g saturated), 52 mg cholesterol, 955 mg sodium.

# Fettuccine with Broccoli Rabe & Italian Sausage

PREP: 10 MINUTES ⟳ COOK: 30 MINUTES

1 package (16 ounces) fettuccine or linguine
1 bunch broccoli rabe (about 1 pound)
12 ounces sweet Italian-sausage links, casings removed
1 medium onion, diced
GH Marinara Sauce (page 154) or 1 jar (32 ounces) marinara sauce
¼ cup chopped fresh basil leaves

1 In large saucepot, prepare fettuccine in *boiling water* as label directs, but do not add salt; drain. Keep warm.

2 Cut off tough stem ends and discard tough leaves from broccoli rabe. Cut broccoli rabe crosswise in half.

3 In nonstick 12-inch skillet, cook sausage over medium-high heat, stirring frequently with spoon to break up sausage. Cook until sausage is well browned. Transfer sausage meat to bowl; discard all but 2 tablespoons drippings from skillet. Add onion and cook until softened. Stir in broccoli rabe; continue cooking until broccoli rabe wilts.

4 Stir in Marinara Sauce and sausage meat; heat to boiling. Reduce heat to low; cover and simmer 10 minutes, stirring occasionally. Stir in basil.

5 Place fettuccine in large bowl; top with sauce. Toss before serving. *Makes 6 servings.*

Each serving: About 470 calories, 20 g protein, 62 g carbohydrate, 15 g total fat (5 g saturated), 35 mg cholesterol, 420 mg sodium.

# Cheese Pierogi with Cabbage & Bacon

PREP: 10 MINUTES ⟳ COOK: 25 MINUTES

1 package (16 ounces) frozen potato and Cheddar pierogi
Salt
4 ounces sliced bacon, cut into ½-inch pieces
1 tablespoon vegetable oil
½ small head green cabbage (1¼ pounds), cut into ½-inch pieces
1 jumbo onion (12 ounces), thinly sliced
2 medium tomatoes
2 teaspoons distilled white vinegar
½ teaspoon sugar

1 In large saucepot, prepare pierogi in *boiling salted water* as label directs; drain.

2 Meanwhile, in 12-inch skillet, cook bacon over medium heat until browned. With slotted spoon, transfer bacon to paper towels to drain. Discard all but 1 tablespoon bacon fat from skillet.

3 Add vegetable oil to skillet and heat over medium-high heat. Add cabbage and onion and cook, covered, 10 minutes, stirring occasionally.

4 Dice 1 tomato; cut remaining tomato into thin wedges. Add diced tomato, white vinegar, sugar, and ½ teaspoon salt to cabbage mixture and cook 5 minutes, uncovered, stirring frequently.

5 Tuck pierogi and tomato wedges into cabbage mixture; heat through. Sprinkle with bacon. *Makes 4 servings.*

Each serving: About 350 calories, 12 g protein, 49 g carbohydrate, 13 g total fat (4 g saturated), 24 mg cholesterol, 965 mg sodium.

# LASAGNA

The quintessential pasta dish. Everybody loves it. For the lasagnas on these pages, we used both the no-boil and regular lasagna noodles. When you assemble a lasagna using no-boil noodles, place the noodles so they do not touch the sides of the baking dish and be sure to completely cover them with sauce (or filling) or they won't cook properly. For all lasagnas, letting them stand for at least 10 minutes after coming out of the oven makes them easier to cut into portions for serving.

## White Lasagna

PREP: 45 MINUTES • BAKE: 45 MINUTES

4 tablespoons margarine or butter
  (½ stick)
⅓ cup all-purpose flour
¼ teaspoon ground nutmeg
1 quart low-fat (1%) milk
1 container (15 to 16 ounces) part-
  skim ricotta cheese
½ cup grated Parmesan cheese
⅓ cup chopped fresh parsley leaves
2 large eggs
2 cups shredded part-skim mozzarella
  cheese (8 ounces)
8 ounces Fontina or Swiss cheese,
  shredded (2 cups)
1 package (8 ounces) no-boil lasagna
  noodles
½ cup chopped oil-packed sun-dried
  tomatoes (no salt added)

1 In 3-quart saucepan, melt margarine or butter over medium heat. Stir in flour and nutmeg until blended; cook 1 minute. Gradually stir in milk; cook, stirring constantly, until sauce boils and thickens. Remove saucepan from heat.
2 In small bowl, mix ricotta, Parmesan, parsley, and eggs. In large bowl, combine mozzarella and Fontina.
3 Preheat oven to 375°F. In 13" by 9" ceramic or glass baking dish, evenly spoon 1 cup white sauce. Arrange one-third of lasagna noodles over sauce, overlapping to fit. Spoon half of ricotta mixture over noodles; spread with 1 cup sauce; top with half of remaining noodles. Place half of shredded cheese over noodles, then sprinkle with sun-dried tomatoes and spread with 1 cup sauce. Arrange remaining noodles over sauce; top with remaining ricotta mix-

ture, remaining sauce, and remaining shredded cheese.
4 Cover baking dish with foil and bake 25 minutes. Remove foil and bake 15 to 20 minutes longer or until lasagna is hot and bubbly and top is lightly browned. Makes 12 servings.

EACH SERVING: ABOUT 355 CALORIES, 21 G PROTEIN, 24 G CARBOHYDRATE, 20 G TOTAL FAT (9 G SATURATED), 84 MG CHOLESTEROL, 465 MG SODIUM.

## Chili Lasagna

PREP: 15 MINUTES • BAKE: 1 HOUR

2 tablespoons vegetable oil
1 medium onion, chopped
2 tablespoons chili powder
1 can (28 ounces) tomatoes in juice
1 can (15¼ to 19 ounces) red kidney
  beans, rinsed and drained
3 tablespoons tomato paste
1 teaspoon salt
1 teaspoon sugar
½ teaspoon coarsely ground black
  pepper
3 medium zucchini (about 1½ pounds),
  chopped
18 no-boil lasagna noodles (about
  12 ounces)
3 cups shredded part-skim mozzarella
  cheese (12 ounces)

1 In 3-quart saucepan, heat 1 tablespoon vegetable oil over medium-high heat until hot. Add onion and cook until tender and lightly browned, stirring occasionally. Stir in chili powder; cook 1 minute.
2 Add tomatoes with their juice, kidney beans, tomato paste, salt, sugar, pepper, and 2½ cups water; heat to boiling over high heat. Reduce heat to low; simmer, uncovered, 15 minutes, stirring sauce occasionally.
3 In 10-inch skillet, heat remaining 1 tablespoon vegetable oil over medium-high heat until hot. Add zucchini and cook until golden brown.

4 Preheat oven to 375°F. In 13" by 9" glass baking dish, evenly spoon one-third of sauce. Arrange half of no-boil lasagna noodles over sauce, overlapping to fit. Top with zucchini, half of mozzarella, and half of remaining sauce. Top with remaining no-boil lasagna noodles, then remaining sauce. Sprinkle remaining mozzarella over sauce.
5 Bake lasagna, covered, 40 to 45 minutes; uncover; bake 15 minutes longer or until hot and cheese is brown and bubbly. Makes 12 servings.

EACH SERVING: ABOUT 255 CALORIES, 14 G PROTEIN, 34 G CARBOHYDRATE, 8 G TOTAL FAT (3 G SATURATED), 17 MG CHOLESTEROL, 530 MG SODIUM.

## Chicken-Filled Lasagna Rolls

PREP: 50 MINUTES • BAKE: 25 MINUTES

2 tablespoons olive oil
1 medium onion, finely chopped
1 can (35 ounces) Italian plum
  tomatoes
1½ teaspoons sugar
1 teaspoon salt
½ teaspoon coarsely ground black
  pepper
1 pound ground chicken or turkey
12 lasagna noodles (about 11 ounces)
1 container (15 to 16 ounces) part-
  skim ricotta cheese
1 cup frozen peas
2 tablespoons grated Parmesan cheese
1 tablespoon chopped fresh parsley
  leaves
1 large egg, lightly beaten
2 cups shredded part-skim mozzarella
  cheese (8 ounces)

1 In 4-quart saucepan, heat 1 tablespoon olive oil over medium-high heat until hot. Add onion and cook until tender. Add tomatoes with their juice, sugar, ¾ teaspoon salt, and ¼ teaspoon pepper; heat to boiling, stirring to break up tomatoes with spoon. Reduce heat to low; cover and simmer sauce 15 minutes, stirring occasionally.
2 Meanwhile, in nonstick 12-inch skillet, heat remaining 1 tablespoon olive oil over medium-high heat until hot. Add ground chicken and cook, stirring frequently, until all pan juices evaporate

and meat is browned, about 10 minutes. Remove skillet from heat.

**3** In large saucepot, prepare lasagna noodles in *boiling water* as label directs, but do not use salt in water. Drain.

**4** Preheat oven to 375°F. Spoon half of sauce into 13" by 9" glass baking dish. Into chicken mixture in skillet, stir ricotta, frozen peas, Parmesan, parsley, egg, 1 cup mozzarella, remaining ¼ teaspoon salt, and remaining ¼ teaspoon pepper until mixed. Spoon 2 heaping tablespoons of chicken filling at end of each lasagna noodle and roll jelly-roll fashion.

**5** Arrange rolls, seam-side down, in baking dish in 1 layer. Spoon remaining sauce over rolls. Top with remaining mozzarella. Cover loosely with foil. Bake 20 minutes. Remove foil and bake, uncovered, 5 minutes longer or until hot and bubbly. Makes 6 servings.

EACH SERVING: ABOUT 635 CALORIES, 42 G PROTEIN, 58 G CARBOHYDRATE, 26 G TOTAL FAT (11 G SATURATED), 144 MG CHOLESTEROL, 770 MG SODIUM.

## Spinach Lasagna

PREP: 50 MINUTES • BAKE: 40 MINUTES

*12 lasagna noodles (about 11 ounces)*
*Salt*
*2 tablespoons olive oil*
*1 small onion, finely chopped*
*2 medium bunches spinach (about 1¾ pounds), tough stems removed*
*1 container (32 ounces) part-skim ricotta cheese*
*¼ cup grated Parmesan cheese*
*⅛ teaspoon ground nutmeg*
*2 large eggs*
*2 tablespoons all-purpose flour*
*2¾ cups low-fat (1%) milk*
*⅛ teaspoon ground white pepper*

**1** In large saucepot, prepare lasagna noodles in *boiling salted water* as label directs; drain.

**2** Meanwhile, in nonstick 12-inch skillet, heat 1 tablespoon olive oil over

*Beef & Sausage Lasagna*

medium heat until hot. Add onion and cook until tender but not browned; add spinach and ¼ teaspoon salt. Cook over high heat until spinach wilts; set aside.

**3** In medium bowl, mix ricotta, Parmesan, nutmeg, eggs, and ½ teaspoon salt; set aside.

**4** In 3-quart saucepan, heat remaining 1 tablespoon olive oil over medium-high heat until hot. Add flour and cook 1 minute. Gradually stir in milk, white pepper, and ¼ teaspoon salt and cook, stirring constantly, until sauce boils and thickens slightly. Remove saucepan from heat.

**5** Preheat oven to 375°F. In 13" by 9" glass baking dish, arrange one-third of lasagna noodles, overlapping to fit. Spread half of ricotta mixture over noodles. Drain off liquid from spinach if any; spoon half of spinach over ricotta mixture; then top with one-third of sauce. Repeat layering. Top with remaining noodles, then remaining sauce.

**6** Bake lasagna, covered, 40 minutes or until hot and bubbly. Makes 10 servings.

EACH SERVING: ABOUT 340 CALORIES, 21 G PROTEIN, 36 G CARBOHYDRATE, 13 G TOTAL FAT (6 G SATURATED), 75 MG CHOLESTEROL, 525 MG SODIUM.

## Beef & Sausage Lasagna

PREP: 30 MINUTES • BAKE: 45 MINUTES

*8 ounces hot Italian-sausage links, casings removed*
*8 ounces lean ground beef (90%)*
*1 medium onion, diced*
*1 can (28 ounces) tomatoes in juice*
*2 tablespoons tomato paste*
*1 teaspoon salt*
*1 teaspoon sugar*
*12 lasagna noodles (about 11 ounces)*
*1 container (15 ounces) part-skim ricotta cheese*
*1 large egg*
*¼ cup chopped fresh parsley leaves*
*2 cups shredded part-skim mozzarella cheese (8 ounces)*

**1** In 4-quart saucepan, cook sausage meat, ground beef, and onion over high heat, stirring frequently, until meat is well browned and onion is tender, stirring to break up sausage with spoon. Spoon off fat if any.

**2** Add tomatoes with their juice, tomato paste, salt, and sugar to saucepan; heat to boiling. Reduce heat to low; cover and simmer 30 minutes, stirring occasionally.

**3** Meanwhile, in large saucepot, prepare lasagna noodles in *boiling water* as label directs, but do not use salt in water; drain. In bowl, mix ricotta, egg, and parsley.

**4** Preheat oven to 375°F. In 13" by 9" glass baking dish, arrange half of lasagna noodles; top with all of ricotta mixture. Sprinkle with half of mozzarella; top with half of meat sauce. Layer with remaining noodles and meat sauce; top with remaining mozzarella.

**5** Cover lasagna with foil and bake 30 minutes. Remove foil and bake 15 minutes longer or until lasagna is hot and bubbly and top is lightly browned. Makes 10 servings.

EACH SERVING: ABOUT 360 CALORIES, 24 G PROTEIN, 32 G CARBOHYDRATE, 15 G TOTAL FAT (7 G SATURATED), 75 MG CHOLESTEROL, 725 MG SODIUM.

## Vegetable Lasagna

PREP: 45 MINUTES • BAKE: 45 MINUTES

*4 tablespoons margarine or butter
   (½ stick)*
*2 medium zucchini (about 8 ounces
   each), diced*
*½ bunch broccoli, coarsely chopped*
*½ teaspoon dried oregano leaves*
*Salt*
*2 cups firmly packed spinach leaves
   (about 4 ounces), coarsely chopped*
*I container (15 ounces) part-skim
   ricotta cheese*
*2 large eggs*
*12 lasagna noodles (about 11 ounces)*
*¼ cup all-purpose flour*
*2½ cups milk*
*¼ cup grated Parmesan cheese*
*8 ounces part-skim mozzarella cheese,
   sliced*

**1** In nonstick 12-inch skillet, melt I tablespoon margarine or butter over medium heat. Add zucchini, broccoli, oregano, and ¼ teaspoon salt and cook, stirring frequently, until vegetables are tender-crisp, about 5 minutes. Add spinach and toss until wilted. Remove skillet from heat.
**2** In medium bowl, mix ricotta and eggs; set aside.
**3** In large saucepot, prepare lasagna noodles in *boiling salted water* as label directs. Drain.
**4** Meanwhile, preheat oven to 350°F. In 2-quart saucepan, melt remaining 3 tablespoons margarine or butter over medium heat. Stir in flour and ¼ teaspoon salt until smooth. Gradually stir in milk; cook, stirring constantly, until sauce boils and thickens. Remove saucepan from heat; stir in Parmesan.
**5** In 13" by 9" glass baking dish, layer half of lasagna noodles, half of ricotta mixture, half of vegetable mixture, and half of mozzarella. Top with half of white sauce, then with remaining noodles, ricotta, and vegetable mixture. Spoon remaining sauce over vegetable layer; arrange remaining mozzarella on top.
**6** Bake lasagna 40 to 45 minutes or until hot and bubbly. Makes 8 servings.

EACH SERVING: ABOUT **455** CALORIES, **26** G PROTEIN, **44** G CARBOHYDRATE, **20** G TOTAL FAT (**9** G SATURATED), **99** MG CHOLESTEROL, **535** MG SODIUM.

## Turkey & Mushroom Lasagna

PREP: 45 MINUTES • BAKE: 30 MINUTES

*12 plain or spinach lasagna noodles
   (about 1.1 ounces)*
*Salt*
*I tablespoon plus ¼ cup olive oil*
*I small onion, minced*
*1½ pounds ground turkey*
*I pound medium mushrooms, sliced*
*4 ounces Jarlsberg or Swiss cheese,
   shredded (1 cup)*
*½ cup all-purpose flour*
*I quart milk*
*2 tablespoons chopped fresh parsley
   leaves*

**1** In large saucepot, prepare lasagna noodles in *boiling salted water* as label directs; drain.
**2** Meanwhile, in nonstick 12-inch skillet, heat I tablespoon olive oil over medium-high heat until hot. Add onion, ground turkey, and ½ teaspoon salt and cook until turkey is browned. With slotted spoon, transfer turkey mixture to bowl.
**3** Add mushrooms and ¼ teaspoon salt to the skillet and cook until mushrooms are golden; add to ground-turkey mixture in bowl. Cool slightly; stir in Jarlsberg.
**4** In 3-quart saucepan, heat remaining ¼ cup olive oil over medium heat. Stir in flour; cook I minute, stirring constantly. Gradually stir in milk and cook, stirring constantly, until sauce boils and thickens. Remove saucepan from heat; stir in parsley.
**5** Preheat oven to 375°F. In 13" by 9" glass baking dish, evenly spoon ½ cup white sauce. Arrange one-third of lasagna noodles over sauce, overlapping to fit. Spoon half of turkey mixture over noodles; top with one-third of remaining sauce. Repeat layering once. Then

*Turkey & Mushroom Lasagna*

top with remaining lasagna noodles and remaining sauce.
**6** Cover lasagna with foil and bake 30 minutes or until hot and bubbly. Makes 12 servings.

EACH SERVING: ABOUT **350** CALORIES, **20** G PROTEIN, **30** G CARBOHYDRATE, **17** G TOTAL FAT (**4** G SATURATED), **59** MG CHOLESTEROL, **435** MG SODIUM.

## Salmon Lasagna

PREP: 35 MINUTES • BAKE: 55 MINUTES

*2 tablespoons vegetable oil*
*¼ cup all-purpose flour*
*3 cups low-fat (1%) milk*
*¼ cup grated Parmesan cheese*
*½ teaspoon coarsely ground black
   pepper*
*2 packages (9 to 9½ ounces) frozen
   creamed spinach, thawed*
*4 cups shredded part-skim mozzarella
   cheese (1 pound)*
*I container (15 ounces) part-skim
   ricotta cheese*
*I package (8 ounces) no-boil lasagna
   noodles*
*I can (14¾ to 15½ ounces) salmon,
   drained and flaked*
*I small tomato, chopped*

**1** In 2-quart saucepan, heat vegetable oil over medium heat until hot; stir in flour; cook 1 minute.

**2** Gradually stir milk into flour mixture, stirring constantly, until mixture boils and thickens. Stir in Parmesan and pepper; set white sauce aside.

**3** In medium bowl, mix creamed spinach with mozzarella and ricotta.

**4** Preheat oven to 375°F. Spread ¼ cup white sauce to cover bottom of 13" by 9" glass baking dish. Arrange one-third of no-boil lasagna noodles over sauce, overlapping to fit. Spoon half of ricotta mixture over noodles; top with half of salmon. Repeat layering once. Top with remaining lasagna noodles and remaining sauce.

**5** Cover baking dish with foil and bake lasagna 40 minutes. Remove foil and bake 10 to 15 minutes longer or until lasagna is hot and bubbly and top is lightly browned. Sprinkle with chopped tomato to serve. Makes 8 servings.

EACH SERVING: ABOUT 535 CALORIES, 39 G PROTEIN, 37 G CARBOHYDRATE, 26 G TOTAL FAT (13 G SATURATED), 84 MG CHOLESTEROL, 935 MG SODIUM.

## Broccoli Lasagna

PREP: 30 MINUTES • BAKE: 40 MINUTES

3 tablespoons margarine or butter
1 small onion, chopped
2 tablespoons all-purpose flour
¼ teaspoon coarsely ground black pepper
⅛ teaspoon ground nutmeg
½ teaspoon salt
2¼ cups low-fat (1%) milk
2 tablespoons chopped fresh parsley leaves
1 container (15 ounces) part-skim ricotta cheese
1 package (10 ounces) frozen chopped broccoli, thawed and squeezed dry
¼ cup grated Parmesan cheese
2 cups shredded part-skim mozzarella cheese (8 ounces)
9 no-boil lasagna noodles (about 5 ounces)

**1** Preheat oven to 350°F. In 2-quart saucepan, melt margarine or butter over medium heat. Add onion and cook until tender and golden, 8 to 10 minutes.

**2** Stir flour, pepper, nutmeg, and ¼ teaspoon salt into onion mixture; cook 1 minute, stirring constantly. Gradually stir in milk and cook, stirring constantly, until sauce boils and thickens slightly. Boil sauce 1 minute longer. Stir in parsley.

**3** In bowl, mix ricotta, broccoli, Parmesan, 1 cup mozzarella, and remaining ¼ teaspoon salt.

**4** In 11" by 7" glass baking dish, spread ¼ cup white sauce. Arrange one-third of no-boil lasagna noodles over sauce, overlapping to fit. Top with one-third of remaining white sauce. Spoon half of ricotta mixture over sauce. Repeat layering once. Then top with remaining lasagna noodles and remaining white sauce. Sprinkle remaining mozzarella on top.

**5** Cover lasagna loosely with foil and bake 40 minutes or until hot and bubbly. Makes 6 servings.

EACH SERVING: ABOUT 420 CALORIES, 29 G PROTEIN, 34 G CARBOHYDRATE, 19 G TOTAL FAT (10 G SATURATED), 56 MG CHOLESTEROL, 925 MG SODIUM.

## Ratatouille Lasagna

PREP: 45 MINUTES • BAKE: 40 MINUTES

3 tablespoons olive oil
1 large green pepper, cut into ¾-inch pieces
1 large red pepper, cut into ¾-inch pieces
1 small eggplant (about 1 pound), cut into ¾-inch pieces
2 medium zucchini (about 8 ounces each), cut into ¾-inch pieces
4 teaspoons sugar
1½ teaspoons salt
1 package (16 ounces) lasagna noodles (about 16 noodles)
1 medium onion, chopped
1 can (35 ounces) Italian plum tomatoes
½ teaspoon dried thyme leaves
1 pound Fontina or mozzarella cheese, shredded (4 cups)

**1** In nonstick 12-inch skillet, heat 2 tablespoons olive oil over medium-high heat until hot. Add peppers and cook until tender-crisp. Stir in eggplant, zucchini, 2 teaspoons sugar, ¾ teaspoon salt, and ¼ cup water; heat to boiling over high heat. Reduce heat to low; cover and simmer 15 minutes or until vegetables are tender. Remove cover and cook vegetables over high heat 5 minutes longer or until any liquid evaporates.

**2** Meanwhile, in large saucepot, prepare lasagna noodles in *boiling water* as label directs, but do not add salt to water; drain.

**3** In 4-quart saucepan, heat remaining 1 tablespoon olive oil over medium heat until hot. Add onion and cook until very tender. Add tomatoes with their juice, thyme, remaining 2 teaspoons sugar, and remaining ¾ teaspoon salt, stirring to break up tomatoes with spoon; heat to boiling over high heat. Reduce heat to medium; cook, uncovered, 15 minutes.

**4** Preheat oven to 375°F. In 13" by 9" glass or ceramic baking dish, arrange one-fourth of lasagna noodles, overlapping to fit. Spread one-third of vegetable mixture over noodles; spoon one-fourth of tomato sauce over vegetables; sprinkle with one-fourth of Fontina. Repeat layering twice. Top with remaining noodles, sauce, and Fontina.

**5** Bake lasagna, uncovered, 40 minutes or until hot and bubbly and top is lightly browned. Makes 10 servings.

EACH SERVING: ABOUT 435 CALORIES, 20 G PROTEIN, 47 G CARBOHYDRATE, 19 G TOTAL FAT (9 G SATURATED), 53 MG CHOLESTEROL, 880 MG SODIUM.

# Pies & Pizzas

# Potato & Onion Pie with Sour-Cream Pastry

PREP: 1 HOUR ～ BAKE: 40 MINUTES

Sour-Cream Pastry (right)
6 medium all-purpose potatoes (about 2 pounds),
   peeled and thinly sliced
2 tablespoons vegetable oil
2 jumbo onions (about 1 pound each), cut into
   ¼-inch-thick slices
3 tablespoons all-purpose flour
1 teaspoon salt
¼ teaspoon coarsely ground black pepper
2¼ cups plus 1 tablespoon milk
6 hard-cooked large eggs, shelled and cut into
   ½-inch-thick slices

1 Prepare Sour-Cream Pastry; set aside.

2 In 4-quart saucepan, heat potatoes and *enough water to cover* to boiling over high heat. Reduce heat to low; cover and simmer 5 minutes; drain.

3 Meanwhile, in nonstick 12-inch skillet, heat vegetable oil over medium-high heat until hot. Add onions and cook until very tender and golden brown, stirring often, about 15 minutes.

4 Stir flour, salt, and pepper into skillet. Gradually stir in 2¼ cups milk and cook, stirring constantly, until sauce boils and thickens slightly. Remove skillet from heat.

5 Preheat oven to 425°F. Lightly grease deep 2½-quart casserole. In casserole, layer half of potatoes, eggs, and onion mixture. Repeat layering.

6 On lightly floured surface, with floured rolling pin, roll Sour-Cream Pastry 1 inch larger all around than top of casserole. Using pastry wheel or knife, cut pastry into ½-inch-wide strips. Follow directions for Quick Lattice Top or Woven Lattice Top (page 169), placing dough strips ¼ inch apart across pie. Brush lattice top and edge with remaining 1 tablespoon milk.

7 Bake pie 40 minutes or until filling is hot and bubbly, potatoes are tender, and crust is golden. Cover casserole with foil after 25 minutes if necessary to prevent overbrowning. ***Makes 8 servings.***

**SOUR-CREAM PASTRY:** In bowl, mix *1 cup all-purpose flour* and *½ teaspoon salt*. With pastry blender or two knives used scissor-fashion, cut in *⅓ cup shortening* until mixture resembles coarse crumbs. With fork, stir in *¼ cup sour cream* and *1 tablespoon cold water* until dough holds together. Shape dough into disk; wrap with plastic wrap; refrigerate until ready to use.

Each serving: About 405 calories, 12 g protein, 43 g carbohydrate, 21 g total fat (6 g saturated), 172 mg cholesterol, 530 mg sodium.

# Greek Pizza

PREP: 30 MINUTES ～ BAKE: 25 MINUTES

3 medium tomatoes (about 1 pound), seeded and
   cut into very thin wedges
8 sheets (about 16" by 12" each) fresh or frozen
   (thawed) phyllo
3 tablespoons margarine or butter, melted
4 ounces feta cheese
¼ cup Kalamata olives, pitted and coarsely
   chopped

1 Drain tomato wedges on paper towels.

2 Place 1 sheet phyllo on large cookie sheet; brush with some margarine or butter. Cover with second sheet of phyllo; brush with margarine or butter. Repeat layering and brushing until all phyllo sheets are used.

3 Preheat oven to 375°F. With scissors, cut 1-inch-square notch from each corner of layered phyllo. Roll each side of layered phyllo 1 inch toward center to make raised edge all around; brush with margarine or butter.

4 Arrange tomato wedges in rows over phyllo. Bake 20 minutes. Crumble feta over pizza; sprinkle with olives. Bake about 5 minutes longer or until edges of phyllo are golden. ***Makes 4 servings.***

Each serving: About 310 calories, 8 g protein, 28 g carbohydrate, 20 g total fat (6 g saturated), 25 mg cholesterol, 760 mg sodium.

*Potato & Onion Pie with Sour-Cream Pastry* ➤

## Seven-Vegetable Pie

PREP: 45 MINUTES ⁓ BAKE: 45 MINUTES

2 cups plus 3 tablespoons all-purpose flour
¾ teaspoon salt
⅔ cup shortening
12 ounces Yukon Gold potatoes, cut into ¾-inch
  pieces
1 tablespoon olive or vegetable oil
2 medium carrots, peeled and thinly sliced
1 large celery stalk, chopped
1 medium onion, chopped
1¾ cups plus 1 tablespoon milk
1 can (11 ounces) vacuum-packed whole-kernel
  corn, drained
1 cup frozen baby lima beans (half 10-ounce
  package)
1 small bunch spinach (about 8 ounces), tough
  stems discarded, coarsely chopped
4 ounces sharp Cheddar cheese, shredded (1 cup)

1 In medium bowl, mix 2 cups flour and ½ teaspoon salt. With pastry blender or two knives used scissor-fashion, cut in shortening until mixture resembles coarse crumbs. Sprinkle *5 to 6 tablespoons cold water*, 1 tablespoon at a time, into flour mixture, mixing lightly with a fork after each addition until dough is just moist enough to hold together. Shape dough into ball.

2 On floured surface, with floured rolling pin, roll two-thirds of dough into round 2 inches larger all around than inverted 9-inch deep-dish pie plate. Gently ease dough into pie plate, allowing dough to hang over edge. Trim pastry edge, leaving 1-inch overhang; reserve trimmings. Cover pie plate and wrap remaining dough with plastic wrap; set aside.

3 In 3-quart saucepan, heat potatoes in *1 inch boiling water* to boiling over high heat. Reduce heat to low; cover and simmer 5 minutes or until potatoes are fork-tender. Drain.

4 Meanwhile, in 12-inch skillet, heat olive oil over medium-high heat until hot. Add carrots, celery, onion, and remaining ¼ teaspoon salt, stirring occasionally, until vegetables are tender-crisp. Stir in remaining 3 tablespoons flour; cook 1 minute, stirring constantly.

5 Stir in 1¾ cups milk, potatoes, corn, and lima beans. Heat to boiling over high heat; boil 1 minute. Remove skillet from heat; stir in spinach and Cheddar cheese. Spoon mixture into pie plate.

6 Preheat oven to 375°F. On floured surface, with floured rolling pin, roll remaining dough into 12-inch round; cut into ½-inch-wide strips. Moisten edge of bottom crust with *water*. Follow the directions for Quick Lattice Top or Woven Lattice Top (opposite page), placing half the dough strips ¼ inch apart.

7 Brush crust with remaining 1 tablespoon milk; bake 45 minutes or until crust is golden brown and filling is hot and bubbly. *Makes 8 servings.*

Each serving: About 505 calories, 13 g protein, 56 g carbohydrate, 26 g total fat (9 g saturated), 23 mg cholesterol, 480 mg sodium.

## Red & Yellow Pepper Pie

PREP: 45 MINUTES ⁓ BAKE: 1 HOUR

2 cups all-purpose flour
¾ teaspoon salt
⅔ cup shortening
2 cups rotelli or rotini pasta (4 ounces)
1 tablespoon olive oil
1 medium onion, chopped
2 medium red peppers, cut into 1-inch pieces
2 medium yellow peppers, cut into 1-inch pieces
1 teaspoon dried basil leaves
¼ teaspoon coarsely ground black pepper
1 large egg
1 container (15 ounces) part-skim ricotta cheese
1 package (10 ounces) frozen chopped spinach,
  thawed and squeezed dry
2 cups shredded part-skim mozzarella cheese
  (8 ounces)
1 cup GH Marinara Sauce (page 154) or bottled
  spaghetti sauce

1 In medium bowl, mix flour and ½ teaspoon salt. With pastry blender or two knives used scissor-fashion, cut in shortening until mixture resembles coarse crumbs. Sprinkle *5 to 6 tablespoons cold water*, 1 tablespoon at a time, into flour mixture, mixing lightly with a fork after each addition until dough is just moist enough to hold together. Shape dough into a disk; wrap with plastic wrap and refrigerate until ready to use.

2 In large saucepot, prepare pasta in *boiling water* as label directs, but do not add salt to water; drain.

**3** Meanwhile, in nonstick 12-inch skillet, heat olive oil over medium heat until hot. Add onion and cook until tender-crisp; add red and yellow peppers, basil, black pepper, and remaining ¼ teaspoon salt and cook, stirring occasionally, until vegetables are tender.

**4** In cup, beat egg slightly. Reserve 1 tablespoon beaten egg; set aside. In another medium bowl, mix remaining egg with ricotta and spinach.

**5** Preheat oven to 400°F. Grease 9" by 2½" springform pan. On lightly floured surface, with floured rolling pin, roll two-thirds of dough into 15-inch round. Gently ease into springform pan, allowing dough to hang over side of pan slightly.

**6** Sprinkle bottom of crust with half of mozzarella; top with half of sautéed-pepper mixture. Spread half of ricotta-spinach mixture over pepper mixture; top

with Marinara Sauce, then pasta. Sprinkle remaining mozzarella over pasta; top with remaining sautéed pepper mixture, then remaining ricotta-spinach mixture.

**7** Roll out remaining dough to 11-inch round; lay dough over filling, allowing dough to hang over side of pan. Fold overhang in toward center, pinching dough all around to make a stand-up edge; flute. Cut slits in top crust to allow steam to escape during baking. Brush top and edge with reserved egg. Bake pie 55 to 60 minutes until crust is golden and filling is hot.

**8** Allow pie to cool 5 minutes for easier slicing. Remove side of springform pan. To serve, cut into wedges. *Makes 8 servings.*

Each serving: About 535 calories, 21 g protein, 46 g carbohydrate, 30 g total fat (10 g saturated), 60 mg cholesterol, 580 mg sodium.

## MAKING A LATTICE TOP

### Quick Lattice Top

Cut the dough into the number of strips specified in the recipe. Place half of strips evenly spaced across the pie (the recipe will specify how far apart they should be). Place the second half of strips on top of the first set of strips, at right angles or obliquely, as shown here. Trim the ends of the strips even with edge of pan or pie plate. Roll any dough overhang from bottom crust up and over ends of strips; crimp to seal.

### Woven Lattice Top

Cut the dough into the number of strips specified in the recipe. Place half of the strips evenly spaced across the pie (the recipe will specify how far apart they should be). Fold every other strip back halfway from the center. Place a strip of dough down the center of the pie, at right angles to the bottom set of dough strips. Replace folded parts of the strips. Now fold back alternate strips. Place second cross strip in place next to the first cross strip (using the same spacing as specified for the bottom strips). Repeat with remaining strips, first completing one half of the lattice, and then moving on to the second half. (Photo at right shows the first two strips in place, with preparations being made to add a third.) Trim ends of strips even with edge of pan or pie plate. Roll overhang up and over ends of strips; crimp to seal.

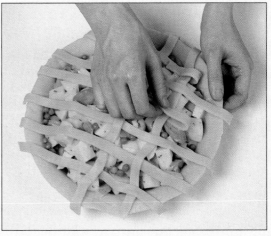

# Greek-Style Broccoli Pie

PREP: 40 MINUTES ∿ BAKE: 1 HOUR

3 packages (10 ounces each) frozen chopped
    broccoli
2 teaspoons margarine or butter
1 bunch green onions, thinly sliced
1 container (16 ounces) reduced-fat cottage
    cheese (2%)
2 cups shredded part-skim mozzarella cheese
    (8 ounces)
4 ounces feta cheese, crumbled
½ cup loosely packed fresh dill, chopped
¼ teaspoon coarsely ground black pepper
Olive-oil nonstick cooking spray
12 sheets (about 16" by 12" each) fresh or frozen
    (thawed) phyllo
2 slices white sandwich bread

1 Prepare broccoli as labels direct, but prepare all 3
packages together. Drain; cool until easy to handle,
then squeeze dry and place in large bowl.

2 Meanwhile, in nonstick 10-inch skillet, melt margarine or butter over low heat. Add green onions and
cook until tender and lightly browned, stirring
frequently.

3 Add green onions, cottage cheese, mozzarella, feta,
dill, and pepper to broccoli; set aside.

4 Spray 9-inch deep-dish pie plate with olive-oil nonstick cooking spray.

5 On a work surface, place 1 phyllo sheet on sheet of
waxed paper. Spray sheet with nonstick cooking spray;
place in pie plate, with edges overhanging. Spray second sheet of phyllo; place over first sheet, with corners
angled slightly away from corners of first sheet. Continue layering (with all but last sheet), spraying each
phyllo sheet with nonstick cooking spray and placing
sheets so that corners are always slightly away from
corners of sheet directly below.

6 Preheat oven to 375°F. Tear bread into small pieces;
sprinkle in pie plate over phyllo; top with broccoli
mixture. Fold overhanging edges of phyllo over broccoli mixture (phyllo will not cover top completely).
Spray last sheet of phyllo with nonstick cooking spray;
crumple slightly and place in space in center of pie.

## QUICK HOMEMADE PIZZA DOUGH

To really save time when making pizza at home,
many neighborhood pizzerias—and some supermarkets—will sell you raw, raised dough ready for
you to roll and top. Or, for a quick homemade version, try this recipe that calls for quick-rise yeast.
After mixing the ingredients, the dough rests for
only 20 minutes and then it's ready. If you are not
using this dough for one of the recipes in this book
and are creating your own pizzas, here's what to do:

SHAPE DOUGH: To make 1 large pizza, roll dough
ball into 14" by 10" rectangle on cookie sheet; add
topping. Bring edges of dough up; fold to make 1-
inch rim. For two 10-inch pizzas, pat and stretch 1
ball into 10-inch round. Add topping; make 1-inch
rim. Repeat to make second pizza. For four 6-inch
pizzas, pat and stretch 1 ball into 6-inch round.
Add topping, make ½-inch rim. Repeat to make 3
more pizzas. Let rest 10 minutes.

COOK: Preheat the oven to 450°F. Grease a 15-inch
pizza pan; sprinkle with yellow cornmeal. Pat
dough onto bottom of pizza pan, shaping dough
into ½-inch-high rim at edge of pan. Layer dough
with toppings and bake 20 to 25 minutes or until
the crust is browned.

PREP: 10 MINUTES PLUS RISING

*2 cups all-purpose flour*
*1 package quick-rise yeast*
*¾ teaspoon salt*
*Yellow cornmeal for sprinkling*

1 In large bowl, combine flour, yeast, and salt. Stir in
*¾ cup very warm water* (120° to 130°F.) until blended and dough comes away from sides of bowl.

2 Turn dough onto lightly floured surface; knead 5
minutes. Sprinkle cookie sheet with cornmeal. Shape
dough into 1, 2, or 4 balls (for 1 large rectangular, two
10-inch, or four 6-inch pizzas); place on large cookie sheets (for 4 balls, use 2 cookie sheets). Cover with
plastic wrap; let rest 10 minutes.

3 Proceed as described in the recipe you are using.
Makes 1 pound.

Spray top of pie with nonstick cooking spray. Bake 1 hour or until pie is hot and phyllo is golden brown.

**7** To serve, cut pie into 8 wedges. *Makes 8 servings.*

Each serving: About 315 calories, 23 g protein, 28 g carbohydrate, 13 g total fat (6 g saturated), 34 mg cholesterol, 730 mg sodium.

# Stuffed Pizza

PREP: 30 MINUTES ⌒ BAKE: 30 MINUTES

Yellow cornmeal for sprinkling
2 pounds pizza dough, homemade (opposite page) or store-bought, divided into 2 balls
1 cup bottled pizza sauce
1 package (10 ounces) frozen chopped broccoli, thawed and squeezed dry
1 package (10 ounces) frozen chopped spinach, thawed and squeezed dry
1 jar (12 ounces) roasted red peppers, drained and chopped
3 medium plum tomatoes (about 8 ounces), cut crosswise into ¼-inch-thick slices
2 cups shredded part-skim mozzarella cheese (8 ounces)
1 tablespoon extravirgin olive oil or olive oil
1 teaspoon coarse salt (optional)

**1** Preheat oven to 400°F. Grease 15-inch pizza pan; sprinkle with yellow cornmeal. Pat first ball of dough onto bottom of pan, shaping dough into ½-inch-high rim at edge of pan. Spread pizza sauce over dough, leaving 1-inch border; top with broccoli, spinach, roasted red peppers, and tomatoes. Sprinkle with mozzarella.

**2** On lightly floured surface, with floured rolling pin, roll second ball of dough into 14-inch round. Fold round in half and transfer to top of pizza; unfold, and with fork, press edges of dough together to seal.

**3** Brush top of pizza with olive oil. Sprinkle with coarse salt if you like. Cut a few short slashes on top to allow steam to escape during baking.

**4** Bake pizza on bottom rack in oven 25 to 30 minutes or until crust is golden brown and filling is hot. *Makes 12 servings.*

Each serving: About 265 calories, 12 g protein, 42 g carbohydrate, 6 g total fat (2 g saturated), 11 mg cholesterol, 525 mg sodium.

# Spinach & Feta Cheese Pizza

PREP: 35 MINUTES ⌒ BAKE: 25 MINUTES

1 tablespoon olive oil
2 large onions (about 8 ounces each), halved lengthwise then cut crosswise into ¼-inch-wide slices
2 bags (10 ounces each) prewashed spinach, tough stems discarded, coarsely chopped
½ teaspoon salt
2 teaspoons yellow cornmeal
1 pound pizza dough, homemade (opposite page) or store-bought
2 ounces feta cheese, crumbled (½ cup)
½ cup shredded part-skim mozzarella cheese (2 ounces)
2 small tomatoes (about 4 ounces each), thinly sliced
¾ teaspoon dried oregano leaves

**1** In nonstick 12-inch skillet, heat olive oil over medium heat until hot. Add onions and cook 10 to 15 minutes or until tender. Add spinach and salt; cook, stirring, just until spinach wilts. Remove from heat.

**2** Grease 15-inch pizza pan; sprinkle with cornmeal. Pat dough onto bottom of pizza pan, shaping dough into ½-inch-high rim at edge of pan.

**3** Preheat oven to 400°F. Spoon onion mixture over dough. Sprinkle crumbled feta over onion mixture; top with mozzarella. Arrange tomato slices over cheese; sprinkle with oregano.

**4** Bake pizza 20 to 25 minutes or until crust is golden and cheese between tomato slices is lightly browned. *Makes 4 servings.*

Each serving: About 445 calories, 18 g protein, 70 g carbohydrate, 11 g total fat (4 g saturated), 21 mg cholesterol, 665 mg sodium.

# Tomato-Pesto Custard Pie

PREP: 35 MINUTES ∼ BAKE: 40 MINUTES

If you make your own pesto, save some small basil sprigs for a garnish.

1 small eggplant (about 12 ounces)
1 tablespoon olive oil
2 cups all-purpose flour
1 teaspoon salt
¾ cup shortening
1 quart milk
8 large eggs
2 cups shredded part-skim mozzarella cheese
   (8 ounces)
½ cup pesto, homemade (page 141) or store-
   bought
3 medium plum tomatoes, seeded and diced

1 Cut ten ¼-inch-thick slices from eggplant. Wrap and refrigerate remaining eggplant to use another day. In nonstick 12-inch skillet, heat olive oil over medium heat until hot. Add eggplant slices in 1 layer and cook until golden brown on both sides, transferring them to paper towels to drain as they brown.

2 Meanwhile, in medium bowl, mix flour and ½ teaspoon salt. With pastry blender or two knives used scissor-fashion, cut in shortening until mixture resembles coarse crumbs. Sprinkle *5 to 6 tablespoons cold water*, 1 tablespoon at a time, into flour mixture, mixing lightly with a fork after each addition until dough is just moist enough to hold together. Shape dough into a disk; wrap with plastic wrap and refrigerate until ready to use.

3 On floured surface, with floured rolling pin, roll dough into rectangle 2 inches larger all around than inverted 13" by 9" glass baking dish. Gently ease dough into baking dish; fold overhang under to make stand-up edge; flute.

4 Preheat oven to 375°F. In large bowl, beat milk, eggs, and remaining ½ teaspoon salt until blended. Stir in mozzarella and pesto. Pour custard mixture into piecrust; sprinkle with tomatoes. Arrange eggplant slices over top of pie. Bake pie 40 minutes or until knife inserted in center of pie comes out clean. *Makes 12 servings.*

Each serving: About 400 calories, 15 g protein, 24 g carbohydrate, 27 g total fat (9 g saturated), 165 mg cholesterol, 450 mg sodium.

# Summer Squash & Spinach Pizza

PREP: 15 MINUTES ∼ BAKE: 25 MINUTES

The tomato for this pizza is seeded so the topping won't be too wet. To seed a tomato, halve the tomato crosswise and then squeeze the halves to force the seeds out. You could also use a small spoon or your finger to scoop the seeds out.

1 tablespoon vegetable oil
1 small zucchini (about 6 ounces), diced
1 small yellow straightneck squash (about
   6 ounces), diced
1 large tomato, seeded and diced
1 package (10 ounces) frozen chopped spinach,
   thawed and squeezed dry
½ teaspoon dried oregano leaves
½ teaspoon salt
¼ teaspoon coarsely ground black pepper
2 teaspoons yellow cornmeal
1 pound pizza dough, homemade (page 170) or
   store-bought
8 ounces smoked mozzarella cheese, shredded
   (2 cups)

1 In 12-inch skillet, heat vegetable oil over medium-high heat until hot. Add zucchini and yellow squash and cook until tender. Stir in tomato, spinach, oregano, salt, and pepper; set aside.

2 Preheat oven to 450°F. Grease 15-inch pizza pan; sprinkle with cornmeal. Pat dough onto bottom of pizza pan, shaping dough into ½-inch-high rim at edge of pan.

3 Top pizza crust with vegetable mixture; sprinkle with mozzarella. Bake pizza on bottom rack of oven 20 to 25 minutes or until crust is golden and crisp. *Makes 8 servings.*

Each serving: About 260 calories, 12 g protein, 32 g carbohydrate, 10 g total fat (5 g saturated), 30 mg cholesterol, 525 mg sodium.

# Asparagus, Mushroom & Gruyère Strudel

PREP: 40 MINUTES ～ BAKE: 25 MINUTES

Assemble the strudels early and refrigerate covered with plastic wrap. Then, just pop them in the oven 25 minutes before serving! They're nice with a salad of mixed baby greens.

12 ounces asparagus
1 teaspoon salt
5 tablespoons margarine or butter
1 pound mushrooms, thinly sliced
2 teaspoons fresh lemon juice
⅓ cup walnuts, toasted and finely chopped
2 tablespoons dried bread crumbs
12 sheets (about 16" by 12" each) fresh or frozen (thawed) phyllo
4 ounces Gruyère or Swiss cheese, shredded (1 cup)

*Asparagus, Mushroom & Gruyère Strudel*

1 Cut asparagus into 6-inch-long spears (reserve ends for use in soup another day). In nonstick 12-inch skillet, heat ½ *inch water* to boiling over high heat. Add asparagus and ½ teaspoon salt; heat to boiling. Reduce heat to medium-low and cook, uncovered, until asparagus is tender, 4 to 8 minutes; drain and wipe skillet dry.

2 In same skillet, melt 1 tablespoon margarine or butter over medium-high heat. Add mushrooms and remaining ½ teaspoon salt; cook until mushrooms are browned and liquid evaporates. Add lemon juice; cook 30 seconds. Remove mushrooms to plate to cool slightly.

3 Preheat oven to 375°F. Lightly grease large cookie sheet. In small saucepan, melt remaining 4 tablespoons margarine or butter (½ stick). In small bowl, mix chopped walnuts and bread crumbs.

4 On work surface, place 1 phyllo sheet on sheet of waxed paper with short side facing you; brush lightly with some melted margarine or butter. Sprinkle with one-sixth of walnut mixture. Top with another phyllo sheet; lightly brush with some margarine or butter, being careful not to tear phyllo. Arrange one-sixth of Gruyère in a strip on phyllo 2 inches from edge facing you and leaving a 1½-inch border on both sides. Arrange one-sixth of asparagus spears on cheese; top with one-sixth of mushrooms. Roll phyllo jelly-roll fashion to enclose filling, then fold left and right sides in toward center and continue rolling phyllo jelly-roll fashion to end. Place packet, seam-side down, on cookie sheet. Brush packet lightly with some margarine or butter. Repeat to make 5 more packets.

5 Bake packets about 25 minutes or until they are slightly puffed and golden brown. Serve immediately. *Makes 6 servings.*

Each serving: About 365 calories, 13 g protein, 28 g carbohydrate, 23 g total fat (6 g saturated), 21 mg cholesterol, 675 mg sodium.

# Cremini Mushroom & Spinach Quiche

PREP: 35 MINUTES ∿ BAKE: 40 MINUTES

1⅓ cups all-purpose flour
1 teaspoon salt
½ cup shortening
1 bunch chives
1 tablespoon olive oil
8 ounces cremini or regular mushrooms, sliced
1 small red pepper, diced
1 small bunch spinach (about 8 ounces), tough
  stems discarded and coarsely chopped
6 large eggs
2 cups milk or half-and-half
¼ teaspoon coarsely ground black pepper
1½ cups shredded Jarlsberg cheese (6 ounces)

1 In medium bowl, stir flour and ¼ teaspoon salt. With pastry blender or two knives used scissor-fashion, cut in shortening until mixture resembles coarse crumbs. Sprinkle *3 to 4 tablespoons cold water*, 1 tablespoon at a time, into flour mixture, mixing lightly with a fork after each addition until dough is just moist enough to hold together. Shape dough into a disk; wrap with plastic wrap and refrigerate until ready to use.

2 On floured surface, with floured rolling pin, roll dough into a square 2 inches larger all around than inverted 8" by 8" glass baking dish. Gently ease dough into baking dish; fold overhang under to make a stand-up edge; flute. Refrigerate.

3 Reserve a few chives for garnish; finely chop enough remaining chives to make about 2 tablespoons. In nonstick 12-inch skillet, heat olive oil over medium-high heat until hot. Add chopped chives, mushrooms, and red pepper, stirring frequently, until vegetables are golden and tender-crisp. Stir in spinach; cook, stirring, until spinach wilts and any liquid evaporates.

4 Preheat oven to 375°F. In large bowl, beat eggs, milk, black pepper, and remaining ¾ teaspoon salt until blended; stir in Jarlsberg. Pour egg mixture into piecrust; top with vegetable mixture. Bake 40 minutes

or until knife inserted in center of quiche comes out clean. Garnish with reserved chives. *Makes 8 servings.*

Each serving: About 390 calories, 16 g protein, 24 g carbohydrate, 26 g total fat (6 g saturated), 181 mg cholesterol, 485 mg sodium.

# Chiles Relleños Pie

PREP: 30 MINUTES ∿ BAKE: 50 MINUTES

For a lower-fat version of this Mexican-inspired pie, use a no- or low-fat bean dip and low-fat milk.

½ cup regular long-grain rice
2 cans (4 to 4½ ounces each) whole mild green
  chiles, rinsed, drained, and patted dry
⅔ cup bean dip (about 6 ounces)
4 large eggs
2 cups milk
½ teaspoon salt
1 cup shredded Monterey Jack cheese (4 ounces)

1 Prepare rice as label directs, but do not add salt to water.

2 Meanwhile, with knife, split each chile lengthwise in half, but not all the way through. Spoon 1 heaping tablespoon bean dip onto half of each chile; fold remaining half of chile over. In medium bowl, mix eggs, milk, and salt until well blended.

3 Preheat oven to 325°F. Spoon rice into shallow 1½-quart casserole or 9½-inch deep-dish pie plate. Place stuffed chiles on top of rice. Pour egg mixture over chiles; sprinkle with Monterey Jack.

4 Bake pie 50 minutes or until knife inserted in center comes out clean. *Makes 6 servings.*

Each serving: About 255 calories, 14 g protein, 23 g carbohydrate, 12 g total fat (6 g saturated), 170 mg cholesterol, 795 mg sodium.

◄ *Chiles Relleños Pie*

# Farmstand Mushroom & Cheese Tart

Although the three types of wild mushrooms add wonderful earthy flavors and a variety of textures, this tart can be made with regular mushrooms. Use a total of 12 to 16 ounces.

1½ cups all-purpose flour
1¼ teaspoons salt
½ cup shortening
1½ cups plus 3 to 4 tablespoons milk
3 large eggs
1 tablespoon chopped fresh parsley leaves
¼ teaspoon coarsely ground black pepper
4 ounces Gruyère or Swiss cheese, shredded
   (1 cup)
1 tablespoon vegetable oil

8 ounces shiitake mushrooms, stems discarded and
   caps thinly sliced
4 ounces cremini or regular mushrooms, thinly
   sliced
4 ounces oyster mushrooms, thinly sliced
Parsley sprigs for garnish

1 In medium bowl, stir flour and ½ teaspoon salt. With pastry blender or two knives used scissor-fashion, cut in shortening until mixture resembles coarse crumbs.

2 Sprinkle 3 to 4 tablespoons milk, 1 tablespoon at a time, into flour mixture, mixing lightly with a fork after each addition until dough is just moist enough to hold together. Shape dough into a disk; wrap with plastic wrap and refrigerate until ready to use.

3 Preheat oven to 400°F. On lightly floured surface, with floured rolling pin, roll pastry to a 13-inch round. Ease pastry into 11" by 1" round tart pan with removable bottom. Trim pastry, leaving ½-inch overhang. Fold overhang in and press against side of tart pan to form a rim ⅛ inch above edge of pan.

4 Line tart shell with foil and fill with pie weights, uncooked rice, or dried beans. Bake tart shell 20 minutes; remove foil with pie weights and bake 10 minutes longer or until crust is golden.

5 While tart shell is baking, in bowl, beat eggs, parsley, pepper, remaining 1½ cups milk, and remaining ¾ teaspoon salt until blended. Stir in half of Gruyère.

6 In nonstick 12-inch skillet, heat olive oil over medium-high heat until hot. Add all 3 kinds mushrooms, stirring frequently, until golden and tender.

7 Sprinkle remaining Gruyère over bottom of tart shell; top with mushrooms. Pour egg mixture over mushrooms.

8 Bake tart 25 to 30 minutes or until egg mixture is set and tart is nicely browned. Serve hot. Or, cool on wire rack and reheat to serve later. Garnish with parsley sprigs. *Makes 6 servings.*

Each serving: About 465 calories, 16 g protein, 32 g carbohydrate, 31 g total fat (11 g saturated), 137 mg cholesterol, 580 mg sodium.

*Farmstand Mushroom & Cheese Tart*

# Roasted Vegetable Cobbler

**PREP: 30 MINUTES  ∾  BAKE: 1 HOUR**

1 medium butternut squash (about 2 pounds), peeled, seeded, and cut into 1½-inch chunks
3 large red potatoes (about 1 pound), unpeeled and cut into 1½-inch chunks
3 medium parsnips, peeled and cut into 1-inch pieces (about 8 ounces)
1 medium red onion, cut into 6 wedges
2 tablespoons olive oil
¾ teaspoon salt
½ teaspoon dried tarragon leaves
1 can (14½ ounces) chicken broth or 1¾ cups homemade (page 24)
½ teaspoon grated lemon peel
1 small bunch broccoli (about 12 ounces), cut into 2" by 1" pieces
½ cup plus ⅔ cup low-fat (1%) milk
1 tablespoon cornstarch
1¾ cups all-purpose baking mix
½ cup yellow cornmeal
¾ teaspoon coarsely ground black pepper

1 Preheat oven to 450°F. In shallow 3½- to 4-quart casserole or 13" by 9" glass baking dish, toss butternut squash, potatoes, parsnips, onion, olive oil, salt, and tarragon together until well coated. Roast, uncovered, 1 hour or until vegetables are fork-tender and lightly browned, stirring once.

2 After vegetables have roasted 45 minutes, in 3-quart saucepan, heat broth and lemon peel to boiling over high heat. Add broccoli; heat to boiling. Reduce heat to low; cover and simmer broccoli 1 minute.

3 In cup, mix ½ cup milk with cornstarch. Stir milk mixture into broccoli mixture, stirring constantly, until mixture boils and thickens slightly; boil 1 minute. Pour broccoli mixture over roasted vegetables; stir until brown bits are loosened from bottom of casserole.

4 In medium bowl, mix baking mix, cornmeal, pepper, and remaining ⅔ cup milk until just combined. Drop 12 heaping spoonfuls of biscuit dough on top of vegetable mixture.

5 Bake cobbler, uncovered, 15 minutes longer or until biscuits are browned. *Makes 6 servings.*

Each serving: About 395 calories, 11 g protein, 67 g carbohydrate, 11 g total fat (2 g saturated), 5 mg cholesterol, 940 mg sodium.

# Fork & Knife Salad Pizza

**PREP: 20 MINUTES  ∾  BAKE: 15 MINUTES**

For this "pizza," the crust is baked separately and then topped with a Mexican-style bean salad laced with taco sauce and sprinkled with shredded Cheddar. As the name of the recipe suggests, you will need a knife and fork to eat this.

1 pound pizza dough, homemade (page 170) or store-bought
1 can (15¼ to 19 ounces) red kidney beans, rinsed and drained
1 teaspoon olive oil
½ teaspoon chili powder
1 jar (16 ounces) medium-hot taco sauce
2 cups thinly sliced iceberg lettuce
4 ounces Cheddar cheese, shredded (1 cup)
1 large tomato, coarsely chopped
½ cup reduced-fat sour cream
¼ cup sliced green onions

1 Preheat oven to 425°F. Grease 15½" by 10½" jelly-roll pan. Press dough to fit jelly-roll pan. Bake about 15 minutes or until golden brown. (If dough puffs up, gently press it to pan with spoon.)

2 Meanwhile, in small bowl, mix kidney beans with olive oil and chili powder.

3 Remove baked pizza crust from pan and place on large cutting board for serving. Spread taco sauce over pizza crust. Arrange iceberg lettuce, kidney-bean mixture, Cheddar, and tomato in diagonal rows across pizza crust to cover, making 2 or 3 rows of each item. Spoon sour cream between several rows; sprinkle green onions over sour cream. *Makes 4 servings.*

Each serving: About 585 calories, 24 g protein, 84 g carbohydrate, 17 g total fat (9 g saturated), 40 mg cholesterol, 1675 mg sodium.

# Shiitake & Rice Quiche

PREP: 20 MINUTES ～ BAKE: 1 HOUR

1 cup all-purpose flour
1 teaspoon salt
7 tablespoons cold margarine or butter
8 ounces shiitake mushrooms, stems discarded and
   caps sliced
1½ cups milk
6 large eggs
5 ounces frozen chopped spinach (half 10-ounce
   package), thawed and squeezed dry
2 ounces roasted red peppers (half 4-ounce jar),
   drained and chopped
4 ounces Jarlsberg cheese, shredded (1 cup)
¼ teaspoon coarsely ground black pepper
1 cup cooked regular long-grain rice

1 In medium bowl, mix flour and ½ teaspoon salt. With pastry blender or two knives used scissor-fashion, cut in 6 tablespoons margarine or butter (¾ stick) until mixture resembles coarse crumbs. Sprinkle *3 to 4 tablespoons cold water*, 1 tablespoon at a time, into flour mixture, mixing lightly with a fork after each addition until dough is just moist enough to hold together.

2 Press dough onto bottom and up side of 9" by 1¾" tart pan with removable bottom. Refrigerate crust while preparing filling.

3 Preheat oven to 400°F. In nonstick 10-inch skillet, melt remaining 1 tablespoon margarine or butter over medium-high heat. Add mushrooms and cook until golden and liquid evaporates.

4 In large bowl, mix sautéed mushrooms with milk, eggs, spinach, roasted red peppers, Jarlsberg, black pepper, and remaining ½ teaspoon salt until well blended.

5 Sprinkle cooked rice over bottom of crust; pour vegetable mixture over rice. Place a sheet of foil underneath tart pan; crimp edges to form rim to catch any drips during baking. Bake quiche 55 to 60 minutes until filling and crust are golden and knife inserted in center comes out clean.

6 Cool quiche slightly on wire rack. Remove side of tart pan; serve warm. ***Makes 6 servings.***

Each serving: About 420 calories, 17 g protein, 31 g carbohydrate, 25 g total fat (5 g saturated), 233 mg cholesterol, 765 mg sodium.

# Plum Tomato & Basil Pie

PREP: 45 MINUTES ～ BAKE: 45 MINUTES

Nonstick cooking spray
8 medium plum tomatoes (about 1½ pounds)
½ teaspoon coarsely ground black pepper
1 teaspoon salt
1½ cups all-purpose flour
⅓ cup shortening
1 small bunch basil, stems discarded, leaves
   coarsely chopped
8 large eggs
3 cups milk
1 package (4 to 5 ounces) soft spreadable cheese
   with garlic and herbs

1 Preheat oven to 450°F. Spray 15" by 10½" jelly-roll pan with nonstick cooking spray. Cut each tomato crosswise into ½-inch-thick slices. Arrange tomato slices in 1 layer on jelly-roll pan; sprinkle with pepper and ½ teaspoon salt. Bake 30 minutes or until tomatoes are golden brown. Remove jelly-roll pan with tomatoes from oven; turn oven control to 375°F.

2 Meanwhile, in medium bowl, mix flour and remaining ½ teaspoon salt. With pastry blender or two knives used scissor-fashion, cut in shortening until mixture resembles coarse crumbs. Sprinkle *5 to 6 tablespoons cold water*, 1 tablespoon at a time, into flour mixture, mixing lightly with a fork after each addition until dough is just moist enough to hold together. Shape dough into a disk; wrap with plastic wrap and refrigerate until ready to use.

3 On floured surface with floured rolling pin, roll dough into a square 2 inches larger all around than inverted 8" by 8" glass baking dish. Gently ease dough into baking dish, allowing dough to hang over edge. Fold overhang under to form stand-up edge; flute. Cover dough loosely with plastic wrap while preparing filling.

4 In large bowl, with wire whisk or fork, mix basil with eggs, milk and cheese until blended. Pour egg mixture into piecrust. With pancake turner, carefully remove tomatoes from jelly-roll pan; arrange tomatoes over custard mixture.

5 Bake pie 40 to 45 minutes or until knife inserted in center of pie comes out clean. ***Makes 8 servings.***

Each serving: About 380 calories, 14 g protein, 28 g carbohydrate, 24 g total fat (10 g saturated), 244 mg cholesterol, 505 mg sodium.

# Bistro Pizza

A winning combination of asparagus, smoked mozzarella, and homemade roasted red peppers brings great flavor to a simple pizza.

2 medium red peppers
2 cups all-purpose flour
1 package quick-rise yeast
1 teaspoon salt
2½ teaspoons olive oil
Yellow cornmeal for sprinkling
8 ounces thin asparagus, trimmed*
6 ounces smoked mozzarella cheese, shredded
 (1½ cups)
¼ teaspoon coarsely ground black pepper

1 Preheat broiler if manufacturer directs. Line broiling pan with foil. Cut each red pepper lengthwise in half; remove and discard stems and seeds. Place peppers, skin-side up, on foil-lined pan and broil, at closest position to source of heat, 10 minutes or until skin is charred and blistered. Remove from broiler. Wrap foil around peppers and allow to steam at room temperature 15 minutes or until cool enough to handle. (Wrapping peppers in foil to steam makes it easier to peel off skin.) Turn oven off.

2 Meanwhile, in large bowl, stir flour, yeast, and ¾ teaspoon salt. Stir in ¾ *cup very warm water* (120° to 130°F.) and 2 teaspoons olive oil until blended and dough comes away from side of bowl. Knead dough 5 minutes.

3 Sprinkle large cookie sheet with cornmeal. Shape dough into 2 balls; place in diagonally opposite corners of cookie sheet, each 3 inches from edges of sheet. Cover; let rest 15 minutes.

4 While dough is resting, remove peppers from foil; peel off skin and discard. Cut pepper halves into thin strips; set aside. Cut each asparagus stalk into 2-inch pieces. In small bowl, toss asparagus with remaining ½ teaspoon olive oil and remaining ¼ teaspoon salt.

5 Preheat oven to 425°F. With dough on cookie sheet, pat and stretch 1 ball into a 10-inch round. Bring edge of dough up, folding to make 1-inch rim. Arrange half of mozzarella, half of red-pepper strips, and half of uncooked asparagus on crust. Repeat to make second pizza. Cover pizzas and let rest 15 minutes.

6 Bake pizzas on bottom rack in oven 25 to 30 minutes or until topping is hot and crust is browned and crisp. Sprinkle pizzas with black pepper. *Makes 4 servings.*

*If thin asparagus is unavailable, use medium asparagus, cutting each stalk lengthwise in half before proceeding with step 4.

Each serving: About 395 calories, 17 g protein, 52 g carbohydrate, 13 g total fat (6 g saturated), 33 mg cholesterol, 730 mg sodium.

## PIZZA ON THE GRILL

Pizza does not have to be a cold-weather-only meal. For an incredibly flavorful pizza crust, and to avoid heating up the kitchen, try making pizza on the grill. A wood-burning or charcoal grill will add an extra flavor bonus, but we've grilled pizza on a gas grill with delicious results. The trick is to keep the pizza rounds small and the toppings on the light side. You may want to grill one pizza at a time until you get the hang of it, since it requires a fair amount of attention. Here are some general guidelines for grilling pizza.

1 Start with about 1 pound of dough for 4 people and divide the dough into 4 portions. Form each portion into a round about 11 inches in diameter and of an even thickness.

2 Brush the bottoms of the dough rounds lightly with oil. Grill the dough rounds over fairly high heat (or about 4 inches above the coals) for about 1 minute or until the top of the dough puffs slightly and the bottom starts to set.

3 Flip the dough rounds over and brush each top with more oil. Sprinkle on the toppings and monitor the pizzas carefully, rotating them often over the heat so the crust doesn't burn.

# Seafood Shepherd's Pies

PREP: ABOUT 1 HOUR ∿ BAKE: 20 TO 25 MINUTES

The tasty filling is a fresh change from the classic ground lamb.

2½ pounds all-purpose potatoes (7 to 8 medium), peeled and cut into 1-inch chunks
3 tablespoons margarine or butter
⅔ cup plus ½ cup milk
1¼ teaspoons salt
2 tablespoons olive oil
2 medium carrots, peeled and sliced
2 medium celery stalks, sliced
1 medium onion, chopped
8 ounces mushrooms, sliced
2 tablespoons dry sherry
¼ teaspoon coarsely ground black pepper
1 can (10¾ ounces) condensed cream of shrimp soup
12 ounces large shrimp, shelled and deveined, and each cut lengthwise in half
12 ounces cod fillet, cut into 1-inch chunks
1 cup frozen peas, thawed

1 Prepare mashed potatoes: In 3-quart saucepan, heat potatoes and *enough water to cover* to boiling over high heat. Reduce heat to low; cover and simmer 12 to 15 minutes or until potatoes are very tender; drain. Return potatoes to saucepan. With potato masher, mash potatoes with margarine or butter, ⅔ cup milk, and ¾ teaspoon salt until smooth. Keep warm.

2 Preheat oven to 400°F. Meanwhile, in 4-quart saucepan, heat 1 tablespoon olive oil over medium-high heat until hot. Add carrots, celery, and onion, and cook 8 to 10 minutes or until browned, stirring frequently; transfer vegetables to medium bowl.

3 In same saucepan, heat remaining 1 tablespoon olive oil until hot. Add mushrooms and cook about 5 minutes until browned. Add sherry; cook 30 seconds, stirring. Add cooked vegetables, pepper, undiluted soup, remaining ½ cup milk, and remaining ½ teaspoon salt; heat to boiling over high heat. Add shrimp, cod, and peas; heat to boiling.

4 Spoon seafood mixture into six 2-cup ceramic ramekins or casseroles. Spoon potatoes over seafood mixture. Use back of spoon to swirl and spread potatoes in an even layer. Place pies on cookie sheet for easier handling and to catch any drips during baking. Bake pies 20 to 25 minutes or until filling is hot and potatoes are lightly browned. *Makes 6 servings.*

Each serving: About 400 calories, 27 g protein, 37 g carbohydrate, 16 g total fat (4 g saturated), 109 mg cholesterol, 1060 mg sodium.

# Summer Salad Pizzas

PREP: 15 MINUTES ∿ BAKE: 15 MINUTES

These would be a great candidate for grilled pizza. Form the dough into 4 rounds instead of 2 rectangles. Grill the rounds on one side (see "Pizza on the Grill," page 179), flip, and sprinkle on the basil and feta as directed in step 2. Proceed with recipe as directed in steps 3 through 5.

Yellow cornmeal for sprinkling
1 pound pizza dough, homemade (page 170) or store-bought
½ cup loosely packed fresh basil leaves, chopped
2 ounces feta cheese, crumbled (½ cup)
¼ cup reduced-fat mayonnaise
2 tablespoons low-fat (1%) milk
¼ teaspoon coarsely ground black pepper
1 small head romaine lettuce (about 12 ounces), thinly sliced
1 small red onion, thinly sliced
2 tablespoons grated Parmesan cheese

1 Preheat oven to 425°F. Grease a large cookie sheet; sprinkle with cornmeal. Divide pizza dough in half. On lightly floured surface, with floured rolling pin, roll each half into an 11" by 6" rectangle. Place on cookie sheet.

2 Sprinkle dough with basil and half of feta. Bake 12 to 15 minutes or until crust is golden brown.

3 Meanwhile, in large bowl, mix mayonnaise, milk, pepper, and remaining feta. Add lettuce and onion to dressing. Gently toss to mix.

4 Pile salad on top of hot pizza crusts; sprinkle with Parmesan. *Makes 4 servings.*

Each serving: About 385 calories, 13 g protein, 64 g carbohydrate, 8 g total fat (3 g saturated), 15 mg cholesterol, 780 mg sodium.

*Seafood Shepherd's Pie* ➤

# Wild Mushroom Quiche

PREP: 40 MINUTES ∿ BAKE: 1 HOUR TO 1 HOUR 5 MINUTES

1¼ cups all-purpose flour
¾ teaspoon salt
3 tablespoons shortening
4 tablespoons cold margarine or butter (½ stick)
4 ounces shiitake mushrooms, stems discarded and
    caps thinly sliced
4 ounces cremini mushrooms, thinly sliced
2 large shallots, minced
¼ teaspoon dried thyme leaves
¼ teaspoon coarsely ground black pepper
Pinch ground nutmeg
¼ cup dry white wine
2 cups milk or half-and-half
3 large eggs
4 ounces Gruyère or Jarlsberg cheese, shredded
    (1 cup)

1 In medium bowl, stir flour and ½ teaspoon salt. With pastry blender or two knives used scissor-fashion, cut in shortening and 3 tablespoons margarine or butter until mixture resembles coarse crumbs. Sprinkle about *3 tablespoons cold water*, 1 tablespoon at a time, into flour mixture, mixing lightly with fork after each addition until dough is just moist enough to hold together. Shape dough into a disk; wrap with plastic wrap and refrigerate 30 minutes or until firm enough to roll.

2 Meanwhile, in nonstick 12-inch skillet, melt remaining 1 tablespoon margarine or butter over medium-high heat. Add both kinds of mushrooms and cook 8 to 10 minutes or until mushrooms are lightly browned and all liquid evaporates, stirring occasionally. Stir in shallots, thyme, pepper, nutmeg, and remaining ¼ teaspoon salt; cook 2 to 3 minutes longer or until shallots are golden. Add white wine; cook 1 to 2 minutes or until all liquid evaporates, stirring constantly.

3 Preheat oven to 425°F. On lightly floured surface, with floured rolling pin, roll dough into a round 1½ inches larger in diameter than inverted 9-inch pie plate. Gently ease dough into pie plate; trim edge, leaving 1-inch overhang. Fold overhang under; pinch to form decorative edge. With fork, prick dough in 1-inch intervals to prevent puffing and shrinking during baking.

4 Line pie shell with foil and fill with pie weights, dried beans, or uncooked rice. Bake pie shell 15 minutes; remove foil with weights and bake 10 minutes longer or until golden. (If crust puffs up during baking, gently press it to pie plate with back of spoon.) Turn oven control to 350°F.

5 In large bowl, mix milk and eggs until well blended.

6 Place Gruyère and cooked mushroom mixture in pie shell. Pour egg mixture over cheese and mushrooms. Bake quiche 35 to 40 minutes or until knife inserted in center comes out clean and top is lightly browned. Serve quiche hot, or cool on wire rack to serve at room temperature later. *Makes 6 servings.*

Each serving: About 400 calories, 15 g protein, 29 g carbohydrate, 24 g total fat (9 g saturated), 134 mg cholesterol, 505 mg sodium.

# Sweet Onion Tart

PREP: 1½ HOURS ∿ BAKE: 55 MINUTES

Destined to be a summer favorite for years to come—the filling is made with caramelized onions, herbs, and Parmesan, and the tart is big enough to serve 12.

3 cups all-purpose flour
2 teaspoons salt
½ cup shortening
½ cup (1 stick) plus 3 tablespoons cold margarine
    or butter
2 pounds sweet onions, thinly sliced
5 large eggs
2½ cups milk
¾ cup grated Parmesan cheese
2 teaspoons chopped fresh thyme leaves
1 tablespoon chopped fresh parsley leaves
½ teaspoon coarsely ground black pepper

1 In large bowl, stir flour and 1 teaspoon salt. With pastry blender or two knives used scissor-fashion, cut in shortening and ½ cup margarine or butter until mixture resembles coarse crumbs. Sprinkle *7 to 8*

*Sweet Onion Tart*

*tablespoons cold water,* 1 tablespoon at a time, into flour mixture, mixing lightly with fork after each addition until dough is just moist enough to hold together. Shape dough into a disk; wrap with plastic wrap and refrigerate until ready to use.

2 On lightly floured surface, with floured rolling pin, roll dough into a rectangle approximately 18" by 13". Gently fold rectangle into fourths and carefully lift onto ungreased 15½" by 10½" jelly-roll pan; unfold. Lightly press dough onto bottom and sides of pan. Fold overhang under and pinch to form decorative edge level with rim of pan. Wrap and refrigerate tart shell about 30 minutes.

3 Meanwhile, in deep 12-inch skillet, melt remaining 3 tablespoons margarine or butter over medium-high heat. Add onions and cook, stirring frequently, until onions are golden brown, about 25 minutes. Remove from heat and cool to room temperature.

4 Preheat oven to 425°F. Line tart shell with foil and fill with pie weights, uncooked rice, or dried beans. Bake tart shell 20 minutes; remove foil and weights and bake 10 minutes longer or until golden. Remove tart shell from oven and turn oven control to 400°F.

5 In bowl, beat eggs, milk, Parmesan, thyme, parsley, pepper, and remaining 1 teaspoon salt.

6 Spread cooled onions over tart shell. Pour egg mixture over onions.

7 Bake tart 25 minutes or until egg mixture is set and edges of tart are nicely browned. Serve hot. Or cool on wire rack; wrap and refrigerate to serve cold later. *Makes 12 servings.*

Each serving: About 400 calories, 11 g protein, 33 g carbohydrate, 25 g total fat (8 g saturated), 100 mg cholesterol, 667 mg sodium.

# Phyllo-Crust Chicken Potpies

PREP: 45 MINUTES ∿ BAKE: 25 MINUTES

2 tablespoons vegetable oil
2 large skinless, boneless chicken-breast halves
    (about 1 pound), cut into 1-inch chunks
1 medium onion, diced
2 medium potatoes (about 8 ounces), peeled and
    cut into ½-inch pieces
2 medium carrots, peeled and sliced
¾ teaspoon salt
½ teaspoon coarsely ground black pepper
¼ teaspoon dried tarragon leaves
1 cup frozen peas
1¼ cups milk
2 tablespoons all-purpose flour
3 sheets (about 16" by 12" each) fresh or frozen
    (thawed) phyllo
1 tablespoon margarine or butter, melted

1 In nonstick 10-inch skillet, heat vegetable oil over medium-high heat until hot. Add chicken and cook, stirring frequently, until tender and chicken just loses its pink color throughout. With slotted spoon, transfer chicken to plate.

2 In drippings in same skillet, cook onion over medium heat until tender. Add potatoes, carrots, salt, pepper, tarragon, and *1 cup water*; heat to boiling. Reduce heat to low; cover and simmer 20 minutes or until vegetables are tender. Stir in frozen peas.

3 In small bowl, mix milk and flour until smooth; stir into vegetable mixture. Cook over medium heat, stirring, until mixture boils and thickens. Stir in chicken; pour mixture into four 10-ounce ovensafe custard cups or ramekins.

4 Preheat oven to 425°F. On work surface, place 1 sheet of phyllo on waxed paper; lightly brush with some melted margarine or butter. Top with second phyllo sheet, lightly brushing with some margarine or butter. Top with remaining phyllo sheet, brushing with remaining margarine or butter. Cut stacked phyllo crosswise in half; cut each half lengthwise in half. Gently arrange 1 phyllo stack on top of each custard cup, scrunching center of phyllo so edge is within rim of custard cup.

5 Place custard cups on jelly-roll pan for easier handling. Bake 20 to 25 minutes until phyllo is golden brown and chicken mixture is hot. **Makes 4 servings.**

Each serving: About 410 calories, 34 g protein, 34 g carbohydrate, 15 g total fat (3 g saturated), 77 mg cholesterol, 705 mg sodium.

# Uptown Turkey Potpie

PREP: 1 HOUR ∿ BAKE: 45 MINUTES

Although this recipe calls for leftover turkey (deli turkey is fine), the addition of a puff pastry top makes this homey dish truly company-worthy.

1 rutabaga (1½ pounds), peeled and cut into
    ¾-inch cubes
2 large carrots, peeled and sliced
1 cup frozen baby lima beans
2 tablespoons margarine or butter
8 ounces mushrooms, halved
1 medium onion, diced
2½ cups milk
¼ cup all-purpose flour
¼ cup grated Parmesan cheese
¾ teaspoon salt
½ teaspoon coarsely ground black pepper
4 cups cut-up cooked turkey
8 ounces frozen puff-pastry sheets, thawed (about
    half 17-ounce package)
1 egg white, beaten

1 In 3-quart covered saucepan, cook rutabaga and carrots in *boiling water* until tender, 10 to 15 minutes. Stir in frozen lima beans until separated. Drain

2 Meanwhile, in nonstick 12-inch skillet, melt 1 tablespoon margarine or butter over high heat. Add mushrooms and brown; transfer to large bowl.

3 In same skillet, melt remaining 1 tablespoon margarine or butter over medium heat. Add onion and *2 tablespoons water* and cook until tender. In medium bowl, mix milk with flour until smooth; stir into onion mixture along with Parmesan, salt, and pepper. Cook, stirring, until sauce boils and thickens. Boil 1 minute.

4 Reserve 1 cup turkey. Stir sauce, rutabaga mixture, and remaining turkey into mushrooms; spoon into a deep 3-quart casserole. Top with reserved turkey.

**5** Preheat oven to 375°F. Roll pastry to 1 inch larger all around than top of casserole; trim as needed. Brush rim of casserole with some egg white. Place pastry over filling; pinch edge for tight seal. Cut 3 slits in pastry top; brush with remaining egg white.

**6** Bake potpie on small cookie sheet 40 to 45 minutes or until filling is hot and pastry is browned; cover with foil if browning too quickly. ***Makes 8 servings.***

Each serving: About 445 calories, 30 g protein, 35 g carbohydrate, 21 g total fat (5 g saturated), 67 mg cholesterol, 500 mg sodium.

## WORKING WITH PHYLLO

When working with phyllo dough, it's important to work quickly and efficiently to prevent the tissue-thin sheets of dough from drying out. Place a sheet of waxed paper on the work surface and place the phyllo on top. Cover the phyllo with damp (not wet) kitchen towel or paper towels to keep the phyllo from drying out. Only expose to the air the phyllo you are working with at the moment. Have the melted margarine or butter in a bowl or small saucepan set next to the phyllo. Place 1 sheet of phyllo on another sheet of waxed paper. Using a pastry brush, brush the phyllo with the melted margarine. Do not use a basting or barbecue brush (or a paintbrush), since the bristles on these brushes are usually coarse and inflexible and may tear the dough.

# Fiesta Turkey Pie

PREP: 35 MINUTES ⌒ BAKE: 45 MINUTES

2 cups all-purpose flour
8 ounces sharp Cheddar cheese, shredded
   (2 cups)
⅔ cup shortening
1 medium potato (about 8 ounces), peeled and cut
   into ½-inch pieces
1 tablespoon vegetable oil
1 medium onion, diced
1 pound cooked turkey, coarsely chopped (about
   3 cups)
1 can (16 ounces) black beans, rinsed and drained
1 can (14 ounces) Mexican-style stewed tomatoes
1 can (11 ounces) whole-kernel corn, drained
1 jar (4 ounces) sliced pimientos, drained
1 teaspoon chili powder

**1** In medium bowl, mix flour and ½ cup Cheddar. With pastry blender or two knives used scissor-fashion, cut in shortening until mixture resembles coarse crumbs. Sprinkle *5 to 6 tablespoons cold water*, 1 tablespoon at a time, into flour mixture, mixing lightly with a fork after each addition until dough is just moist enough to hold together. Shape dough into a disk; wrap with plastic wrap and refrigerate until ready to use.

**2** In 2-quart saucepan, heat potato and *enough water to cover* to boiling over high heat. Reduce heat to low; cover and simmer 5 minutes or until tender; drain.

**3** In 12-inch skillet, heat vegetable oil over medium-high heat until hot. Add onion and cook, stirring occasionally, until tender. Stir in turkey, black beans, stewed tomatoes, corn, pimentos, chili powder, and potato; heat to boiling over high heat. Remove skillet from heat; stir in remaining 1½ cups Cheddar.

**4** Preheat oven to 400°F. On lightly floured surface, with floured rolling pin, roll out two-thirds of dough into a round 2½ inches larger all around than inverted deep-dish 9-inch pie plate. Gently ease dough into pie plate; trim edge, leaving 1-inch overhang.

**5** Spoon turkey mixture into pie plate. Roll remaining dough into 11-inch round; lift onto pie. Trim edge, leaving 1-inch overhang. Fold overhang under; flute edge. Cut slits in top crust to allow steam to escape during baking. Bake pie 40 to 45 minutes or until filling bubbles and crust is golden. ***Makes 8 servings.***

Each serving: About 595 calories, 31 g protein, 46 g carbohydrate, 32 g total fat (11 g saturated), 73 mg cholesterol, 530 mg sodium.

# Moroccan Chicken Pie

PREP: 1 HOUR ～ BAKE: 35 TO 40 MINUTES

The filling for this famous dish, known as *bistilla*, is traditionally made with ground and sweetened nuts, softly scrambled eggs, a flaky phyllo crust, and pigeon or squab (but we used shredded chicken). It combines sweet and savory flavors in an unusual but delicious dish.

3 medium onions
1¼ pounds skinless, boneless chicken thighs
1 can (13¾ to 14½ ounces) chicken broth or
    1¾ cups homemade (page 24)
5 tablespoons margarine or butter
1 teaspoon ground ginger
¼ cup chopped fresh cilantro leaves
¼ teaspoon loosely packed saffron threads,
    crumbled
3 large eggs, lightly beaten
1 cup slivered blanched almonds, toasted
1 tablespoon sugar
1 teaspoon grated orange peel
½ teaspoon salt
¾ teaspoon ground cinnamon
8 sheets (about 16" by 12" each) fresh or frozen
    (thawed) phyllo
1 teaspoon confectioners' sugar

**1** Cut 1 onion into quarters; chop remaining 2 onions. Set chopped onions aside. In 3-quart saucepan, heat onion quarters, chicken thighs, and chicken broth to boiling over high heat. Remove saucepan from heat; cover and let chicken sit in poaching liquid 20 minutes or until chicken loses its pink color throughout. With slotted spoon, transfer chicken to plate; cool until easy to handle. Discard onion quarters, reserving broth.

**2** Meanwhile, in 10-inch skillet, melt 2 tablespoons margarine or butter over medium heat. Add chopped onions and cook until tender and lightly browned, about 15 minutes, stirring occasionally. Add ginger; cook 1 minute. Stir in cilantro, saffron, and reserved broth; heat to boiling over high heat. Boil 10 minutes, stirring occasionally. Reduce heat to medium; add eggs and cook, stirring, 1 to 2 minutes or just until eggs are softly scrambled. Remove skillet from heat; let mixture stand 15 minutes or until most of liquid is absorbed.

**3** In food processor, with knife blade attached, pulse almonds with sugar, orange peel, salt, and ¼ teaspoon cinnamon until almonds are finely ground.

**4** When chicken is cool, pull into thin shreds. Stir chicken into egg mixture.

**5** Preheat oven to 375°F. In small saucepan, melt remaining 3 tablespoons margarine or butter over low heat. Brush bottom and side of 9-inch round cake pan with some melted margarine or butter. Place 1 phyllo sheet on sheet of waxed paper. Lightly brush 1 phyllo sheet with some melted margarine or butter; place in cake pan, allowing edges to overhang side of pan. Brush second sheet with some melted margarine; place over first sheet with corners angled slightly away from corners of first sheet. Continue layering, brushing each sheet with margarine and placing sheets so that corners are always angled slightly away from corners of sheet directly underneath.

**6** Spoon half of almond mixture over phyllo in cake pan; top with chicken mixture, then remaining almond mixture. One by one, fold overhanging edges of phyllo over filling until top of pie is covered. Brush top with remaining melted margarine. Bake pie 35 to 40 minutes or until golden. Invert onto platter.

## ▌ FOOD EDITOR'S TIP ▐

**Q.** How can I tell if eggs are fresh when I buy them? And what's the best way to store them?

**A.** Most markets stamp egg cartons with a "use by" or "sell by" date, which is the clearest indication of freshness; the later the date, the longer you can use the eggs, and the fresher they are when you buy them. If there's no "use by" date (or to be extra sure the eggs are fresh), look for a "pack date," which appears on all USDA-inspected (not state- or producer-inspected) cartons. This three-digit number, ranging from 001 to 365 (corresponding to the days of the year), indicates the day on which the eggs were packed; they are safe to use for at least four to five weeks beyond this date. (The market's "use by" date must be no more than 30 days past the "pack date.")

The best way to store eggs for optimum quality is in their original carton in a cold section of your refrigerator—not on the refrigerator door, even if it has a special egg-holder section, since the temperature on the door will fluctuate every time the door is opened.

**7** To decorate top of bistilla if you like, cut six ¾-inch wide strips of waxed paper. Place waxed-paper strips, ¾ inch apart, over bistilla; sprinkle spaces between strips with remaining ½ teaspoon cinnamon. Remove strips of waxed paper. Place more waxed-paper strips over cinnamon and sprinkle spaces between strips with confectioners' sugar. Remove waxed paper and discard. *Makes 6 servings.*

Each serving: About 455 calories, 28 g protein, 27 g carbohydrate, 28 g total fat (4 g saturated), 170 mg cholesterol, 745 mg sodium.

# Chicken Potpie with Cornmeal Crust

PREP: 1½ HOURS ∾ BAKE: 40 MINUTES

1 whole chicken (about 3½ pounds)
2 large celery stalks with leaves
1 tablespoon olive oil
1 medium rutabaga (about 1¼ pounds), peeled and diced
3 medium carrots (about 12 ounces), peeled and diced
1 large onion, diced
2 large potatoes (about 1¾ pounds), peeled and diced
1¾ teaspoons salt
1 package (10 ounces) frozen peas
1 cup milk
1¾ cups all-purpose flour
¼ teaspoon coarsely ground black pepper
¼ cup yellow cornmeal
⅔ cup shortening
1 large egg white, slightly beaten

**1** In 4-quart saucepan, heat chicken, breast-side down, and *3 cups water* to boiling over high heat. Reduce heat to low; cover and simmer 30 minutes or until chicken just loses its pink color throughout. Transfer chicken to bowl to cool slightly.

**2** Into 4-cup measuring cup, strain chicken cooking broth through fine sieve. (You should have 3 cups broth, or add *enough water* to make 3 cups.) Skim fat from broth. Return broth to saucepan; set aside.

**3** Remove skin and bones from chicken. Cut chicken into bite-size pieces. Dice celery; mince enough celery leaves to equal ½ cup.

**4** In nonstick 12-inch skillet, heat olive oil over high heat until hot. Add rutabaga, carrots, and onion and cook 10 minutes, stirring often.

**5** Stir in potatoes, diced celery, and ½ teaspoon salt; cook mixture 10 minutes longer or until vegetables are tender-crisp, stirring often. Stir in frozen peas and chicken; spoon mixture into 13" by 9" glass baking dish.

**6** In small bowl, mix milk and ¼ cup flour until smooth. Heat chicken broth in saucepan to boiling; stir in milk mixture, pepper, and ¼ teaspoon salt. Cook, stirring, until sauce boils and thickens. Stir sauce into chicken-vegetable mixture in baking dish.

**7** Preheat oven to 425°F. Prepare crust: In large bowl, mix cornmeal, remaining 1½ cups flour, and remaining 1 teaspoon salt. With pastry blender or two knives used scissor-fashion, cut in shortening until mixture resembles coarse crumbs. Sprinkle *6 to 7 tablespoons cold water*, 1 tablespoon at a time, into flour mixture, mixing with a fork after each addition until dough is just moist enough to hold together. Shape dough into a disk; wrap with plastic wrap and refrigerate until ready to use.

**8** On lightly floured surface, with floured rolling pin, roll dough into rectangle 2 inches larger all around than top of baking dish; sprinkle with celery leaves. With rolling pin, gently press celery leaves into dough. Arrange dough rectangle over filling; trim edge, leaving 1-inch overhang. Fold overhang under; flute. Brush crust with some egg white. If you like, reroll trimmings; cut into decorative shapes to garnish top of pie. Brush garnish with remaining egg white. Cut slits in crust to allow steam to escape during baking.

**9** Tear off a 15-inch piece of foil; crimp edges slightly. Place foil on second oven rack directly below pie to catch any drips while baking. Bake pie 35 to 40 minutes or until crust is golden brown and filling is hot and bubbling; during end of baking time, cover edge of crust with foil to prevent overbrowning. *Makes 10 servings.*

Each serving: About 450 calories, 24 g protein, 46 g carbohydrate, 19 g total fat (5 g saturated), 57 mg cholesterol, 550 mg sodium.

# Shepherd-Style Chicken Pie

PREP: 45 MINUTES ∾ BAKE: 20 TO 25 MINUTES

This delicious variation of the classic favorite has lots of well-browned carrots and red pepper pieces to flavor the ground chicken. Top with our special mashed potatoes and bake until browned.

6 medium all-purpose potatoes (about 2 pounds), peeled and cut into 1-inch chunks
2 tablespoons vegetable oil
2 medium carrots, peeled and diced
1 large onion, diced
1 large red pepper, diced
2 tablespoons margarine or butter
1 teaspoon salt
¾ cup milk
2 tablespoons chopped fresh chives or green onion tops

8 ounces medium mushrooms, thickly sliced
1¼ cups chicken broth, canned or homemade (page 24)
1 tablespoon all-purpose flour
1½ pounds ground chicken
¼ teaspoon coarsely ground black pepper
¼ teaspoon dried thyme leaves
2 tablespoons ketchup
1 tablespoon Worcestershire sauce

1 In 3-quart saucepan, heat potatoes and *enough water to cover* to boiling over high heat. Reduce heat to low; cover and simmer 15 minutes or until potatoes are fork-tender.

2 Meanwhile, in 12-inch skillet, heat 1 tablespoon vegetable oil over medium-high heat. Add carrots; cook 5 minutes. Add onion and red pepper and cook until vegetables are golden, about 15 minutes longer. Transfer vegetables to medium bowl.

3 When potatoes are done, drain. With potato masher, mash potatoes in saucepan with margarine or butter and ½ teaspoon salt. Gradually add milk; mash until mixture is smooth. Stir in chives; set aside.

*Shepherd-Style Chicken Pie*

**4** Add remaining 1 tablespoon vegetable oil and mushrooms to skillet and cook until well browned and liquid evaporates, 5 to 10 minutes; transfer to bowl with vegetables.

**5** In 2-cup glass measuring cup, mix chicken broth and flour until blended; set aside.

**6** Preheat oven to 400°F. Add ground chicken, black pepper, thyme, and remaining ½ teaspoon salt to skillet and cook over high heat until chicken is lightly browned and any liquid evaporates, 7 to 10 minutes. Stir in ketchup, Worcestershire sauce, cooked vegetables, and chicken-broth mixture. Cook, stirring, until liquid thickens, 3 to 5 minutes.

**7** Spoon chicken mixture into shallow 2-quart ceramic or glass casserole; top with mashed potatoes. Place sheet of foil underneath casserole; crimp edges to catch any drips during baking. Bake 20 to 25 minutes or until mashed potato topping is lightly browned. *Makes 6 servings.*

Each serving: About 385 calories, 30 g protein, 37 g carbohydrate, 14 g total fat (3 g saturated), 86 mg cholesterol, 735 mg sodium.

# White Pizza

PREP: 15 MINUTES ～ BAKE: 15 MINUTES

1 jar (6 ounces) marinated artichoke hearts
8 ounces sweet or hot Italian turkey-sausage links, casings removed
1 medium onion, chopped
4 ounces medium mushrooms, sliced
Yellow cornmeal for sprinkling
1 pound pizza dough, homemade (page 170) or store-bought
6 ounces Swiss or Jarlsberg cheese, shredded (1½ cups)

**1** Drain artichoke hearts, reserving marinade; coarsely chop artichokes.

**2** In 10-inch skillet, heat 2 tablespoons marinade from artichokes over medium-high heat. Add sausage meat and onion and cook until lightly browned; transfer to bowl. In same skillet, heat 2 more tablespoons marinade; cook mushrooms until lightly browned. Stir mushrooms and artichokes into sausage mixture.

**3** Preheat oven to 425°F. Grease large cookie sheet; sprinkle with cornmeal. Press dough into 15" by 10"

rectangle. Sprinkle half of Swiss cheese over crust; top with sausage mixture, then remaining cheese. Bake pizza on bottom rack in oven 15 minutes or until crust browns and cheese is bubbly. *Makes 4 servings.*

Each serving: About 575 calories, 31 g protein, 63 g carbohydrate, 23 g total fat (10 g saturated), 70 mg cholesterol, 1140 mg sodium.

# Skillet Polenta Pizza

PREP: 20 MINUTES ～ COOK: 1 HOUR

6 ounces hot Italian-sausage links
8 ounces mushrooms, sliced
1 tablespoon olive oil
2 medium onions, sliced
3 cups milk
½ teaspoon salt
1 cup yellow cornmeal
1½ cups shredded whole-milk mozzarella cheese (6 ounces)
¾ cup GH Marinara Sauce (page 154) or bottled spaghetti sauce

**1** In 10-inch skillet, heat sausages and *¼ cup water* to boiling over medium heat. Cover and cook 5 minutes, Remove cover; continue cooking, turning sausages frequently, until water evaporates and sausages are well browned, about 20 minutes. Transfer sausages to paper towels to drain; thinly slice.

**2** In drippings in same skillet, cook mushrooms over medium-high heat about 10 minutes or until tender and browned; remove from skillet. In same skillet, heat olive oil; add onions and cook 15 minutes or until tender and lightly browned.

**3** Meanwhile, in 2-quart saucepan, heat milk and salt to boiling over medium-high heat. Gradually sprinkle in cornmeal, stirring constantly with wire whisk. Cook over low heat, stirring frequently, about 10 minutes or until mixture is very thick. Remove saucepan from heat; stir in all but ¾ cup mozzarella.

**4** Spoon cornmeal mixture into skillet over onions, piling higher around edge to form rim. Spread Marinara Sauce over polenta to rim; top with remaining mozzarella, then sausage and mushrooms. Cover and cook over low heat 10 minutes or until heated through. *Makes 4 servings.*

Each serving: About 610 calories, 26 g protein, 50 g carbohydrate, 34 g total fat (15 g saturated), 91 mg cholesterol, 1040 mg sodium.

## Cheddar-Crust Chili Pie

PREP: 45 MINUTES ⌢ BAKE: 45 MINUTES

1 tablespoon vegetable oil
1½ pounds lean ground beef (90%)
1 medium onion, chopped
2 tablespoons chili powder
1 can (15¼ to 19 ounces) red kidney beans, rinsed
   and drained
1 can (15 to 16 ounces) Great Northern beans,
   rinsed and drained
1 can (14½ ounces) stewed tomatoes
1 package (10 ounces) frozen whole-kernel corn
1 package (10 ounces) frozen cut green beans
1 tablespoon chopped fresh cilantro
2¾ cups all-purpose flour
2 ounces Cheddar cheese, shredded (½ cup)
½ teaspoon salt
1 cup shortening
1 large egg, slightly beaten

1  In 12-inch skillet, heat vegetable oil over medium-high heat until hot. Add ground beef and onion and cook, stirring frequently, until pan juices evaporate and beef is browned. Stir in chili powder; cook 1 minute.

2  Add red kidney beans, Great Northern beans, stewed tomatoes, frozen corn. frozen green beans, and cilantro. In 2-cup measuring cup, mix ¼ cup flour with 1¼ cups water; stir into ground beef mixture. Heat to boiling over high heat.

3  Spoon meat mixture into 13" by 9" glass or ceramic baking dish. Cool slightly.

4  Meanwhile, prepare Cheddar crust: In large bowl, stir Cheddar, salt, and remaining 2½ cups flour. With pastry blender or two knives used scissor-fashion, cut in shortening until mixture resembles coarse crumbs. Sprinkle 6 to 7 tablespoons cold water, 1 tablespoon at a time, into flour mixture, mixing lightly with a fork after each addition until dough is just moist enough to hold together. Shape dough into a disk; wrap with plastic wrap and refrigerate until ready to use.

5  Preheat oven to 375°F. On lightly floured surface, with floured rolling pin, roll dough into a rectangle about 2 inches larger all around than top of baking dish. Gently arrange dough rectangle over filling. Trim edge, leaving 1-inch overhang. Fold overhang under;

flute edge. Cut slits in crust to allow steam to escape during baking. Brush top of pie and edge with egg.

6  Place sheet of foil underneath baking dish; crimp edges to form a rim to catch any drips during baking. Bake 40 to 45 minutes or until crust is golden and filling is hot. **Makes 8 servings.**

Each serving: About 765 calories, 34 g protein, 69 g carbohydrate, 41 g total fat (12 g saturated), 87 mg cholesterol, 490 mg sodium.

## Skillet Pizza with Prosciutto

PREP: 15 MINUTES ⌢ COOK: 25 MINUTES

2 tablespoons vegetable oil
1 medium onion, thinly sliced
1 medium yellow pepper, thinly sliced
¼ teaspoon coarsely ground black pepper
1 pound pizza dough, homemade (page 170) or
   store-bought
¾ cup GH Marinara Sauce (page 154) or bottled
   pizza sauce
8 ounces Monterey Jack cheese, shredded (1 cup)
1 ounce thinly sliced prosciutto
2 tablespoons sliced fresh basil leaves

1  In nonstick 12-inch skillet, heat 1 tablespoon vegetable oil over medium heat until hot. Add onion and yellow pepper and cook 15 minutes or until tender and lightly browned. Transfer onion mixture to small bowl; toss with black pepper. Set aside.

2  On lightly floured surface, roll pizza dough into 12-inch circle. In same skillet, heat remaining 1 tablespoon vegetable oil over medium-low heat. Press pizza dough onto bottom and partway up side of skillet to fit. Cook pizza crust, covered, 5 to 6 minutes or until bottom is lightly browned.

3  Remove skillet from heat; spoon Marinara Sauce over crust. Top with half of onion mixture, all of Monterey Jack, then remaining onion mixture. Cover skillet and cook pizza 3 to 5 minutes longer or until crust is golden and cheese melts. Top with prosciutto; sprinkle with basil. **Makes 4 servings.**

Each serving: About 595 calories, 25 g protein, 62 g carbohydrate, 27 g total fat (11 g saturated), 66 mg cholesterol, 1060 mg sodium.

*Skillet Pizza with Prosciutto* ➤

## Macaroni & Mozzarella Pie with Parmesan Crust

~~~~~~~~~~~~~~~~~~~~~~~~~~

PREP: 55 MINUTES ⌁ BAKE: 1 HOUR

3 cups elbow macaroni (12 ounces)
3 tablespoons olive oil
1½ pounds mushrooms, sliced
1 pound smoked ham, in ½-inch-thick slices, cut
   into ½-inch cubes
1 container (15 ounces) part-skim ricotta cheese
2 cups shredded part-skim mozzarella cheese
   (8 ounces)
½ cup chopped fresh parsley leaves
⅛ teaspoon coarsely ground black pepper
½ cup plus 1 tablespoon milk
3 cups all-purpose flour
1 cup grated Parmesan cheese
1 cup shortening

1 In large saucepot, prepare macaroni in *boiling water* as label directs, but do not add salt to water; drain.

2 Meanwhile, in 12-inch skillet, heat olive oil over medium-high heat until hot. Add mushrooms and cook, stirring occasionally, until browned and all liquid evaporates, about 15 minutes. Remove skillet from heat.

3 In large bowl, mix ham, ricotta, mozzarella, parsley, pepper, cooked macaroni, and ½ cup milk; set aside.

4 Prepare pastry: In medium bowl, mix flour and Parmesan. With pastry blender or two knives used scissor-fashion, cut in shortening until mixture resembles coarse crumbs. Sprinkle *7 to 9 tablespoons of cold water*, 1 tablespoon at a time, into flour mixture, mixing lightly with fork after each addition until dough is just moist enough to hold together. Shape dough into a disk; wrap with plastic wrap and refrigerate until ready to use.

5 On lightly floured surface, with floured rolling pin, roll two-thirds of dough into 17-inch round; use to line bottom and side of 10" by 2½" springform pan; trim dough to 1-inch overhang.

6 Spoon half of macaroni mixture into springform pan; top with mushrooms, then with remaining macaroni mixture, pressing down gently with spoon.

7 Preheat oven to 375°F. Roll remaining dough into 20" by 10" rectangle; cut dough crosswise into twenty

1-inch-wide strips. Moisten edge of bottom crust in springform pan with *water*. Follow the directions for a Quick Lattice Top or a Woven Lattice Top (page 169), placing half the dough strips next to each other, almost touching. Flute edge of pastry inside rim of springform pan. Brush top and edge of pastry with remaining 1 tablespoon milk.

8 Bake 1 hour or until crust is golden and filling is hot. Cover loosely with foil if crust begins to brown too quickly.

9 Cool on wire rack 10 minutes. Carefully loosen crust from side of pan with knife or metal spatula; remove side of pan. *Makes 12 servings.*

Each serving: About 605 calories, 27 g protein, 52 g carbohydrate, 32 g total fat (11 g saturated), 55 mg cholesterol, 810 mg sodium.

## Unstuffed Cabbage Pie with Potato Topping

~~~~~~~~~~~~~~~~~~~~~~~~~~

PREP: 1 HOUR ⌁ BAKE: 35 MINUTES

6 large potatoes (about 3 pounds), peeled and cut
   into 1-inch pieces
2 tablespoons vegetable oil
7 cups loosely packed thinly sliced green cabbage
   (about 1 small head)
½ teaspoon caraway seeds, crushed
2 teaspoons salt
12 ounces lean ground beef (90%)
1 medium onion, chopped
8 ounces mushrooms, thinly sliced
1 can (8 ounces) tomato sauce
½ teaspoon sugar
¾ cup low-fat (1%) milk
2 tablespoons margarine or butter

1 In 4-quart saucepan, heat potatoes and *enough water to cover* to boiling over high heat. Reduce heat to low; cover and simmer 10 to 15 minutes or until potatoes are tender. Drain potatoes; cover saucepan and set aside.

2 Meanwhile, in nonstick 12-inch skillet, heat 1 tablespoon vegetable oil over high heat until hot. Add cabbage and cook 1 minute, stirring constantly. Add caraway seeds, ½ teaspoon salt, and *¾ cup water*. Reduce heat to medium-low; cover and cook 15 minutes, stirring occasionally, until cabbage is tender. Spoon cabbage into 11" by 7" glass baking dish.

**3** In same skillet, heat remaining 1 tablespoon vegetable oil over high heat; cook ground beef, onion, and mushrooms until all pan juices evaporate and meat is browned. Stir in tomato sauce, sugar, and ½ teaspoon salt. Spoon beef mixture over cabbage in baking dish.

**4** Preheat oven to 375°F. Using potato masher, mash potatoes with milk, margarine or butter, and remaining 1 teaspoon salt until potatoes are smooth.

**5** Spoon or pipe mashed potatoes on top of beef mixture, making sure to cover surface entirely and seal edges. Bake pie 35 minutes or until cabbage mixture is hot and potatoes are lightly browned. *Makes 6 servings.*

Each serving: About 380 calories, 19 g protein, 46 g carbohydrate, 15 g total fat (4 g saturated), 36 mg cholesterol, 1140 mg sodium.

cook until golden brown and carrots are tender. In 1-cup measuring cup, mix flour and *1 cup water* until blended. Return meat mixture to skillet; stir in Worcestershire sauce and flour mixture. Heat to boiling over high heat; boil 1 minute.

**4** Preheat oven to 425°F. Peel potatoes; return to saucepan. With potato masher, mash potatoes with milk, Parmesan, salt, and pepper until smooth.

**5** Spoon meat mixture into shallow 2½-quart casserole. Spoon mashed-potato mixture into decorating bag with large writing tube (½ inch wide). Pipe mashed-potato mixture over meat mixture in lattice design and around edge of casserole. Bake 10 to 15 minutes or until potatoes are golden brown. *Makes 6 servings.*

Each serving: About 330 calories, 19 g protein, 45 g carbohydrate, 9 g total fat (3 g saturated), 40 mg cholesterol, 375 mg sodium.

## Shepherd's Pie

PREP: 45 MINUTES ～ BAKE: 15 MINUTES

7 medium potatoes (about 2 pounds)
12 ounces extralean ground beef
1 large celery stalk, finely chopped
1 medium onion, finely chopped
½ teaspoon dried thyme leaves
2 teaspoons vegetable oil
1 pound carrots, peeled and cut into ½-inch chunks
1½ pounds medium mushrooms, quartered
2 teaspoons all-purpose flour
2 tablespoons Worcestershire sauce
⅔ cup milk
2 tablespoons grated Parmesan cheese
½ teaspoon salt
⅛ teaspoon coarsely ground black pepper

**1** In 3-quart saucepan, heat potatoes and *enough water to cover* to boiling over high heat. Reduce heat to low; cover and simmer 25 to 30 minutes until potatoes are fork-tender; drain.

**2** Meanwhile, in nonstick 12-inch skillet, cook ground beef, celery, onion, and thyme over high heat until all juices evaporate and meat is browned, stirring frequently. Transfer meat mixture to plate.

**3** In same skillet, heat vegetable oil over medium-high heat until hot. Add carrots and mushrooms and

### GOOD NEWS ABOUT GROUND BEEF

Ground meat is rarely considered a lean choice, since it typically contains between 15 and 30 percent fat, by weight. But ground beef with less than 10 percent fat is now available. To taste-test it, we made three dishes—hamburgers, meat loaf, and chili—with 93 percent lean ground beef. The burgers, both broiled and pan-fried, tended to be dry and somewhat tough—though acceptable on hamburger buns, camouflaged with ketchup—but we never missed the fat in the chili and meat loaf. The best news: Four ounces of 93 percent lean ground beef (a typical burger, uncooked) contains 8 grams of fat and 160 calories—less than even most ground turkeys (9 fat grams and 170 calories).

**TIP** Fat savings are greatest for dishes like meat loaf and casseroles, from which excess fat cannot readily be skimmed. A meat loaf's fat drips into the pan and then is soaked back up; so if you start with meat that contains less fat, you end up eating less fat.

# Easy as Pie

Here is a collection of "pizzas" that use pita breads, tortillas, and Italian bread shells as a starting point. There are other breads that could also be used as the base for a quickie pizza, such as Italian focaccia and pocketless pitas (see "Bread Winners," page 209).

## Individual Smoked-Salmon Pizzas

PREP: 10 MINUTES • BAKE: 8 MINUTES

4 small Italian bread shells (4 ounces each)
8 tablespoons whipped cream cheese
6 ounces smoked salmon, cut into bite-size pieces
¼ cup minced red onion
4 teaspoons capers, rinsed and chopped
Parsley leaves for garnish

1 Preheat oven to 450°F. Place bread shells on large cookie sheet; bake 8 minutes.
2 Spread each hot crust with 2 tablespoons whipped cream cheese. Top with smoked salmon, red onion, and capers. Garnish with parsley leaves. Makes 4 servings.

EACH SERVING: ABOUT 455 CALORIES, 24 G PROTEIN, 52 G CARBOHYDRATE, 18 G TOTAL FAT (9 G SATURATED), 46 MG CHOLESTEROL, 1655 MG SODIUM.

## Individual Mushroom & Onion Pizzas

PREP: 20 MINUTES • BAKE: 10 MINUTES

1 tablespoon olive oil
12 ounces mushrooms, thinly sliced
1 large onion, thinly sliced
1 can (14½ ounces) pizza-style chunky tomatoes
4 small Italian bread shells (4 ounces each)
2 cups shredded part-skim mozzarella cheese (8 ounces)
1 teaspoon dried oregano leaves
½ teaspoon coarsely ground black pepper
1 tablespoon chopped fresh parsley leaves

1 Preheat oven to 450°F. In nonstick 12-inch skillet, heat olive oil over medium-high heat until hot. Add mushrooms and onion and cook until tender and golden.
2 Stir in tomatoes; heat to boiling over high heat. Reduce heat to medium-low; cover and simmer sauce 10 minutes to blend flavors.
3 Place bread shells on large cookie sheet. Top shells with mushroom sauce. Sprinkle with mozzarella, oregano, and pepper. Bake pizzas on bottom rack of oven 8 to 10 minutes or until hot and bubbly. Sprinkle pizzas with parsley. Makes 4 servings.

EACH SERVING: ABOUT 560 CALORIES, 31 G PROTEIN, 69 G CARBOHYDRATE, 19 G TOTAL FAT (8 G SATURATED), 39 MG CHOLESTEROL, 1500 MG SODIUM.

## Shiitake & Three-Pepper Pizza

PREP: 15 MINUTES • BAKE: 10 MINUTES

1 tablespoon plus 1 teaspoon olive oil
1 medium red pepper, cut into thin strips
1 medium green pepper, cut into thin strips
1 medium yellow pepper, cut into thin strips
1 small onion, thinly sliced
12 ounces shiitake mushrooms, stems discarded and caps thinly sliced
¼ teaspoon salt
1 large Italian bread shell (16 ounces)
6 ounces smoked mozzarella cheese, shredded (1½ cups)
1 teaspoon dried oregano leaves
½ teaspoon coarsely ground black pepper

1 Preheat oven to 450°F. In nonstick 12-inch skillet, heat 1 tablespoon olive oil over medium-high heat until hot. Add red, yellow, and green peppers and onion and cook until tender-crisp.
2 Add shiitakes, salt, and remaining 1 teaspoon olive oil; cook until all liquid evaporates and vegetables are tender and golden.
3 Place bread shell on large cookie sheet. Top with smoked mozzarella, then vegetable mixture. Sprinkle with oregano and black pepper. Bake pizza on bottom rack of oven 8 to 10 minutes or until hot and bubbly. Makes 6 servings.

EACH SERVING: ABOUT 345 CALORIES, 17 G PROTEIN, 41 G CARBOHYDRATE, 14 G TOTAL FAT (6 G SATURATED), 34 MG CHOLESTEROL, 615 MG SODIUM.

## Chicken-Topped Pita Pizzas

PREP: 20 MINUTES • BROIL: 2 MINUTES

2 teaspoons vegetable oil
1 medium red pepper, thinly sliced
1 medium green pepper, thinly sliced
1 medium onion, thinly sliced
¾ cup bottled marinara sauce
¼ teaspoon crushed red pepper
3 (6-inch diameter) pitas
6 ounces smoked chicken, torn into fine shreds
1 cup shredded part-skim mozzarella cheese (4 ounces)
2 tablespoons sliced fresh basil leaves

1 In nonstick 12-inch skillet, heat vegetable oil over medium-high heat until hot. Add red and green peppers and onion and cook until vegetables are tender-crisp. Stir in marinara sauce and crushed red pepper; heat through.
2 Preheat broiler if manufacturer directs. Split each pita horizontally into 2 halves. Place pita halves, split-side up, on cookie sheet. Place cookie sheet in broiler at closest position to source of heat; broil pitas until lightly browned.
3 Spoon sauce on pita halves; top with chicken and mozzarella. Broil until cheese melts. Sprinkle with basil. Makes 6 servings.

EACH SERVING: ABOUT 215 CALORIES, 14 G PROTEIN, 25 G CARBOHYDRATE, 7 G TOTAL FAT (3 G SATURATED), 26 MG CHOLESTEROL, 735 MG SODIUM.

*Broccoli Pizzas*

## Tomato, Basil & Goat Cheese Tortilla Pizzas

PREP: 15 MINUTES • BAKE: 5 MINUTES

*2 medium plum tomatoes, thinly sliced*
*4 (10-inch diameter) flour tortillas*
*1½ cups shredded part-skim*
*    mozzarella cheese (6 ounces)*
*10 large fresh basil leaves*
*2 ounces goat cheese or feta cheese,*
*    crumbled (½ cup)*
*2 tablespoons pine nuts (optional)*

**1** Preheat oven to 450°F. Arrange tomato slices on paper towels to drain.
**2** Place 2 tortillas in single layer on each of 2 large cookie sheets; place cookie sheets on 2 oven racks and bake 4 to 5 minutes or until tortillas are crisp but not brown. Remove from oven.
**3** Sprinkle ½ cup mozzarella on 1 tortilla on each cookie sheet. Top with second tortillas and remaining mozzarella. Arrange basil leaves and tomato slices on tortilla pizzas; sprinkle with goat cheese and pine nuts if using. Bake pizzas on cookie sheets 5 minutes or until edges begin to brown.
**4** To serve, cut each pizza into 4 wedges. Makes 4 servings.

EACH SERVING: ABOUT 340 CALORIES,
18 G PROTEIN, 33 G CARBOHYDRATE,
15 G TOTAL FAT (8 G SATURATED),
36 MG CHOLESTEROL, 535 MG SODIUM.

## Broccoli Pizzas

PREP: 20 MINUTES • BAKE: 10 MINUTES

*1 tablespoon light corn-oil spread*
*1 package (16 ounces) sliced*
*    mushrooms*
*1 large garlic clove, crushed with garlic*
*    press*
*1 package (16 ounces) broccoli*
*    flowerets*
*½ teaspoon salt*
*⅔ cup part-skim ricotta cheese*
*½ cup packed basil leaves, chopped*
*4 (6-inch diameter) pitas, split and*
*    toasted*
*½ cup refrigerated plum tomato sauce*

**1** Preheat oven to 425°F. In nonstick 12-inch skillet, melt light corn-oil spread over medium-high heat. Add mushrooms and garlic and cook until mushrooms are golden brown.
**2** Meanwhile, in 10-inch skillet, heat *1 inch water* to boiling over high heat. Place steamer basket in skillet; add broccoli. Reduce heat to low; cover and steam until tender, about 8 minutes.
**3** Remove broccoli; add to mushrooms with ¼ teaspoon salt and toss well to mix.
**4** In small bowl, mix ricotta, basil, and remaining ¼ teaspoon salt.
**5** Spoon broccoli mixture over each pita half. Spoon ricotta mixture in dollops on top. Drizzle pizza with tomato sauce. Bake 8 to 10 minutes or until heated through. Makes 4 servings.

EACH SERVING: ABOUT 320 CALORIES,
17 G PROTEIN, 49 G CARBOHYDRATE,
7 G TOTAL FAT (3 G SATURATED),
13 MG CHOLESTEROL, 805 MG SODIUM.

## California-Style Tortilla Pizzas

PREP: 20 MINUTES • BROIL: 5 MINUTES

*4 (8-inch diameter) flour tortillas*
*8 ounces Port du Salut or Monterey*
*    Jack cheese, shredded (2 cups)*
*2 large plum tomatoes, sliced*
*⅓ cup pitted ripe olives, chopped*
*1 small green pepper, cut into paper-*
*    thin slices*

*½ teaspoon coarsely ground black*
*    pepper*
*¼ cup grated Parmesan cheese*

**1** Preheat broiler if manufacturer directs. Place tortillas on large cookie sheet. Place cookie sheet at closest position to source of heat. Broil tortillas about 3 minutes or until golden brown, turning once.
**2** Sprinkle Port du Salut over toasted tortillas. Top with tomato slices, olives, green pepper, black pepper, and Parmesan. Broil until cheeses melt, about 2 minutes. Makes 4 servings.

EACH SERVING: ABOUT 370 CALORIES,
19 G PROTEIN, 23 G CARBOHYDRATE,
22 G TOTAL FAT (12 G SATURATED),
64 MG CHOLESTEROL, 665 MG SODIUM.

## Caramelized Onion Pizza

PREP: 40 MINUTES • BAKE: 12 MINUTES

*1 tablespoon olive oil*
*2 jumbo onions (about 12 ounces*
*    each), sliced ¼ inch thick*
*¼ teaspoon salt*
*½ cup packed fresh basil leaves,*
*    chopped*
*1 large Italian bread shell (16 ounces)*
*6 ounces Gruyère or Swiss cheese,*
*    shredded (1½ cups)*

**1** Preheat oven to 450°F. In nonstick 12-inch skillet, heat olive oil over medium heat. Add onions and salt and cook, stirring occasionally, until onions are golden brown and very tender, about 25 minutes. Remove skillet from heat; stir in basil.
**2** Place bread shell on large cookie sheet. Spoon onion mixture on bread shell; sprinkle with Gruyère. Bake pizza 10 to 12 minutes or until cheese melts. Makes 4 servings.

EACH SERVING: ABOUT 570 CALORIES,
27 G PROTEIN, 65 G CARBOHYDRATE,
24 G TOTAL FAT (9 G SATURATED),
49 MG CHOLESTEROL, 880 MG SODIUM.

# Sandwiches

# Double Tomato & Brie Sandwiches

Great for a summer buffet table—plain or fancy. If you make the sandwiches ahead of time, wrap the uncut loaves in plastic wrap and refrigerate. Then cut them into portions when ready to serve.

1 jar (6.5 ounces) oil-packed sun-dried tomatoes, drained (¾ cup) and finely chopped*
2 tablespoons extravirgin olive oil
2 tablespoons white wine vinegar
2 long loaves (about 8 ounces each) Italian bread
1 pound Brie cheese, sliced (with rind left on)
2 medium tomatoes, sliced
1 cup packed fresh basil leaves

1 In small bowl, combine sun-dried tomatoes, olive oil, and white wine vinegar.

2 Cut each loaf of Italian bread horizontally in half. Evenly spread dried-tomato mixture on cut sides of bread. Arrange Brie on bottom halves of both loaves; top with tomato slices and basil leaves. Replace tops of loaves. Cut each loaf into 4 portions. *Makes 8 servings.*

*For this recipe, we used dried tomatoes marinated in lightly salted olive oil with herbs.

Each serving: About 400 calories, 18 g protein, 34 g carbohydrate, 22 g total fat (12 g saturated), 56 mg cholesterol, 720 mg sodium.

# Ratatouille Heros

1 bunch basil
3 tablespoons olive oil
2 medium onions, chopped
1 large red pepper, cut into 2-inch pieces
1 large yellow pepper, cut into 2-inch pieces
1 medium eggplant (about 1½ pounds), cut into 1½-inch chunks
1 garlic clove, minced
1 can (14½ to 16 ounces) tomatoes in juice
2 tablespoons sugar
2 tablespoons red wine vinegar
½ teaspoon salt
4 hero rolls (8 inches long)

1 Chop enough basil to equal ¼ cup; reserve remaining basil leaves.

2 In 12-inch skillet, heat 1 tablespoon olive oil over medium-high heat until hot. Add onions and peppers and cook until lightly browned, about 10 minutes.

3 Add remaining 2 tablespoons olive oil to skillet. Add eggplant and garlic and cook until eggplant is lightly browned, about 5 minutes. Add tomatoes with their juice, sugar, red wine vinegar, and salt; heat to boiling over high heat. Reduce heat to low; cover and simmer 15 minutes or until eggplant is tender. Uncover and cook until liquid evaporates. Stir chopped basil into ratatouille mixture.

4 Cut each hero roll horizontally in half. Line bottom of each roll with some reserved basil leaves. Spoon ratatouille over basil leaves; replace tops of rolls. *Makes 4 servings.*

Each serving: About 460 calories, 12 g protein, 76 g carbohydrate, 14 g total fat (2 g saturated), 0 mg cholesterol, 975 mg sodium.

*Fruited Barley Salad (page 133), Double Tomato & Brie Sandwiches (above), with a side of Asian Coleslaw (page 133)* ➤

# Grilled Vegetable Sandwiches

PREP: 20 MINUTES ⌒ BROIL: 10 MINUTES

Nonstick cooking spray
1 small eggplant (about 1 pound), cut lengthwise
     into ¼-inch-thick slices
2 medium zucchini (about 8 ounces each), cut
     lengthwise into ¼-inch-thick slices
1 tablespoon olive oil
½ teaspoon dried oregano leaves
¼ teaspoon salt
2 tablespoons Dijon mustard
2 tablespoons balsamic vinegar
½ teaspoon sugar
½ bunch watercress, tough stems trimmed
8 slices (½ inch thick) multigrain bread (each
     5" by 3")
1 large tomato, thinly sliced
2 slices Muenster cheese (each about 6" by 3½"),
     each slice cut crosswise in half

1 Preheat broiler if manufacturer directs. Spray rack
in large broiling pan with nonstick cooking spray.

2 Place eggplant and zucchini slices on rack in broiling pan. Brush one side of the vegetable slices with
olive oil; sprinkle with oregano and salt.

3 With rack at closest position to source of heat, broil
zucchini and eggplant until tender and golden, turning once, about 10 minutes.

4 Meanwhile, in cup, mix mustard, vinegar and sugar.

5 Assemble sandwiches: Place watercress on 4 slices
bread. Top each with eggplant, zucchini, tomato, and
Muenster. Brush mustard mixture on remaining bread
slices and place on top of sandwiches. Cut each sandwich diagonally in half. *Makes 4 servings.*

Each serving: About 335 calories, 15 g protein, 39 g carbohydrate,
15 g total fat (6 g saturated), 27 mg cholesterol, 775 mg sodium.

# French Tuna Sandwiches

PREP: 20 MINUTES

¼ cup extravirgin olive oil
2 tablespoons red wine vinegar
5 flat anchovies, rinsed and finely chopped
2 teaspoons capers, rinsed and finely chopped
1 teaspoon dried oregano leaves
½ teaspoon sugar
¼ teaspoon crushed red pepper
1 loaf (12 ounces) French or Italian bread,
     16 inches long
4 lettuce leaves
1 jar (7 ounces) roasted red peppers, drained
1 can (12¼ ounces) chunk white tuna in water,
     drained
8 oil-cured olives, pitted and slivered

1 In small bowl, mix olive oil, red wine vinegar,
anchovies, capers, oregano, sugar, and crushed red
pepper until dressing is blended.

*French Tuna Sandwich*

**2** Slice bread horizontally in half; drizzle three-fourths of dressing on cut sides of bread halves. Arrange lettuce leaves on bottom half of bread, then top with roasted red peppers, chunks of tuna, and slivered olives. Drizzle tuna with remaining dressing; replace top half of bread. Cut sandwich crosswise into 4 pieces. ***Makes 4 servings.***

Each serving: About 510 calories, 31 g protein, 50 g carbohydrate, 21 g total fat (3 g saturated), 37 mg cholesterol, 1305 mg sodium.

# Waldorf Pita Sandwiches

PREP: 30 MINUTES

A takeoff on famous Waldorf salad (traditionally made with apples, celery, mayonnaise, and walnuts), served in a pita pocket to eat out of hand.

1 package (3 ounces) cream cheese, softened
¼ cup reduced-fat sour cream
¼ cup fresh lemon juice
2 tablespoons honey
¼ teaspoon salt
¼ teaspoon ground cinnamon
2 celery stalks, diced
2 medium McIntosh apples, unpeeled, cored, and diced
⅓ cup walnuts, toasted and chopped
1 bunch spinach (about 8 ounces), tough stems discarded, sliced
4 ounces Jarlsberg or Swiss cheese, cut into matchstick-thin strips
6 (6- to 7-inch diameter) pitas

**1** In large bowl, stir cream cheese, sour cream, lemon juice, honey, salt, and cinnamon until smooth. Add celery, apples, walnuts, spinach, and Jarlsberg; toss well.

**2** Cut off top third of each pita to form pocket. Fill pockets with salad mixture. ***Makes 6 servings.***

Each serving: About 400 calories, 14 g protein, 51 g carbohydrate, 16 g total fat (7 g saturated), 36 mg cholesterol, 550 mg sodium.

# Open-Faced Roasted Eggplant & Mozzarella Sandwiches

PREP: 15 MINUTES ~ BROIL: 12 MINUTES

1 medium eggplant (about 1½ pounds), cut crosswise into ¼-inch-thick slices
3 tablespoons olive oil
1 loaf (18 inches long) semolina or Italian bread
1 teaspoon dried oregano leaves
¼ teaspoon crushed red pepper
¼ teaspoon salt
8 ounces part-skim mozzarella cheese, thinly sliced
8 oil-packed sun-dried tomatoes, drained*
1 small bunch basil

**1** Preheat broiler if manufacturer directs.

**2** Place eggplant slices on rack in broiling pan; brush both sides of slices with 1 tablespoon olive oil. Broil eggplant 10 to 12 minutes or until browned, turning once halfway through broiling time.

**3** Diagonally slice both ends from loaf of semolina bread; reserve for making bread crumbs another day. Slice remaining bread diagonally into 8 slices.

**4** In a small bowl, mix oregano, crushed red pepper, salt, and remaining 2 tablespoons olive oil. Brush each bread slice with herb mixture.

**5** Arrange the bread slices on a large platter. Top with broiled eggplant, mozzarella, and sun-dried tomatoes; tuck basil leaves in between mozzarella slices. ***Makes 4 servings.***

*For this recipe we used imported dried tomatoes, marinated with herbs and other seasonings.

Each serving: About 585 calories, 26 g protein, 66 g carbohydrate, 25 g total fat (8 g saturated), 33 mg cholesterol, 1055 mg sodium.

# Chicken & Avocado Sandwiches

PREP: 25 MINUTES ~ COOK: 15 MINUTES

I medium lemon
I medium avocado, peeled and coarsely chopped
¼ teaspoon hot pepper sauce
½ teaspoon salt
I tablespoon plus 2 teaspoons olive oil
I medium red onion, cut into ¼-inch-thick slices
4 skinless, boneless chicken-breast halves (about
   I pound)
2 tablespoons all-purpose flour
½ teaspoon coarsely ground black pepper
4 large sandwich or kaiser rolls
I medium tomato, sliced
½ small bunch spinach, tough stems discarded

**I** From lemon, grate ½ teaspoon peel and squeeze 1 tablespoon juice. In medium bowl, mix avocado, lemon juice, hot pepper sauce, and ¼ teaspoon salt. Cover and refrigerate until ready to use.

**2** In nonstick 12-inch skillet, heat 2 teaspoons olive oil over medium-high heat until hot. Add onion and cook until tender and golden. With slotted spoon, remove onion to plate.

**3** Meanwhile, with meat mallet, pound each chicken-breast half to ¼-inch thickness. On sheet of waxed paper, mix flour, lemon peel, pepper, and remaining ¼ teaspoon salt; use to coat chicken-breast halves.

**4** Add remaining 1 tablespoon olive oil to skillet and heat over medium-high heat; cook chicken until golden brown on both sides and juices run clear when pierced with tip of knife, about 6 minutes.

**5** To serve, slice each sandwich roll horizontally in half. Top bottom halves of rolls with tomato slices, then with spinach leaves, chicken, and sautéed onion. Spread avocado mixture over sautéed onion; replace top halves of rolls. *Makes 4 servings.*

Each serving: About 465 calories, 35 g protein, 43 g carbohydrate, 17 g total fat (3 g saturated), 66 mg cholesterol, 715 mg sodium.

# Fancy Grilled Cheese Sandwiches

PREP: 5 MINUTES ~ COOK: 5 MINUTES

I loaf (16 ounces) unsliced white bread
4 ounces Brie cheese, softened
4 ounces thinly sliced prosciutto or cooked ham
I medium tomato, thinly sliced
4 teaspoons Dijon mustard
2 tablespoons margarine or butter

**I** From loaf of bread, slice eight ¾-inch-thick slices. Reserve remaining bread for use another day.

**2** Cut rind from Brie. Spread Brie on 4 bread slices; top with ham and tomato. Spread mustard on remaining 4 bread slices; place on top of sandwiches, mustard-side down.

**3** In nonstick 12-inch skillet, melt 1 tablespoon margarine or butter over medium-low heat. Add sandwiches; cover and cook until golden brown on both sides, carefully turning sandwiches once and adding remaining 1 tablespoon margarine or butter after turning. *Makes 4 servings.*

Each serving: About 420 calories, 20 g protein, 39 g carbohydrate, 20 g total fat (3 g saturated), 52 mg cholesterol, 1295 mg sodium.

# Roasted Pepper & Mozzarella Sandwiches with Basil Puree

PREP: 30 MINUTES ~ COOK: 20 MINUTES

Home-roasted peppers* require a little more effort than the store-bought kind but the flavor is worth it! They can be roasted several days ahead of time and then refrigerated.

3 medium red peppers
⅓ cup olive oil
2 cups packed basil or watercress leaves
½ teaspoon salt
I loaf (12 ounces) French bread

*Roasted Pepper & Mozzarella Sandwiches with Basil Puree (opposite page) and Smoked Turkey Lahvash Sandwiches with Chutney Mayonnaise (page 208)*

1 pound fresh mozzarella cheese or 1 package (16 ounces) whole-milk mozzarella cheese, cut into ¼-inch slices

1 Preheat broiler if manufacturer directs. Cut each pepper lengthwise in half; discard stem and seeds. Arrange peppers, cut-side down, on 15½" by 10½" jelly-roll pan. Place jelly-roll pan in broiler at closest position to source of heat and broil peppers 15 minutes or until charred and blistered. Turn peppers and broil 5 minutes longer.

2 Transfer peppers to clean brown paper bag; fold top of bag over to seal it and let stand at room temperature 15 minutes (keeping peppers in bag to steam makes them easier to peel). Remove peppers from bag and peel off skin. Cut each pepper half lengthwise into thirds.

3 In blender or food processor, with knife blade attached, blend olive oil, basil, and salt until almost smooth.

4 Cut French bread horizontally in half. Remove and discard some soft bread from each half. Evenly spread basil mixture on cut side of both halves. Arrange mozzarella slices on bottom half of loaf; top with roasted peppers. Replace top half of loaf. Cut into 8 sandwiches. *Makes 8 servings.*

*Or, you can substitute store-bought roasted red peppers for the home-roasted ones and omit steps 1 and 2 at left. Prepare recipe as in steps 3 and 4 but use 1½ jars (7 to 7¼ ounces each) roasted peppers, drained and cut into 2-inch-wide strips.

Each serving: About 350 calories, 14 g protein, 24 g carbohydrate, 22 g total fat (8 g saturated), 44 mg cholesterol, 400 mg sodium.

## Hot Barbecued Chicken Sandwiches

PREP: 10 MINUTES ～ COOK: 20 MINUTES

2 tablespoons vegetable oil
1 medium green pepper, chopped
1 medium onion, chopped
1 teaspoon chili powder
1 can (8 ounces) tomato sauce
8 ounces cooked chicken breast, pulled into shreds
1 tablespoon Worcestershire sauce
1 tablespoon cider vinegar
2 teaspoons brown sugar
½ teaspoon dry mustard
¼ teaspoon salt
4 kaiser rolls

**1** In 3-quart saucepan, heat vegetable oil over medium heat until hot. Add green pepper and onion and cook until tender and lightly browned. Stir in chili powder; cook 1 minute.

**2** Add tomato sauce, chicken, Worcestershire sauce, cider vinegar, brown sugar, mustard, salt, and *¼ cup water*; to boiling over high heat. Reduce heat to low; cover and simmer 10 minutes to blend flavors.

**3** Serve barbecued chicken on kaiser rolls. *Makes 4 servings.*

Each serving: About 375 calories, 25 g protein, 43 g carbohydrate, 12 g total fat (2 g saturated), 48 mg cholesterol, 890 mg sodium.

## California Grilled Sandwiches

PREP: 20 MINUTES ～ COOK: 10 MINUTES

1 loaf (16 ounces) unsliced white bread
8 ounces Monterey Jack cheese, thinly sliced
8 ounces roasted turkey breast, thinly sliced
2 medium tomatoes, thinly sliced
1 medium avocado, thinly sliced
4 teaspoons Dijon mustard
2 tablespoons margarine or butter

## OATMEAL BATTER BREAD

This is a super easy, slightly sweet, tender bread with a delicate oatmeal flavor. The recipe doubles easily and it's perfect for sandwiches!

PREP: 15 MINUTES PLUS COOLING
BAKE: 55 TO 60 MINUTES

1 cup milk
1 cup plus 1 tablespoon quick-cooking oats, uncooked
2 large eggs, lightly beaten
6 tablespoons margarine or butter (¾ stick), melted
¼ cup packed light brown sugar
2 cups all-purpose flour
2¼ teaspoons baking powder
½ teaspoon salt

**1** Preheat oven to 350°F. Grease 8½" by 4½" or 9" by 5" loaf pan. In large bowl, combine milk and 1 cup oats; let stand 5 minutes.

**2** Add eggs, melted margarine or butter, and brown sugar to oat mixture; mix well, making sure there are no lumps of brown sugar. Stir in flour, baking powder, and salt just until blended.

**3** Spoon batter into loaf pan. Sprinkle top with remaining 1 tablespoon oats. Bake 55 to 60 minutes in 8½" by 4½" pan (bake 35 to 40 minutes in 9" by 5" pan) or until toothpick inserted in center of loaf comes out clean. Cool bread in pan on wire rack 10 minutes; remove from pan and cool completely on wire rack. Makes 12 servings.

Each serving: About 225 calories, 6 g protein, 31 g carbohydrate, 8 g total fat (2 g saturated), 38 mg cholesterol, 255 mg sodium.

1 From loaf of bread, slice eight ¾-inch-thick slices. Reserve remaining bread for use another day.

2 On 4 bread slices, layer Monterey Jack, turkey, tomatoes, and avocado. Spread remaining 4 slices of bread with mustard; place on top of sandwiches, mustard-side down.

3 In nonstick 10-inch skillet, melt 1 tablespoon margarine or butter over medium-low heat. Add 2 sandwiches; cover and cook until golden brown on both sides, carefully turning sandwiches once. Repeat with remaining 1 tablespoon margarine or butter and remaining 2 sandwiches. To serve, slice sandwiches in half with serrated knife. *Makes 4 servings.*

Each serving: About 670 calories, 38 g protein, 44 g carbohydrate, 38 g total fat (14 g saturated), 103 mg cholesterol, 940 mg sodium.

# Quick BBQ Turkey Sandwiches

PREP: 10 MINUTES ∽ COOK: 10 MINUTES

Make this with shredded roast pork instead of turkey.

2 teaspoons vegetable oil
1 medium onion, diced
1 cup chili sauce
3 tablespoons light brown sugar
2 tablespoons Worcestershire sauce
1 pound roasted turkey breast
4 sandwich buns
4 lettuce leaves

1 In 3-quart saucepan, heat vegetable oil over medium heat until hot. Add onion and cook, stirring occasionally, until tender and golden. Stir in chili sauce, brown sugar, Worcestershire sauce, and *3 tablespoons water*; heat to boiling over high heat. Reduce heat to low; simmer, uncovered, 5 minutes to blend flavors.

2 Meanwhile, tear turkey into fine shreds; stir into barbecue-sauce mixture.

3 On bottom half of each sandwich bun, place lettuce leaf; top with turkey mixture. Replace tops of buns. *Makes 4 servings.*

Each serving: About 470 calories, 42 g protein, 60 g carbohydrate, 6 g total fat (1 g saturated), 97 mg cholesterol, 1280 mg sodium.

# Sesame Chicken Sandwiches

PREP: 15 MINUTES ∽ COOK: 15 MINUTES

1 tablespoon cornstarch
¼ teaspoon salt
1 large egg white
⅔ cup sesame seeds
4 medium skinless, boneless chicken-breast halves (about 1¼ pounds)
2 tablespoons plus 2 teaspoons vegetable oil
1 loaf (10 ounces) French bread, 17 inches long
1 small onion, chopped
1 medium red pepper, cut into ¼-inch-wide strips
1 bunch spinach, tough stems discarded
2 tablespoons teriyaki sauce

1 On sheet of waxed paper, mix cornstarch and salt. In pie plate, beat egg white and *1 teaspoon water* until blended. Place sesame seeds on another sheet of waxed paper. Dip each chicken-breast half in cornstarch mixture, then egg-white mixture, then sesame seeds to coat.

2 In nonstick 12-inch skillet, heat 2 tablespoons vegetable oil over medium-high heat until hot. Add chicken-breast halves and cook until sesame seeds are golden brown. Turn chicken; reduce heat to medium. Cook chicken until sesame seeds are golden and juices run clear when chicken is pierced with tip of knife, about 5 minutes longer. Transfer chicken to plate; keep warm.

3 Preheat broiler if manufacturer directs. Cut French bread crosswise into 4 pieces. Cut each piece horizontally in half. Arrange bread, cut-side up, on large cookie sheet. With oven rack at closest position to source of heat, broil bread about 30 seconds or until lightly toasted.

4 In same skillet, heat remaining 2 teaspoons vegetable oil over medium-high heat. Add onion and cook 5 minutes or until it begins to soften. Add red pepper and cook until onion and red pepper are tender. Add spinach and teriyaki sauce; cook just until spinach wilts.

5 Arrange half of vegetable mixture on bottom halves of bread. Top with chicken-breast halves, remaining vegetable mixture, then top halves of bread. *Makes 4 servings.*

Each serving: About 615 calories, 47 g protein, 51 g carbohydrate, 25 g total fat (4 g saturated), 82 mg cholesterol, 1075 mg sodium.

# Bistro Chicken & Roasted Vegetable Sandwiches

PREP: 20 MINUTES ⌇ COOK: 20 MINUTES

Nonstick cooking spray
1 small eggplant (12 ounces), cut lengthwise into
    ½-inch-thick slices
1 medium red onion, cut crosswise into ½-inch-
    thick slices
1 teaspoon dried basil leaves
2 tablespoons plus 1½ teaspoons balsamic vinegar
2 tablespoons extravirgin olive oil or olive oil

½ teaspoon salt
¾ teaspoon coarsely ground black pepper
2 teaspoons all-purpose flour
4 medium skinless, boneless chicken-breast halves
    (about 1¼ pounds)
1 large round loaf crusty bread
3 tablespoons Dijon mustard

1 Preheat oven to 500°F. Spray 15½" by 10½" jelly-roll pan with nonstick cooking spray. Arrange eggplant and onion slices in 1 layer on jelly-roll pan.

2 In cup, mix basil with 2 tablespoons balsamic vinegar, 1 tablespoon olive oil, salt, and ½ teaspoon pepper. Brush half of balsamic vinegar mixture over vegetables.

3 Roast vegetables 10 to 12 minutes, turning them once and brushing with remaining balsamic vinegar mixture, until tender and beginning to brown.

## STEAK & PEPPER FAJITAS

Not a sandwich in the strictest sense, but all of the components are there: bread, meat, vegetables, cheese, and condiments. Try this with chicken or turkey instead of round steak.

PREP: 10 MINUTES ⌇ COOK: 20 MINUTES

1 beef top round steak, 1 inch thick (about 12 ounces),
    well trimmed
1 cup medium-hot chunky salsa
1 tablespoon margarine or butter
1 medium red onion, thinly sliced
1 medium green pepper, thinly sliced
1 medium red pepper, thinly sliced
2 tablespoons chopped fresh cilantro leaves
8 (6- to 7-inch diameter) flour tortillas, warmed
    according to package directions
1 cup reduced-fat sour cream
4 ounces sharp Cheddar cheese, shredded (1 cup)
Lime wedges and cilantro sprigs for garnish

1 Preheat broiler if manufacturer directs. Place steak on rack in broiling pan; spread steak with ¼ cup salsa. Place pan in broiler at closest position to source of heat; broil steak 8 minutes. Turn steak over and spread with ¼ cup salsa; broil 8 minutes longer for medium-rare or until of desired doneness.

2 Meanwhile, in nonstick 12-inch skillet, melt margarine or butter over medium-high heat. Add red onion and peppers and cook until vegetables are ten-der-crisp. Stir in chopped cilantro. Spoon mixture into serving bowl.

3 To serve, place steak on cutting board; with knife held in slanting position almost parallel to cutting surface, thinly slice steak. Serve sliced steak with pepper mixture, flour tortillas, sour cream, Cheddar, and remaining salsa. Garnish with lime wedges and cilantro. Makes 4 servings.

Each serving: About 530 calories, 36 g protein, 37 g carbohydrate, 26 g total fat (12 g saturated), 103 mg cholesterol, 1115 mg sodium.

**4** Meanwhile, on sheet of waxed paper, mix flour, remaining ¼ teaspoon pepper; use to coat chicken-breast halves. In 12-inch skillet, heat remaining 1 tablespoon olive oil over medium-high heat until hot. Add chicken and cook until golden brown on both sides and juices run clear when pierced with tip of knife, turning chicken once, about 7 minutes. With knife held in slanting position, almost parallel to the work surface, cut each breast half into 3 slices.

**5** To serve, from center of loaf of bread, cut four ¾-inch-thick slices (reserve remaining bread for use another day). Top bread with eggplant slices, slightly overlapping, onion slices, separated into rings, and chicken.

**6** In cup, mix Dijon mustard with remaining 1½ teaspoons balsamic vinegar; drizzle over chicken. *Makes 4 servings.*

Each serving: About 505 calories, 42 g protein, 53 g carbohydrate, 12 g total fat (2 g saturated), 82 mg cholesterol, 1160 mg sodium.

# Hot Turkey Sandwiches Monterey

PREP: 15 MINUTES ∼ BAKE: 30 MINUTES

4 tablespoons margarine or butter (½ stick)
1 large onion, sliced
¼ cup all-purpose flour
¼ teaspoon ground red pepper (cayenne)
2 cups milk
6 ounces Monterey Jack cheese, shredded
   (1½ cups)
Half of 14-inch-long loaf Italian bread, cut into
   ½-inch-thick slices
8 ounces roast turkey, thinly sliced
2 medium tomatoes, sliced

**1** In 2-quart saucepan, melt 3 tablespoons margarine or butter over medium heat. Add onion and cook until tender, stirring occasionally. With slotted spoon, transfer onion to small bowl.

**2** Add remaining 1 tablespoon margarine or butter to saucepan. Stir in flour and ground red pepper. Cook over medium heat 1 minute. Gradually stir in milk; cook until slightly thickened and smooth, stirring constantly. Remove saucepan from heat. Stir in Monterey Jack, stirring until cheese melts.

**3** Preheat oven to 350°F. Arrange Italian-bread slices on cookie sheet; toast in oven until lightly browned on both sides, about 10 minutes.

**4** In 11" by 7" glass baking dish, arrange toast slices in single layer; spoon a small amount of cheese sauce over toast; top with turkey and tomato slices, remaining sauce, then onion. Cover baking dish with foil; bake 30 minutes or until mixture is hot and bubbly. *Makes 6 servings.*

Each serving: About 430 calories, 25 g protein, 32 g carbohydrate, 22 g total fat (9 g saturated), 70 mg cholesterol, 535 mg sodium.

# Turkey Sloppy Joes

PREP: 15 MINUTES ∼ COOK: 25 MINUTES

2 tablespoons vegetable oil
1 medium green pepper, chopped
1 pound ground turkey
1 can (15 ounces) tomato sauce
¼ cup cider vinegar
3 tablespoons light brown sugar
1 tablespoon Worcestershire sauce
1 jumbo onion (about 1 pound)
4 kaiser rolls, cut in half
4 green-leaf lettuce leaves

**1** In nonstick 12-inch skillet, heat 1 tablespoon vegetable oil over medium-high heat until hot. Add green pepper and cook until tender and golden. Stir in ground turkey. Cook turkey over high heat until pan juices evaporate and turkey is browned. Stir in tomato sauce, cider vinegar, brown sugar, Worcestershire sauce, and ¼ *cup water*, heat to boiling. Reduce heat to low; cover and simmer 15 minutes to blend flavors.

**2** Meanwhile, cut onion into ½-inch-thick slices. In 10-inch skillet, heat remaining 1 tablespoon vegetable oil over high heat; cook 4 center slices of onion until golden and tender; wrap and refrigerate remaining onion slices for use another day.

**3** To serve, on each kaiser roll, arrange 1 lettuce leaf, some turkey mixture, and cooked onion slice. *Makes 4 servings.*

Each serving: About 515 calories, 29 g protein, 61 g carbohydrate, 18 g total fat (4 g saturated), 83 mg cholesterol, 1110 mg sodium.

# Chicken-Cutlet Sandwiches with Eggplant-Pepper Relish

PREP: 15 MINUTES ～ COOK: 25 MINUTES

1 tablespoon vegetable oil
1 small eggplant (about 12 ounces), cut into ½-inch pieces
1 medium red pepper, cut into ½-inch pieces
1 medium yellow pepper, cut into ½-inch pieces
1 medium onion, cut into ½-inch pieces
1 teaspoon salt
2 tablespoons light brown sugar
2 tablespoons red wine vinegar
1 tablespoon coarsely chopped fresh parsley leaves
4 chicken cutlets (1 pound)
Nonstick cooking spray
1 bunch arugula, stems trimmed, or 1 small head Boston lettuce, torn into bite-size pieces
4 kaiser rolls

1 In 3-quart saucepan, heat vegetable oil over medium-high heat until hot. Add eggplant, peppers, onion, and ¾ teaspoon salt and cook, stirring frequently, until vegetables are lightly browned. Stir in ½ cup water; heat to boiling over high heat. Reduce heat to low; cover and simmer 15 minutes or until vegetables are very tender. Stir in brown sugar and red wine vinegar. Remove saucepan from heat; stir in parsley.

2 Sprinkle chicken cutlets with remaining ¼ teaspoon salt. Spray nonstick 12-inch skillet with nonstick cooking spray; cook chicken over medium-high heat until lightly browned on both sides, and chicken loses its pink color throughout, about 3 to 4 minutes.

3 Place arugula on kaiser rolls; top with eggplant-pepper relish, then chicken cutlets. *Makes 4 servings.*

Each serving: About 405 calories, 34 g protein, 49 g carbohydrate, 8 g total fat (1 g saturated), 66 mg cholesterol, 980 mg sodium.

# Smoked Turkey Lahvash Sandwiches with Chutney Mayonnaise

PREP: 20 MINUTES

This easy-to-fix sandwich is even easier if you mix the chutney mayonnaise and clean the arugula or watercress the day before serving.

⅓ cup reduced-fat mayonnaise
3 tablespoons mango chutney, large pieces chopped
½ teaspoon curry powder
¼ teaspoon coarsely ground black pepper
1 package (14 ounces) lahvash (2 soft Armenian flatbread loaves)
1 pound smoked turkey, thinly sliced
1 bunch arugula or watercress (4 ounces), stems removed

1 In small bowl, combine mayonnaise, chutney, curry powder, and pepper.

2 Unfold 1 loaf lahvash; spread with half of mayonnaise mixture, then half of smoked turkey, then half of arugula. Roll lahvash jelly-roll fashion. Repeat with remaining lahvash, mayonnaise mixture, smoked turkey, and arugula to make a second sandwich. If not serving right away, wrap each sandwich in plastic wrap and refrigerate up to 4 hours.

3 To serve, cut each sandwich into 6 pieces. *Makes 6 servings.*

Each serving: About 405 calories, 23 g protein, 60 g carbohydrate, 8 g total fat (1 g saturated), 39 mg cholesterol, 970 mg sodium.

FRENCH-BREAD VERSION: Instead of lahvash, slice one *12-ounce loaf French bread* horizontally in half. Remove and discard some soft bread from each half. Evenly spread mayonnaise mixture on cut side of both halves. Arrange smoked turkey on bottom half of loaf; top with arugula. Replace top half of loaf. Cut into 6 sandwiches. (If not serving right away, wrap uncut sandwich with plastic wrap and refrigerate up to 4 hours.) *Makes 6 servings.*

Each serving: About 285 calories, 19 g protein, 36 g carbohydrate, 7 g total fat (2 g saturated), 39 mg cholesterol, 1250 mg sodium.

# Roast Beef Pitas

¼ cup reduced-fat sour cream
1 tablespoon reduced-fat mayonnaise
2 tablespoons prepared white horseradish, well
   drained
2 teaspoons Dijon mustard
¼ teaspoon coarsely ground black pepper
4 (8-inch diameter) pitas
12 ounces roast beef, thinly sliced

1 small head Boston lettuce, torn into bite-size
   pieces
½ bunch watercress, stems removed

1 Prepare horseradish sauce: In small bowl, mix sour cream, mayonnaise, horseradish, Dijon mustard, and pepper.

2 Cut each pita in half. Tuck roast beef, lettuce leaves, and watercress into pita halves.

3 Arrange sandwiches on large platter. Serve with horseradish sauce to spoon over each sandwich. *Makes 4 servings.*

Each serving: About 440 calories, 34 g protein, 51 g carbohydrate, 10 g total fat (3 g saturated), 74 mg cholesterol, 625 mg sodium.

## BREAD WINNERS:
## GREAT FINDS FROM THE SUPERMARKET

Grocery stores now carry a variety of fresh breads made by local bakeries that can turn even the plainest ingredients into a memorable meal. Look for the following types (and use within a few days, since most are made without preservatives). Note that calories for all breads are approximate and may vary by brand.

*Afghan Snowshoe Naan* A larger version of tender Indian naan, this bread gets its name from its long, oval shape. Sprinkled with black caraway seeds and white sesame seeds, it's an excellent companion for grilled veggies or meat. [150 calories per serving.]

*Focaccia* This thick, tender Italian flatbread is brushed or drizzled with olive oil, sprinkled with salt, and often flavored with fresh rosemary, which is tucked into the dough before baking. It comes in large rounds or rec-

tangles, and is a good match for tuna salad. Focaccia is generally low-fat, except when it's soaked with olive oil. [150 calories per serving.]

*Italian Bread Shell* Similar to a plain pizza crust, this makes a nice base for all kinds of toppings (see "Easy as Pie," page 194). Don't miss the newer Italian-style grilled flatbread, which can be used like a bread shell but is also slender enough to wrap around such fillings as pan-fried steak and onions. [150 calories per serving.]

*Lahvash* When unfolded, this soft version of Armenian cracker bread ranges from 9 to 16 inches in diameter. Its thin texture is especially good with creamy spreads, like goat cheese or guacamole. [130 calories per serving.]

*Pita* The well-known pocket bread, in white or whole wheat, is enjoying a resurgence; it's the perfect catch for everything from Greek salad

to pan-browned portobello mushrooms. In addition to the classic version, which opens into a pocket when you cut off the top, there are thicker pocketless pitas, which are used uncut. These are often warmed and wrapped around fillings, as in the popular Greek gyro sandwich. [150 calories per medium white pita; 130 per medium whole-wheat pita; and 200 per medium pocketless pita.]

*Tortillas* These staples of Mexican cooking are made from wheat, blue corn, or corn flour and baked on a griddle. They range in diameter from 7 to 12 inches; we prefer the larger ones for meal-size servings. Also on the market: flavored tortillas made with spinach, tomatoes, or red chiles; they have a subtle flavor and a green or reddish color, and are stocked near regular tortillas, usually in the refrigerated section. [90 calories per tortilla.]

# Barbecued Beef Sandwiches with Carrot Salad

PREP: 40 MINUTES ～ COOK: 20 MINUTES

Carrot Salad (below)
1 beef flank steak or round steak (about 1 pound), well trimmed
1 tablespoon vegetable oil
2 medium red peppers, cut into ½-inch-wide strips
1 large onion, cut into ¼-inch-thick slices
1 tablespoon chili powder
1 can (8 ounces) tomato sauce
2 tablespoons Worcestershire sauce
2 tablespoons cider vinegar
1 tablespoon light brown sugar
4 hamburger buns

1 Prepare Carrot Salad; cover and refrigerate until ready to serve.

2 With knife held in slanting position, almost parallel to cutting surface, cut steak crosswise into paper-thin slices.

3 In nonstick 12-inch skillet, heat vegetable oil over high heat until hot. Add steak and cook, stirring quickly and frequently, until steak loses its pink color throughout, about 2 to 3 minutes. Transfer steak to bowl.

4 In drippings in skillet, cook peppers, onion, and *1 tablespoon water* until the vegetables are tender-crisp and lightly browned. Stir in chili powder; cook 1 minute.

---

## LOW-CHOLESTEROL WESTERN-OMELET SANDWICH

We cut the fat and cholesterol in this classic diner favorite by using turkey-ham and packaged liquid whole eggs (with 90 percent of the cholesterol removed). Sandwich-size English muffins really turn this omelet into a hearty, two-handed meal!

PREP: 10 MINUTES ～ COOK: 25 MINUTES

*4 teaspoons olive oil*
*8 ounces mushrooms, sliced*
*½ teaspoon salt*
*1 small onion, diced*
*1 large green pepper, diced*
*1½ containers (8 ounces each) liquid whole eggs (reduced cholesterol)*
*4 ounces turkey-ham, finely diced*
*4 sandwich-size English muffins, split*

1 In nonstick 10-inch skillet, heat 2 teaspoons olive oil over medium-high heat until hot. Add mushrooms and ¼ teaspoon salt and cook until any liquid evaporates and mushrooms are golden brown; transfer to bowl; keep warm.

2 Reduce heat to medium. Add remaining 2 teaspoons olive oil and onion and cook 5 minutes, stirring occasionally. Stir in green pepper and cook until onion is very tender and pepper is lightly browned, about 5 minutes longer.

3 In medium bowl, beat liquid whole eggs, remaining ¼ teaspoon salt, turkey-ham, and *2 tablespoons water*. Pour egg mixture into onion mixture. Reduce heat to medium-low and cook until eggs are set around edge; with spatula, gently lift edge as it sets, tilting skillet to allow uncooked portion to run under egg mixture. When egg mixture is set, remove skillet from heat.

4 Meanwhile, preheat broiler if manufacturer directs. Place English muffins, cut-side up, on cookie sheet. Broil English muffins until lightly browned.

5 Cut omelet into quarters. On bottom half of each English muffin, place 1 quarter of omelet, folding omelet over slightly to fit. Spoon sautéed mushrooms over omelet quarters. Replace tops of English muffins. Makes 4 servings.

Each serving: About 340 calories, 16 g protein, 46 g carbohydrate, 8 g total fat (1 g saturated), 18 mg cholesterol, 995 mg sodium.

5 Add tomato sauce, Worcestershire sauce, cider vinegar, brown sugar, and ¾ *cup water*; heat to boiling over high heat. Reduce heat to low; cover and simmer 15 minutes or until vegetables are very tender. Return steak to skillet; heat through.

6 Serve barbecued-beef mixture in hamburger buns. Serve with Carrot Salad. *Makes 4 servings.*

CARROT SALAD: Cut *1½ pounds carrots* and *½ European cucumber*, peeled, into matchstick-thin strips. In large bowl, mix carrots and cucumber with *2 tablespoons olive oil, 2 tablespoons cider vinegar, 1 tablespoon chopped fresh dill* or 1 teaspoon dried dillweed, *1 tablespoon Dijon mustard, 1 teaspoon sugar, ½ teaspoon salt,* and *½ teaspoon ground ginger.*

Each serving: About 580 calories, 30 g protein, 59 g carbohydrate, 25 g total fat (7 g saturated), 59 mg cholesterol, 1210 mg sodium.

# Turkey-Meatball Pitas

PREP: 15 MINUTES ∿ BAKE: 12 TO 15 MINUTES

Nonstick cooking spray
1 pound ground turkey
2 slices firm-textured white bread, chopped
2 tablespoons grated onion
1 large egg white
1½ teaspoons ground cumin
¾ teaspoon salt
4 (6-inch-diameter) whole-wheat pitas
½ large cucumber, peeled, seeded, and coarsely chopped
1 container (8 ounces) nonfat plain yogurt
2 tablespoons chopped fresh mint or 1 teaspoon dried mint leaves
4 cups thinly sliced romaine lettuce

1 Preheat oven to 425°F. Spray 15½" by 10½" jelly-roll pan with nonstick cooking spray.

2 In large bowl, mix ground turkey, bread, onion, egg white, cumin, ½ teaspoon salt, and *3 tablespoons water.*

3 Shape turkey mixture into 25 meatballs. (For easier shaping, use wet hands.) Place meatballs on jelly-roll pan and bake 12 to 15 minutes or until cooked through (meatballs will not brown).

4 Cut about 1 inch from top of each pita; reserve cut-off pieces for use another day. Wrap pitas in foil. After meatballs have baked 5 minutes, warm pitas in oven until meatballs are done.

5 Meanwhile, mix cucumber, yogurt, mint, and remaining ¼ teaspoon salt.

6 To serve, fill pitas with lettuce and meatballs; top with cucumber sauce. *Makes 4 servings.*

Each serving: About 425 calories, 33 g protein, 50 g carbohydrate, 11 g total fat (3 g saturated), 84 mg cholesterol, 1025 mg sodium.

# Antipasto Heros

PREP: 15 MINUTES

2 tablespoons extravirgin olive oil
2 tablespoons balsamic vinegar
1 teaspoon sugar
¾ teaspoon dried oregano leaves
¼ teaspoon crushed red pepper
4 large hero rolls (8 inches long)
½ small head escarole, coarsely chopped
½ small head radicchio, coarsely chopped
6 ounces provolone cheese, thinly sliced
4 ounces baked ham, thinly sliced
6 ounces roast turkey, sliced
2 medium tomatoes, sliced
12 peperoncini, cut into rings

1 In small bowl, mix olive oil, balsamic vinegar, sugar, oregano, and crushed red pepper until blended.

2 Slice hero rolls horizontally in half. Spoon oil-vinegar dressing onto cut sides of bread halves. Arrange escarole and radicchio on bottom halves of bread. Top with provolone, ham, turkey, tomatoes, peperoncini rings, and remaining bread. *Makes 4 servings.*

Each serving: About 600 calories, 39 g protein, 52 g carbohydrate, 26 g total fat (11 g saturated), 79 mg cholesterol, 1555 mg sodium.

# Steak & Peppers Sandwiches

PREP: 15 MINUTES ～ COOK: 20 MINUTES

1 tablespoon vegetable oil
1 boneless beef sirloin steak, about ¾ inch thick
  (12 ounces), well trimmed
1 medium yellow pepper, cut into ¼-inch-wide
  strips
8 ounces mushrooms, sliced
1 medium onion, sliced
4 sandwich-size English muffins
⅓ cup ketchup
1 tablespoon Worcestershire sauce
1 teaspoon light brown sugar
1 bunch arugula
1 large tomato, sliced

1 In nonstick 12-inch skillet, heat vegetable oil over medium-high heat until hot. Add steak and cook 8 to 10 minutes for medium-rare or until of desired doneness, turning once. Transfer steak to plate.

2 In drippings in same skillet, cook pepper, mushrooms, and onion until tender and lightly browned.

3 Meanwhile, preheat broiler if manufacturer directs. Split each English muffin horizontally in half; place halves, cut-side up, on rack in broiling pan. Broil 1 minute or until lightly toasted; set aside. Slice steak crosswise into thin slices.

4 In small bowl, mix ketchup, Worcestershire sauce, and brown sugar. Add steak and sauce to sautéed vegetables; heat through.

5 To serve, place arugula and tomato slices on bottom halves of English muffins; top with steak mixture, then top halves of English muffins. *Makes 4 servings.*

Each serving: About 415 calories, 22 g protein, 56 g carbohydrate, 10 g total fat (2 g saturated), 52 mg cholesterol, 623 mg sodium.

# Steak Sandwiches with Jicama Salad

PREP: 30 MINUTES PLUS MARINATING
COOK: 45 MINUTES

¼ cup chili sauce
1 tablespoon chili powder
2 tablespoons red wine vinegar
1 teaspoon sugar
1 boneless beef top round steak, about 1¼ inches
  thick (1 pound), well trimmed
Jicama Salad (opposite page)
Nonstick cooking spray
1 package (10 ounces) mushrooms, thinly sliced
2 French-bread rolls, 6 inches long (about 4 ounces
  each)
2 medium tomatoes, sliced
1 small head Boston lettuce

1 In large zip-tight plastic bag or 11" by 7" glass baking dish, combine chili sauce, chili powder, red wine vinegar, and sugar. Add round steak, turning to coat. Seal bag or cover dish with plastic wrap and place in refrigerator at least 6 hours or overnight, turning meat occasionally.

2 Meanwhile, prepare Jicama Salad; cover and refrigerate until ready to serve.

3 Preheat broiler if manufacturer directs. Spray nonstick 12-inch skillet with nonstick cooking spray. In hot skillet, cook mushrooms over medium-high heat 10 to 12 minutes or until golden, stirring frequently. Transfer mushrooms to large bowl.

4 Place steak on rack in broiling pan; pour marinade into same skillet. With broiling pan at closest position to source of heat, broil steak 8 to 10 minutes for medium-rare or until of desired doneness, turning steak once. Remove steak to cutting board; thinly slice. Add meat to mushrooms.

5 Add *¼ cup water* to skillet; heat to boiling over high heat. Reduce heat to medium-low; boil 2 minutes. Pour sauce into meat-mushroom mixture, tossing to coat well.

6 Slice each roll horizontally in half. Top cut sides of rolls with tomato slices, lettuce leaves, and beef mixture. Serve open-face sandwiches with Jicama Salad. *Makes 4 servings.*

JICAMA SALAD: With knife or vegetable peeler, remove peel from *1 small jicama (about 8 ounces)*. Dice jicama; place in large bowl. Stir in *1 large red pepper, chopped, 1 cup frozen whole-kernel corn, thawed, 2 tablespoons lime juice, 2 tablespoons chopped cilantro* or parsley leaves, *1 small fresh jalapeño chile*, seeded and minced, *1 teaspoon sugar, ½ teaspoon salt*, and *¼ teaspoon coarsely ground black pepper*.

Each serving: About 445 calories, 37 g protein, 59 g carbohydrate, 8 g total fat (2 g saturated), 71 mg cholesterol, 855 mg sodium.

# Teriyaki Steak Sandwiches

PREP: 20 MINUTES ～ COOK: 10 MINUTES

1 tablespoon plus 1 teaspoon vegetable oil
1 medium red pepper, cut into ¼-inch slices
1 medium onion, cut into ¼-inch slices
1 beef flank steak (1 pound), cut across the grain into thin slices
1 tablespoon cornstarch
2 tablespoons teriyaki sauce
4 sandwich-style English muffins or 4 onion rolls, split and toasted

1 In nonstick 12-inch skillet, heat vegetable oil over medium-high heat until hot. Add pepper and onion and cook until tender and golden. Transfer to bowl. Meanwhile, in another bowl, toss flank steak with cornstarch.

2 In same skillet, cook flank steak over high heat, stirring constantly, just until steak loses its pink color, about 5 minutes. Add teriyaki sauce and *¼ cup water*; heat to boiling.

3 Spoon steak mixture over bottom halves of English muffins; top with pepper mixture, then top halves of English muffins. *Makes 4 servings.*

Each serving: About 470 calories, 24 g protein, 46 g carbohydrate, 19 g total fat (6 g saturated), 59 mg cholesterol, 705 mg sodium.

# Toasted Cheese & Roast Beef Sandwiches

PREP: 15 MINUTES ～ COOK: 25 MINUTES

To give the sandwich kick, use Monterey Jack with jalapeño chiles instead of Cheddar.

1 tablespoon vegetable oil
2 large onions (about 1½ pounds), cut into ¼-inch-thick slices
¼ teaspoon salt
1 loaf (18 ounces) Italian bread, about 16 inches long
¼ cup reduced-fat sour cream
1 tablespoon prepared white horseradish, well drained
8 ounces Cheddar cheese, sliced
8 ounces roast beef, thinly sliced
⅛ teaspoon coarsely ground black pepper
Lettuce leaves
1 large tomato, thinly sliced

1 In nonstick 12-inch skillet, heat vegetable oil over medium heat until hot. Add onions and salt and cook until onions are golden brown, about 20 minutes. With slotted spoon, transfer onions to bowl.

2 Meanwhile, preheat broiler if manufacturer directs. Slice Italian bread horizontally in half. In small bowl, mix sour cream and horseradish. Spread cut sides of bread with horseradish sauce. Place bread halves, cut-side up, on cookie sheet; top with Cheddar. Broil until cheese melts.

3 In same skillet, cook beef slices and pepper over medium heat just until heated through.

4 Arrange several lettuce leaves over Cheddar on bottom half of bread. Top with sliced beef, onions, then tomatoes. Replace top half of loaf. Cut loaf crosswise into 4 sandwiches. *Makes 4 servings.*

Each serving: About 620 calories, 39 g protein, 48 g carbohydrate, 31 g total fat (15 g saturated), 111 mg cholesterol, 885 mg sodium.

# BURGERS & SPUDS

The sandwich of all sandwiches, and an American institution, the burger is seen here wearing a bunch of different disguises. Also, what would a burger be without some kind of potato? A good potato salad? Or roasted new potatoes? Or maybe home fries. Take your pick.

## Spicy Cheese-Stuffed Burgers

PREP: 15 MINUTES • GRILL: 10 MINUTES

1 pound lean ground beef (90%) or ground turkey
16 saltine crackers with unsalted tops, crushed (about ½ cup)
1 small green pepper, minced
1 small red pepper, minced
1 teaspoon grated onion
¼ teaspoon salt
¼ teaspoon coarsely ground black pepper
3 ounces Monterey Jack cheese with jalapeño chiles, shredded (¾ cup)
4 sesame-seed hamburger buns, split
4 lettuce leaves
1 small tomato, diced

**1** Prepare outdoor grill for barbecuing.
**2** Meanwhile, in medium bowl, mix ground beef, crackers, green and red peppers, onion, salt, and black pepper. Shape meat mixture into 4 balls. Make indentation in center of each ball; place 1 heaping tablespoon Monterey Jack into each indentation. Shape beef mixture around cheese, making sure to enclose cheese completely. Flatten each into a ¾-inch-thick round patty.
**3** Grill burgers over medium heat 7 to 10 minutes for medium or until of desired doneness, turning burgers occasionally with pancake turner. During last few minutes of cooking time, top burgers with remaining Monterey Jack and arrange buns, cut-side down, on grill; cook until cheese melts and buns are lightly browned and toasted.
**4** To serve, arrange lettuce leaves on bottom halves of toasted buns; top with burgers. Spoon diced tomato on top of burgers. Replace tops of buns. Makes 4 servings.
TO BROIL: Preheat broiler if manufacturer directs. Broil burgers at closest position to source of heat for about 7 to 10 minutes for medium or

until of desired doneness, turning burgers once. Top burgers with cheese, toast buns, and serve as above.

EACH BEEF BURGER: ABOUT 465 CALORIES, 33 G PROTEIN, 34 G CARBOHYDRATE, 22 G TOTAL FAT (9 G SATURATED), 93 MG CHOLESTEROL, 720 MG SODIUM.

EACH TURKEY BURGER: ABOUT 465 CALORIES, 31 G PROTEIN, 34 G CARBOHYDRATE, 22 G TOTAL FAT (7 G SATURATED), 80 MG CHOLESTEROL, 705 MG SODIUM.

## Teriyaki Burgers

PREP: 5 MINUTES • GRILL: 12 MINUTES

1 pound lean ground beef (90%)
¼ cup chopped green onions
2 tablespoons plus 1 teaspoon reduced-sodium soy sauce
1 tablespoon light brown sugar
¼ teaspoon ground red pepper (cayenne)
2 tablespoons apple jelly, melted
2 teaspoons minced, peeled fresh ginger
8 thick slices whole-grain bread, toasted

**1** Prepare outdoor grill for barbecuing.
**2** In medium bowl, mix ground beef, green onions, 2 tablespoons soy sauce, brown sugar, and ground red pepper. Shape into 4 patties, each ¾ inch thick. In small bowl, mix remaining 1 teaspoon soy sauce, apple jelly, and ginger; set aside to use as glaze.
**3** Grill burgers over medium heat for 10 to 12 minutes, turning once. Brush both sides of burgers with glaze and cook 2 minutes longer for medium or until of desired doneness. Serve with whole-grain bread. Makes 4 servings.
TO BROIL: Preheat broiler if manufacturer directs. Broil burgers at closest position to source of heat for 7 to 10 minutes for medium or until of desired doneness. Turn burgers once. Glaze as directed.

EACH SERVING: ABOUT 370 CALORIES, 29 G PROTEIN, 36 G CARBOHYDRATE, 13 G TOTAL FAT (5 G SATURATED), 70 MG CHOLESTEROL, 690 MG SODIUM.

## Herb-Roasted Baby Potatoes

PREP: 5 MINUTES • BAKE: 25 MINUTES

1½ pounds small red potatoes, cut into quarters, or eighths if large
Olive-oil nonstick cooking spray
¾ teaspoon salt
½ teaspoon dried thyme leaves
¼ teaspoon coarsely ground black pepper

**1** Preheat oven to 450°F. In 13" by 9" metal baking pan, arrange potatoes in single layer. Spray potatoes with olive-oil nonstick cooking spray to coat; toss with salt, thyme, and pepper.
**2** Roast potatoes 20 to 25 minutes, turning once with metal spatula, until golden and fork-tender. Makes 4 accompaniment servings.

EACH SERVING: ABOUT 130 CALORIES, 4 G PROTEIN, 28 G CARBOHYDRATE, 0 G TOTAL FAT (0 G SATURATED), 0 MG CHOLESTEROL, 410 MG SODIUM.

## Teriyaki Salmon Burgers

PREP: 15 MINUTES • COOK: 10 MINUTES

5 sesame-seed hamburger buns
1 salmon fillet* (1 pound), skin removed
2 tablespoons teriyaki sauce
2 medium green onions, chopped
1½ teaspoons grated, peeled fresh ginger

**1** Coarsely grate 1 hamburger bun to make bread crumbs. Measure ⅓ cup bread crumbs; set aside. Reserve remaining crumbs to coat patties.
**2** With tweezers, remove any bones from salmon. Finely chop salmon and place in medium bowl. Add teriyaki sauce, green onions, ginger, and reserved ⅓ cup bread crumbs.
**3** On waxed paper, shape salmon mixture into four 3-inch round patties. Coat patties with remaining bread crumbs.
**4** In nonstick 10-inch skillet, cook patties 10 minutes over medium heat, turning once, until golden and cooked through. Serve patties on hamburger buns. Makes 4 servings.

*If you don't want to buy fresh salmon, substitute 14¾-ounce can of salmon, drained, and add 1 large egg to mixture.

EACH SERVING: ABOUT 340 CALORIES, 28 G PROTEIN, 38 G CARBOHYDRATE, 12 G TOTAL FAT (2 G SATURATED), 61 MG CHOLESTEROL, 695 MG SODIUM.

## Chunky Home Fries

PREP: 10 MINUTES • COOK: 20 MINUTES

2 tablespoons olive oil
1½ pounds medium red potatoes, cut into 1½-inch chunks
½ teaspoon salt

1 In nonstick 12-inch skillet, heat olive oil over medium-high heat until hot. Add potatoes and salt and cook until potatoes are golden brown, turning them occasionally.
2 Reduce heat to medium; cover skillet and continue cooking until potatoes are fork-tender. Makes 4 accompaniment servings.

EACH SERVING: ABOUT 195 CALORIES, 3 G PROTEIN, 31 G CARBOHYDRATE, 7 G TOTAL FAT (1 G SATURATED), 0 MG CHOLESTEROL, 305 MG SODIUM.

## Grilled Greek Burgers

PREP: 5 MINUTES • GRILL: 12 MINUTES

1 pound lean ground beef (90%)
¼ cup chopped fresh parsley leaves
1 teaspoon dried mint leaves
½ teaspoon salt
¼ teaspoon coarsely ground black pepper
4 (6-inch diameter) pitas

1 Prepare outdoor grill for barbecuing.
2 In medium bowl, mix ground beef, parsley, mint, salt, and pepper. Shape into 4 patties, each ¾ inch thick.
3 Grill burgers over medium heat for 10 to 12 minutes for medium or until of desired doneness, turning once. Serve in pitas. Makes 4 servings.

TO BROIL: Preheat broiler if manufacturer directs. Broil burgers at closest position to source of heat for 7 to 10 minutes for medium or until of desired doneness. Turn burgers once.

EACH SERVING: ABOUT 360 CALORIES, 29 G PROTEIN, 34 G CARBOHYDRATE, 12 G TOTAL FAT (5 G SATURATED), 70 MG CHOLESTEROL, 695 MG SODIUM.

*Jumbo Chicken Burgers*

## Jumbo Chicken Burgers

PREP: 15 MINUTES • COOK: 10 MINUTES

1 pound ground chicken
2 green onions, chopped
1 small zucchini (about 5 ounces), grated
1 medium carrot, peeled and grated
1 tablespoon chili powder
½ teaspoon salt
¼ teaspoon ground cumin
⅛ teaspoon ground red pepper (cayenne)
Nonstick cooking spray
4 whole-grain sandwich rolls
Lettuce leaves

1 In medium bowl, mix ground chicken, green onions, zucchini, carrot, chili powder, salt, cumin, and ground red pepper until well mixed.
2 Shape ground-chicken mixture into four 3½-inch round patties.
3 Spray heavy 12-inch skillet with nonstick cooking spray. Heat skillet over medium-high heat until very hot. Add chicken patties and cook 5 minutes; turn

patties and cook 5 minutes more or until no longer pink inside. Serve burgers on sandwich rolls with lettuce. Makes 4 servings.

EACH SERVING: ABOUT 295 CALORIES, 25 G PROTEIN, 23 G CARBOHYDRATE, 12 G TOTAL FAT (3 G SATURATED), 94 MG CHOLESTEROL, 620 MG SODIUM.

## Stuffed Mushroom-Beef Burgers

PREP: 10 MINUTES • COOK: 10 MINUTES

1 teaspoon olive oil
8 ounces mushrooms, coarsely chopped
¼ teaspoon salt
¼ teaspoon coarsely ground black pepper
1 pound lean ground beef (90%)
2 tablespoons bottled steak sauce
1 ounce mild goat cheese (¼ cup)
4 sandwich-size English muffins, split and toasted

1 In nonstick 10-inch skillet, heat oil over medium heat until hot. Add mushrooms, salt, pepper, and 1 tablespoon water. Cook, stirring, until the mushrooms are tender and the liquid has evaporated (pour off any mushroom liquid remaining in pan). Cool slightly.
2 In medium bowl, combine mushrooms, ground beef, and steak sauce. Shape beef mixture into 4 balls. Make indentation in center of each ball; place 1 tablespoon goat cheese into each indentation. Shape beef mixture around goat cheese, making sure to enclose cheese completely. Flatten each ball into a ¾-inch-thick round patty.
3 Heat nonstick 12-inch skillet over medium-high heat until hot. Add cheese-stuffed beef patties to hot skillet and cook 5 minutes for medium-rare or until of desired doneness, turning once. Serve burgers on English muffins. Makes 4 servings.

EACH SERVING: ABOUT 435 CALORIES, 26 G PROTEIN, 42 G CARBOHYDRATE, 16 G TOTAL FAT (6 G SATURATED), 74 MG CHOLESTEROL, 660 MG SODIUM.

## Pepper & Potato Home Fries

PREP: 15 MINUTES • COOK: 20 MINUTES

3 tablespoons vegetable oil
5 medium red potatoes (about
   1½ pounds), each cut lengthwise
   into 6 wedges
1 large onion, diced
½ teaspoon salt
3 medium red peppers, cut into
   ½-inch-wide slices
2 medium yellow peppers, cut into
   ½-inch-wide slices
2 medium green peppers, cut into
   ½-inch-wide slices
½ teaspoon coarsely ground black
   pepper

**1** In 5-quart Dutch oven, heat 2 table-spoons vegetable oil over medium heat until hot. Add potatoes, onion, and ¼ teaspoon salt and cook until potatoes and onion are golden brown and tender, turning potato wedges occasionally, about 20 minutes.
**2** Meanwhile, in nonstick 12-inch skillet, heat remaining 1 tablespoon vegetable oil over medium-high heat until hot. Add red, yellow, and green peppers, black pepper, and remaining ¼ teaspoon salt and cook until peppers are golden brown and tender, stirring occasionally.
**3** Stir pepper mixture into potato mixture; spoon onto platter. Makes 8 accompaniment servings.

EACH SERVING: ABOUT 145 CALORIES,
3 G PROTEIN, 22 G CARBOHYDRATE,
5 G TOTAL FAT (1 G SATURATED),
0 MG CHOLESTEROL, 155 MG SODIUM.

## Tex-Mex Burgers

PREP: 5 MINUTES • GRILL: 12 MINUTES

1 pound lean ground beef (90%)
2 tablespoons minced onion
2 tablespoons bottled salsa
½ teaspoon salt
1 teaspoon chili powder
4 seeded rolls, split and toasted

**1** Prepare outdoor grill for barbecuing.
**2** In medium bowl, mix ground beef, onion, salsa, salt, and chili powder. Shape into 4 patties, each ¾ inch thick.
**3** Grill burgers over medium heat for

10 to 12 minutes for medium or until of desired doneness, turning once. Serve on seeded rolls. Makes 4 servings.
TO BROIL: Preheat broiler if manu-facturer directs. Broil burgers at closest position to source of heat for 7 to 10 minutes for medium or until of desired doneness. Turn burgers once.

EACH SERVING: ABOUT 330 CALORIES,
27 G PROTEIN, 23 G CARBOHYDRATE,
14 G TOTAL FAT (5 G SATURATED),
70 MG CHOLESTEROL, 700 MG SODIUM.

*Tex-Mex Burger*

## Chicken Burgers with Black-Bean Salsa

PREP: 30 MINUTES • COOK: 10 MINUTES

2 tablespoons plus 2 teaspoons
   vegetable oil
1 medium carrot, peeled and finely
   chopped
1 medium celery stalk, finely chopped
½ small red onion, minced
2 tablespoons fresh lime juice
¼ teaspoon coarsely ground black
   pepper
¼ teaspoon salt
1 large tomato, seeded and diced
1 medium avocado, peeled and diced
1 can (15 to 16 ounces) black beans,
   rinsed and drained
1 can (8¾ ounces) whole-kernel corn,
   drained
1 pound ground chicken
1 slice white bread, torn into coarse
   crumbs
1 can (4 to 4½ ounces) chopped mild
   green chiles, drained

4 (8-inch diameter) flour tortillas
1 small head Boston or romaine
   lettuce

**1** In nonstick 12-inch skillet, heat 2 teaspoons vegetable oil over medium heat until hot. Add carrot, celery, and all but 1 tablespoon onion and cook until very tender, about 10 minutes.
**2** Meanwhile, in small bowl, mix lime juice, pepper, 1 tablespoon vegetable oil, and ⅛ teaspoon salt. Stir in tomato, avocado, black beans, corn, and reserved 1 tablespoon minced onion. Set aside.
**3** In medium bowl, mix sautéed vegetable mixture with ground chicken, bread crumbs, chopped green chiles, and remaining ⅛ teaspoon salt. Shape chicken mixture into 4 patties, each ¾ inch thick.
**4** In same skillet, heat remaining 1 tablespoon vegetable oil over medium heat; cook chicken patties about 10 minutes or until thoroughly cooked throughout and lightly browned on both sides, turning patties occasionally.
**5** Meanwhile, preheat broiler if manu-facturer directs. Place flour tortillas on cookie sheet. Place cookie sheet on rack in broiler at closest position to source of heat; broil tortillas until lightly toasted, turning them once.
**6** To serve, place 1 flour tortilla on each of 4 dinner plates. Top each tortilla with a few Boston lettuce leaves and a chicken patty. Spoon black-bean salsa over chicken patties. Makes 4 servings.

EACH SERVING: ABOUT 600 CALORIES,
31 G PROTEIN, 54 G CARBOHYDRATE,
31 G TOTAL FAT (6 G SATURATED),
94 MG CHOLESTEROL, 920 MG SODIUM.

## Roquefort Burgers

PREP: 5 MINUTES • GRILL: 12 MINUTES

1 pound lean ground beef (90%)
1 tablespoon Worcestershire sauce
½ teaspoon coarsely ground black
   pepper
2 ounces Roquefort or blue cheese,
   crumbled (½ cup)
4 sandwich-size English muffins, split
   and toasted

**1** Prepare outdoor grill for barbecuing.
**2** In medium bowl, mix ground beef,

Worcestershire sauce, and pepper. Shape mixture into 4 balls. Make indentation in center of each ball; place one-fourth of Roquefort into each indentation. Shape mixture around cheese to completely enclose; flatten each into ¾-inch-thick patty.

**3** Grill burgers over medium heat for 10 to 12 minutes for medium or until of desired doneness, turning once. Serve on English muffins. Makes 4 servings. TO BROIL: Preheat broiler if manufacturer directs. Broil at closest position to source of heat for 7 to 10 minutes for medium or until of desired doneness. Turn burgers once.

EACH SERVING: ABOUT 440 CALORIES, 26 G PROTEIN, 39 G CARBOHYDRATE, 18 G TOTAL FAT (7 G SATURATED), 83 MG CHOLESTEROL, 660 MG SODIUM.

## Apple-Turkey Burgers

PREP: 10 MINUTES • BROIL: 10 MINUTES

1 pound ground turkey
2 tablespoons prepared white
    horseradish, well drained
1 medium Granny Smith apple, peeled
    and shredded
½ small onion, grated
½ teaspoon salt
1 tablespoon chopped fresh parsley
    leaves
Nonstick cooking spray
4 (6-inch diameter) pitas, split

**1** Preheat broiler if manufacturer directs. In medium bowl, mix ground turkey, horseradish, apple, onion, salt, and parsley.

**3** Shape turkey mixture into four 1-inch-thick patties. Spray rack in broiling pan with nonstick cooking spray; place patties on rack.

**4** With broiling pan at closest position to source of heat, broil patties 4 minutes. Turn patties; broil 5 to 6 minutes longer until cooked through.

**5** Serve turkey patties on pitas. Makes 4 servings.

EACH SERVING: ABOUT 385 CALORIES, 26 G PROTEIN, 40 G CARBOHYDRATE, 13 G TOTAL FAT (3 G SATURATED), 57 MG CHOLESTEROL, 690 MG SODIUM.

## Steakhouse Burgers with Horseradish Sour Cream

PREP: 10 MINUTES • COOK: 6 MINUTES

1¼ pounds ground beef chuck
½ teaspoon plus ⅛ teaspoon salt
1 teaspoon plus ⅛ teaspoon coarsely
    ground black pepper
⅓ cup sour cream
2½ teaspoons prepared white
    horseradish, well drained
4 English muffins, split and toasted
4 Boston lettuce leaves

**1** Shape ground beef into 4 patties, each ½ inch thick. Sprinkle patties with ½ teaspoon salt, then with 1 teaspoon pepper, pressing pepper lightly into patties.

**2** Heat nonstick 12-inch skillet over medium-high heat until hot. Add patties and cook about 6 minutes for medium or until of desired doneness, shaking skillet occasionally and turning patties once.

**3** Meanwhile, in small bowl, combine sour cream, horseradish, remaining ⅛ teaspoon salt, and remaining ⅛ teaspoon pepper.

**4** Serve patties on English muffins with lettuce and horseradish sauce. Makes 4 servings.

EACH SERVING: ABOUT 505 CALORIES, 32 G PROTEIN, 31 G CARBOHYDRATE, 27 G TOTAL FAT (11 G SATURATED), 104 MG CHOLESTEROL, 880 MG SODIUM.

## Lemon-Chive Potato Salad

PREP: 25 MINUTES PLUS COOLING
COOK: 10 TO 12 MINUTES

5 pounds medium red potatoes, cut
    into 1½-inch chunks
Salt
2 medium lemons
3 tablespoons olive oil
1 teaspoon sugar
¾ cup light mayonnaise
½ cup milk
⅓ cup sour cream
5 large celery stalks, thinly sliced
½ cup chopped chives or green-onion
    tops
Chopped chives for garnish

**1** In 8-quart saucepot, heat potatoes, 2 teaspoons salt, and *enough water to cover* to boiling. Reduce heat to low; cover and simmer 10 to 12 minutes or until potatoes are fork-tender.

**2** Meanwhile, from lemons, grate 1½ teaspoons peel and squeeze ¼ cup juice. In large bowl, mix lemon peel, lemon juice, olive oil, sugar, and 1 teaspoon salt.

**3** Drain potatoes. Add hot potatoes to lemon dressing. With rubber spatula, stir gently to coat. Let potatoes cool at room temperature 30 minutes, stirring occasionally.

**4** In small bowl, stir mayonnaise, milk, sour cream, and ¼ teaspoon salt until smooth. Add mayonnaise mixture, celery, and chives to potatoes; stir gently to coat well. If not serving right away, cover and refrigerate. Garnish with chopped chives. Makes 16 accompaniment servings.

EACH SERVING: ABOUT 165 CALORIES, 4 G PROTEIN, 28 G CARBOHYDRATE, 5 G TOTAL FAT (1 G SATURATED), 3 MG CHOLESTEROL, 327 MG SODIUM.

## Roast Potato Duo

PREP: 5 MINUTES • BAKE: 20 MINUTES

Nonstick cooking spray
2 large baking potatoes (1 pound)
2 small sweet potatoes (12 ounces)
1 tablespoon olive oil
½ teaspoon salt
¼ teaspoon dried rosemary leaves,
    crushed

**1** Preheat oven to 450°F. Spray 15½" by 10½" jelly-roll pan with nonstick cooking spray.

**2** Cut each unpeeled baking potato and sweet potato lengthwise into 6 wedges. Arrange on jelly-roll pan; sprinkle with olive oil, salt, and rosemary. Bake 20 minutes, stirring occasionally, until potatoes are golden brown and tender Makes 4 servings.

EACH SERVING: ABOUT 205 CALORIES, 4 G PROTEIN, 40 G CARBOHYDRATE, 4 G TOTAL FAT (1 G SATURATED), 0 MG CHOLESTEROL, 310 MG SODIUM.

# Simple Desserts

## Autumn Fruit Compote

PREP: 20 MINUTES PLUS CHILLING ∽ COOK: 20 MINUTES

Great with fresh pears in place of apples.

4 medium Golden Delicious or Jonagold apples
1 medium orange
1 medium lemon
1 package (8 ounces) mixed dried fruit (with pitted prunes)
4 ounces dried Calimyrna figs
½ cup sugar
1 cinnamon stick (3 inches long)

1 Peel, core, and cut each apple into 16 wedges. With vegetable peeler, remove peel from orange and lemon in 1-inch-wide strips. Squeeze juice from lemon to equal 2 tablespoons (refrigerate peeled orange for use another day).

2 In 4-quart saucepan, heat apples, orange and lemon peels, lemon juice, mixed dried fruit, figs, sugar, cinnamon stick, and *3 cups water* to boiling over high heat. Reduce heat to low; cover and simmer 15 to 20 minutes or until apples are tender.

3 Pour fruit mixture into bowl and refrigerate at least 4 hours to blend flavors. Serve chilled or at room temperature. Store compote in refrigerator to use up within 4 days. *Makes 8 servings.*

Each serving: About 195 calories, 1 g protein, 50 g carbohydrate, 0 g total fat (0 g saturated), 0 mg cholesterol, 5 mg sodium.


## Easy Minted Peaches & Pears with Ginger

PREP: 5 MINUTES

1 can (16 ounces) pear halves in their own juice
1 can (16 ounces) sliced cling peaches in their own juice
1 tablespoon chopped crystallized ginger
1 tablespoon chopped fresh mint
Mint sprigs for garnish

1 Drain pears, reserving ½ cup juice. Drain peaches.

2 In medium bowl, mix pears with their reserved juice, peaches, crystallized ginger, and chopped mint. Garnish with mint sprigs. *Makes 4 servings.*

Each serving: About 120 calories, 1 g protein, 31 g carbohydrate, 0 g total fat (0 g saturated), 0 mg cholesterol, 15 mg sodium.


## Mixed Fruit with Fresh Strawberry Sauce

PREP: 30 MINUTES

Perfect for a picnic or a potluck dinner. In a pinch, you can make the sauce with frozen (not syrup-packed) strawberries.

2 pints strawberries
¼ cup sugar
3 tablespoons anise-flavor liqueur (optional)
3 medium peaches or nectarines
1 small cantaloupe (2½ pounds), peeled and cut into 1-inch chunks
1 pound seedless green grapes, halved if large
3 small plums, cut into thin wedges
1 small pineapple, peeled, cored, and cut into 1-inch chunks
1½ pints blueberries

1 In medium bowl, with potato masher, mash strawberries and sugar; stir in anise liqueur if using. Place sauce in serving bowl; cover and refrigerate.

2 Peel peaches (do not peel nectarines); cut into thin wedges.

3 Assemble fruit: In 3-quart straight-sided glass dish, begin with cantaloupe chunks, then grapes, plums, pineapple, and all but ½ cup blueberries. Arrange peaches in decorative pattern over blueberries; pile remaining blueberries in center. Cover and refrigerate if not serving right away. Serve fruit with strawberry sauce to spoon over. *Makes 12 servings.*

Each serving: About 145 calories, 2 g protein, 36 g carbohydrate, 1 g total fat (0 g saturated), 0 mg cholesterol, 5 mg sodium.

*Autumn Fruit Compote* ➤

# Minted Melon Cups

PREP: 20 MINUTES

Mint and melon are natural partners.

¼ cup mint jelly
½ small cantaloupe, peeled and cut into bite-size chunks
½ small honeydew melon, peeled and cut into bite-size chunks
Mint leaves for garnish

1 In small saucepan, melt mint jelly over low heat. Set aside to cool.

2 In medium bowl, toss cantaloupe and honeydew chunks with mint jelly; let stand 10 minutes for flavors to blend. Spoon cantaloupe and honeydew and any liquid into 4 dessert glasses. Garnish with mint leaves. *Makes 4 servings.*

Each serving: About 110 calories, 1 g protein, 29 g carbohydrate, 0 g total fat (0 g saturated), 0 mg cholesterol, 25 mg sodium.

# Strawberries in White Wine

PREP: 15 MINUTES

Sparkling wine makes a festive substitute.

⅓ cup fruity white wine, such as Riesling
2 tablespoons sugar
1 pint strawberries, halved

1 In small bowl, mix white wine and sugar until sugar dissolves.

2 Place strawberries in 4 goblets. Pour white-wine mixture over strawberries. *Makes 4 servings.*

Each serving: About 60 calories, 1 g protein, 12 g carbohydrate, 0 g total fat (0 g saturated), 0 mg cholesterol, 0 mg sodium.

# Grilled Pineapple Wedges

PREP: 20 MINUTES ⌇ BROIL: 10 TO 15 MINUTES

1 medium pineapple
3 tablespoons light or dark brown sugar
2 tablespoons margarine or butter

1 Preheat broiler if manufacturer directs. Cut pineapple lengthwise through crown to stem end into 4 wedges, leaving on leafy crown. Loosen fruit from each pineapple wedge by cutting close to rind. Leaving fruit in shell, cut flesh crosswise into ½-inch-thick slices for easier serving.

2 Line broiling pan with foil (do not use rack). Place pineapple wedges, cut-side up, in broiling pan; set aside.

3 In small saucepan, heat brown sugar and margarine or butter over low heat until melted and smooth.

4 With pastry brush, brush pineapple wedges with brown sugar mixture. Place pan in broiler at closest position to source of heat. Broil pineapple 10 to 15 minutes or until golden brown. *Makes 4 servings.*

Each serving: About 220 calories, 1 g protein, 43 g carbohydrate, 7 g total fat (1 g saturated), 0 mg cholesterol, 75 mg sodium.

# Peachy Melon Soup

PREP: 10 MINUTES

1 small cantaloupe (about 2½ pounds), peeled and cut into bite-size chunks
1 cup peach nectar or apricot nectar
2 tablespoons fresh lime juice
Lime slices for garnish

In blender, at medium speed, blend cantaloupe, peach nectar, and lime juice until smooth, stopping blender occasionally and scraping down sides of container with rubber spatula. Increase speed to high; blend 1 minute. If not serving right away, pour soup into bowl; refrigerate. Garnish with lime slices. *Makes 4 servings.*

Each serving: About 90 calories, 1 g protein, 21 g carbohydrate, 0 g total fat, 0 mg cholesterol, 20 mg sodium.

# Tropical Magic

PREP: 10 MINUTES

Easily doubled or tripled, but make this frozen dessert drink in two-serving batches.

1 small mango, peeled and cut into bite-size chunks
1 can (8 ounces) pineapple chunks in pineapple juice
¼ teaspoon coconut extract
1 cup chilled seltzer or club soda
3 ice cubes

1 In blender, at high speed, blend mango, pineapple with its juice, and remaining ingredients 1 minute. Pour into 2 chilled glasses. *Makes 2 servings.*

Each serving: About 125 calories, 1 g protein, 33 g carbohydrate, 0 g total fat, 0 mg cholesterol, 30 mg sodium.

## MICROWAVE LEMON CURD

Spoon this sweet, tangy treat on fruit, spread on toast—or put in a pie. (Just fill a baked shell with the curd and top with berries.)

From *2 lemons,* grate 1 tablespoon peel and squeeze ⅓ cup juice. In medium bowl, melt *½ cup margarine or butter* (1 stick) on High 45 seconds to 1 minute. Stir in *⅓ cup sugar,* lemon peel, and juice, then *4 large eggs.* Cook on Medium-Low (30% power) 5 to 8 minutes until mixture is very thick, stirring twice during cooking. Refrigerate. Makes 2 cups. [Each tablespoon: About 45 calories, 1 g protein, 2 g carbohydrate, 4 g total fat (1 g saturated), 27 mg cholesterol, 40 mg sodium.]

# Peach Granita

PREP: 20 MINUTES PLUS 5 HOURS TO FREEZE

Be sure the peaches or nectarines are as ripe as possible.

1 cup sugar
5 medium peaches or nectarines (about 1¾ pounds), unpeeled and cut into wedges
2 tablespoons fresh lemon juice

1 In 1-quart saucepan, heat sugar and *1¼ cups water* to boiling over high heat, stirring occasionally. Reduce heat to medium; cook mixture about 1 minute or until sugar dissolves completely. Transfer to small bowl to cool.

2 In blender, at medium speed, blend unpeeled peach wedges until smooth. Pour fruit puree into medium-mesh sieve set over medium bowl. With spoon, press peach puree against sieve to push through pulp and juice. You should have 3 cups puree; discard skin.

3 Stir lemon juice and sugar syrup into puree. Pour peach mixture into 9" by 9" metal baking pan.

4 Cover with foil or plastic wrap. Freeze until partially frozen, about 2 hours; stir with fork. Freeze until completely frozen, at least 3 hours longer or overnight.

5 To serve, let granita stand at room temperature 15 minutes to soften slightly. Then, with spoon or fork, scrape across surface of granita to create pebbly texture. *Makes about 8 cups or 16 servings.*

Each serving: About 65 calories, 0 g protein, 17 g carbohydrate, 0 g total fat, 0 mg cholesterol, 0 mg sodium.

# Strawberry Cloud

PREP: 10 MINUTES

Simple but irresistible.

1 package (10 ounces) frozen quick-thaw
    strawberries in light syrup
½ cup heavy or whipping cream

1 Thaw strawberries as label directs.

2 In small bowl, with mixer at medium speed, whip heavy cream; fold in strawberries with their syrup. Spoon into 4 dessert bowls. *Makes 4 servings.*

Each serving: About 170 calories, 1 g protein, 19 g carbohydrate, 11 g total fat (7 g saturated), 41 mg cholesterol, 15 mg sodium.

# Raspberry Granita

PREP: 20 MINUTES PLUS 5 HOURS TO FREEZE

1 cup sugar
6 half-pints raspberries
2 tablespoons fresh lime juice

1 In 1-quart saucepan, heat sugar and *1¼ cups water* to boiling over high heat, stirring occasionally. Reduce heat to medium; cook mixture about 1 minute or until sugar dissolves completely. Transfer to small bowl to cool.

2 In blender, at medium speed, blend raspberries until smooth. Pour fruit puree into fine-mesh sieve set over medium bowl. With spoon, press raspberry puree against sieve to push through pulp and juice. You should have 3 cups puree; discard seeds.

3 Stir lime juice and sugar syrup into puree. Pour raspberry mixture into 9" by 9" metal baking pan.

4 Cover with foil or plastic wrap. Freeze until partially frozen, about 2 hours; stir with fork. Then freeze until completely frozen, at least 3 hours longer or overnight.

5 To serve, let granita stand at room temperature 15 minutes to soften slightly. Then, with spoon or fork, scrape across surface of granita to create pebbly texture. *Makes about 8 cups or 16 servings.*

Each serving: About 70 calories, 0 g protein, 18 g carbohydrate, 0 g total fat, 0 mg cholesterol, 0 mg sodium.

# Blueberry Granita

PREP: 20 MINUTES PLUS 5 HOURS TO FREEZE

1 cup sugar
3 pints blueberries
2 tablespoons fresh lemon juice

1 In 1-quart saucepan, heat sugar and *1¼ cups water* to boiling over high heat, stirring occasionally. Reduce heat to medium; cook mixture about 1 minute or until sugar dissolves completely. Transfer to small bowl to cool.

2 In blender, at medium speed, blend blueberries until smooth. Pour fruit puree into medium-mesh sieve set over medium bowl. With spoon, press blueberry puree against sieve to push through pulp and juice. You should have 3 cups puree; discard skin.

3 Stir lemon juice and sugar syrup into puree. Pour blueberry mixture into 9" by 9" metal baking pan.

4 Cover with foil or plastic wrap. Freeze until partially frozen, about 2 hours; stir with fork. Then freeze until completely frozen, at least 3 hours longer or overnight.

5 To serve, let granita stand at room temperature 15 minutes to soften slightly. Then, with spoon or fork, scrape across surface of granita to create pebbly texture. *Makes about 8 cups or 16 servings.*

Each serving: About 80 calories, 0 g protein, 20 g carbohydrate, 0 g total fat, 0 mg cholesterol, 5 mg sodium.

*From top to bottom: Watermelon Granita* ➤
*(page 226), Raspberry Granita, Blueberry*
*Granita, Peach Granita (page 223)*

# Applesauce-Yogurt Parfaits

PREP: 10 MINUTES ～ COOK: 15 TO 20 MINUTES

6 small McIntosh or Winesap apples (about 1½
   pounds), peeled, cored, and cut into 1-inch
   chunks
½ cup apple juice
½ cup fresh or frozen cranberries
¼ cup sugar
¼ teaspoon ground cinnamon (optional)
2 containers (8 ounces each) vanilla low-fat yogurt

1  In 3-quart saucepan, heat apples, apple juice, cranberries, sugar, and cinnamon to boiling over high heat. Reduce heat to low; simmer, uncovered, 15 to 20 minutes, stirring occasionally, until apples are very tender. Cover and refrigerate until chilled.

2  Spoon 1 container of yogurt into five 8-ounce goblets. Then spoon about ⅓ cup applesauce into each goblet over yogurt. Repeat with remaining yogurt and applesauce. *Makes 5 servings.*

Each serving: About 210 calories, 4 g protein, 46 g carbohydrate, 2 g total fat (1 g saturated), 5 mg cholesterol, 55 mg sodium.

# Fried Apples à la Mode

PREP: 10 MINUTES ～ COOK: 10 MINUTES

Substitute pears in this delightful autumn dessert.

2 tablespoons margarine or butter
3 large Golden Delicious apples, cored and cut
   into wedges
⅓ cup maple syrup
1 pint vanilla low-fat frozen yogurt
¼ cup chopped walnuts

1  In 10-inch skillet, melt margarine or butter over medium heat. Add apples and cook until browned. Reduce heat to medium-low; cover, cook until tender.

2  Stir in maple syrup; spoon into 4 bowls; top with frozen yogurt and walnuts. *Makes 4 servings.*

Each serving: About 335 calories, 4 g protein, 56 g carbohydrate, 12 g total fat (2 g saturated), 5 mg cholesterol, 130 mg sodium.

# Watermelon Granita

PREP: 20 MINUTES PLUS 5 HOURS TO FREEZE

1 cup sugar
1 piece (5½ pounds) watermelon, seeded and cut
   into chunks (about 9 cups)
2 tablespoons fresh lime juice

1  In 1-quart saucepan, heat sugar and ¾ *cup water* to boiling over high heat, stirring occasionally. Reduce heat to medium; cook mixture about 1 minute or until sugar dissolves completely. Transfer to small bowl to cool.

2  In blender, at medium speed, blend watermelon until smooth. Pour fruit puree into medium-mesh sieve set over medium bowl. With spoon, press puree against sieve to push through pulp and juice. You should have 3 cups puree; discard any seeds.

3  Stir lime juice and sugar syrup into puree. Pour watermelon mixture into 9" by 9" metal baking pan.

4  Cover with foil or plastic wrap. Freeze until partially frozen, about 2 hours; stir with fork. Freeze until completely frozen, at least 3 hours longer or overnight.

5  To serve, let granita stand at room temperature 15 minutes to soften slightly. Then, with spoon or fork, scrape across surface of granita to create pebbly texture. *Makes about 8 cups or 16 servings.*

Each serving: About 70 calories, 1 g protein, 17 g carbohydrate, 0 g total fat, 0 mg cholesterol, 2 mg sodium.

# Easy Banana-Coconut Parfaits

PREP: 10 MINUTES

If you have more time, make this with noninstant vanilla pudding mix.

⅓ cup shredded coconut
2 medium bananas
1 package vanilla-flavor instant pudding and pie-filling for 4 servings
2 cups low-fat (1%) milk
¼ cup pistachios, chopped

**1** In small saucepan, toast coconut over medium heat; cool.

**2** Slice bananas. Prepare pudding as label directs but use low-fat milk.

**3** Into 4 parfait glasses, spoon half of pudding; top with bananas and half of coconut, then remaining pudding. Top with pistachios and remaining coconut. *Makes 4 servings.*

Each serving: About 260 calories, 7 g protein, 45 g carbohydrate, 8 g total fat (3 g saturated), 5 mg cholesterol, 245 mg sodium.

# Fruit & Orange Cream

PREP: 15 MINUTES

2 small oranges
1 pint strawberries, halved
½ cup vanilla frozen yogurt, softened
¼ teaspoon orange extract

**1** From oranges, grate enough peel for 1 tablespoon. Peel and section oranges. Arrange orange sections and strawberries in 4 dessert glasses.

**2** In small bowl, mix frozen yogurt with orange peel and orange extract. Spoon orange cream on fruit. *Makes 4 servings.*

Each serving: About 75 calories, 2 g protein, 17 g carbohydrate, 1 g total fat (0 g saturated), 1 mg cholesterol, 15 mg sodium.

## THE ULTIMATE BAKED APPLE

Our microwave version is ready in minutes (instead of the hour the oven takes), looks brighter, plumper, and less shriveled—and tastes sweeter and juicier than when baked. It makes a nutritious fall breakfast or dessert.

Core large cooking apples, like Romes (about 10 ounces each), but don't cut all the way through to the bottom. Peel one-third of the way down. In center of each apple, place 1 teaspoon margarine or butter and 1 tablespoon brown sugar. In small individual bowls or 8" by 8" baking dish, cook, covered, on Medium-High (70% power) until tender; turn apples halfway through cooking. Let stand, covered, 5 minutes.

### Cooking Times
• 1 apple: 3½ to 4½ minutes
• 2 apples: 7 to 8 minutes
• 4 apples: 13 to 14 minutes

Each apple: About 250 calories, 1 g protein, 55 g carbohydrate, 5 g total fat (1 g saturated), 0 mg cholesterol, 50 mg sodium.

# Shortcakes with Fruit Compote

PREP: 30 MINUTES ～ BAKE: 15 MINUTES

3 cups all-purpose flour
1 tablespoon baking powder
1 teaspoon salt
5 tablespoons plus 2 teaspoons sugar
¾ cup margarine or butter (1½ sticks)
1⅓ cups plus 1 tablespoon milk
1 package (12 ounces) pitted prunes
1¼ cups apple cider
1 cup dried apricots
½ teaspoon ground cinnamon
1 can (16 ounces) pear halves in juice
1 can (16 ounces) peach halves in juice, drained
    and cut into 1-inch pieces
1 can (15¼ to 20 ounces) pineapple slices in juice,
    drained and cut into 1-inch pieces

1 Preheat oven to 400°F. In medium bowl, mix flour, baking powder, salt, and ¼ cup sugar.

2 With pastry blender or two knives used scissor-fashion, cut in margarine or butter until mixture resembles coarse crumbs. With fork, stir in 1⅓ cups milk; quickly mix just until mixture forms soft dough that leaves side of bowl.

3 Turn dough onto lightly floured surface; with lightly floured hands, gently knead 4 to 5 times to mix thoroughly. With floured rolling pin, roll dough 1 inch thick.

4 With floured 3-inch round biscuit cutter, cut out as many biscuits as possible. With pancake turner, place biscuits on ungreased large cookie sheet. Press trimmings together; roll and cut as above to make 8 biscuits in all.

5 Brush tops of biscuits with remaining 1 tablespoon milk; sprinkle with 1 tablespoon sugar. Bake biscuits 15 minutes or until golden.

6 Meanwhile, in 3-quart saucepan, heat prunes, apple cider, apricots, cinnamon, and remaining 2 teaspoons sugar to boiling over medium heat. Reduce heat to low; cover and simmer 15 minutes, gently stirring occasionally with rubber spatula.

7 While dried fruits are simmering, drain pear halves, reserving ¼ cup juice; cut pear halves into 1-inch pieces.

8 Stir pears, peaches, pineapple, and reserved pear juice into fruit mixture in saucepan; heat through.

9 With serrated knife, cut each biscuit horizontally in half but do not separate halves. Place a split biscuit, cut-side up, on each of 8 dessert plates and top each with some warm compote. *Makes 8 servings.*

Each serving: About 645 calories, 9 g protein, 115 g carbohydrate, 19 g total fat (4 g saturated), 6 mg cholesterol, 705 mg sodium.

# Puffy Apple Pancake

PREP: 25 MINUTES ～ BAKE: 15 MINUTES

2 tablespoons margarine or butter
½ cup plus 2 tablespoons sugar
6 medium Granny Smith or Newtown Pippin
    apples (about 2 pounds), peeled, cored, and each
    cut into 8 wedges
3 large eggs
¾ cup milk
¾ cup all-purpose flour
¼ teaspoon salt

1 Preheat oven to 425°F. In 12-inch skillet, with oven-safe handle, heat margarine or butter, ½ cup sugar, and ¼ *cup water* to boiling over medium-high heat. Add apple wedges; cook about 15 minutes, stirring occasionally, until apples are golden and sugar mixture begins to caramelize.

2 Meanwhile, in blender, at medium speed, or in food processor, with knife blade attached, blend eggs, milk, flour, salt, and remaining 2 tablespoons sugar until batter is smooth.

3 When apple mixture is golden and lightly caramelized, pour batter over apples. Place skillet in oven; bake pancake 15 minutes or until puffed and golden. Serve immediately. *Makes 8 servings.*

Each serving: About 225 calories, 5 g protein, 40 g carbohydrate, 6 g total fat (1 g saturated), 83 mg cholesterol, 140 mg sodium.

*◄ Puffy Apple Pancake*

# Blueberry-Peach Shortcakes

PREP: 30 MINUTES ～ BAKE: 16 TO 22 MINUTES

A fresh take on everyone's favorite mid-summer dessert.

2 tablespoons fresh lemon juice
1 tablespoon cornstarch
1½ pints blueberries (about 3½ cups)
1 cup plus 3 tablespoons sugar
2 pounds peaches (about 6 medium), peeled and
    each cut into 8 wedges
3 cups all-purpose flour
4½ teaspoons baking powder
¾ teaspoon salt
9 tablespoons cold margarine or butter plus
    1 tablespoon margarine or butter, melted

1 cup plus 2 tablespoons milk
1 cup heavy or whipping cream

1 Preheat oven to 425°F. In cup, mix lemon juice and cornstarch until smooth.

2 In 3-quart saucepan, heat blueberries, ⅔ cup sugar, and lemon juice mixture to boiling over medium-high heat. Reduce heat to medium; cook 1 minute. Stir in peaches; set aside.

3 Prepare biscuits: In large bowl, mix flour, baking powder, salt, and ⅓ cup sugar. With pastry blender or two knives used scissor-fashion, cut in 9 tablespoons cold margarine or butter until mixture resembles coarse crumbs. Stir in milk; quickly mix just until mixture forms a soft dough that leaves side of bowl.

4 Turn dough onto lightly floured surface; knead 6 to 8 strokes to mix thoroughly. With lightly floured hands, pat dough 1 inch thick.

5 With floured 3-inch round biscuit cutter, cut out shortcakes. With pancake turner, place shortcakes, 1 inch apart, on ungreased large cookie sheet.

*Blueberry-Peach Shortcakes*

**6** Press trimmings together; cut as above to make 8 shortcakes in all. With pastry brush, brush shortcakes with 1 tablespoon melted margarine or butter and sprinkle with 1 tablespoon sugar. Bake 15 to 20 minutes or until golden.

**7** Beat cream with remaining 2 tablespoons sugar until soft peaks form. With fork, split warm shortcakes horizontally in half. Spoon some blueberry-peach mixture onto each split shortcake; top with sweetened whipped cream, then some more blueberry-peach mixture. *Makes 8 servings.*

Each serving: About 615 calories, 8 g protein, 88 g carbohydrate, 27 g total fat (10 g saturated), 45 mg cholesterol, 630 mg sodium.

# Cherry-Almond Clafouti

PREP: 20 MINUTES ～ COOK: 40 TO 45 MINUTES

This French classic—sweet cherries with a custardlike topping—should be served hot.

1 pound dark sweet cherries, pitted
⅔ cup all-purpose flour
⅓ cup sugar
2 tablespoons amaretto (almond-flavor liqueur)
4 large eggs
2 cups half-and-half or light cream
Confectioners' sugar for garnish

**1** Preheat oven to 350°F. Grease a 10" by 1½" round ceramic baking dish.

**2** Place pitted cherries in baking dish. In blender, at low speed, blend flour, sugar, amaretto, eggs, and 1 cup half-and-half 30 seconds. With motor running, gradually add remaining 1 cup half-and-half; blend 30 seconds longer.

**3** Pour egg mixture over cherries. Bake 40 to 45 minutes or until custard is set and knife inserted 1 inch from edge comes out clean (center will still jiggle). Serve hot, sprinkled with confectioners' sugar. *Makes 12 servings.*

Each serving: About 150 calories, 4 g protein, 19 g carbohydrate, 6 g total fat (3 g saturated), 84 mg cholesterol, 40 mg sodium.

# Nectarine & Cherry Crisp with Oatmeal Topping

PREP: 30 MINUTES PLUS 15 MINUTES TO COOL
BAKE: 65 TO 75 MINUTES

The topping is actually oatmeal cookie dough! You can prepare it up to a day ahead and store it in the refrigerator.

½ cup sugar
3 tablespoons cornstarch
3 pounds nectarines (about 10 medium), each cut into 6 wedges
1½ pounds dark sweet cherries, pitted
2 tablespoons fresh lemon juice
2 tablespoons cold margarine or butter, cut into small pieces
Oatmeal Cookie-Crisp Topping (below)

**1** Preheat oven to 375°F. In small bowl, mix sugar and cornstarch.

**2** In large bowl, toss nectarines, cherries, lemon juice, and sugar mixture until fruit is evenly coated.

**3** Spoon fruit mixture into 13" by 9" glass baking dish; dot with margarine or butter. Cover with foil and bake 40 to 50 minutes or until mixture is gently bubbling.

**4** Meanwhile, prepare Oatmeal Cookie-Crisp Topping. Cover and refrigerate until ready to use.

**5** Drop topping by scant ¼ cups over hot fruit. Bake, uncovered, 20 to 25 minutes or until topping is browned. Cool slightly on wire rack to serve warm. Or, cool completely to serve later. Reheat if desired. *Makes 12 servings.*

**OATMEAL COOKIE-CRISP TOPPING:** In large bowl, with mixer at medium-high speed, beat *⅔ cup packed light brown sugar* and *6 tablespoons margarine or butter* (¾ stick), softened, until smooth. Add *1 large egg* and *2 teaspoons vanilla extract*; beat until light and fluffy. With spoon, stir in *1½ cups old-fashioned oats, uncooked, ¾ cup all-purpose flour, ¼ teaspoon salt,* and *¼ teaspoon baking soda.*

Each serving: About 360 calories, 6 g protein, 63 g carbohydrate, 11 g total fat (2 g saturated), 18 mg cholesterol, 185 mg sodium.

# Nectarine-Cream Parfaits

PREP: 20 MINUTES

2 medium nectarines, peeled and cut into small
  pieces
2 tablespoons raspberry- or orange-flavor liqueur
1 pint vanilla low-fat frozen yogurt
¼ cup seedless red raspberry preserves
Raspberries and mint sprigs for garnish

**1** In blender, at medium speed, blend nectarines until smooth. Add raspberry liqueur and 1 cup frozen yogurt; blend until smooth.

**2** Into 4 parfait glasses, pour nectarine-yogurt mixture. Top with raspberry preserves. Spoon remaining frozen yogurt over preserves.

**3** To serve right away, garnish each parfait with raspberries and mint sprigs. To serve later, cover and freeze parfaits without garnish. When ready to serve, let par-

faits stand 30 minutes to soften slightly; garnish with raspberries and mint sprigs just before serving. ***Makes 4 servings.***

Each serving without garnish: About 190 calories, 4 g protein, 40 g carbohydrate, 2 g total fat (1 g saturated), 5 mg cholesterol, 70 mg sodium.

*Rhubarb-Strawberry Cobbler*

# Rhubarb-Strawberry Cobbler

PREP: 20 MINUTES PLUS 15 MINUTES COOLING
BAKE: 20 MINUTES

We like the filling sweet-tart. If you prefer it a little sweeter, just increase the sugar in the filling to ¾ cup. Delicious served warm with vanilla ice cream!

1¼ pounds rhubarb, cut into 1-inch chunks
  (4 cups)
¾ cup plus 1 teaspoon sugar
1 tablespoon cornstarch
1 pint strawberries, quartered
1½ cups all-purpose flour
1½ teaspoons baking powder
½ teaspoon baking soda
¼ teaspoon salt
¼ teaspoon ground cinnamon
⅛ teaspoon ground nutmeg
4 tablespoons margarine or butter (½ stick)
¾ cup plus 1 tablespoon heavy or whipping cream

**1** Prepare filling: In 3-quart saucepan, heat rhubarb and ½ cup sugar to boiling over high heat, stirring constantly. Reduce heat to medium-low and continue cooking until rhubarb is tender, about 8 minutes.

**2** In cup, mix cornstarch with *¼ cup water*. Stir cornstarch mixture and strawberries into rhubarb mixture; continue cooking 2 minutes until mixture thickens slightly. Remove from heat.

**3** Meanwhile, preheat oven to 400°F. In bowl, mix flour, baking powder, baking soda, salt, cinnamon, nutmeg, and ¼ cup sugar. With pastry blender or two knives used scissor-fashion, cut in margarine or butter until mixture resembles coarse crumbs. Add ¾ cup cream; quickly stir just until mixture forms a soft dough that pulls away from side of bowl.

**4** Turn dough onto lightly floured surface; knead 6 to 8 strokes to mix thoroughly. With floured rolling pin, roll dough ½ inch thick. With floured 3-inch star-shaped cookie cutter, cut out as many biscuits as possible. Reroll trimmings and cut as above to make 8 biscuits in all.

**5** Reheat rhubarb filling until hot; pour into 11" by 7" glass baking dish or shallow 2-quart casserole. Place biscuits on top of rhubarb. Brush biscuits with remaining 1 tablespoon cream and sprinkle with remaining 1 teaspoon sugar. Place sheet of foil under baking dish; crimp edges to form rim to catch any drips during baking. Bake 20 minutes or until biscuits are golden brown and rhubarb filling is bubbly. Cool slightly on wire rack to serve warm, about 15 minutes. *Makes 8 servings.*

Each serving: About 325 calories, 4 g protein, 45 g carbohydrate, 15 g total fat (7 g saturated), 33 mg cholesterol, 305 mg sodium.

# Superquick Strawberry Turnovers

PREP: 10 MINUTES  〰  BAKE: 16 TO 20 MINUTES

Try this with other fruit preserves.

1 package (8 ounces) refrigerated crescent dinner
   rolls
Confectioners' sugar
⅓ cup whipped cream cheese
¼ cup strawberry preserves
1 large egg white, beaten

**1** Preheat oven to 375°F. On cookie sheet, separate dough into 4 rectangles; pinch diagonal seams closed; sprinkle with 1 tablespoon confectioners' sugar. Spoon one-fourth of cream cheese and one-fourth of strawberry preserves in center of each. Brush edges with some egg white. Fold corners to center; press.

**2** Brush tops with remaining egg white. Bake 16 to 20 minutes or until golden. Sprinkle with confectioners' sugar. *Makes 4 servings.*

Each serving: About 335 calories, 6 g protein, 39 g carbohydrate, 18 g total fat (7 g saturated), 20 mg cholesterol, 515 mg sodium.

# Rice-Pudding Surprise

PREP: 10 MINUTES PLUS 1 HOUR TO CHILL
COOK: 50 TO 55 MINUTES

For a subtle flavor twist, make this with basmati or jasmine rice.

3½ cups low-fat (1%) milk
½ cup regular long-grain rice
4 teaspoons sugar
½ teaspoon salt
1 package (10 ounces) frozen sliced strawberries in
   syrup, thawed
1¼ cups vanilla low-fat frozen yogurt

**1** In 3-quart saucepan, heat milk, rice, sugar, and salt to boiling over medium heat. Reduce heat to low; cover and simmer 50 to 55 minutes, stirring occasionally, until rice is very tender and mixture is creamy. Pour rice mixture into a large bowl; refrigerate about 1 hour or until well chilled.

**2** Drain syrup from strawberries. In blender, at medium speed, or in food processor, with knife blade attached, blend strawberries until smooth. Pour pureed strawberries into small bowl.

**3** Stir 2 tablespoons frozen yogurt into pureed strawberries. Stir remaining frozen yogurt into rice-pudding mixture.

**4** Into six 8-ounce dessert bowls or goblets, spoon strawberry mixture; top with rice-pudding mixture. Refrigerate if not serving right away. *Makes 6 servings.*

Each serving: About 210 calories, 7 g protein, 41 g carbohydrate, 2 g total fat (1 g saturated), 8 mg cholesterol, 290 mg sodium.

# Strawberry "Cheesecake" Pudding

PREP: 15 MINUTES

A 15-minute dessert!

1 pint strawberries
1 container (8 ounces) strawberry-flavor soft
    cream cheese
½ cup low-fat (1%) milk
2 tablespoons confectioners' sugar

1 Slice all but 4 berries.

2 Mix cream cheese, milk, and confectioners' sugar until smooth.

3 In 4 goblets, layer half of sliced berries, then half of cheese mixture. Repeat layering. Garnish with whole berries. *Makes 4 servings.*

Each serving: About 230 calories, 4 g protein, 19 g carbohydrate, 17 g total fat (10 g saturated), 51 mg cholesterol, 135 mg sodium.

# Quick Yogurt Spumoni

PREP: 10 MINUTES PLUS FREEZING TIME

1 quart vanilla frozen yogurt, softened
⅓ cup chopped dried cherries
⅓ cup slivered blanched almonds
½ teaspoon almond extract
3 tablespoons diced candied citron or golden
    raisins

1 Place softened frozen yogurt in large bowl. Stir in cherries, almonds, almond extract, and 2 tablespoons candied citron.

2 Spoon yogurt mixture into 6 dessert dishes. Garnish with remaining 1 tablespoon citron. Freeze until ready to serve. *Makes 6 servings.*

Each serving: About 210 calories, 6 g protein, 36 g carbohydrate, 6 g total fat (2 g saturated), 7 mg cholesterol, 105 mg sodium.

# Valentine Sundaes

PREP: 10 MINUTES PLUS 2 HOURS TO FREEZE

Special finale: frozen yogurt hearts drizzled with ruby red raspberry sauce. To soften the frozen yogurt for spooning into the molds, place in a microwave and heat, uncovered, on Medium-Low (30% power) for 45 seconds to 1 minute.

1 pint vanilla frozen yogurt, softened.
1 package (12 ounces) frozen raspberries, thawed
¼ cup sugar
Fresh raspberries for garnish

1 Line four 4-ounce heart-shaped molds (or small bowls) with plastic wrap. Spoon the softened frozen yogurt into molds. Fold wrap over to cover. Freeze about 2 hours or until firm.

2 In food processor, with knife blade attached, or blender, puree thawed frozen raspberries and sugar. Pour raspberry puree into fine-mesh sieve set over medium bowl. With spoon, press raspberry puree against sieve to push through pulp and juice. Discard seeds.

3 Unmold hearts and serve drizzled with raspberry sauce and garnished with fresh berries. *Makes 4 servings.*

Each serving: About 225 calories, 4 g protein, 52 g carbohydrate, 2 g total fat (1 g saturated), 5 mg cholesterol, 60 mg sodium.

*Valentine Sundaes* ➤

# Frozen Toffee Mousse

PREP: 10 MINUTES PLUS 20 MINUTES TO FREEZE
COOK: 5 MINUTES

A great trick for a last-minute mousse. Try the peanut version below, too.

1 envelope unflavored gelatin
½ cup milk
¾ cup heavy or whipping cream
½ cup English toffee bits for baking
Unsweetened cocoa for garnish

**1** In 1-quart saucepan, evenly sprinkle gelatin over milk; let stand 1 minute to soften.

**2** Cook over medium heat until tiny bubbles form around edge of pan and gelatin completely dissolves, stirring frequently.

**3** Pour hot mixture into blender; add heavy cream, toffee bits, and 3 ice cubes; blend until smooth. Pour into 4 dessert dishes; freeze 20 minutes. Sprinkle with cocoa. *Makes 4 servings.*

Each serving: About 340 calories, 3 g protein, 21 g carbohydrate, 28 g total fat (14 g saturated), 75 mg cholesterol, 205 mg sodium.

# Quick Pumpkin Mousse with Sugared Pecans

PREP: 15 MINUTES PLUS 30 MINUTES TO CHILL

½ cup pecans, chopped
1 tablespoon plus ⅓ cup packed light brown sugar
1 can (16 ounces) solid-pack pumpkin (not pumpkin-pie mix)
1 package vanilla-flavor instant pudding and pie filling for 4 servings
1 cup milk
1 teaspoon vanilla extract
¾ teaspoon ground cinnamon
½ teaspoon ground ginger
½ teaspoon ground allspice
2 cups heavy or whipping cream

**1** Prepare sugared pecans: In 2-quart saucepan, cook pecans over medium-high heat until lightly browned,

stirring occasionally. Remove saucepan from heat; stir in 1 tablespoon brown sugar until sugar melts and evenly coats pecans, about 1 minute. Set saucepan aside to cool pecans.

**2** In large bowl, mix pumpkin, pudding mix, milk, vanilla extract, cinnamon, ginger, allspice, and remaining ⅓ cup brown sugar until well blended.

**3** In small bowl, with mixer at medium speed, beat cream until stiff peaks form. Refrigerate 1 cup whipped cream for garnish. Fold remaining whipped cream into pumpkin mixture.

**4** Spoon pumpkin mixture into eight 10-ounce goblets; cover and refrigerate until ready to serve. (Pumpkin mixture tastes best if refrigerated for at least 30 minutes before serving.)

**5** To serve, spoon reserved whipped cream onto pumpkin mixture; sprinkle with sugared pecans. *Makes 8 servings.*

Each serving: About 380 calories, 3 g protein, 31 g carbohydrate, 28 g total fat (15 g saturated), 86 mg cholesterol, 225 mg sodium.

# Frozen Peanut Mousse

PREP: 10 MINUTES PLUS 20 MINUTES TO FREEZE
COOK: 5 MINUTES

1 envelope unflavored gelatin
1 cup milk
⅔ cup peanut-butter bits for baking
3 tablespoons sugar
½ cup heavy or whipping cream

**1** In blender, sprinkle gelatin over ½ cup milk. Let stand 2 minutes.

**2** In saucepan, heat remaining ½ cup milk just to boiling. Add hot milk to blender; blend 1 minute. Add ½ cup peanut-butter bits; blend until melted.

**3** Add sugar, cream, and 3 ice cubes to blender; blend until smooth. Pour into 4 dessert dishes; freeze 20 minutes. Garnish with remaining peanut-butter bits. *Makes 4 servings.*

Each serving: About 395 calories, 12 g protein, 32 g carbohydrate, 24 g total fat (19 g saturated), 49 mg cholesterol, 140 mg sodium.

# Stir & Bake Carrot Cake

PREP: 15 MINUTES PLUS COOLING
BAKE: 1 HOUR 10 MINUTES

A supereasy cake. If you can get preshredded carrots in your supermarket, you can cut the prep time to almost nothing.

3 cups all-purpose flour
1¾ cups sugar
2 teaspoons ground cinnamon
2 teaspoons baking powder
1 teaspoon baking soda
1 teaspoon salt
4 large eggs
1¼ cups vegetable oil
1 teaspoon vanilla extract
3 cups loosely packed shredded carrots (about 7 medium carrots)
1 box (12 ounces) pitted prunes, chopped
1 cup chopped pecans
Cream-Cheese Drizzle (below)

**1** Preheat oven to 350°F. Grease and flour 10-cup fluted baking mold or 10-inch Bundt pan. In large bowl, mix flour, sugar, cinnamon, baking powder, baking soda, and salt.

**2** In small bowl, beat eggs slightly; stir in vegetable oil and vanilla extract. Stir egg mixture, shredded carrots, prunes, and pecans into flour mixture just until flour is moistened.

**3** Spoon batter into pan. Bake 65 to 70 minutes or until toothpick inserted in center of cake comes out clean. Cool cake in pan on wire rack 10 minutes; remove cake from pan; cool completely on rack.

**4** When cake is cool, prepare Cream-Cheese Drizzle. Spoon drizzle on top of cake. *Makes 16 servings.*

**CREAM-CHEESE DRIZZLE:** In small bowl, with mixer at medium speed, beat *one 3-ounce package cream cheese, softened, ¾ cup confectioners' sugar, 3 tablespoons milk, 1 tablespoon margarine or butter, softened, and ½ teaspoon vanilla extract* until smooth.

Each serving: About 430 calories, 4 g protein, 48 g carbohydrate, 26 g total fat (4 g saturated), 59 mg cholesterol, 340 mg sodium.

# No-Bake Peanut-Butter Chocolate Bars

PREP: 30 MINUTES PLUS 3 HOURS TO CHILL

20 chocolate wafers (half 9-ounce package)
¾ cup salted peanuts
½ cup margarine or butter (1 stick), softened
1¼ cups graham-cracker crumbs (eleven 5" by 2½" graham crackers, crushed)
1 cup confectioners' sugar
¾ cup creamy peanut butter
1 teaspoon vanilla extract
½ cup semisweet-chocolate mini pieces

**1** In blender, at medium speed, or in food processor, with knife blade attached, blend chocolate wafers and ½ cup peanuts to fine crumbs.

**2** In 11" by 7" metal baking pan, with hand, mix chocolate-crumb mixture and 4 tablespoons margarine or butter (½ stick) until well blended; firmly press mixture onto bottom of pan. Refrigerate to set crust.

**3** In large bowl, stir graham-cracker crumbs, confectioners' sugar, peanut butter, vanilla extract, and remaining 4 tablespoons margarine or butter (½ stick) until blended. With hand, knead mixture until smooth; pat peanut-butter mixture evenly over chilled crust.

**4** Chop remaining ¼ cup peanuts. Sprinkle chopped peanuts and semisweet-chocolate pieces over peanut-butter mixture. Cover with plastic wrap; with hands, firmly press down chopped peanuts and chocolate pieces. Refrigerate, covered, at least 3 hours.

**5** When cold, cut lengthwise into 4 strips, then cut each strip crosswise into 6 pieces. Store refrigerated in tightly covered containers. *Makes 2 dozen.*

Each bar: About 195 calories, 4 g protein, 18 g carbohydrate, 12 g total fat (2 g saturated), 0 mg cholesterol, 190 mg sodium.

# THE COOKIE JAR

Bake a batch of cookies on the weekend for a quick and easy weeknight dessert. Serve with applesauce, cut-up fruit, frozen yogurt or ice cream. Or, make one of our refrigerator cookie doughs so you can bake the cookies up fresh.

## Hazelnut Shortbread

PREP: 45 MINUTES PLUS COOLING
BAKE: 40 TO 45 MINUTES

1 cup hazelnuts (also called filberts), about 4 ounces
2¼ cups all-purpose flour
1 cup butter (2 sticks), softened
½ cup sugar
½ teaspoon vanilla extract
¼ teaspoon salt

1 Preheat oven to 375°F. Place hazelnuts in 9" by 9" baking pan. Bake 10 to 15 minutes until toasted. Wrap hot hazelnuts in clean cloth towel. With hands, roll hazelnuts back and forth to remove skins. Cool.
2 Turn oven control to 300°F. In food processor, with knife blade attached, finely chop hazelnuts with ¼ cup flour.
3 In large bowl, with mixer at low speed, beat butter and sugar until light and creamy. Beat in vanilla extract, salt, hazelnuts, and remaining 2 cups flour just until blended.
4 Pat dough evenly into 3 ungreased 8-inch round cake pans. With fork, prick dough in many places. Press edges with tines of fork to form a decorative border.
5 Bake shortbread 40 to 45 minutes or until lightly browned. Let cool in pans on wire racks 10 minutes; remove from pans.
6 While still warm, cut each shortbread round into 12 wedges. Cool shortbread wedges completely on wire racks. Store in tightly covered container. Makes 3 dozen cookies.

EACH COOKIE: ABOUT 100 CALORIES, 1 G PROTEIN, 9 G CARBOHYDRATE, 7 G TOTAL FAT (3 G SATURATED), 14 MG CHOLESTEROL, 65 MG SODIUM.

## Slice-and-Bake Chocolate-Orange Cookies

PREP: 15 MINUTES PLUS CHILLING
BAKE: 12 MINUTES PER BATCH

1 cup sugar
1 cup shortening
1 teaspoon baking powder
¾ teaspoon salt
1½ teaspoons orange extract
1 large egg
2½ cups all-purpose flour
2 tablespoons unsweetened cocoa

1 In large bowl, with mixer at low speed, beat sugar, shortening, baking powder, salt, orange extract, and egg until well blended. Increase speed to high; beat until mixture is light and fluffy, scraping bowl often with rubber spatula.
2 With wooden spoon, gradually stir in flour to make soft dough. Wrap half of dough with plastic wrap. Knead cocoa into remaining half of dough; wrap with plastic wrap. Chill plain and chocolate doughs until firm enough to handle: 1 hour in refrigerator or 30 minutes in freezer.
3 On sheet of waxed paper, with floured rolling pin, roll chocolate dough into 14" by 6" rectangle. Roll plain dough into 14-inch-long cylinder. Place cylinder on one long end of chocolate dough. Starting from same long end, roll doughs together, jelly-roll fashion, to enclose cylinder completely. Wrap roll in plastic wrap and chill until firm enough to slice: 1 hour in refrigerator or 30 minutes in freezer. (Dough can be refrigerated up to 1 week before slicing and baking.)
4 Preheat oven to 350°F. Cut roll crosswise into ¼-inch-thick slices. Place slices, 1 inch apart, on 2 ungreased large cookie sheets. Bake cookies 12 minutes or until lightly browned. Transfer cookies to wire racks to cool. Store cookies in tightly covered container. Makes about 2½ dozen cookies.

EACH COOKIE: ABOUT 130 CALORIES, 1 G PROTEIN, 15 G CARBOHYDRATE, 7 G TOTAL FAT (2 G SATURATED), 7 MG CHOLESTEROL, 75 MG SODIUM.

## Double-Chocolate Chunk Cookies

PREP: 40 MINUTES PLUS COOLING
BAKE: 25 TO 30 MINUTES PER BATCH

1 package (12 ounces) semisweet-chocolate chunks (2 cups)
1 cup margarine or butter (2 sticks), softened
⅔ cup packed light brown sugar
⅓ cup granulated sugar
1 teaspoon baking soda
2 teaspoons vanilla extract
½ teaspoon salt
1 large egg
2 cups all-purpose flour
2 cups walnuts, coarsely chopped

1 In heavy small saucepan, heat 1 cup chocolate chunks over low heat until melted and smooth, stirring frequently. Remove saucepan from heat; cool to room temperature.
2 In large bowl, with mixer at low speed, beat margarine or butter, brown sugar, granulated sugar, baking soda, vanilla extract, and salt until crumbly. Add melted chocolate and egg; beat until well blended, occasionally scraping bowl with rubber spatula. With spoon, stir in flour, walnuts, and remaining chocolate chunks.
3 Preheat oven to 350°F. Drop dough by level ¼ cups, about 3 inches apart, on 2 ungreased large cookie sheets. Place cookie sheets on 2 oven racks. Bake 25 to 30 minutes or until edges of cookies are set but centers are still soft, rotating cookie sheets between upper and lower racks halfway through baking time. Transfer cookies to wire racks to cool completely. Store cookies in tightly covered container. Makes about 1½ dozen cookies.

EACH COOKIE: ABOUT 365 CALORIES, 5 G PROTEIN, 38 G CARBOHYDRATE, 23 G TOTAL FAT (3 G SATURATED), 12 MG CHOLESTEROL, 285 MG SODIUM.

## Sesame Crisps

PREP: 15 MINUTES PLUS CHILLING & COOLING • BAKE: 15 MINUTES PER BATCH

⅔ cup sesame seeds (about 2½ ounces)
2½ cups all-purpose flour
1 cup margarine or butter (2 sticks), softened
¾ cup packed light brown sugar
¾ cup granulated sugar
½ cup cornstarch
1 teaspoon baking soda
½ teaspoon salt
1 large egg

**1** In 2-quart saucepan, cook sesame seeds over medium heat until golden, 5 to 7 minutes, shaking saucepan and stirring frequently. Remove saucepan from heat; set aside to cool.
**2** In large bowl, with mixer at low speed, beat flour, margarine or butter, brown sugar, granulated sugar, cornstarch, baking soda, salt, and egg until well blended (mixture will be crumbly). Stir in toasted sesame seeds; with hands, knead dough just until it holds together.
**3** Divide dough in half. Pat each half into 7½" by 3" rectangle (about 1 inch thick). Wrap each rectangle in plastic wrap and chill until firm enough to slice: 1 hour in refrigerator or 30 minutes in freezer. (Dough can be refrigerated up to 1 week before slicing and baking.)
**4** Preheat oven to 350°F: Cut 1 rectangle of dough crosswise into ¼-inch-thick slices, keeping remaining dough refrigerated. Place slices, 1 inch apart, on 2 ungreased large cookie sheets Bake 15 minutes or until golden. Transfer cookies to wire racks to cool. Repeat with remaining rectangle. Store cookies in tightly covered container. Makes about 5 dozen cookies.

EACH COOKIE: ABOUT 80 CALORIES, 1 G PROTEIN, 10 G CARBOHYDRATE, 4 G TOTAL FAT (1 G SATURATED), 4 MG CHOLESTEROL, 80 MG SODIUM.

*Macadamia Snaps*

## Macadamia Snaps

PREP: 10 MINUTES PLUS COOLING BAKE: 15 MINUTES PER BATCH

2 cups all-purpose flour
1 cup margarine or butter (2 sticks), softened
¾ cup sugar
1½ teaspoons vanilla extract
¼ teaspoon salt
1 jar (3½ ounces) macadamia nuts, chopped

**1** Preheat oven to 350°F. In large bowl, with mixer at low speed, beat flour, margarine or butter, sugar, vanilla extract, and salt until well blended.
**2** Place macadamia nuts on waxed paper. Roll level tablespoons of dough into balls; press 1 side of each ball into chopped macadamia nuts. Place flattened balls, nut-side up, on ungreased large cookie sheet, about 2 inches apart. Bake cookies about 15 minutes or until lightly browned; transfer to wire racks to cool. Store in tightly covered container. Makes about 2 dozen cookies.

EACH COOKIE: ABOUT 160 CALORIES, 2 G PROTEIN, 15 G CARBOHYDRATE, 11 G TOTAL FAT (2 G SATURATED), 0 MG CHOLESTEROL, 115 MG SODIUM.

## Chunky Black & White Oaties

PREP: 25 MINUTES PLUS CHILLING BAKE: 15 MINUTES PER BATCH

1½ cups all-purpose flour
¾ cup shortening
¾ cup granulated sugar
¾ cup packed light brown sugar
1 teaspoon baking soda
2 teaspoons vanilla extract
¾ teaspoon salt
2 large eggs
6 ounces semisweet chocolate, chopped
1 cup pecans, chopped
¾ cup quick-cooking oats, uncooked
1 package (6 ounces) white baking bar, * chopped

**1** Preheat oven to 375°F. In large bowl, with mixer at low speed, beat flour, shortening, granulated sugar, brown sugar, baking soda, vanilla extract, salt, and eggs until blended, scraping bowl frequently with rubber spatula. With spoon, stir in semisweet chocolate, pecans, and oats.
**2** Drop about one-third of mixture by 2 heaping tablespoons, 3 inches apart, onto ungreased large cookie sheet to make about 5 cookies. Bake 13 to 15 minutes or until nicely browned. Transfer cookies to wire racks to cool. Repeat with remaining dough.
**3** In heavy 1-quart saucepan, heat white baking bar over low heat, stirring occasionally, until melted and smooth. On sheet of waxed paper, arrange cookies in one layer. Using spoon, drizzle melted baking bar randomly over each cookie.
**4** Refrigerate cookies at least 1 hour to allow drizzle to set. Store cookies, with waxed paper between layers, in tightly covered containers. Makes about 15 cookies.
*Or, use two 3-ounce Swiss confectionery bars.

EACH COOKIE: ABOUT 405 CALORIES, 5 G PROTEIN, 49 G CARBOHYDRATE, 23 G TOTAL FAT (7 G SATURATED), 28 MG CHOLESTEROL, 225 MG SODIUM.

## Frosted Pecan Squares

PREP: 45 MINUTES PLUS FREEZING & COOLING
BAKE: 12 TO 15 MINUTES PER BATCH

¾ cup packed dark brown sugar
½ cup margarine or butter (1 stick), softened
1 large egg
2 teaspoons vanilla extract
4 tablespoons plus 2 teaspoons milk
2½ cups all-purpose flour
½ teaspoon baking soda
½ teaspoon salt
1¼ cups pecans, toasted and chopped
2 cups confectioners' sugar
About 1¼ cups toasted pecan halves
    for garnish

1 In large bowl, with mixer at medium-high speed, beat brown sugar and margarine or butter until light and fluffy. Add egg, vanilla extract, and 2 tablespoons milk; beat until mixture is smooth.
2 With wooden spoon, stir in flour, baking soda, and salt. When flour is almost all incorporated, stir in chopped pecans. (Dough will be very stiff.)
3 Divide dough in half. On lightly floured surface, shape each half of dough into 4-sided log, 1½ inches on all sides and 8 inches in length, using pancake turner to help flatten sides. Wrap each log in plastic wrap and slide onto small cookie sheet for easier handling. Chill dough until very firm: at least 24 hours in refrigerator or 2 hours in freezer. (Dough can be refrigerated up to 1 week before slicing and baking.)
4 Preheat oven to 350°F. Grease 2 large cookie sheets. Cut each log into slightly less than ¼-inch-thick slices. Place slices, about 1½ inches apart, on cookie sheets. Place cookie sheets on 2 oven racks. Bake cookies 12 to 15 minutes until browned around edges, rotating cookie sheets between upper and lower racks halfway through baking time. Transfer cookies to wire racks to cool.
5 When cookies are cool, prepare icing: In medium bowl, mix confectioners' sugar and remaining 2 tablespoons plus 2 teaspoons milk to make a thick icing, adding more milk if necessary.

6 With small metal spatula or knife, spread some icing on top of one cookie; then top with a pecan half. Repeat with remaining cookies, icing, and pecan halves. Set cookies aside to allow icing to dry completely. Store cookies in tightly covered container. Makes about 5 dozen cookies.

EACH COOKIE: ABOUT 90 CALORIES, 1 G PROTEIN, 12 G CARBOHYDRATE, 5 G TOTAL FAT (1 G SATURATED), 4 MG CHOLESTEROL, 50 MG SODIUM.

*Frosted Pecan Squares (top) and Toffee-Nut Squares*

## Toffee-Nut Squares

PREP: 20 MINUTES PLUS COOLING
BAKE: 20 TO 25 MINUTES

2 cups all-purpose flour
¾ cup shortening
¾ cup sugar
2 teaspoons vanilla extract
1 large egg
1 cup walnuts, chopped
1 bag (6 ounces) chocolate-covered toffee chips
2 ounces semisweet chocolate

1 Preheat oven to 350°F. Grease 15½" by 10½" jelly-roll pan.
2 In large bowl, with mixer at low speed, beat flour, shortening, sugar, vanilla extract, and egg just until blended, occasionally scraping bowl with rubber spatula. Increase speed to medium; beat

until well mixed. With spoon, stir in walnuts and toffee chips.
3 With fingertips, pat dough evenly into pan. Bake 20 to 25 minutes or until lightly browned. Transfer pan to wire rack to cool.
4 In heavy small saucepan, heat chocolate over very low heat until melted and smooth, stirring frequently. Spoon melted chocolate into paper cone with tip cut to make ⅛-inch-diameter hole, or use decorating bag with small writing tube. Drizzle chocolate over top layer in zigzag pattern. Let chocolate drizzle dry.
5 When drizzle is dry, cut toffee-nut rectangle lengthwise into 5 strips, then cut each strip crosswise into 8 pieces. Store in tightly covered container. Makes 40 squares.

EACH SQUARE: ABOUT 120 CALORIES, 2 G PROTEIN, 13 G CARBOHYDRATE, 8 G TOTAL FAT (2 G SATURATED), 8 MG CHOLESTEROL, 15 MG SODIUM.

## Chocolate Biscotti

PREP: 10 MINUTES PLUS COOLING
BAKE: 1 HOUR

¾ cup walnuts
1⅓ cups all-purpose flour
1 cup sugar
½ cup unsweetened cocoa
1 tablespoon instant espresso-coffee powder
¾ teaspoon baking soda
½ teaspoon baking powder
¼ teaspoon salt
3 large eggs, lightly beaten
1 teaspoon vanilla extract
Nonstick cooking spray

1 In 10-inch skillet, toast walnuts over medium heat, shaking skillet frequently, until golden; remove skillet from heat. Cool walnuts.
2 Meanwhile, into large bowl, measure flour, sugar, cocoa, espresso-coffee powder, baking soda, baking powder, and salt.
3 Chop walnuts. With spoon, stir walnuts, eggs, and vanilla extract into

flour mixture just until blended. With floured hands, knead mixture until it holds together (mixture may appear dry or crumbly).

**4** Preheat oven to 325°F. Spray large cookie sheet with nonstick cooking spray. On lightly floured surface, divide dough in half. With lightly floured hands, roll each half of dough into 8" by 2½" loaf. Place loaves, about 3 inches apart, on cookie sheet. Bake 35 to 40 minutes or until toothpick inserted in center of loaf comes out clean.

**5** Remove cookie sheet from oven. Turn oven control to 300°F. Cool loaves 10 minutes for easier slicing.

**6** Transfer loaves to cutting board. With serrated knife, cut loaves crosswise into ¼-inch-thick diagonal slices. Arrange slices, cut-side down, on same cookie sheet, making sure they do not touch. Return to oven and bake 10 to 15 minutes longer (biscotti will seem cakelike in center but will become characteristically crisp and dry when cooled). Transfer biscotti to wire racks to cool. Store biscotti in tightly covered container. Makes about 3½ dozen cookies.

EACH COOKIE: ABOUT 55 CALORIES, 1 G PROTEIN, 9 G CARBOHYDRATE, 2 G TOTAL FAT (0 G SATURATED), 15 MG CHOLESTEROL, 45 MG SODIUM.

## Jumbo Gingersnaps

PREP: 15 MINUTES • BAKE: 15 MINUTES

½ cup plus 2 tablespoons sugar
2¼ cups all-purpose flour
¾ cup vegetable oil
¼ cup dark unsulphured molasses
¼ cup maple syrup
2 teaspoons baking soda
1 teaspoon ground ginger
½ teaspoon ground cinnamon
½ teaspoon ground cardamom
¼ teaspoon salt
1 large egg

**1** In large bowl, with mixer at low speed, beat ½ cup sugar, flour, vegetable oil, molasses, maple syrup, baking soda, ginger, cinnamon, cardamom, salt, and egg until well blended, occasionally scraping bowl with rubber spatula.

**2** Preheat oven to 350°F. Place remaining 2 tablespoons sugar on waxed paper. Shape ¼ cup dough into ball; roll in sugar to coat evenly. Repeat with remaining dough to make 10 balls in all. Place balls, 3 inches apart, on ungreased cookie sheet. (Dough is very soft; balls will flatten slightly.) Bake cookies 15 minutes. Transfer cookies to wire racks to cool. Store cookies in tightly covered container. Makes 10 cookies.

EACH COOKIE: ABOUT 345 CALORIES, 4 G PROTEIN, 45 G CARBOHYDRATE, 17 G TOTAL FAT (2 G SATURATED), 21 MG CHOLESTEROL, 320 MG SODIUM.

## Peanut-Butter Shortbread

PREP: 15 MINUTES
BAKE: 12 MINUTES PER BATCH

2¾ cups all-purpose flour
¾ cup granulated sugar
½ cup packed light brown sugar
1½ teaspoons baking powder
½ teaspoon salt
1¼ cups creamy peanut butter
¾ cup margarine or butter
   (1½ sticks), softened

**1** In large bowl, combine flour, granulated sugar, brown sugar, baking powder, and salt. With pastry blender or two knives used scissor-fashion, cut in peanut butter and margarine or butter until mixture resembles coarse crumbs. With hand, knead mixture just until dough forms ball.

**2** Preheat oven to 350°F. Roll level tablespoons of dough into balls (if dough is crumbly, work with hand until pliable). Place balls, 3 inches apart, on 2 ungreased large cookie sheets. With floured metal spatula, flatten each ball to ¼-inch thickness. (If desired, use small cookie or canapé cutters to press shapes into each cookie, halfway but not all the way through, to make decorative designs.)

**3** Bake cookies 12 minutes or until lightly browned. Transfer cookies to wire racks to cool. Store cookies in tightly covered container. Makes about 4½ dozen cookies.

EACH COOKIE: ABOUT 100 CALORIES, 2 G PROTEIN, 11 G CARBOHYDRATE, 6 G TOTAL FAT (1 G SATURATED), 0 MG CHOLESTEROL, 95 MG SODIUM.

## McIntosh-Oatmeal Cookies

PREP: 20 MINUTES • BAKE: 25 MINUTES

1½ cups sugar
1 cup margarine or butter (2 sticks), softened
1½ cups all-purpose flour
1 teaspoon baking soda
1 teaspoon ground cinnamon
1 teaspoon vanilla extract
½ teaspoon salt
2 large eggs
2 medium McIntosh apples, peeled, cored, and diced (about 2 cups)
3 cups quick-cooking oats, uncooked
1 cup dark seedless raisins
¾ cup walnuts, chopped

**1** In large bowl, with mixer at medium speed, beat sugar and margarine or butter until light and fluffy, about 5 minutes. Add flour, baking soda, cinnamon, vanilla extract, salt, and eggs; beat just until blended, occasionally scraping bowl with rubber spatula. With spoon, stir in apples, oats, raisins, and walnuts.

**2** Preheat oven to 350°F. Drop batter by level ¼ cups, about 3 inches apart, on 2 ungreased large cookie sheets.

**3** Place cookie sheets on 2 oven racks. Bake cookies 20 to 25 minutes until golden, rotating cookie sheets between upper and lower racks halfway through baking time. Transfer cookies to wire racks to cool.

**4** Repeat until all batter is used. Store cookies in tightly covered container. Makes about 2 dozen cookies.

EACH COOKIE: ABOUT 275 CALORIES, 5 G PROTEIN, 39 G CARBOHYDRATE, 12 G TOTAL FAT (2 G SATURATED), 18 MG CHOLESTEROL, 205 MG SODIUM.

## Raspberry-Star Sandwich Cookies

PREP: 45 MINUTES PLUS CHILLING & COOLING
BAKE: 10 TO 12 MINUTES PER BATCH

2¼ cups all-purpose flour
¾ cup granulated sugar
1 teaspoon baking powder
1 teaspoon vanilla extract
½ teaspoon salt
¾ cup butter (1½ sticks), softened
½ cup seedless raspberry preserves
⅓ cup confectioners' sugar

1 In large bowl, combine flour, granulated sugar, baking powder, vanilla extract, and salt. With pastry blender or two knives used scissor-fashion, cut in butter until mixture resembles coarse crumbs. Sprinkle *4 to 5 tablespoons cold water*, 1 tablespoon at time, into flour mixture, mixing lightly with fork after each addition until dough is just moist enough to hold together. Shape dough into ball. Wrap with plastic wrap and refrigerate until firm enough to roll: 1 hour in refrigerator or 30 minutes in freezer.
2 Preheat oven to 350°F. On lightly floured surface, with floured rolling pin, roll one-third of dough at a time ⅛ inch thick, keeping remaining dough refrigerated. With floured 4-inch star-shaped cookie cutter, cut dough into as many stars as possible. Place stars, ½ inch apart, on ungreased large cookie sheet. Reserve trimmings. With floured 1½-inch star-shaped cookie cutter, cut out centers from half of stars. Remove cut-out centers and add to dough trimmings.
3 Bake cookies 10 to 12 minutes or until lightly browned. Transfer cookies to wire racks to cool. Roll dough trimmings and remaining dough together to cut out more cookies; bake.
4 When cookies are cool, sprinkle cookies that have star cutouts with confectioners' sugar. Spread center of each solid, uncut cookie with 1 rounded teaspoon raspberry preserves; top each with cookie with star cutout, gently

pressing cookies together to form sandwich. Store in tightly covered container. Makes about 1½ dozen sandwich cookies.

EACH COOKIE: ABOUT 190 CALORIES, 2 G PROTEIN, 29 G CARBOHYDRATE, 8 G TOTAL FAT (5 G SATURATED), 21 MG CHOLESTEROL, 160 MG SODIUM.

## Cranberry-Nut Biscotti

PREP: 1 HOUR PLUS COOLING
BAKE: 45 TO 55 MINUTES

1⅓ cups hazelnuts (also called filberts)
3¾ cups all-purpose flour
2 cups sugar
1 teaspoon baking powder
½ teaspoon salt
5 large eggs
2 teaspoons vanilla extract
½ cup dried cranberries or currants

1 Preheat oven to 350°F. Place hazelnuts on 15½" by 10½" jelly-roll pan. Bake about 20 minutes or until toasted. Wrap hot hazelnuts in clean cloth towel. With hands, roll hazelnuts back and forth to remove skins. Coarsely chop hazelnuts.
2 Grease and lightly flour 2 large cookie sheets. In large bowl, combine flour, sugar, baking powder, and salt. In small bowl, beat 4 whole eggs, 1 egg yolk (reserve egg white for use later), vanilla extract, and *1 tablespoon water*. Pour egg mixture into flour mixture; stir with wooden spoon, then use hands to knead dough together (dough will be very stiff). Knead in hazelnuts and dried cranberries.
3 Divide dough into 4 equal pieces. On lightly floured surface, with floured hands, shape each piece of dough into 11" by 2" log. Place 2 logs, about 4 inches apart, on each cookie sheet. Lightly beat reserved egg white. With pastry brush, brush logs with egg white.

4 Place cookie sheets on 2 oven racks. Bake logs 35 to 40 minutes until toothpick inserted in center comes out clean, rotating cookie sheets between upper and lower racks halfway through baking time. Let loaves (during baking, logs will spread and become loaf shaped) cool 10 minutes on cookie sheets on wire racks.
5 Transfer loaves to cutting board. With serrated knife, cut each loaf crosswise into ½-inch-thick diagonal slices. Place slices, cut-side down, on same cookie sheets. Place cookie sheets on 2 oven racks. Bake slices 10 to 15 minutes to allow biscotti to dry out, turning biscotti once and rotating cookie sheets between upper and lower racks halfway through baking time. Transfer biscotti to wire racks to cool completely. (Biscotti will harden as they cool.) Store biscotti in tightly covered container. Makes about 4½ dozen biscotti.

EACH BISCOTTI: ABOUT 90 CALORIES, 2 G PROTEIN, 16 G CARBOHYDRATE, 2 G TOTAL FAT (0 G SATURATED), 20 MG CHOLESTEROL, 35 MG SODIUM.

## Jumbo Pecan-Date Cookies

PREP: 30 MINUTES PLUS COOLING
BAKE: 20 TO 25 MINUTES PER BATCH

1 cup margarine or butter (2 sticks), softened
¾ cup granulated sugar
¾ cup packed light brown sugar
1½ cups all-purpose flour
1 teaspoon baking soda
1 teaspoon vanilla extract
½ teaspoon salt
½ teaspoon ground cinnamon
2 large eggs
3 cups quick-cooking oats, uncooked
2 cups (10 ounces) pitted dates, chopped
1 cup pecans, chopped

1 In large bowl, with mixer at medium speed, beat margarine or butter, granulated sugar, and brown sugar until light and fluffy, about 5 minutes. Reduce

speed to low; add flour, baking soda, vanilla, salt, cinnamon, and eggs; beat just until blended, occasionally scraping bowl with rubber spatula. With spoon, stir in oats, dates, and pecans.

**2** Preheat oven to 350°F. Drop cookie dough by level ¼ cups, 3 inches apart, on 2 ungreased large cookie sheets.

**3** Place cookie sheets on 2 oven racks. Bake cookies 20 to 25 minutes or until golden, rotating cookie sheets between upper and lower racks halfway through baking time. Transfer cookies to wire racks to cool.

**4** Repeat until all batter is used. Store cookies tightly covered for up to 1 week. Makes about 2 dozen cookies.

EACH COOKIE: ABOUT 255 CALORIES, 4 G PROTEIN, 35 G CARBOHYDRATE, 12 G TOTAL FAT (2 G SATURATED), 18 MG CHOLESTEROL, 205 MG SODIUM.

## Chewy Chocolate-Chip Oatmeal-Raisin Cookies

PREP: 15 MINUTES PLUS COOLING
BAKE: 10 TO 12 MINUTES PER BATCH

*Nonstick cooking spray*
*½ cup margarine or butter (1 stick)*
*¾ cup packed dark brown sugar*
*½ cup granulated sugar*
*2 large egg whites*
*1 large egg*
*2 teaspoons vanilla extract*
*2 cups all-purpose flour*
*1 cup quick-cooking oats, uncooked*
*1 cup semisweet-chocolate pieces*
*½ cup dark seedless raisins*
*1 teaspoon baking soda*
*½ teaspoon salt*

**1** Preheat oven to 375°F. Spray 2 large cookie sheets with nonstick cooking spray.

**2** In large bowl, with mixer at low speed, beat margarine or butter, brown sugar, and granulated sugar until combined. Increase speed to high; beat until light and fluffy.

**3** Add egg whites, whole egg, and vanilla extract; beat until smooth.

**4** With spoon, stir in flour, oats, chocolate pieces, raisins, baking soda, and salt until combined.

**5** Drop dough by level tablespoons, about 2 inches apart, on cookie sheets. Place cookie sheets on 2 oven racks. Bake cookies 10 to 12 minutes or until golden, rotating cookie sheets between upper and lower racks halfway through baking time. Transfer cookies to wire racks to cool.

**6** Repeat until all batter is used. Store cookies in tightly covered containers. Makes about 4 dozen cookies.

EACH COOKIE: ABOUT 90 CALORIES, 1 G PROTEIN, 14 G CARBOHYDRATE, 3 G TOTAL FAT (1 G SATURATED), 4 MG CHOLESTEROL, 80 MG SODIUM.

*Chewy Chocolate-Chip Oatmeal-Raisin Cookies*

## Spicy Almond Slices

PREP: 15 MINUTES PLUS CHILLING
BAKE: 10 TO 12 MINUTES PER BATCH

*1 cup margarine or butter (2 sticks), softened*
*1 cup granulated sugar*
*¾ cup packed dark brown sugar*
*1 tablespoon ground cinnamon*
*1 teaspoon ground cloves*
*1 teaspoon baking soda*
*1 teaspoon vanilla extract*
*¾ teaspoon ground nutmeg*
*½ teaspoon salt*
*2 large eggs*
*3½ cups all-purpose flour*
*2 cups sliced blanched almonds*

**1** In large bowl, with mixer at medium speed, beat margarine or butter, granulated sugar, brown sugar, cinnamon, cloves, baking soda, vanilla extract, nutmeg, salt, eggs, and 2 cups flour until well mixed.

**2** With wooden spoon, stir in almonds and remaining 1½ cups flour; use hands, if necessary, to mix thoroughly as dough will be very stiff.

**3** Divide dough in half. Shape each half into 10" by 3" by 1" brick. Wrap each brick in plastic wrap and chill until firm enough to slice: 2 hours in refrigerator or 1 hour in freezer. (Dough can be refrigerated up to 1 week before slicing and baking.)

**4** Preheat oven to 375°F. Cut 1 brick into ¼-inch-thick slices. Place slices, 1 inch apart, on ungreased cookie sheets. Bake 10 to 12 minutes or until browned around the edges. Transfer cookies to wire racks to cool. Repeat with remaining brick. Store cookies in tightly covered container. Makes about 80 cookies.

EACH COOKIE: ABOUT 75 CALORIES, 1 G PROTEIN, 9 G CARBOHYDRATE, 4 G TOTAL FAT (1 G SATURATED), 5 MG CHOLESTEROL, 60 MG SODIUM.

# INDEX

# CREDITS

Cover: Mark Thomas. Page 11: Steven Mark Needham. Page 14: Peter Ardito. Pages 18, 20, and 23: Steven Mark Needham. Page 24: Ann Stratton. Page 27: Steven Mark Needham. Pages 28 and 39: Brian Hagiwara. Page 40: David Hamsley. Pages 45 and 47: Alan Richardson. Pages 48, 50, and 54: Brian Hagiwara. Pages 57 and 61: Alan Richardson. Pages 62 and 63: Martin Jacobs. Page 67: Charles Gold.

Page 68: Alan Richardson. Page 71: Brian Hagiwara. Page 74: Alan Richardson. Page 79: Mark Thomas.

Page 81: Steven Mark Needham. Page 82: Martin Jacobs. Pages 85, 86, and 88: Brian Hagiwara.

Page 92: Charles Gold. Page 94: Steven Mark Needham. Page 97: Brian Hagiwara. Page 98: Charles Gold.

Pages 103 and 106: Brian Hagiwara. Page 108: Lisa Koenig. Page 113: David Hamsley. Page 115: Arthur Beck. Page 116: Martin Jacobs. Pages 118 and 120: Lisa Koenig. Page 123: Mark Thomas. Page 126: Steven Mark Needham. Page 128: Lisa Koenig. Page 130: Alan Richardson. Page 133: Steven Mark Needham.

Page 137: Mark Thomas. Pages 139, 142, 147, and 152: Brian Hagiwara. Page 157: Mark Thomas.

Pages 161 and 162: Lisa Koenig. Page 167: Charles Gold. Page 169: Lisa Koenig. Page 173: Alan Richardson. Page 174: Brian Hagiwara. Page 176: Steven Mark Needham. Page 181: Ann Stratton.

Page 183: Steven Mark Needham. Page 185: Elizabeth Watt. Page 188: Alan Richardson. Page 191: Brian Hagiwara. Page 195: Mark Thomas. Page 199: Steven Mark Needham. Page 200: Lisa Koenig. Pages 203 and 204: Brian Hagiwara. Pages 206 and 215: Mark Thomas. Page 216: Brian Hagiwara. Page 221: Steven Mark Needham. Page 223: Ann Stratton. Page 224: Steven Mark Needham. Page 227: Peter Ardito.

Pages 228 and 230: Steven Mark Needham. Page 232: Alan Richardson. Page 235: Steven Mark Needham.

Page 239: Lisa Koenig. Page 240: Steven Mark Needham. Page 243: Mark Thomas.